The Company-State

The Company-State

Corporate Sovereignty and the
Early Modern Foundations of the
British Empire in India

PHILIP J. STERN

OXFORD
UNIVERSITY PRESS

OXFORD
UNIVERSITY PRESS

Oxford University Press is a department of the University of Oxford.
It furthers the University's objective of excellence in research, scholarship,
and education by publishing worldwide.

Oxford   New York
Auckland   Cape Town   Dar es Salaam   Hong Kong   Karachi
Kuala Lumpur   Madrid   Melbourne   Mexico City   Nairobi
New Delhi   Shanghai   Taipei   Toronto

With offices in
Argentina   Austria   Brazil   Chile   Czech Republic   France   Greece
Guatemala   Hungary   Italy   Japan   Poland   Portugal   Singapore
South Korea   Switzerland   Thailand   Turkey   Ukraine   Vietnam

Oxford is a registered trade mark of Oxford University Press
in the UK and certain other countries.

Published in the United States of America by
Oxford University Press
198 Madison Avenue, New York, NY 10016

Library of Congress Cataloging-in-Publication Data
Stern, Philip J.
The company-state: corporate sovereignty and the early modern foundations
of the British Empire in India /Philip J. Stern.
p. cm.
Includes bibliographical references and index.
ISBN 978-0-19-539373-6 (hardcover); 978-0-19-993036-4 (paperback)
1. East India Company—History.
2. Corporations, British—India.
3. India—History—British occupation, 1765–1947. I. Title.
HF486.E6S73 2011
382'.094205—dc22
2010032527

Printed in the United States of America
on acid-free paper

CONTENTS

PREFACE

Over the decade that has spanned from the first conception of this project to its ultimate conclusion in this book, the East India Company has enjoyed a posthumous quartercentenary, museum exhibits, specialist and general histories, and collected volumes. Its name has been attached to a line of tropical clothing and the Company itself resurrected in a London shop selling high-end foodstuffs including, of all things, tea. There is now an East India Company video game, and the Company was cast as the corporate archvillain in the final two blockbuster *Pirates of the Caribbean* movies. In the meantime, the Company, long of interest to British imperial historians, has experienced an academic resurgence, from the history of British domestic culture to its diffusion in the Atlantic and elsewhere.[1]

Clearly, given the great contemporary concerns, both political and historiographical, with globalization, multinational corporations, private mercenaries and outsourced warfare, colonialism and neocolonialism, and, of course, pirates, the renewed interest in the Company should be unsurprising. Yet, amid all this publicity, there still seems to be one fundamental assumption about the Company itself that has been near impossible to shake: that it was essentially a trading corporation, which became an empire only with its acquisition of territory in the middle of the eighteenth century. The understanding of its early history as an institution has thus tended to be focused on its roles in commerce or domestic politics, its driving motivations and institutional culture summarized in the words uttered by the Company's fictive representative in that final *Pirates of the Caribbean* film, just before he was blown to bits: "It's nothing personal . . . It's just good business." This vision of the Company is rooted in, and reinforces, some deeply seated and enduring chronological, geographical, and conceptual divisions in the historiography of the British Empire, between a "trading" and "imperial" period in British India, "first" and "second" British empires, a colonial Atlantic and a commercial Asia, and the state, on the one hand, and the variety of other bodies politic that governed over people, places, and things across the early modern world. Perhaps most fundamentally, it reflects the remarkable ideological power the modern state has had in shaping our historiographical and political imagination. That the national form of state is, and has been, the final and ultimate form of sovereignty and political community has underscored some fundamental distinctions—between nations and empires, politics and commerce, companies and states—that increasingly seem neither intuitive nor tenable.

This is thus a book about a "trading" corporation that has much less to say about trade and far more to say about corporations. Great amounts of ink have been spilt on the early Company's commerce in Asia as well as its role in shaping British history, much of it quite good and useful. However, this book approaches the early Company differently: as a form of government, a corporation, a jurisdiction, and a colonial proprietor. In exploring the constitutional, institutional, and ideological foundations for this Company-State, it suggests a vision of early modern overseas activity driven by a variety of forms of political community that were only later incorporated into their ally and competitor, a national state and empire, which itself was only in the process of formation. *The Company-State* is thus a proposition and an experiment in the notion that companies, corporations, and other non-national bodies often act as political communities in their own rights, and their motivations, allegiances, and even ideologies can only be understood when we take seriously the possibility that they have intellectual and political histories as institutions on their own terms.

The best argument for seeing the East India Company as a state is actually one that sits behind rather than inside this book, namely, the vast archive it has left behind. Even within a decade of its creation, Samuel Purchas noted the countless hours he had to spend transcribing Company records for his *Pilgrims*, "the tediousnesse of which," he complained, "wearied me."[2] Two centuries later, James Mill found the Company's library to be "appalling by its magnitude, that many years appeared to be inadequate to render the mind familiar with it."[3] While aspiring to render my mind familiar with only one part of this archive, and to write about it, I inevitably have incurred innumerable debts, for which this book is hardly adequate compensation. Thankfully, unlike Purchas, I was not left to my own devices and received indispensable assistance from staff at a variety of archives and libraries, including the British Library, Guildhall Library, Lambeth Palace Archives, Library of Congress, Oxford University's Bodleian Library, Scottish National Archives, Scottish National Library, Royal Bank of Scotland, UK Parliamentary Archives, the UK National Archives, Yale University's Beinecke Rare Books and Manuscript Library and University Manuscripts and Archives; particular gratitude must also go to the various kind souls over the years behind the book delivery desk in the Oriental and India Office (now

Asian & African Studies) reading room, as well as archivists Antonia Moon, Penny Brook, Margaret Makepeace, Andrew Cook, and Anthony Farrington, all of whom, though they will not remember it, have set me straight on several matters at many crucial points. Staff at the British Library, British Museum, National Maritime Museum, Bodleian Library, and Duke University Libraries were remarkable in helping to locate and secure permission to reprint the images in this book. At various points, research, writing, and thinking was made possible by funding, fellowships, and support from Columbia University, the U.S. Department of Education, the Huntington Library, American University, and Duke University. My year at the Society for the Humanities at Cornell University deserves particular mention as a remarkable experience, without which this book and its related work would never have taken its present shape. I am eternally grateful for the support and friendship of Brett DeBary, Tim Murray, the Society's staff, and all of my fellow fellows. This work has also been presented in parts to scores of conferences, symposia, and colloquia, and all the co-panelists, commentators, and audiences at these have had a hand in shaping the final product; I wish I had the space to thank them all appropriately here. I must, however, single out my particular appreciation for the Duke University Franklin Humanities Institute, the Andrew Mellon Foundation, Srinivas Aravamudan, Ian Baucom, and all the other participants in the discussion of this manuscript, in its embarrassingly engorged form, at the Fall 2009 FHI faculty book manuscript workshop. Although no one chapter or section has been reprinted, some ideas, quotations, and possibly inadvertently turns-of-phrase strewn throughout have appeared previously in articles in the *William and Mary Quarterly* (October 2006), *Journal of British Studies* (April 2008), *Journal of Imperial and Commonwealth History* (March 2007), and book chapters in Sameetah Agah and Elizabeth Kolsky, eds., *The Fringes of Empire* (Oxford University Press, 2009), and Rafael Torres Sánchez, ed., *War, State, and Development: Fiscal-Military States in the Eighteenth Century* (Eunsa, 2007). My great thanks go to all of the readers, editors, and other interlocutors who helped shaped these pieces, and thus inevitably this book. Where drawn upon, these have been cited in appropriate places in the text.

A stunning number of colleagues, friends, and confidants have contributed, willingly or not, knowingly and not, to this project, in reading articles, chapters and even the manuscript at various points, or in offering their own work and work-in-progress, perspectives, references, research, suggestions, comfortable guest rooms, moral support, fine meals, strong drinks, and smirking indulgence of yet another conversation about how companies can be states. So, thank you: Ed Balleisen, Lauren Benton, Shailen Bhandare, Bill Bulman, Trevor Burnard, Huw Bowen, Dirk Bonker, Margaret Brill, Laurent Dubois, Kumkum Chatterjee, Partha Chatterjee, Matt Cook, Duane Corpis, Emily Erikson, Jan

Ewald, Eileen Findlay, Mitch Fraas, Rich Freeman, Alison Games, Barry Gaspar, Durba Ghosh, Marc Jason Gilbert, David Gilmartin, Travis Glasson, Chris Grasso, Malachi Hacohen, Bruce Hall, David Hancock, Kate Haulman, Santhi Hejeebu, Engseng Ho, Maya Jasanoff, Dane Kennedy, Christian Lentz, Adriane Lentz-Smith, Andrew Lewis, Matt Levinger, Andrew Mackillop, Daniel H.A. Maksymiuk, Elizabeth Mancke, Jenny Mann, John Martin, Marty Miller, Tillman Nechtman, Guy Nelson, Katharine Norris, Miles Ogborn, Guy Ortolano, Sasha Pack, Gunther Peck, Patrick Peebles, Susan Pennybacker, Vijay Pinch, Richard Price, Sumathi Ramaswamy, Bill Reddy, Tom Robisheaux, Anupama Rao, Suman Seth, April Shelford, Kim Sims, Brent Sirota, Stacey Sloboda, Tristan Stein, Sanjay Subrahmanyam, Rajani Sudan, Susan Thorne, Erin Williams-Hyman, Hannah Weiss-Muller, Carl Wennerlind, Kathleen Wilson, Anna Winterbottom, Phil Withington, Karin Wulf, Nuala Zahedieh, and all the other people I will, embarrassingly, have left off this list in my haste to get the book to press. Rick Elphick deserves particular mention, having been a remarkable mentor to me since I first staged a Wesleyan-style sit-in in his office to persuade him to be my undergraduate advisor many years ago. Nicholas Dirks, Paul Halliday, Peter Marshall, Robert Travers, and Deborah Valenze have offered their support and friendship over the years in countless ways, and allowed me constantly to test that friendship by forcing this work and my troubles on them in various forms; I owe them each far more than this one line of thanks can encapsulate. Susan Ferber has been an indefatigable editor, a tireless BlackBerrier, a culinary confidant, and a remarkably patient friend throughout, without whom I am certain I would not have survived any of this. Yet, I must reserve this last line of thanks here for David Armitage, who has tolerantly watched this project grow (and shrink, grow, and shrink again) for quite some time, and whose unflinching support, counsel, mentorship, and friendship has meant so very much to me; I can only hope he will come to regard this book as, so to speak, the statue inside the block of stone.

As this book for better and worse has been seamlessly integrated into my life for upwards of a decade, my greatest debts go to my family—grandparents, aunt, uncle, cousins, brothers- and sisters-in-law, nieces, and nephews—who have provided so much over the years. To John, who I very much think would have liked seeing this book in print, and Carole, who tolerated this book's (and my) constant and uninvited intrusion into their lives, thank you, for everything. There is really no way to express my gratitude and love for my parents, Elliot and Sharon, who, though undoubtedly bewildered at my peculiar fascinations and long trips abroad to sit in libraries for hours on end, have supported me without limits, generously, unwaveringly, and unhesitatingly in everything I have done; I could not have done any of this without them. Anyone who knows me well will likely not be surprised if I take at least one line to acknowledge with deep affection the indelible pawprint Mina has left on my work and my life. And, I suppose the only thing I can say to Kim—who has read, edited, listened, humored, D.J'd, consulted, consoled, cajoled, and otherwise endured my shiny happy fits of rage on an almost daily basis—is that I dedicate this book to her.

NOTE ON SPELLING AND DATES

Spellings in quotations have been, for the most part, left unaltered, though for the sake of ease of reading, contemporary shorthand has been expanded and modernized (e.g., "ye" replaced with "the"; Compa rendered "Company"; and so on). Spelling in this period, even of names and especially of non-English terms, was variable; the use of [*sic*] or any other marker has been reduced to an absolute minimum and employed only where absolutely necessary. Place and personal names in nonquoted text have mostly been modernized but contemporary usage retained where there exists a common or familiar historical usage (e.g., Bengkulu not Bencoolen, but Bombay not Mumbai). All emphasis in quotations (italics and capitalizations) is original, unless otherwise noted.

All dates appear in the English ("old") style. Years in the text have been rendered with the calendar year beginning 1 January, though dates in the notes have been cited using contemporary convention, with the year beginning 25 March (e.g., 4 February 1677 in the text but 4 February 1676/7 in the notes).

The Company-State

Introduction

"A State in the Disguise of a Merchant"

"It is strange, very strange," reflected the author, statesman, and East India Company employee Thomas Babington Macaulay in 1833, "that a joint stock society of traders . . . which, judging a priori from its constitution, we should have said was as little fitted for imperial functions as the Merchant Tailors' Company or the New River Company, should be intrusted with the sovereignty of a larger population, the disposal of a larger clear revenue, the command of a larger army, than are under the direct management of the Executive Government of the United Kingdom."[1] For many then and since, the English East India Company's victory over the *nawab* of Bengal at the Battle of Plassey in 1757 and its assumption eight years later of the Mughal office of *diwan* (revenue collector and administrator) in eastern India had transformed a commercial body into something novel, unnatural, and, in Adam Smith's words, a "strange absurdity": that is, a Company-State and a merchant-empire.[2] Yet, the constitutional, institutional, and ideological roots of what Edmund Burke pilloried as "a state in the disguise of a merchant" traced to an era when such a thing was not so much "strange" as typical: an early modern world filled with a variety of corporate bodies politic and hyphenated, hybrid, overlapping, and composite forms of sovereignty.[3] While the English East India Company may have become a territorial power in South Asia in the mid-eighteenth century, it had actually been a form of government, state, and sovereign in Asia for some time.

From its inception in 1600, the East India Company, as a corporation, was by its very organization a government over its own employees and corporators. It claimed jurisdiction over English trade and traffic in Asia and thus over English goods, ships, and subjects throughout the Eastern Hemisphere. By the second half of the seventeenth century, the Company had also become a colonial proprietor, governing a small but growing network of plantations in Asia and the South Atlantic and their polyglot European, Asian, and African populations. In these capacities, the Company did what early modern governments did: erect and administer law; collect taxes; provide protection; inflict punishment; perform stateliness; regulate economic, religious, and civic life; conduct diplomacy

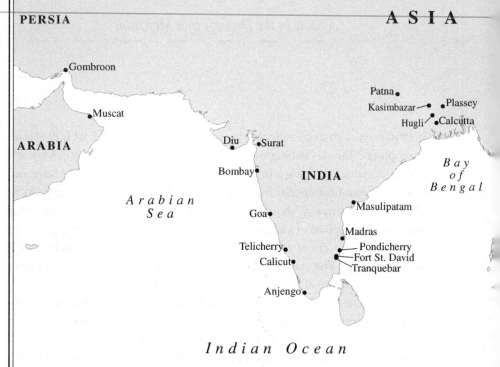

World of the
East India Company before 1757

PERSIA

ASIA

Gombroon

Muscat

ARABIA

Diu •Surat

Bombay•

INDIA

Patna•
Kasimbazar• •Plassey
Hugli• •Calcutta

*Bay
of
Bengal*

*Arabian
Sea*

Goa•

•Masulipatam

Madras•

Telicherry•
Calicut•

Pondicherry
Fort St. David
Tranquebar

Anjengo•

Indian Ocean

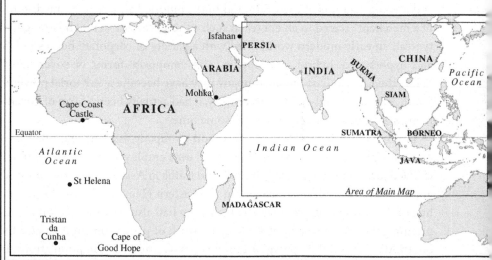

Isfahan•
PERSIA

CHINA

ARABIA   INDIA

BURMA

*Pacific
Ocean*

Mohka•

Cape Coast
Castle

AFRICA

SIAM

Equator

SUMATRA   BORNEO

*Atlantic
Ocean*

Indian Ocean

JAVA

•St Helena

Area of Main Map

MADAGASCAR

Tristan
da
Cunha
•

Cape of
Good Hope

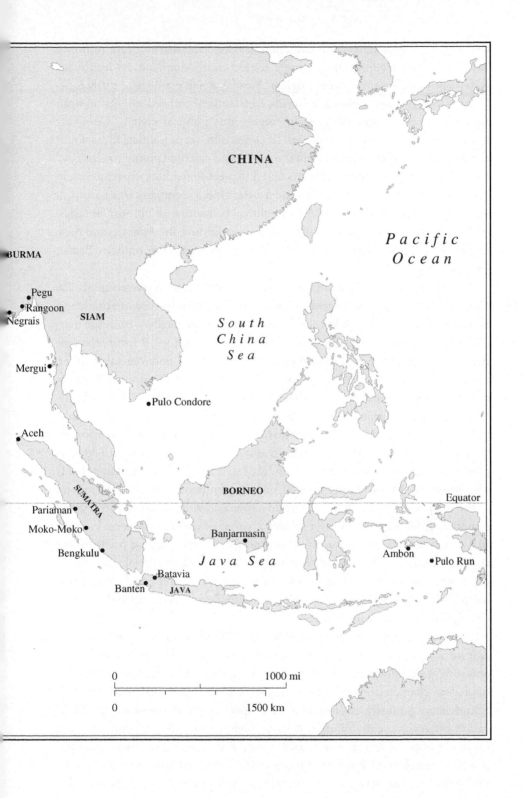

CHINA

BURMA

Pegu
Rangoon
Negrais   SIAM

Pacific
Ocean

South
China
Sea

Mergui

Pulo Condore

Aceh

SUMATRA

BORNEO

Equator

Pariaman

Moko-Moko

Banjarmasin

Ambon
Pulo Run

Bengkulu

Java Sea

Batavia
Banten   JAVA

0		1000 mi

0		1500 km

and wage war; make claims to jurisdiction over land and sea; cultivate authority over and obedience from those people subject to its command. Its legitimacy rested in a complex amalgam of English charters, Asian grants, and its own deliberate and aggressive political behavior, constantly negotiated with its subordinates, allies, rivals, and subjects. In forging this political system, Company leadership were guided by a coherent, if composite, set of political ideas about the duties of subjects and rulers and the nature and extent of political authority.[4] Even if many of its early experiments failed to meet immediate expectations, in both form and function the early modern East India Company was hardly an anomaly. It reflected the same sort of political behaviors, ambitions, fantasies, and imagination evident in its contemporaries in Europe, the Atlantic, and Asia, not to mention its famous and most obvious progeny: the modern British Empire in India.

In focusing on the Company as a form of early modern government, *The Company-State* proposes to move it—along with companies, corporations, and a variety of non-national political communities more generally—from the margins to the center of its own political and intellectual history. It resists the tendency to envision the early Company as either merely a commercial body or, when exhibiting political behaviors, in conditional, metaphorical, and ultimately imperfect terms: state-*like*, *semi*-sovereign, *quasi*-governmental.[5] Instead, this book takes the early Company as a body politic on its own terms, neither tethered to supposedly broader national histories nor as an imitation, extension, or reflection of the national state, which was itself still in formation through this period.[6] It therefore offers neither a model of state and empire formation that is a projection of the will of a pre-formed, imperial center outward nor a discussion of the ways in which the British state and national identity emerged through the imperial experience, but rather explores a vision of an early modern "empire" that was constituted by a variety of competing and overlapping political and constitutional forms in both alliance and tension with the national state and its claims to coherent and central power, and a modern state and empire that was in many ways formed by the process of incorporating, co-opting, and undermining the legitimacy of those institutions.

Envisioning a more composite and decentered constitution for early modern empire ironically encourages at the same time a healthy skepticism about the enduring geographical, conceptual, and chronological distinctions that have tended to characterize both the Company's history and that of the British Empire more generally. The notion of a Company-State questions any fast bifurcation between an early modern Atlantic, defined by colonial plantation and European imperial rivalry, and a "trading world" of Asia and the Indian Ocean.[7] It also challenges the long-standing assumptions about the contrasts among Europeans in Asia between, on the one hand, supposedly modern, capitalist northern European companies and an antediluvian Portuguese *Estado da India*[8] and, on the other, an aggressive, monopolistic state-building Dutch *Vereenigde Oost-Indische Compagnie* (United East India Company, or VOC) and a weak, peaceful, and commercial English Company.[9] As in the Atlantic, European experiences in Asia were both historiographically comparable and historically entangled.[10] Thinking in this way about the early modern Company further undermines traditionally stark divisions between "trading" and "imperial" eras in Asia and rethinks the dynamics of transition between the "first" and "second" British empires, pointing instead to a more continuous, gradual, and contingent story that envisions the evolution of empire as part of the transformation from early modern to modern forms of state, sovereignty, and political power.

The early English East India Company laid the necessary though not sufficient conditions for its later transformation into a territorial empire. Its origins were admittedly far more humble, but they were no less political. The charter Queen Elizabeth I granted on 31 December 1600 for the *Governor and Company of Merchants of London, Trading into the East-Indies* announced it from the start to be "one body corporate and politick," that is, a corporation.[11] The concept of the "corpus politicum et corporatum" or "communitas perpetua" went back to Roman law and formed the bedrock for political and associational life in early modern England. There were corporations for municipal government, domestic and regional trades, public works, ecclesiastical establishments and religious confraternities, universities and educational societies, charities, and, of course, for overseas English commerce, settlement, and colonization from Europe to the Atlantic, Russia to the Mediterranean and Africa.[12] Legally and conceptually speaking, the early modern national state and even the monarch herself were forms of corporation.[13] Whatever their immediate purposes and particular organization, all corporations shared a common purpose: to bind a multitude of people together into a legal singularity, an artificial person that could maintain common rights, police community standards and behavior, and administer over and on behalf of the collectivity.[14] In the words of an early eighteenth-century digest of corporation laws, "The general Intent and End of all Civil Incorporation is for better Government; either general or special."[15]

As governments, corporations possessed complex legal personalities, both subject and resistant to other forms of political power. The artificial man could be neither loyal nor treasonous, pious nor apostate; he could sue and be sued but not commit a crime, take an oath, or even really appear when summoned. People, quite obviously, could belong to, and even govern, multiple corporations at once. Some corporations stretched over or between various jurisdictions, while some were nested within other corporations, such as guilds, churches, or universities in incorporated municipalities, like London or Oxford.[16] In principle, many were immortal, and certainly the idea of the corporation itself was that it would outlive any individual member: "in like manner," as the eighteenth-century English legal scholar William Blackstone described it, "as the river Thames is still the same river, though the parts which compose it are changing every instance."[17] In fact, a corporation's government in theory only got stronger with age. As Blackstone observed, the corporation of London did not have a charter but existed by the prescription of time; the lawyer Charles Molloy, writing in 1677, insisted the Merchant Adventurers, which had been founded as recently as the early fifteenth century, were a "Society . . . of Ancient estimation, so is their Government very commendable."[18]

If the corporation was a body politic, it was, as the East India Company's charter announced, a "fellowship" as well.[19] As a form of society, it possessed an inescapably social character.[20] Like the corporation, the idea of a "company" was etymologically and conceptually rooted in principles of association, as in keeping the company of others, whether a company of infantry troops or the company of a theater troupe. In the civil law tradition, as the seventeenth-century jurist Edward Coke observed, the corporation was simply and broadly compre-hended as a "*collegium* or *universitas*," that is, a group bound together for a com-munal purpose under a shared set of rules and laws.[21] This public and associational character was not merely theoretical. All corporations possessed and employed distinct forms of franchise, ceremony, privileges, and overt and secret rituals that created social bonds and shaped institutional cultures. Such practices inevitably generated their own allegiances and identities, compatible but also potentially in competition with others, including the Crown.[22] Corporations frequently resented, resisted, and, from the Civil War to the American Revolution, even rebelled against that hierarchy: "like some Frankenstein," the twentieth-century political theorist Harold Laski waxed sardonically, showing "ingratitude to their creators."[23] Thomas Hobbes, for one, believed the largest and most well-armed municipal corporations to be such a threat to the sovereignty of his Leviathan that he regarded them as an "infirmity" in the body politic and, in his famous phrase, as "lesser commonwealths in the bowels of a greater, like wormes in the entrayles of a naturall man."[24]

Whether seen as a person or a parasite, the idea of the corporation and asso-ciation confounds modern assumptions about the nation-state as the ultimate political and social community. Both Max Weber's very influential notion of the state—as a territorially bounded bureaucracy with a monopoly on legitimate violence—and the so-called Westphalian model of sovereignty—a system of purely autonomous and independent territorial states that supposedly emerged out of the treaties that ended the Thirty Years' War in 1648—have been more myth and argument than reality and inevitability.[25] Meanwhile, the German po-litical theorist Carl Schmitt's modern notion that the political realm was defined by the presence of friends and enemies, but "in the domain of economics there are no enemies, only competitors, and in a thoroughly moral and ethical world perhaps only debating adversaries" is certainly complicated by a globalizing, postmodern world where it is clear states have competitors and companies can have friends, enemies, and possibly even sovereignty.[26] As different as Weber and Schmitt's visions were, they both pointed to the exclusivity of a transcendent national state, yet, even in its supposed modern heyday, this was hardly the only available model of political community. As the mid-nineteenth-century German historian and legal scholar Otto von Gierke argued, fellowships, associations, and corporations had deep historical roots in Europe as legal and moral communities, which were in "total antagonism" with the relatively novel notion of an absolutist state; even their modern iteration, the joint-stock company, was simultaneously public and private in its corporate personality.[27] In von Gierke's wake, a number of English legal and political theorists, like Frederic William Maitland, John Neville Figgis, and Harold Laski (in his early work) similarly offered a powerful critique of the nation-state's claim to unity and coherence; their understanding of society was one rooted in a pluralism defined as well by varieties of corporate and associational life.[28] "The groups [the state] has claimed to control seem, often enough, to lead a life no less full and splendid than its own," Laski observed;[29] "everywhere we find groups within the state, a part of it; but one with it they are not. . . . Whether we will or no, we are bundles of hyphens."[30]

Such a vision of political fragmentation undoubtedly characterized an early modern world defined not by singular, sovereign monocracies but intersecting empires, pluralistic legal cultures, and a variety of shapes and forms of hybrid and competing jurisdictions.[31] The sorts of "absolutism" described by thinkers like Hobbes and the French theorist Jean Bodin, so often taken to represent a norm of early modern politics, were more prescription than description. They were indeed anxious responses to the practice and theory of an early modern sovereignty, which was divisible, uneven, and exemplified by competing claims over people and the corridors, passageways, and spaces in which they lived and on which they traveled.[32] What the historian J. H. Elliott has termed "a Europe of composite monarchies," a system of conglomerate, diverse, and overlapping forms of political power, actually characterized imperial polities across Eurasia, such as the British, Spanish, Holy Roman, Russian, Ottoman, or Mughal empires.[33] Moreover, from popery to piracy, one found within and among these empires a cacophony of enclaved, self-governing communities, from city-states to merchants, mercenaries, masons, mendicants, and many others.[34] Certainly early modern England appears upon closer examination to be not so much a clear hierarchy as an interlocking matrix of commonwealths, churches, associations, communities, office-holders, agencies, and families.[35]

This was perhaps no more true than in early modern European overseas empires, which more often than not were pioneered and governed not by states alone but in cooperation and competition with a medley of companies and corporations, *conquistadores*, explorers, privateers, proprietors, and itinerant merchant, family, and religious networks. Political community in this extra-European world looked far more like Laski's bundles of hyphens than Weber's "territorial bundles."[36] Accordingly, the governance of the "English" empire at home and abroad was a layered and hybrid affair, resting on multiple constitutional foundations and constantly negotiated among a variety of royal agencies, local governors, councils, assemblies, courts, and corporate and legal communities.[37] With some notable exceptions, like Jamaica and Tangier, this was an empire founded and often administered by corporations, companies, and proprietors, each built on multiple contrasting ideological, religious, political, and legal foundations.[38] Though theoretically dependent upon the Crown, in both principle and practice, these corporate colonies exercised a great deal of autonomy; some were even literally self-constituting, such as the *Mayflower* "compact," which set the foundation for colonial government in New England and its relative independence from the English state at least through the 1680s.[39] This was an English empire that was not clearly and at all times governed by or from England, one in which charters and other such instruments were often more tenuous claims on than authoritative dispensations of authority. As Maitland perceived it, "the king was no more a corporator of Rhode Island than he was a corporator of the city of Norwich or of the East India Company."[40]

As a corporation, a joint-stock company, and proprietor over English government and colonies in Asia, the English East India Company thus needs to be approached as a form of political community and polity. Like other English corporations, it was empowered and obligated to construct "Laws, Constitutions, Orders and Ordinances" to govern itself and those under its command, to administer oaths, and offer its "freedom," which essentially conferred on its holder a share of the Company's rights and privileges but also served as a form of allegiance and identity.[41] Though its first charter was experimental, limited to fifteen years, by 1607 the Crown had agreed the Company could expect a "perpetual succession," a corporate immortality that preceded the establishment of a fixed, permanent capital stock by fifty years. Unlike a guild or other forms of company, where leadership and governance inhered in those who actually did the trading, the joint-stock organization meant that the Company was administered by shareholders. Stock functioned in many ways as land did in the territorial polity: it was a requirement for the franchise, a testimony of loyalty, and a literal and symbolic investment in the corporation's well-being. It was also open to the same sorts of patronage and clientage, split stocks—that is, large shareholdings alienated in trust to friends, family, and allies to shore up voting blocs—serving in essence as the Company's rotten boroughs.[42]

Like similar organizations, the Company was led by an executive council constituted by twenty-four large stockholders, known individually as "committees."[43] At the helm of this Court of Committees, as it was known, was a governor
and deputy governor, limited to two-year terms and elected annually by those
holding a minimum amount of stock out of a General Court, the main body of
Company shareholders that William Pitt would later deride as a "Little Parliament."[44] The committees were organized into subcouncils to which were delegated particular tasks, such as letter writing or supervising lawsuits, all meeting
and working at its imposing headquarters in London's Leadenhall Street. A secretary managed its day-to-day business, as did a growing staff, including, by the
1680s, a solicitor and standing counsel.[45] Although its politics were at times
characterized by great disagreement, acrimony, and the domination of particularly powerful or persuasive voices, its decisions and policies, as reflected in minutes, letters, rules, and orders, self-consciously insisted on the representation of
institutional unity and unanimity. Letters were signed by the whole. Conclu-
sions rather than debates were often recorded. As in early modern English politics, great purchase was placed on government by council, counsel, consensus,
and decisions made by the whole as a whole, or, in the language of the time,
nemine contradicente.[46]

This governing structure was mirrored in the Company's government abroad.
Ships, trading factories, and settlements were all headed by a captain, agent, president, or governor, each of whom sat at the head of a council, which itself was, in
theory, located in a chain of command that ultimately led back to London. Except
under extenuating circumstances, correspondence, orders, and minutes (known
as "consultations") were considered invalid without the consent and signature of
an entire council; one individual who refused to put his name to an outgoing letter
could bring all business to a halt. Company government at every level was thus a
delicate balance of strict hierarchy and consultative government, conditioned by
an institutional culture defined and constantly reinforced by ritual, procedure, and
ceremony. Even seemingly pragmatic exercises, like letter writing, were imbued
with political significance. Superiors scrutinized subordinates' writing, down to
proper margins and handwriting: orderly letters signaled obedient behavior.
Writing was also the backbone of a global network, crucial to imagining such a
geographically dispersed political system as coherent and to supervising and governing it. Company committees regarded writing as capable in both form and content of revealing the state of a place on the other side of the world as clearly as if
they were "to observe them with their own eyes."[47]

This hierarchical system of councils bound together by a constant circulation
of people, things, and documents was the backbone of the Company's political
system. The tendency to approach the Company as a private commercial concern, however, has led scholars most often to imagine its politics as a subset of

seventeenth-century English and European politics, political economy, and state formation.[48] Its system of governance has been treated, at best, as what the historian K. N. Chaudhuri called a "business constitutionalism," a sophisticated administrative structure primarily concerned with predicting markets, managing commercial exchange, and confronting the "agency" problem faced by all large companies: namely, how to control and discipline employees and minimize inefficiencies and corruption. Meanwhile, political institutions and behavior, especially violence, are assumed to be a "politics of trade" in which the bottom line was the only ideology and the balance sheet the only manifesto.[49] In this view, ideology seems purely instrumental in the service of that commerce, devoid of coherent principles even if occasionally punctuated by the sorts of lofty sentiments Macaulay sarcastically dismissed as an "admirable code of political ethics."[50] When combined with imperial historians' long-standing concern with the ways in which the private trading of Company employees precipitated the expansion of empire in the eighteenth century, the pre-Plassey Company in Asia has tended to be approached as commercially transformative but politically anemic and hollow, plagued by short-term and instrumental thinking driven from within by its particular political and commercial concerns or those of its employees and manipulated from without by its rivals.[51]

Yet, taking the Company seriously as a political institution and its writing as a body of ideological work reveals something else entirely: a preoccupying concern with government that extended far beyond regulating trade and its "servants," as employees were known. The Company's charter, which encompassed all the trade and traffic between the Cape of Good Hope and the Strait of Magellan, translated into a claim to jurisdiction over all English subjects in Asia and the Eurasian populations resident in its growing network of settlements. Grant after grant from English monarchs progressively expanded this purview, giving the Company leave to establish fortifications, make law, erect courts, issue punishment, coin money, conduct diplomacy, wage war, arrest English subjects, and plant colonies.[52] This was hardly unique. As the former governor of Massachusetts Thomas Pownall observed in 1773, such a constitution could "be found to stand upon the same grounds and base [and] to have moved in the same line as all other like emigrations and settlements *in partibus caeteris*"—that is, the world beyond Europe, namely in the Atlantic.[53] At the same time, the Company's vast claim to jurisdiction over the entire Eastern Hemisphere, and ultimately even parts of the South Atlantic, far more resembled those of its European rivals than its Atlantic brethren. This large and vaguely defined jurisdiction, Company leaders, advocates, and lawyers came to argue, demanded an even greater range of independence from metropolitan ambitions than those other English overseas ventures.[54] In this, the Company's Portuguese, Dutch, and Asian contemporaries, with their sophisticated governmental and martial organization and capacious claims to sovereignty formed both the principal exemplars and adversaries for efforts to expand the early political foundations for the English in India.[55]

Like those other Europeans in Asia, the Company's claims to jurisdiction and authority were framed by a range of instruments and behaviors beyond their charters and powers from home, and particularly by numerous grants, treaties, alliances, and agreements with Asian polities establishing an array of commercial and political powers and immunities.[56] Company leadership placed particular value on the Mughal imperial *farman*, which they imagined as somewhat analogous to English charters and patents.[57] While this analogy often led to serious interpretive differences over the nature of such grants, the Company's vision of that parity did not arise so much from a chauvinistic imposition of European expectations on alien Asian forms as a sense that there was in fact some commonality and translatability across early modern Eurasian political cultures. Like the charter, the *farman* provided certain protections and exceptions from legal and financial obligations and impositions, such as customs duties or restrictions on the movement of people and goods. Like the *farman*, the charter was a tool that could establish political legitimacy and provide leverage against rivals.[58] Both were also terms Company officials used loosely and colloquially to refer to a range of documents and dispensations; what the Company called "charters" were quite often more properly letters patents or like instruments, while "*Phirmaund*" frequently stood in for a host of imperial and local grants like a *sanad, husb-ul-hukm, ziman, kaul,* even referring sometimes to those derived from other than the Perso-Arabic legal tradition, like the Tamil *ola.* The process and practices involved in acquiring all of these were indeed strikingly similar, requiring persistent acts of political supplication and incorporation, lobbying at court and with courtiers, outmaneuvering rivals, performances of obsequiousness and supplication, and the disbursement of great sums of money, whether in the form of goods, gifts, loans, or *peskash* tributary payments.[59]

With its roots planted in both hemispheres, the Company's constitution could be volatile and fragile, dependent as it was on constantly changing regimes in both Europe and Asia as well its own inchoate and often resource-starved political institutions and practices.[60] At the same time, the ability to borrow and balance these various sources of authority and legitimacy potentially offered a remarkably flexible and robust form of political power. Unlike a monarchical state, the Company could modulate between positions of deference and defiance, between claims to be a "mere merchant" and an independent "sovereign." Grants and other instruments as well as the Company's own political practices could both amplify and be set against one another. The ability to do this came not just from the Company's constitution as a corporation but its unique position occupying the space between England and Asia, serving as the commercial, political, and diplomatic intermediary between the two. From such a position,

Company leaders could imagine and increasingly forge an autonomous political system, which was dependent on multiple political relationships and thus subject entirely to none—a precarious but potentially potent form of "structural autonomy" and thus corporate sovereignty.[61]

Approaching the Company as a form of state and sovereign, which claimed final jurisdiction and responsibility over people and places, suggests that the history of state formation and of political thought, only relatively recently extended to include the ideas and institutions of empire, might be extended even further, beyond the national form of those states and empires to apply to a range of corporate communities.[62] Such bodies politic possessed institutional and political cultures that both shaped and were shaped by the ideas, expectations, and behaviors of their leaders, corporators, and subjects.[63] Though undoubtedly conditioned by the prolific political economists and philosophers within its ranks, the ideologies of the Company-State, and perhaps even the ideas of those thinkers, arose not in abstraction but in direct response to the opportunities, challenges, and problems that Company leaders confronted. Pursuing a history of political thought and political economy for non-national political communities thus requires taking seriously as political thinkers in their own right those that did the governing and, in turn, regarding the act of governing itself as equally productive a site of political thought as the sorts of theoretical work more often studied.[64] This means reading the products of that government—such as pamphlets and propaganda, correspondence, minutes, laws and orders, petitions, commissions, diaries, court proceedings, and even material objects like coins and flags—as ideological texts. Intended for a variety of audiences and produced under a variety of circumstances, such texts can be traced for a set of theoretical principles, reflective of a shared set of political ideas and political culture that shaped policymaking. In the early East India Company's case, one finds leadership drawing liberally and fruitfully on examples and evidence ranging from the Bible to Batavia to Barbados, mirroring familiar doctrines of European and Asian political thought but adapting them to particular circumstances. Their ideas ranged from the pragmatic and severe to the quixotic and impractical. They were at times sober, modest, and conservative in their expectations, and at others, possessed of grand, utopian projects. Things also rarely worked out as planned. Ideas were shaped as much by failure as success. Projects were sharpened, negotiated, challenged, and elaborated across a hemispheric political system and amongst multiple layers of government, in dialogue with a host of allies, rivals, and contingent circumstances, both predicted and unforeseen.

This book traces the establishment and development of this Company-State, possessed of political institutions and underscored by coherent principles about the nature of obligations of subjects and rulers, good government, political economy, jurisdiction, authority, and sovereignty. Part 1 explores its foundations, particularly in the second half of the seventeenth century. Chapter 1 details the origins of the Company's ambitions for a network of fortified settlements in Asia and the South Atlantic, which came to be understood by its leadership as colonies, which required peopling, planting, and good and effective government. Chapter 2 in turn examines the basis for the Company's claims to be a government in Asia more broadly and thus to an extra-territorial jurisdiction on land and across the sea. Paying particular attention to the infamous case of *East India Company v. Thomas Sandys* (1682–84), it shows how Company governors in London and Asia took their exclusive trade to imply the responsibility to govern over that trade and thus over English subjects and even souls in Asia. The following three chapters scrutinize the three crucial concerns that emerged out of those colonial and jurisdictional foundations: the use of diplomacy and war to protect and expand those rights over subjects; the political and economic theory, institutions, and policies that constituted this brand of Company government; and the guiding concern among Company leadership with their role in protecting and expanding Protestantism and morality in Asia, and its fundamental relationship to political authority, power, and sovereignty.

Part 2 analyzes the transformations of this system from the 1690s up to the acquisition of territorial power in the eighteenth century, as the Company had to negotiate rapidly changing political circumstances in both Europe and Asia. Chapters 6 and 8 trace the continuities between the institutional and ideological regime established in the seventeenth century and the Company's response to continuing challenges from European, Asian, and English rivals. As the Company was expanding in fits and starts in Asia, however, it was increasingly coming under assault in Britain. Chapter 7 argues that the attack the Company faced by its rivals in England and Scotland, particularly the English Parliament, in the aftermath of the Glorious Revolution was fundamentally a dispute not only over political economy but the proper nature of colonial sovereignty; as such, the debate that ensued was instrumental in laying the groundwork for the Company's slow incorporation into the British state and empire in the eighteenth century. The final chapter returns to Asia, tracing the ways in which the core principles behind the Company's seventeenth-century political operation adapted to new circumstances in the following century. This book concludes by reflecting schematically on the connections between the Company's later eighteenth-century expansion and its pre-Plassey history. In the end, it suggests that while territorial power was hardly inevitable or prefigured, the conditions that made a British Empire in India possible—that is, both the expansion of the Company-State in India and the expansion of the British state's power over the Company—had deep roots in a seventeenth-century when the Company's "establishment in *India*" had already become, as one contemporary observed, "another Common-Wealth."[65]

PART ONE

FOUNDATIONS

1

"Planting & Peopling Your Colony"

Building a Company-State

If the English East India Company began in 1600 as essentially a body of London commercial investors and trading ships on the move, it did not remain that way for very long. Commerce from the very start required diplomacy. The Company's very first fleet was sent with royal and Company letters to negotiate for the foundations for its first "factory" (warehouse and trading post) in the Javanese sultanate of Banten. Other such outposts soon followed: at the western Mughal port of Surat, the southern Indian trading entrepot of Masulipatam, and short-lived efforts at Japan and China. Within decades, however, both in competition with and emulation of its European and Asian rivals, the East India Company would define stability in the East Indies as maintaining independent and thus fortified settlements of its own. By the end of the century, it had conceived, planted, and begun to govern a relatively scattered but coherent network of towns and islands that stretched from the south Atlantic to southeast Asia. Even if initially responding to the need to preserve a commercial network, Company leadership almost immediately came to imagine these garrisoned enclaves, like those of their contemporaries, not simply as trading posts secured by arms but as "forts places and Colonies," the foundations for sovereign settler plantations governed by sound civic institutions.[1]

Like most colonial efforts, the Company's early ambitious projects frequently failed to meet their high expectations. Its first attempted fortification was in 1626 at Armagon, just north of the southeastern Indian Dutch settlement of Pulicat; poorly constructed, costly, and both commercially and martially untenable, the project was soon abandoned, proving, in the words of its factors, to be "better lost then found." Company officials next contemplated purchasing the nearby Danish settlement of Tranquebar, also to no avail. Finally, in 1634, the head of the Armagon factory, Francis Day, initiated negotiations with Darmala

Venkatappa, a *nayak* under the waning south Indian Vijayanagara empire, for a small grant of territory a bit farther to the south. Five years later, in August 1639, in exchange for an annual tribute of half the customs raised on the port, Day received Darmala's *kaul* for the rights to build a "fort and Castle," to trade customs-free, and to "perpetually Injoy the priviledges of mintag[e]" in the coastal territory of Madraspatnam, soon known simply as Madras.[2]

From its very origins, Madras was understood as a secure base and harbor for the Company's trade in southeastern India, which could at the same time provide cheaper and more reliable access to labor, such as weavers, brokers, and translators, necessary for prosecuting that trade. A populous city was also in itself a potential market for Company goods. Yet, the very act of settling required the Company, as the court of committees confidently observed decades later, to become "Governors and Legislators" of "our Fort and towne of Madrass-patam and all that numerous people under our Government there."[3] Madras's first governor and his council set immediately about the work of building its fort, styled Fort St. George, erecting a small civil administration, and enticing settlers from nearby jurisdictions. Over the next half-century, Madras's leadership was quite successful in confirming and expanding its authority, autonomy, and even boundaries, especially remarkable given the constant political upheaval in its environs caused by ongoing war, succession struggles, conflict with other European powers, and a carousel of ruling dynasties and their feudatory officials, from Vijayanagara to Golkonda to finally, the Mughal Empire. In 1645 the Company received a new grant from Raja Sri Ranga, who had replaced Darmala as *nayak*, which now explicitly "surrender[ed]" further territory as well as "the government and justice of the towne into your hands."[4] By 1658 the Company's obligation of half-customs had been commuted into a fixed tribute, which was raised in 1672 to an annual payment of 1,200 pagodas in return for a grant "to hold this Fort & Tow[ne] free from any Aveldar [*havaldar*] or Divans [*diwan's*] People or any Imposition for ever." Within the decade, these instruments would be again confirmed and the village of Triplicane was acknowledged as part of the city's jurisdiction, while the Madras council pursued, with varying success, other neighboring villages "rent free or at moderate Rents . . . for ever."[5]

Across Asia, the early Company periodically pursued similar establishments. In 1617 the Company acquired grants in the name of King James I from local rulers in the Banda Islands for a settlement at Pulo Run. In 1622 a joint offensive with forces under the Persian *shah* ousted the Portuguese from the Gulf island of Hormuz, for which the Company was granted a perpetual share of the annual customs at the lucrative nearby port of Gombroon (Bandar-i-'Abbas).[6] In 1649 the Company supported plans for a colony in Madagascar, known as Assada, using English Barbados as their model and motivated by the recent efforts of a consortium of English interlopers led by William Courteen to establish their own rival settlement there.[7]

None of these projects was particularly successful. The Dutch had forcibly expelled the English from Run by 1620 and, more infamously, from its factory at Amboina three years later. Persian officials through the century obfuscated and delayed payment of customs from Gombroon. The Assada plantation failed. Yet, Company leadership remained committed to such an establishment abroad, especially after its brief four-year loss of exclusive rights over the East Indian trade in the mid-1650s. Oliver Cromwell's grant in 1657 of a new, vastly expanded charter emboldened investors to the tune of £739,782 in new subscriptions and propelled the committees, among whom were several prominent Atlantic projectors and proprietors, to look for new opportunities for settlement.[8] The Company purchased from the Guinea Company its monopoly and Fort Cormantine on the Gold Coast, and entered into negotiations for Cape Coast Castle as well.[9] In 1659, the factory at Surat led a failed initiative to acquire the outpost of Muscat on the Arabian coast.[10] Meanwhile, the year before, Captain John Dutton was selected to lead a return to Pulo Run. The island had theoretically been restored to the Company at the end of the (first) Anglo-Dutch war in 1654, and by 1655 the committees were resolved once more to "plant, fortify and people" it.[11] Dutton was also given a commission as governor for the south Atlantic island of St. Helena, for which the Protector Richard Cromwell had recently granted the Company a charter similarly to "settle, fortifie, and plant."[12]

As before, most of these plans would never come to fruition. The chartering of the Royal African Company at the Restoration under the patronage of the Duke of York, the King's brother and future James II, mooted the Company's new acquisitions on the eastern African coast. Continued Dutch prevarications, delays, and resistance prevented Dutton's resettlement at Pulo Run; the island was finally recovered in 1665 only to become a casualty to the peace of the second Anglo-Dutch war, swapped for Dutch New Amsterdam (restyled, after its proprietor James, as New York). Though the court of committees did not abandon hope for a plantation at Run or nearby to challenge Dutch domination over the nutmeg trade, their attention thus turned to the South Atlantic.

Ever since the island had been claimed, and soon after abandoned, by the Portuguese in the very early sixteenth century, writers had lauded St. Helena's convenient situation, abundant produce, and potential fecundity.[13] Richard Boothby, a promoter of the Courteen Madagasacar scheme, proposed it as an ideal place for colonial plantation: "pleasant, healthfull, frutifull, and commodious," perfect for "trading with all Nations" and naturally "invincible and impregnable."[14] In reality, the forty-seven-square-mile, vacant, volcanic island was hardly paradise on earth, yet this did not stop the Company from making grand plans for its future. It was most immediately useful as port of call, not only for English East India shipping but for other Europeans, who it was imagined would bring business and traffic to the island and reciprocate in kind at their own stations, particularly the recently planted Dutch Cape colony.[15] Especially after its recovery from a brief Dutch occupation and its rechartering in 1673, St. Helena became to Company leadership far more than a place to repair ships and take in water. Constant hardship, consistent failure, and frequent rebellions of soldiers and settlers could not dissuade them of their grand plans for constructing a colonial plantation at the crossroads between East and West, populated with European settlers and African slaves, the latter governed on an Atlantic model as chattel and under a harsh code modeled quite explicitly on "a Barbados discipline." Such a plantation could produce goods of both hemispheres, while serving as the lynchpin in a wider, interconnected transhemispheric commercial and political system.[16]

If St. Helena was this global network's lynchpin, the Company's third major settlement was to be its axle: the archipelago of Bombay, just off the western Indian coast not far from Surat. Just as at St. Helena and Madras, Company leaders' ambitions for "some place that wee might call our owne" in the region were hardly new. Also like in those earlier efforts, previous projects had not come to much. A joint expedition of four hundred English and Dutch soldiers failed to take the island from the Portuguese by force in 1626. A proposal in 1654 to Oliver Cromwell for the acquisition, either through purchase or seizure, of one of the Portuguese colonies of Bassein, Bombay, or Mozambique went unrealized.[17] As recently as 1658, amid their other objectives in the Atlantic, Pacific, and Africa, the committees had commissioned the Surat factory council to acquire a footing at Danda Rajpuri, Bassein, or Bombay, "if they be in a capacitie to keep possession of the same."[18]

Finally, in 1661, "Bombay"—the actual shape and extent of which would be in dispute for years—was transferred from Portugal to the English King Charles II, as part of the dowry and treaty occasioned by his marriage to the Portuguese *infanta*, Catherine of Braganza.[19] Not many in England considered it much of a prize. Edward Hyde, the Earl of Clarendon and Lord High Chancellor, was rumored to have thought it was located somewhere near Brazil (something not helped, but hardly explained, by the fact that someone had lost the map accompanying the treaty), while the naval official and infamous diarist Samuel Pepys regarded the "poor little island" as vastly inferior to Tangier, the other major overseas possession that came from the Portuguese match.[20] As at Tangier, a Crown governor—in Bombay's case, Abraham Shipman—and a garrison were sent to take possession of the colony and instructed to govern "according to such good, just and reasonable Customes and Constitutions as are exercised and settled in Our other Colonies and Plantations."[21] Unlike Tangier, state officials almost immediately sought to unload the island. The Crown had little experience governing in India and at such a distance, and even the short royal tenure at Bombay had incited jurisdictional tensions with the Company. In December 1667, the Privy Council ordered the attorney general to draft a charter giving the Company "full Power to Governe, Order and direct in the said Island, as is Usuall in any other his Majesty's Plantations"; the patents that followed the next year transferred to the Company the island's sole proprietorship, along with command of a fort, a small English garrison and its stores, and about ten or twelve thousand inhabitants, mostly Portuguese and *mestizo* Indo-Portuguese Catholics and western Indian Hindus and Muslims, all in exchange for a nominal tribute of £10 a year.[22]

Although the London committees had actually expressed initial hesitation to take the island, once obtained, they nonetheless seemed enthusiastic, eager, and ambitious for their charge over, as the traveler John Fryer, who visited the island several years later, put it, "the Martial as well as the civil Affairs . . . the Sword as well as the Quill."[23] Bombay presented a remarkable opportunity to remove the Company's presidency, the head of its affairs in Western Asia, from Surat, where it was vulnerable both to the vicissitudes of Mughal politics in the town and the ongoing war between the Mughal and Maratha empires without it. To accomplish this, Bombay was to be "settled in the way of a colony," along the lines of Dutch Batavia and "as considerable as the great Cittie of our neighbours," Portuguese Goa.[24] Before even acquiring formal power on the island, London had advised Surat "to seriously consider, what is fitt to be done . . . for the setling of a Christian Collony, in good order and safety, under a good government and for the increase of all Manufactures and to encourage trade to and from the place."[25]

The royal patents for Bombay, like the one for St. Helena, delivered to the East India Company what Courtenay Ilbert, the late-nineteenth-century government of India lawyer, called "the attributes of sovereignty."[26] This included rights to dispose of and alienate land, to draw rents and assess taxes, to defend the island and use martial force, to appoint and dismiss its governors, and to make laws "for the good Government, and other Use of the said Port and Island *Bombay*," as long as they were "not repugnant or contrary, but as near as may be agreeable to the Laws of this Our Realm of *England*."[27] Such language was consistent with those found in Atlantic charters and proprietorships, and, despite its superficial implication of legal uniformity, in fact provided for a great deal of variation, flexibility, and independence in the styles and practice of colonial government. What was "near as may be agreeable" to English law was clearly a matter of interpretation. Laws, such as those governing property and inheritance, differed dramatically from one plantation to another. Some, such as policies on slavery and religious toleration, could even be quite "repugnant" to established English law and custom. In fact, as St. George Tucker, the early American republic legal scholar, suggested, to make the laws of the realm of England actually *conform* in and among the colonies "would require the talents of an Alfred . . . united with the coercive arm of the Norman tyrant."[28] A similar implication

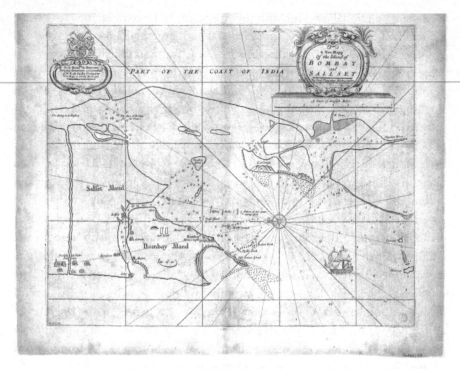

Samuel Thornton, "A New Mapp Of the Island of Bombay and Sallset" (London, 1734), National Maritime Museum, G254:6/8. The map is identical to the one published by John Thornton in 1685. © National Maritime Museum, Greenwich, London.

could be found in the way Bombay and St. Helena's patents, again as in the western Atlantic, situated the islands "as of the Manor of *East-Greenwich*, in the County of *Kent*."[29] While seemingly constructing a legal geography in which the entire English world overseas was within a stone's throw of the Thames, such language in fact served to strengthen rather than diminish a proprietor's autonomy and independence. It established lands and jurisdiction held "in free and common Soccage, and not in Capite, nor by Knight's Service," that is, held freely in exchange for a fixed rent, neither directly of the Crown nor with any expectation of feudal service. Locating property as of East Greenwich, whether overseas or in England, essentially rendered any previous claims, whether by local landholders or other sovereign powers, in legal oblivion, permitting its conversion to allodial, freehold property completely subject to the rule and regulation of its "true Lords and Proprietors."[30]

As proprietors, colonial governors and councils were in this sense like manorial lords, who could alienate land, administer justice, exact fines, and control populations within the bounds of their estates. The Court of Committees regarded its rights at Bombay and St. Helena, for example, to issue fines for "all

"The English Fort of Bombay," from Philippus Baldaeus, *A True and Exact Description of the Most Celebrated East-India Coasts of Malabar and Coromandel* (London, 1703), Duke University Libraries, E f#88 v. 3 c. 1. This is a translation of the Dutch edition of 1672. Reprinted courtesy of Rare Book, Manuscript, and Special Collections Library, Duke University.

cases of trespass, misbehaviour, breach of the peace, or high misdemeanor," as akin to those of royal or seigniorial courts.[31] As both a property and jurisdictional right, such patents could not be summarily recalled. Unlike a viceroyalty, they did not behold the patent holder to the immediate supervision of the Crown. In short, instruments like the "repugnancy" and "Manor of Greenwich" formulae implied a significant latitude of rights and immunities for a proprietor, which were only more pronounced overseas, where relationships to the Crown that granted the patent and theoretically retained sovereignty over its holder proved potentially ambiguous in both theory and practice.[32]

Such a wide sense of a proprietors' prerogative abroad certainly limited the reach of statute law, and thus Parliament.[33] This is not to say that English law was not extremely useful and pervasive in shaping Company law. European legal texts were periodically sent from London; when Sir William Langhorn was replaced as governor of Madras in 1677, the council there anxiously negotiated with him to buy his personal law library of twenty-eight titles.[34] Nonetheless, the committees held fast to the notion that English common and statute law was a useful model but not a binding one abroad, extending as it did no "further then to England, Wales, & Berwick upon Tweed." In their estimation, in overseas plantations, the Crown's power was absolute, as long as "he has not bounded it by some Charter of his own to the first Planters or Adventurers, as in the Plantations of the Matathusis or Boston in New England and that of Pistataqua or Plimouth in New England."[35] The corporation thus had a dual personality: subject to the English Crown in one sense but possessed of a supreme rule abroad in another: "wee act by his authority, so their dependence is on us, and they act by ours."[36] As London contended, "the Company must always have the Preference in India as his Majesty justly hath here," though in some ways they implied it was even greater, as St. Helena's laws and constitutions, which they had drafted, were also to be regarded "as good Law as Magna Charta is to England."[37]

The importance of establishing regular and demonstrable forms of *Company* administration and justice in these overseas plantations could not be overstated. Bombay's new council immediately began to hear inhabitants' complaints against previous, including Crown, governments on the island. It set about restoring property that had been confiscated by the last formally appointed royal governor, Gervase Lucas, both "to endear the inhabitants to us, for fear of depopulation" and to "keepe the people in good order and obedience."[38] By late 1668, the committees had composed a digest of laws for Bombay, covering a range of "civill, military or religious" matters, including observance of the Sabbath, judicial procedures, property laws, systems of probate, civil and criminal offences, and military discipline. These also included instructions for building fortifications and organizing government.[39] (A similar set for St. Helena followed in 1680.[40]) Before Bombay could even complain that the island needed a judge "for deciding the causes of meum and teum among these litigious people," the committees had sent out several factors who they boasted were "not only schollers, but have studied something both of civill and common law" to serve in such a capacity.[41]

To settle this transfer, Gerald Aungier, Bombay's second governor, made two visits to the island from Surat, where he normally resided. He came first for a couple of months in 1670 and then, in 1672, for a couple of years. During both stays, he primarily concerned himself with replacing the Portuguese system with Company law and otherwise establishing a regular system of civil government.[42] He had the code of laws sent from London published in English, Portuguese, and Canarin (Konkani). Three different courts were proposed for enforcing them: a "court of conscience" to hear cases worth twenty Xeraphins or less, "where the Poore may have justice done them gratis"; a lesser court, to adjudicate all civil cases worth less than two hundred Xeraphins; and a high judicature court with jurisdiction over all cases directly affecting the island's governance, criminal cases, greater civil cases, and appeals from the other courts. George Wilcox, one of the "schollers" sent from London, was appointed its first chief judge, at the relatively lucrative salary of two thousand rupees, and relieved of all his duties of "trade & commerce," as he put it, "appointing me wholly to the study of the law & to spend my time in reading such bookes, as might advantage me to performe my duty in so high a place."[43] As at its other two settlements, the Company insisted that its garrisoned settlement not be a garrison government: as Aungier and his council put it, Bombay was "a politie military and civill," that must "grounde itself on maxims answerable to the exigences of each respective species." The use of martial law to try non-soldiers was forbidden.[44] London sent orders for the organization of a civilian militia.[45] Aungier created an "English" civil administration of clerks, clerk's criers, constables, church wardens, a probate office, and an attorney and solicitor general. He even subdivided the island into Anglo-Saxon jurisdictions of "hundreds"—Bombay, Mahim, Mazagon, and Sion—each with a justice of the peace (Bombay had two), who were to hold monthly assizes.

Of course, Company Bombay was also built on and over existing infrastructure as well as legal, political, and social traditions. Wilcox understood the island's charter required courts and laws be "as neare as possible, according to the Custome and constitution of England," but to him this seemed to mean English law would step in when no appropriate Company law or local custom could be found to do a better job. For Aungier, Company law was an "Excellent Abridgement" of the "nationall Laws of England," in so far as both were "grounded on the laws of God written in his holy word, and on the Laws of nature, stamped on the heart of man."[46] Bombay's hundreds were subdivided not into parishes but "packerys" (*pakhadi*). The lesser civil court was to be presided over by "country justices," who inevitably mixed this new English law with existing Portuguese legal traditions. Though the island would not have representative bodies, like American assemblies, Aungier did envision a system of *panchayats*, caste-based consultative and judicial bodies for the Portuguese, Hindu, and Muslim populations, so that the island's population would cease to be "a mixed confused body, a garden planted with severall sorts of flowers promiscuously growing up among one another without order and decorum, and having no head nor chiefe among themselves." Their election was authorized in 1674, and the Portuguese council for Bombay was established the next year.[47]

These experiments at Bombay served as models for the Company's other colonies. Madras's high judicature court was established in 1678, "agreeable to the forme and Method of the proceedings in the Court of Judicature at Bombay." It did not, however, replace the existing court, in operation since the 1650s. Where the new judicature drew its authority from the Company's royal charters and the committees' commissions, the "choultry," as it was known, was grounded on the rights to administer justice found in the town's original South Indian grants. It principally tried cases according to equity and in consultation with local caste heads and community leaders. Like at Bombay, the new high court was intended for more substantial civil or criminal cases, especially originating from the "white" or "Christian" town, as well as issues more directly related to matters of state and to serve as a court of appeal from the choultry.[48] St. Helena also had a high judicature court, presided over by the governor and council. The court heard both criminal and civil causes, ranging from probate and property disputes to murder, slander, adultery, fornication, assault, and, on one occasion, the odd case of a corporal in the garrison's "catching and holding [a planter] by his privy members to his greate paine and griefe."[49]

These Company courts were designed first and foremost to maintain respect for government, from within and without, and satisfy the needs of inhabitants for both public order and the resolution of civil conflict. The ability to mete out justice and the willingness of inhabitants to submit to and seek it out justified and buttressed claims to jurisdiction and authority. Punishment, as in one case of a Jesuit and his servant who aided in a jailbreak at Bombay, served as "a Severe reproofe that they may knowe under whose Government they Live."[50] Aungier compared Bombay's laws to those of ancient Israel, Greece, Persia, and Rome. George Wilcox went so far as to insist that the reputation of Company government rested entirely on the reputation of its court, almost reveling in the conviction of a Company soldier for rape, a decision that supposedly gave "a General Satisfaction to the people and has brought such a repute to our Justice that they think themselves happy under our Government."[51] In 1687 the Madras council boasted in similar terms that the choultry was a key to the "great reputation of this Government."[52]

If the administration of justice made implicit claims about the Company's authority over its settlements and their inhabitants, it simultaneously limited others' ability to do the same. In 1671 the Madras council refused to allow Portuguese inhabitants to have "judges of their owne Nation," because, as it wrote London, such a concession would "intrench upon your jurisdiction." The council also resisted strong pressure from a *havaldar* with military jurisdiction over neighboring territories who insisted he was "to have jurisdiction in this Towne."[53] In 1678 the Madras government specifically forbid any private inhabitant to collect taxes or administer justice without permission of the council, the judicature court, or the choultry, specifically to assert authority over the customary prerogatives of local temple management and patronage.[54] Gerald Aungier was even reluctant to allow Bombay inhabitants to appeal decisions to the then-superior Surat council, since, in the words of one of his successors, "it takes a great deale of the Respect from you that is due."[55] Crucially, none of the Company's seventeenth-century settlements, even the royally chartered governments of St. Helena and Bombay, permitted formal appeals to authorities in England; on the rare occasion when an appeal did happen, as in the case of one

Portuguese resident accused of murder at Madras, it was treated a matter of clemency, not a right. In 1677 even the Lords Commissioners of Trade and Plantations agreed, advising Charles II on the complaint of a Portuguese inhabitant from Bombay that "it does not consist with your Majesty's justice to give sentence in this place upon a cause which does originally belong to the courts of Bombay"; to do so would have diminished the power of the law, the Company's proper "jurisdiction," and, perhaps paradoxically, even the King's "sovereignty."[56]

As law and justice served to buttress the Company's authority within a settlement, it also reinforced a broader vision of a system of settlements, bound together in a network of exchange and movement. Laws, like much experience and experiments in governance from ecological policies to measures for preventing, suppressing, and punishing rebellion, were though to be easily transferable from colony to colony. People—governors, soldiers, clerics, settlers, prisoners, and slaves—could also be shuffled from one place to another.[57] The Company transported its own convicted felons from one settlement to another; in 1687 Madras vacated the death sentence for all but the "ringleader" of thieves condemned for murder, opting to send them to the Company's new colony at Sumatra "where they are to remain Slaves to the Right Honorable Company during life & never to return."[58] In that same year, the committees considered sparing condemned rebels at St. Helena from death by exporting them to Madras, as "they shall no longer live upon the Island where their crime was committed according to the usuall Custom of the Romans of old."[59]

Laws and courts were in themselves potent symbols of authority; it was not incidental that Bombay's chief judge was afforded a *palanquin*, an umbrella-bearer, and a gown.[60] This fit into a broadly pervasive concern in the Company, and in the early modern world more generally, with the use of ceremony and display to represent and constitute stateliness and political power.[61] Even in others' jurisdictions, where the Company only had factories and warehouses, it carefully protected rights to fly its flag, use *palanquins*, and exercise other perquisites; as the Surat council noted, it was simply "not seemly" to be seen without a trumpeter.[62] In settlements, such punctilios were taken even more seriously, marking both hierarchy and authority. Foreigners at Madras and civilians at St. Helena were generally forbidden to wear swords without special permission. The Madras government limited the carrying of "rundells," or umbrellas of state, to chaplains, garrison officers, Company officials and their wives so "that there may be Some distinction in persons and ceremonies."[63]

Pomp and pageantry were in fact integral to the constitution of Company government. The delivery of the Company's laws and commission to Bombay had all the trappings of a coronation, including a procession led by Aungier accompanied by horses, trumpets, drummers, the judge, warden, constable, attorney general, church wardens, one hundred island civilians, including twenty each of Hindus, Muslims, and Christians marching two by two, along with two infantry companies; Aungier even tossed commemorative medals into the crowd.[64] Fryer described Aungier's normal "state" as equally lavish:

> The President has a large Commission, and is *Vice-Regis*; he has a Council here also and a Guard when he walks or rides abroad, accompanied with a Party of Horse, which are constantly kept in Stables, either for Pleasure or Service. He has Chaplains, Physician, Chyrurgeons, and Domesticks; his Linguist, and Mint-Master: At Meals he has Trumpets usher in his Courses, and Soft Musick at the Table: If he move out of his Chamber, the Silver Staves wait on him; if down Stairs, the Guard receive him; if he go abroad, the *Bandarines* and *Moors* under two Standards march before him: He goes sometimes in his Coach, drawn by large Milk-White Oxen, sometimes on Horseback, other times in *Palenkeens*, carried by *Cohors*, *Musslemen* Porters: Always having a *Sumbrero* of State carried over him: And those of the *English* inferior to him, have a suitable Train.[65]

When the Governor of Madras traveled outside the town, he did so with a retinue of attendants and soldiers, horses, fife and drums, flag and umbrella bearers, and *palanquins*. Joseph Collet, who held that post in the early eighteenth century, lamented the "pomp and Grandeur which I am oblig'd to assume in order to the discharge of my Duty," insisting that "A Retir'd Walk with a Sincere Friend would be more agreeable to me, than to be encompass'd with Guards, and entertain'd with the Noise of Drums and Trumpets." Thomas Salmon, who was at the town a few years earlier, noted that the governor "has as much respect paid him at his going abroad as a sovereign Prince."[66]

Representations and symbols of Company political authority surrounded not only its governors but could be found in a range of seemingly mundane and practical acts of government. Even the tombs of particularly important Company leaders in India could be read as attempts to impress and awe visitors.[67] Certainly the projects for ordering the physical space of the Company's towns with gridlike street plans, for example, resembled the concerns for authority and deference found throughout the Restoration's "urban renaissance," which was also reflected in contemporary Atlantic colonial cities such as Charleston and Philadelphia.[68] Madras's central "white" town had been laid out on a grid, so that the fort would clearly remain the dominating architectural structure.[69] The Bombay council was even sent a copy of the 1667 Parliamentary Act for the Rebuilding of London, passed following the fire of the previous year, to guide their efforts in "directing a regular form of building, that it may be uniforme," which ironically only began to be implemented after a 1671 fire

accidentally destroyed a number of houses in the town.[70] St. Helena was similarly instructed to model its efforts on postfire London, to raze all irregular
buildings, and order its street plan for the "publique good and accommodation
of the generality of the Inhabitants."[71]

Much like the law, such ideals, born in London, could not simply be implemented without negotiating local circumstances. Outside of the town surrounding the fort, Bombay sprawled. St. Helena's residents were often recalcitrant
and its plantations were irregular and not surveyed until the 1690s. Madras's
growth, particularly at its edges, was unplanned and contingent, especially as it
incorporated piecemeal existing neighboring villages into its environs.[72] The
very fundamental division of its space between the "white" or "Christian" town
centered on the fort, and the "black" or "Gentue" town to its north, was unknown
to other English plantations in the Atlantic, and reflected instead the sort of divisions based on religion, occupation, and wealth found in Iberian, Dutch, and
other large trading ports and polities in Asia.[73] Within these towns existed communities that often organized themselves, and even planned architecture and
urban design often responded to contingent administrative and governmental
needs, such as taxation, public health, and most particularly defense.[74] The size
and location of buildings at Madras, for example, were restricted by the height of
Fort St. George and the reach of its guns.[75] The town's street names were themselves only systematized after 1688, in the hopes of reducing potential confusion
during an attack or siege as well as regularizing property deeds and the assessment of ground rents and taxes.[76]

Within these towns existed a variety of spaces that reflected both the relationship between urban life and state authority as well as the negotiation between
central planning and the contingent developments that shaped it. Gardens, for
instance, served a number of purposes, as recreational sites, as political spaces
for formal and diplomatic ceremonies, and, as in other English colonial cities,
symbols in themselves of plantation and colonial possession.[77] Here one found
English crops mingling with local vegetation; Fryer, for one, found such fusion
in Madras's garden as profoundly foreboding as a Catholic cathedral.[78] As sites
of agricultural production, gardens also served as another means of linking
Company settlements to one another in a system of cultivation and circulation.
In 1673 Bombay requested a variety of seeds and plants from London, as crucial
for "settlement, building, and planting."[79] The committees imagined Madras's
gardens and nursery could "from time to time supply our Plantations."[80] St. Helena
in particular was conceived of as a potential emporium for crops of both Indies:
indigo, aloe, cotton, ginger, tobacco, sugar and sugar products (like rum and
molasses), and limes.[81] Both Bombay and Bengal were to raise pepper plants
and obtain indigo and cotton seeds, cloves, and rice to transplant to the South
Atlantic.[82] A 1668 order to recruit Bengali servants for St. Helena also came with

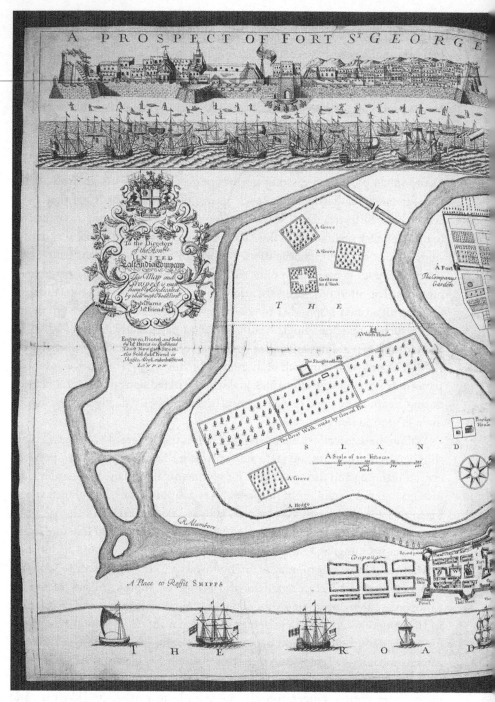

"A Prospect of Fort St. George and Plan of the City of Madras," Bodleian Library Gough Maps 41°, no. 138. Reprinted courtesy of The Bodleian Libraries, University of Oxford.

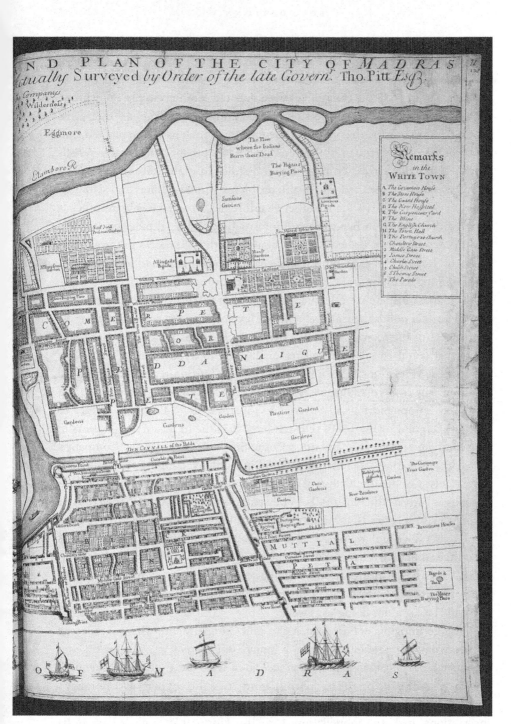

The Companys
Wildernefs

Eggmore

Elembore R.

The Place
where the Indians
Burn their Dead

The Pagod:
Burying Place

Santome
Garden

S. of Jua's
Princes Garden

Allingails
Pagod:

Remarks
in the
WHITE TOWN

A. The Governor House
B. The Store House
C. The Guard House
D. The New Hospital
E. The Carpenters Yard
F. The Mint
G. The English Church
H. The Town Hall
I. The Portuguze Church
1. Chaulter Street
2. Middle Gate Street
3. James Street
4. Charles Street
5. Church Street
6. S. Thomas Street
7. The Parade

C O M P E T E R P E T E

C O D D A N A I G U E

P E T E

Gardens

Gardens

Garden

Pauline Gardens

Gardens

DIE CINNALL of the Pidds

Queens Point

Cuculds Point

The Campanys
Fruit Garden

Garden

B L A K

M U T T I A L

P E T A

Pegods &
Thos

The Moors
Burying Place

a request for "any Plants or seeds fitt for the nourishment of man . . . and also some Cotton seed."[83] The island attempted to raise both European and Western Indian varieties of wheat. Tobacco seeds were sent from both England and Madagascar. In 1688 the committees even debated sending twenty Frenchmen to St. Helena to investigate the feasibility of planting vineyards; by 1691 it seems that not just grapevines but some Huguenot Frenchmen had been planted, and by 1714 the "improvement of the vines" seemed a prospectively viable substitute for importing arrack, a rumlike liquor distilled in south and southeast Asia, which was blamed for a range of health problems among soldiers and settlers.[84] This circulation also extended to other technologies, as when Company officials ordered the council in Bengal to cull information about saltpeter production and to encourage one or two Bengalis familiar with the process to travel to St. Helena.[85] Robert Knox, a Company ship captain, was instructed to learn about iron smithing techniques at Ceylon, for similar purposes.[86]

Even the most apparently practical commercial instruments, like coins, served distinct political purposes.[87] On one level, coinage was a crucially important aspect of the Company's trade, necessary for translating specie into currency that could pass locally and regionally and to bypass sarrafs, or money changers, at Mughal and other mints.[88] Yet, in both European and Asian political traditions, the rights of mintage were, as the court of committees recognized, "so necessary an appendix to all Sovereign Governments."[89] Bombay's failure to establish its mint by the 1680s thus rendered it in the minds of its superiors in London "lame of one foot, and not an intire Soveraign State."[90] The Company's coins, like its justice, also reflected the multiple and overlapping sources of that sovereignty. On the foundation of its original kaul, Madras began issuing gold pagodas as early as the mid-1640s. While patents in 1676 from Charles II, later reconfirmed by James II, for liberty to coin in India theoretically provided the same rights for Bombay, the court of committees had announced themselves interested in having "coyne of our owne," particularly rupees, there as early in 1671.[91] They had also already been striking coins there anyway and continued to express a desire not only for an English charter but "the Mogulls Phirmaund and Husball Hookum" for doing so as well.[92]

This intermingling of European, Asian, and Company authority was reflected in these coins' iconography. Bombay's "tinny" or budgrook, a low-value tin coin meant only for local circulation, was inscribed with the Company's balemark and the year of issue on the back, while from 1672 the copperoon—Bombay's version of the copper paise—was struck with the Company's crest, with the inscriptions, in Latin abbreviation, for "The Honorable English East India Company" and "Money of the English Government of Bombay," encircled by "a deo pax & incrementum" (from God comes peace and expansion). The 1672 "Angelina," the island's silver rupee, was similar, though it was simplified in 1676 to show just the Company's arms on the obverse and the inscription of *"pax deo"* and *"moneta bombaiensis"* on the reverse.[93] Emboldened by the royal patents, in February 1677, the court of committees commissioned a new stamp and restyled the coin a rupee, now marked by the words "1677 By Authority of Charles the Second," with the royal arms and the encircling words "King of Great Britaine France and Ireland" on the reverse.[94] However, these rupees were minted only in 1677 and 1678 and did not circulate much.[95] Thereafter, the Company took to striking two versions of its rupee, one in Persian and another in English, which by the 1680s had reverted to the 1676 *"pax deo"* design.[96]

Coins at Madras, since they both rested in the original grants for its settlement and had to pass current in South India, tended instead to reflect somewhat different sources of authority.[97] Its earliest gold *pagodas*, up to the 1670s, featured imagery common in Vijayanagar, with the diety Hanuman on the reverse, while other less valuable coins on occasion were stamped with various versions of the

Early East India Company coins. Counterclockwise from top *left*: (1) 1672 Bombay Angelina; (2) 1676 Bombay rupee; (3) 1678 Bombay rupee; (4) 1714 St. Helena penny, minted at Madras; (5) 1695 Sumatra fanam, minted at Madras; (6) Madras pagoda, minted between 1691–1740. © The Trustees of the British Museum.

Company's balemark; later pagodas featured the god Visnu, having taken the form of Venkateswara, flanked by his wives.[98] The council received instructions in 1685 to coin silver rupees inscribed with the words "English rupee" and the Company's Arms but to use their "fancies" for smaller denominations.[99] However, when in 1692 Madras reached another agreement with Muhammad Kam Bakhsh, the Mughal *subahdar*, for minting pagodas and rupees, these coins were to display Persian Mughal iconography and be struck in the name of the emperor Alamgir (Aurangzeb); he even provided the iron stamps to strike them.[100]

From streets and gardens to courts and coins, the Company's efforts at Madras, St. Helena, and Bombay were focused on establishing a form of effective colonial government. This was, of course, all premised on the notion that these colonies could attract settlers to govern in the first place. Initially, Company leadership seemed hopeful they could engage English and European Protestants to emigrate to India. This was particularly important at Bombay, where such a population, it was thought, would help to diffuse the Portuguese majorities on the island and draw Englishmen living elsewhere in India back into the fold of the Company's authority.[101] The committees did in fact entertain a few early proposals from Englishmen who wished to settle at Bombay as "merchants and free planters."[102] They also hatched schemes of their own. The original establishment of both Bombay and St. Helena included the offer of land for any "persons as shalbe willing to come and build."[103] The committees provided free passage from the British Isles to the wives, older children, and servants of any married men who would commit to settling and planting on either island.[104] There was even one ill-fated plan to entice a community of English fishmongers and their families to Bombay to build up its maritime economy.[105]

As in other European overseas plantations, the Court of Committees understood attracting women to these settlements as a key to sustaining a solid colonial population and particularly sought out English "maidens" who could be persuaded to settle, marry, and procreate in these colonies.[106] In 1674 the committees approached officials of London's Christ's Hospital to see if any girls or women of "virtuous education," between twelve and thirty years old, would be willing to emigrate to Bombay and St. Helena; the following year, Bombay requested "20 or 30 poore Country girles or hospitall girles," and the committees promptly ordered the shipping committee to draw another list of twenty single women "of honest and civil behaviour," who might be persuaded to go.[107] Women sent out who could not marry immediately were to be offered some form of employment, one year of free victuals, and clothing. Many were destined for Bombay, though three did seem to make their way to Madras in 1678. The Fort St. George council voted them a small pension until they were married, which all three were by 1681. Two others who arrived that year married by 1683. Within five years, there had been fourteen English marriages in the town.[108]

It was not enough just to attract settlers; one had to convince them to stay. After 1671, any man who wanted a marriage license at Bombay had to sign an indenture, committing to reside on the island for at least seven years. English widows, "especially those of Ordinary Quallity," were forbidden from leaving either for Surat or England, and, though it is not clear if they implemented it, Aungier and his council also recommended to London that all widows be bound by their husbands' indentures. The thought was that persuading people to marry and reside for a minimum period would lead them to plant estates and invest in them; as evidence the council cited "the Successful examples of New England, Virginia, Barbados & Jamaica, [and] the no less Successful examples of the Portuguese & Dutch in India."[109]

By 1675, the Bombay council reported that the English population there consisted of 219 men, 27 women, and 6 children (all girls), a considerable increase over the 90 when it came into the Company's possession. Still, this was hardly what one might regard as a flourishing plantation filled with English subjects, especially when considering the fact that another 175 English people had died on the island over the previous two years.[110] A visitor to Bombay in 1690 insisted optimistically that were it not for the great infant mortality, "the Island might in time be peopled with the *Europeans* transmitted thither, as the Western Islands are, which belong to the Crown of England."[111] The Bombay council was also not terribly impressed with the "lives and conversation" of those settlers they did receive, many of whom they regarded as "a great scandal to our religion and Nation."[112] Much the same could be said about Madras, where the civilian English population rose from just under 40 in the late 1670s to only about 150 by 1699, one-quarter of whom were Company employees.[113]

It would frankly have been unrealistic to hope that a place like Bombay could become "an English Collony," with "free Burghers in trading, building and planting there," that is, if an "English" colony meant only a colony consisting mostly of "English" people.[114] With the exception of St. Helena, it did not. The vast majority of the Company's colonists in Asia would ultimately be drawn not from Europe but out of a highly competitive market for itinerant South, Central, and East Asian artisans, soldiers, merchants, and laborers, including a large Indo-Portuguese *mestizo* population, sometimes called black Christians or, when soldiers, *topasses.* The committees regarded a colony of artisans, merchants, weavers, and others "under our owne Government" as an extremely effective way of ensuring a cheap and reliable supply of goods for its European trade, particularly calico.[115] Yet population was also, a number of political economists including Company committee Josiah Child argued, the core source of a polity's wealth.[116] Immigrants planted land and produced for a local economy. In turn, they provided tax revenue, a source of labor and soldiery, defense in the form of militia service, and served in a range of capacities that were fundamentally necessary for the very existence, let alone success, of a plantation.

Company governments thus regarded it as critical to attract and sustain these populations, though such a policy was not without its risks. In particular, some feared potentially divided loyalties. The Indo-Portuguese inhabitants were constantly under suspicion for affiliation with both Jesuit priests and the *Estado da India*. Company officials were extremely wary of entanglements with the Mughal empire over Muslim residents. Gerald Aungier worried *bhandaris*, the western Indian soldiering caste, many of whom migrated from Maratha territories, would prove "snakes in our bosome."[117] Still, Company councils had little choice but to promote local immigration and policies that would both attract and root artisans, skilled workers, merchants, and "moneyed men" in these towns. Like the Dutch at Batavia and the Portuguese at Goa (and as some, like William Petty, had even proposed for the English Atlantic), the Company ultimately abandoned plans to bring European women in favor of accepting and at times encouraging unions between English men and "native" women; one early scheme even suggested offering financial incentive for such marriages.[118] More commonly, incentives for immigration came in the form of land or tax relief and security. The Company promoted Madras and Bombay in particular as safe havens, protected by arms from the growing upheavals caused by ongoing Mughal and Portuguese wars with the Marathas.[119]

Councils also targeted specific populations and occupations. Aungier's government worked to attract at least one hundred western Indian weavers in order to seed a domestic calico industry at Bombay.[120] As early as 1641, Madras offered migrant workers and settlers a variety of incentives including customs exemptions and land under the protection of the fort; between three and four hundred families soon arrived, many from nearby Portuguese San Thomé and Armagon.[121] A number of these Indo-Portuguese lived rent free in the white town, since, as the Madras council observed, "giving ground for houses & gardens to any that will build or plant upon it" was common policy in jurisdictions throughout Golkonda and absolutely necessary for the Company to compete with its neighbors for settlers.[122] Both Madras and Bombay also facilitated the creation of corporate trading bodies, modeled on English guilds and Surat's *mahajan* system, hoping to advance the Company's trade and attract more settlers through the encouragement of local economic infrastructure. Aungier even suggested the Company invest money in these corporations, as, he noted, the Duke of Florence had done at Livorno.[123] In 1687, Madras established a maritime insurance office modeled on such efforts in England, and London proposed one for Bombay as well, sending ledger books and blank policy forms. The committees also observed that, as in England, a post office could bring in revenue, encourage private commerce, and increase naval traffic to and from a settlement and thus its security.[124] Furthermore, security was in itself an industry that provided employment in garrisons and aboard ships. Bombay also took several measures to encourage a domestic shipbuilding industry while requiring its ships to careen in its port, so as to encourage "all manner of workmanship as well as trade" and thus "encrease our Inhabitants."[125]

While much of this effort to attract settlers was oriented toward the regions near Bombay and Madras, the Company also deliberately tried a variety of experiments to draw people from even farther afield. In 1684 Madras specifically entreated traders from Taiwan, ordering four shops built in the bazaar for the "Honorable Company's Interest and proffitt of the towne."[126] A few years later, Josiah Child with the assistance of Jean Chardin, the Huguenot traveler in Persia and now European agent for the Company, began to solicit Armenians to immigrate to both Bombay and Madras. Though "no new thought or project of the present Age," but rather a project their predecessors had considered as early as the 1610s, the committees had for at least a decade envisioned such an alliance as a crucial opportunity "for the planting & peopling your Colony at Bombay."[127] Not only were Armenians Christians but, London believed, they would bring wealth, mercantile skill, and be "as good a Security to our Garrison and trade as 100 hired English Soldiers." Child also seemed to think the relationship would "doe the Company great service" in undermining the "falsitys & untruths" spread by Company enemies in India.[128] Hoping as well to divert the Levant Company's overland Persian silk trade to the Company, Child, Chardin, and others struck a deal with Khwaja Panous Kalantar, an Isfahani-Armenian merchant living in London, which permitted Armenian merchants a liberal amount of private trade between India, Persia, and England in addition to the privileges any free settler had in Company India, including travel and freight on Company ships, free practice of religion, and the right to move among Company settlements and even hold offices there "as if they were Englishmen born."[129] Madras was then instructed to create an Armenian quarter called "Julpha," after the Armenian town and self-consciously imitating what the Persian Shah Abbas had done, for the very same purpose, in Isfahan almost a century earlier.[130]

These projects for encouraging colonial immigration reflected a vision of plantation as a multidimensional process, in which settlements acted as nodes within a global Company system crosscut by a variety of English, European, and Asian commercial and migratory diasporic networks and labor markets.[131] While some of these schemes, like the relationship with the Armenians, were fairly successful in the long term, more immediately the grandiloquent projects that emerged in the correspondence, consultations, and other communications about this inchoate Company plantation system were ideas, not achievements. As it turned out, forts took a very long time to build. Labor and materials were scant. Disease was rampant. Justice was imperfect, piecemeal, and inconsistent. The loyalties of soldiers and settlers could prove extremely difficult to decipher. Local, regional, and geopolitics seemed constantly to militate against the utopian fantasies that emerged out of correspondence and discourse in London, Asia, and the South Atlantic.

It was also extremely expensive. While the Court of Committees frequently pushed their subordinates to build faster, it also seemed frequently dismayed by the attendant costs. Even as celebrated a figure as Gerald Aungier was not safe from scrutiny. Upon returning to Surat from his long stay at Bombay, he received a letter from London, chiding him for being "too apt to be led into a way of grandeur, answerable to those Princes who have a great rule and government." He was reminded that "our business is to advantage ourselves by trade and what government we have is but the better to carry on and support that."[132] Still, if a sense remained that the original purpose of these colonies was to secure trading factories and vertically integrate production within a Eurasian commercial system, the very fact that these fortified towns had settlers requiring government had inescapably affected the Company's nature and objectives. The East India Company was now the proprietor over plantations in Asia and the South Atlantic, peopled by a growing Eurasian population and, like all colonies in their early days, constantly under threat from within and without. This was something Aungier and his council understood, as they boldly responded to their superiors, liberally paraphrasing from the book of Ecclesiastes:

> There is a time and season for all things under the sunn: a time to plant, to build, to fortifie, to defend in warr, to be liberall, show the solemnity of Government, to give God thanks for the mercys rec[eive]d and for their contrarys; and as there is a time soe there are proper meanes to be used; according to number, weight, measure, and place, the due application or misapplication whereof are the surest marks (if anything can be sure) to judge of humane actions by.[133]

While certain tensions between "commerce" and "territory" would consistently remain, and London would never abandon its desire to rein in costs, an East India Company firmly committed to a system of colonial plantation unavoidably required a different way of doing business. Even the most ambitious among the Company's committees understood this would be neither quick nor easy, but as Aungier's predecessor at Bombay, George Oxinden, observed "story tells us, Rome was not built in a day."[134]

"A Sort of Republic for the Management of Trade"

The Jurisdiction of a Company-State

Although much about the East India Company's efforts to establish colonial government resembled the contemporary Atlantic world, the Company was also quite unique among other English overseas and colonial experiences. Bombay and St. Helena were the only seventeenth-century Company settlements chartered by the English Crown; the rest would find their foundations in Asian, not English, grants and treaties. Furthermore, unlike many Atlantic proprietors, the Company owed its corporate existence not to its colonial patents but rather an antecedent charter; any colonial grants had to be read in the context of the other rights and responsibilities embodied in a series of royal patents to the Company. Thus, while the grant for Bombay legally situated it "as of the manor of East Greenwich," the island was actually identified as "lying and being within the Limits of Our said Charter." The patents for St. Helena similarly noted that they followed from the Company's general prerogative "to erect such Colonies, and make such Plantations . . . within the Limits and Bounds of Trade, granted unto The said Governor and Company."[1]

The Company possessed general charters and patents as a corporation, which were indeed far more expansive than all but perhaps the very earliest Atlantic proprietorships, encompassing the world "beyond the *Cape of Bona Esperanza*, to the Streights of *Magellan*." Even this hemispheric charge, however, was rendered powerfully ambiguous by the Company's pursuit of particular grants for plantation and fortification, especially when they fell beyond those "limits and bounds." For example, soliciting for a new charter at the Restoration, the Company maintained that its recent acquisitions of Guinea Company trading rights and a fortification in Africa should justify relocating the western point of demarcation for its jurisdiction from the Cape of Good Hope to an imaginary boundary line from Cape de Tres Puntas in present-day Argentina to the central African coast.[2] Though these efforts were nullified by the creation of the Royal African Company, in practice the proprietorship of St. Helena had a similar effect of extending Company jurisdiction into the South Atlantic. Thus, when the committees insisted in 1674 that a new Admiralty regulation, which required all English commercial shipping to fly only the English merchant flag, should not apply to Company ships within the boundaries of its charter, they and the Admiralty under Samuel Pepys reached a compromise: Company captains would simply switch their flag for the English "red ensign" when outside of the East Indies. The point specified for the transition, however, was not the Cape of Good Hope but St. Helena.[3] While contemporary maps might have located the island geographically in the Atlantic or Africa, for the Court of Committees it quite clearly was situated conceptually and jurisdictionally "in India."[4]

This jurisdiction Company officials fought so vigilantly to protect was also itself a fairly expansive concept. Obviously, the royal charters rendered the Company the only body capable of undertaking licit English trade with Asia, but, despite how it is often characterized, this implied a range of rights and responsibilities far beyond those of commercial monopoly. Charters for overseas enterprises were in themselves a delegation and limitation of monarchical prerogative over the mobility of subjects; those under the auspices of the East India Company, and bodies like it, had what amounted to blanket permission to enter and exit the realm.[5] Over the course of the seventeenth century, the Company's charters and patents provided for a range of other political rights and immunities—to constitute governors and governments abroad, to make war and peace on non-Europeans, to plant and fortify, to make law, to coin money, and so on—that implied that overseas merchants, especially in Asia, did far more than simply barter goods. As Gerard de Malynes had observed, merchants were the vanguard of a nation abroad, since "by them Countreys are discovered, Familiaritie betweene Nations is procured, and politike Experience is attained."[6] Certainly, the right to trade itself implied a right to access that trade. Thus, Company charters acknowledged the freedom to explore and navigate all "Ways and Passages ... Islands, Ports, Havens, Cities, Creeks, Towns and Places of *Asia* and *Africa* and *America*, or any of them" wherever such trade was to "be discovered, established or had." For this right to be exclusive, such navigation had to be restricted to the Company and those under its aegis. Company charters accordingly prohibited any other English subject to "visit, haunt, frequent, or trade, traffick or adventure" into Asia without the Company's permission and license.[7]

Charters were thus as valuable for what they permitted one set of subjects to do as for what they proscribed all others from doing. From this followed an intertwined jurisdiction over trade, people, places, and passageways within a

"Two views of an East Indiaman of the Time of King William III," National Maritime Museum BHC1676. The ship, possibly the *Charles the Second*, flying both the English and East India Company's flags. © National Maritime Museum, Greenwich, London.

vast and often fungible hemispheric jurisdiction. Such a claim was embodied in the actual licenses the Company granted for individuals and ships traveling to, from, and in the East Indies. Like Portuguese *cartazes* or Dutch *pascedullen*, the Company issued passes, for a fee, to some private shipping from England, to residents of its settlements, and to other European and Asian ships in the Indian Ocean.[8] Part protection racket and part passport, such documents were an expression of fairly aggressive claims over the sea lanes and those people on them.[9] Passes for foreigners in Asia were an attempt to fold those ships into a sort of Company security regime and establish deference to Company sea power. Passes for English subjects and inhabitants of colonies expressed a claim to extraterritorial authority and jurisdiction over them. Such passes required their holders to "[conform] themselves in all things to the orders and rules" of the Company; in turn the holder could expect rights and protection as if he "were actually in the said Right Honorable Company's service."[10] Thus, following a Danish attack in 1692 on a ship owned by private merchants at Bombay, the island's governor demanded restitution, since they carried a Company pass and were in his words "Subjects to the Right Honorable East India Company."[11]

If the shipping pass expressed the idea that a Company "subject" existed and that the privileges and obligations of subjecthood traveled with it, failure to take such a pass could mark one's conscious rejection of that status, and thus status as an enemy instead. Absence of a pass served as potential justification for boarding or attacking a European or Asian ship, but even more importantly differentiated unequivocally between an Englishman who sailed to Asia with the Company's "Approbation or Licence" and an interloper, whose activities were considered a "publick acting against authority." Interlopers were in this sense more than just smugglers. They were pernicious, "evill *Engines*," Edward Misselden had observed, which worked "to subvert *Companyes*, yea, *Kingdomes*, also."[12] For Company officials, interlopers caused faction, dissention, disorderliness, and even rebellion. They were "unstable minds" and "ungovernable persons" who "to [the] Utmost of their power in India endeavoured to bannish all reverence of Government out of the mindes of men."[13] Simply put, interlopers were "worse . . . then Pirates & deserve as much to be hanged."[14]

Like piracy, interloping was hardly a self-evident category. If the Company reckoned its jurisdiction as being not just over trade but over English traffic to and within the East Indies, an interloper conversely meant any English subject—and at times, any British subject—that traveled to or resided in Asia without Company permission. There were thus multiple kinds of "interloper," each of whom reflected different ideological positions. Even those who sought access to the trade between England and Asia, often indeed through smuggling, did not necessarily agree on their objectives and justification for doing so. Some of these were free traders who argued that commercial monopolies were patently illegal by the common law and, as one crewmember of an interloping ship at Surat put it in 1684, that as Englishmen "they had as good right and Priviledge to trade into the Easterne parts as any Company had by the vertue of any Pretended Charter."[15] Many others had no objection to monopoly, but simply sought to expand the Company's stock so they could purchase shares. Still others objected to the particular governance of the Company, insisting it was fundamentally mismanaged and in need of reform. This meant either replacing its leadership, forming another joint-stock company altogether, or, as had happened with the Levant Company years earlier, transforming the Company from a joint stock into a "regulated" company, a sort of East India trading consortium, which, like a guild, would have pooled rights, responsibilities, and resources among authorized but independent commercial syndicates.[16]

As far as the Company was concerned, there was yet another, entirely different species of interloper: the English subject, often a former and dismissed Company employee, who had taken to residing in Asia without Company license. Some assisted the illicit traders to England by freighting ships or facilitating relationships in Asia, though many had far more interest in trade to the Atlantic, for example in Madagascar slaves, or the lucrative intra-Asian, later known as the "country," trade. Whether captaining their own ships, setting up residence in bustling port towns like Surat, or seeking the employ of other Asian or European powers as soldiers, pilots, and administrators, this sort of interloper was, for the Company, objectionable not for his mercantile activity per se. By the second half of the seventeenth century, the Company had come to allow unrestricted private trade in India among its servants and even the perquisite of a limited "permissive" trade back to Europe. As an institution, it did not even partake in the intra-Asian trade. What made these interlopers so odious was the fact that their blatant rejection of Company authority and their attempts to forge their own diplomatic and commercial relationships in Asia, as the Bombay council noted to one ship captain, rendered "us a people in the Eyes of all these Eastern Princes without Government."[17]

Yet, even the people the Company grouped together under this category did not necessarily share the same ideological foundations. Some simply rejected any English authority over them at all, like Thomas Eatman at Surat who allegedly did "not care a fart for the King and Company."[18] Others like John Petit, a former deputy governor of Bombay who took up residence in Surat in the 1680s after he was acrimoniously dismissed under accusations of corruption, rejected the Company's interpretation of the scope of its power. Petit accepted that the "the Kings Charter Is butt a Monopoly to restraine others from tradeing to India," but insisted that it "doth not concerne persons that trade to & fro in Indias" and "gives them nott the least Magistraticall power noe nott to touch the haire off any mans head." The Company was simply a "parcel of Merchants Congregated by their owne call"; it was thus as absurd to believe they had any more jurisdictional rights than a monopoly company in Europe. Even if it might justifiably claim political authority at Bombay, the Company could not justly do so "butt One mile out of Itt."[19] "Interlopers" like Petit and his sometime partner George Bowcher regarded themselves as perfectly obedient English subjects, whose activities in Asia were primarily subject to those Asian jurisdictions in which they resided and traded. Thomas Haggerston, who had absconded with the property of several merchants from Surat to Bengal in 1683, even demanded a hearing in front of the nawab's court, the *adalat*, at Hugli rather than appear before the Madras judicature.[20]

What all of these various activities shared in common, and what made them all "interloping," was not any particular commercial interest but their rejection of Company government and jurisdiction. Interloping of all stripes had been a problem for the Company from its very origins, but by the late 1670s in London, "the interloper," in the words of one nineteenth-century historian, had become "as familiar a topic of conversation as the weather."[21] The prospects seemed just as gloomy. The reinstatement of the Company's exclusive rights and the establishment of a permanent capital stock in 1657, followed by the reconfirmation and expansion of these rights under Charles II, had led to enviable profits and growth. The Company's growing interest in the Persian silk trade inspired jurisdictional squabbles with its once close ally, the Levant Company. Meanwhile, conflicts in its own ranks and an attempt to placate the Stuart monarchs by displacing prominent Whigs from its leadership in the early 1680s had led a coterie of Company committees, headed by the London merchant Thomas Papillon, to leave the Company and sell off their shares at remarkable profit. Meanwhile, given the Company's anxieties about obedience and loyalty among its employees, there was an ever-present supply of discontented, dismissed Company servants, often casualties of political struggles within the governments of factories and settlements, who either returned to England or, like Petit, ensconced themselves in various places in India.

By October 1680, a subgroup of the Court of Committees was appointed to develop a strategy "against the insinuations aspersions & practices of Interlopers & others."[22] In September the following year, the committees resolved to give the king a gift of 10,000 guineas for his support in the matter; the sum not long after transmuted into an expected, annual tribute, the king two years later even requesting his "present" early.[23] Meanwhile, the Company launched a vigilant public relations campaign in print. It maintained two solicitors as well as standing counsel on its payroll, rewarded intelligence on suspected interlopers before setting out or on their return, issued civil claims against their proprietors, and brought information and complaint to initiate suits in defense of its rights by charter.[24] One such suit arose in 1682 when the Court of Committees received information that Thomas Sandys was outfitting a ship and intending to make an unauthorized voyage to the East Indies. The Company had the ship stopped on the Thames and proceedings brought in the Court of Chancery to have his goods forfeited. For the Company, this was a fairly routine matter, but Sandys's response soon turned it into a *cause célèbre*. Sandys challenged the Admiralty's right to seize his ship, arguing that its civil law jurisdiction extended only to the high seas.[25] Before the Chancery, he similarly made no effort to deny he planned an eastward voyage. He insisted instead that, according to common law, he had every right to do so, since the Company's charter, being for a monopoly, was "in it self void."[26]

The Lord Keeper was skeptical of the argument but the core issues it raised over the nature of royal authority were legitimate enough to be forwarded as a constitutional matter to be heard before the Court of King's Bench. The resulting *East India Company v. Sandys*, soon known colloquially as the "Great Case of Monopolies," was argued by some of London's most prominent lawyers on both sides: the Company retained the services of the attorney general Robert Sawyer, the solicitor general Heneage Finch (also, the son-in-law of Company committee and governor John Banks), and John Holt, the future chief justice of King's Bench, while James II's later solicitor general, William Williams, and two future chief justices of Common Pleas, George Treby and Henry Pollexfen, served as counsel for Sandys. None of them was a stranger to the legal questions surrounding corporate rights, as each had been deeply involved as well in the ongoing controversies over the Crown's use of writs of *quo warranto* to diminish the autonomy of municipal corporations, like London, though many now found themselves representing opposite sides of the question.[27] For its part, the *Sandys* case came to be cited as precedent in the following centuries in cases ranging from procedural injunctions to immigration policy, but it has most often been viewed as a watershed moment in the history of political economy, which put mercantilism, monopolies, the Crown's prerogative, and other of the most critical issues of the late Restoration and subsequently the Glorious Revolution themselves on trial.[28] Yet, the arguments offered in the case even more fundamentally raised long-standing debates over the politics of empire and overseas activity. They touched on questions relating to the nature of the corporation, the definition of public and private, the tension between the common and the civil law, the applicability of European law, canon law and the law of nations to English legal practice, the propriety of trade and intercourse with non-Christians, and the constitution of extra-territorial authority over English subjects abroad. As such, the Company's position in the case was in essence a manifesto for its rights in Asia, recalling the striking ways in which its leadership had come to regard themselves as bearing a responsibility not just for trade but for government in the East Indies.

At first blush, Sandys's line of reasoning was fairly straightforward. Monopolies were illegal. This argument followed from a long line of common-law precedent—from Magna Carta through statutes under Edward III and Elizabeth I—which suggested trade, and thus the seas, were by nature open to English subjects. In the Chancery suit, the Company had countered that its exclusive trade needed to be seen as something akin to a patent on public works, which maintained ships, factories, trading relationships, and other infrastructure for the advantage of the whole of investors, as well as the public indirectly, through customs and other benefits of the trade. In capitalizing on those public works but not contributing to them, interlopers were essentially freeloaders who could not rightly expect to profit.[29]

Confronting a much broader constitutional issue before King's Bench, Company lawyers expanded this argument significantly. They did not quibble with Sandys's premise that monopolies were illegal. The East India Company, they insisted, was simply *not* a monopoly. By their definition, a monopoly was the restriction to one party of a right possessed by all. The Company, however, had pioneered and maintained the trade for almost a century; it also governed over it and secured it, through infrastructure, diplomacy, and traffic. The trade thus existed by virtue of the Company rather than antecedent to it. In short, there would be no English trade in the East Indies without the East India Company, so there was no extant right to be restricted. While the Company might be said to have an exclusive privilege, it could not accurately be called a monopoly. Had it been, the lawyers noted in a polemical counterfactual, it was unlikely it could ever have been first chartered without objection from Elizabeth's famously vigorous anti-monopoly Parliament. However, "in all the catalogue, and in all the debates of parliament at that time, there's not one word mentioned of the East-India company's charter."[30]

It would be all too easy to dismiss this as a sort of legal acrobatic, but the argument was not novel or without foundation.[31] Advocates of the Company and of joint-stock exclusive trades generally had long maintained that the essential difference between a monopoly and a licit exclusive privilege was that the former served private interest, the latter public good, a debate that spoke to broader concerns about the importance of proper government over trade.[32] A Hobbesian vision of human nature as inherently self-interested implied that trade as much as civil society required a controlling power to patrol individual interests on behalf of the common good.[33] This mirrored deep early modern suspicions of "masterless men" and the anarchic tendencies of democracy.[34] "Interest more then reason commonly sways most mens affections," Samuel Fortrey argued in 1663; thus it was absolutely "necessary . . . that the publick profits should be in a single power to direct, whose Interest is onely the benefit of the whole."[35] In 1681 the pamphleteer "Philopatris," possibly Josiah Child, similarly argued on the Company's behalf that not only private merchants but guilds and even regulated companies were concerned only with "the busie and eager prosecution of their particular Trades" and could not, by their very nature, consider the common good. This, he noted, citing Cicero, Bodin, and the seventeenth-century jurist Oliver St. John for authority, was why one had government in the first place.[36] Under his own name, Child reinforced this point. Policy had to be oriented toward the general not the particular interest. "Trade," he insisted, "should be regulated and governed by wise, honest and able men."[37] As another Company propagandist, Robert Ferguson, waxed proverbially, "*That which is every mans business, will be no mans business;* when there is none by particular obligation of place, duty, and interest, engaged to mind the general security and priviledg of the *English*-Trade, but every one minds only his own private concern, the National Honour and Interest will decline."[38]

Such concerns were amplified in the extra-European world. In a place seen as so distant and dangerous, lawless trade seemed to be an invitation to chaos, catastrophe, and corruption. Philopatris likened ungoverned free trade in the East to sending untrained conscripts against a wealthy, organized army or defending against popery without a national church.[39] Long-held stereotypes about the untrustworthiness of Muslims, fears of bodily and moral infection, and the more practical concerns of managing commerce and markets across a hemispheric system recommended that some form of government had to exist to supervise and authorize commercial activity in Asia. As trade was at its root a form of trust and interchange, Holt insisted in *Sandys*, one could not understand how to organize trade properly without "consideration of the persons that are to be traded withal."[40]

For its defenders, the joint-stock company provided such a government. Child and others envied the Dutch for including merchants in their "Councils of State and War," and, later recalling Philopatris's arguments, noted that in fact a "mixt Assembly of *Noblemen, Gentle-men* and *Merchants* are the best *Constitution* for the making *Rules, Orders* and *By-Laws*, for the carrying on any *Trade* for the publick utility of the *Kingdom*."[41] In theory, as a body funded and governed by stockholders rather than individual traders, the joint-stock company involved a far broader cross-section of society—"Noblemen, Clergy-men, Gentlemen, Widows, Orphans, Shop-keepers and all others," Ferguson hyperbolized—in its profits than would an open trade or a regulated consortium of monopoly merchants.[42] Many so-called monopolists, including Child, actually resisted monopolies and even companies, as Charles Molloy put it, "on this side the Line," that is in Europe, but regarded them as indispensable in the world outside the supervision of responsible Christian princes.[43] As the Court of Committees argued to its subordinates in Bengal, it was only "the Deluded World of the Vanity and Folly of those persons that would persuade them the trade of England in India is to be preserved by any other Means than the strict Rules and Discipline of an United Stock governed by a Select & authorized council."[44]

All of those words were critical to understanding the Company leadership's own conception of the nature of their charge. "Rules and discipline" preserved the trade as well as those who prosecuted it. A "united stock" provided the capital and the corporate institution necessary to provide those rules. Finally, recalling the importance of consultative government, that institution had to be governed at every level by "a Select & authorized council." For Company leadership, all of this reflected the fact that they regarded their charge as a distinctly public one. In administering and protecting the English trade, the Company insisted it served the English public, acting somewhat like a Board of Trade for Asia. As a corporation and joint-stock company, it served its own public in the form of shareholders, investors, employees, and freemen. Furthermore, in the East Indies, it was a public authority in its own right over, as one chief of Surat stated in 1692, "all Affairs of our English Nation both in Government & Trade."[45] Finally, in possessing colonies, the Company leaders had come to understand themselves as "in effect our own Law-makers" in Asia.[46] Thus, when the Persia factory failed to properly gather intelligence, London indicted its council as acting "not like Merchants much less like Publick Persons, that represent the English Nation in that place."[47] A newly appointed member of the Bombay council wrote his superiors that he had "Acquited all particular Affairs & private Interest purely to Serve the Publick & intreat your Honnours."[48] Meanwhile, one deputy governor on the island announced his intentions to resign his post by explaining that he sought "not to concerne myselfe any more in publique Affairs."[49]

This pervasive sense that the Company was something quite other than a private monopoly merchant underscored all of its arguments in the *Sandys* case. Among the first evidence Company lawyers offered in the original Chancery suit was to "[set] forth what Places and Towns they had in the *East Indies*, and that they had there above 150000 Men under their Government."[50] Governing towns and fortifications represented a massive investment of time, men, and money. It was also the basic infrastructure that made trade possible. Yet it revealed the complexity of a Company's constitution founded in both English grants and a diplomatic regime in Asia. Thomas Exton, the advocate general and later Admiralty judge, argued before the Court of Admiralty that Sandys's offense was a violation of an English charter as well as "severall contracts treaties & Articles of Alliance" the Company had with "Severall Princes in the East Indies."[51] Advocates for the Company maintained that only a corporate body could establish and keep the sorts of relationships necessary to support trade in Asia, such as customs-free trading or the rights to issue *dastaks*. Often citing the disastrous consequences of the brief revocation of its exclusive trade in 1653, the Company insisted that Asian merchants and states would take advantage of competition among English traders to drive up prices. Yet, *farmans, kauls, olas,* and the like were also political instruments. Warehouses, factories, and settlements like Madras depended on them, as well as constantly negotiated and tenuous relationships with their neighbors. The very reason for having an exclusive company in the first place was that somebody had to maintain these relationships; this was especially true when that trade was with people, as Josiah Child wrote, "with which his *Majesty* hath no *Alliance*, nor can have any by reason of their distance, or Barbarity, or non-Communication with the *Princes of Christendom*."[52]

Crucially, the Company's jurisdiction was also categorically unlike English trade with non-Christians elsewhere, such as in the Mediterranean and the Ottoman empire; there, Philopatris explained, like the French, the Venetians, and the Dutch, the English monarch had diplomatic relations and an ambassador, while in India "There are above 100 Kings and Raja's, which are Gentu Princes, but governing with absolute Power in their own Dominions," and with whom it would have been impossible for the monarch to maintain envoys and proper relations.[53]

In practice, the Company had much to be anxious about. Interlopers did in fact pursue a separate diplomacy in Asia, primarily as a means of establishing trade and evading the Company's authority. Sometime around 1682, Thomas Pitt acquired a *perwana* from Shaista Khan, the *nawab* of Bengal, to establish his own factory at Hugli. At Surat, John Petit and George Bowcher also set about procuring "a Phirmaund in as large & authentick a manner from the Mogull for theire residence & Privileges of trade in his Countrey as the Honorable Company themselves had"; by 1684 Bowcher was rumored in fact to have obtained a grant "in the form Phirmaun given the Europe Nations."[54] To the Company, this was as absurd and illegal as individual English subjects negotiating their own treaties with European monarchs. It ordered Bowcher's goods seized at sea. When he complained, the ship's captain replied that his "protests . . . are soe Common that they Hang in Severall Commanders Shyting Houses, to make them Laugh when they have the Occasion." He also encouraged Bowcher either to "make the same use of" his *farman* or to "keep itt like a Ba[u]ble which Pleases Children and Fooles."[55]

Diplomacy in Asia was thus a double-edged sword, capable of either reinforcing or confounding claims made by virtue of English charters and other instruments. For the Company, it was critical to keep that diplomacy in its hands alone. This imperative rested at the core of the Company's arguments in *Sandys*. Its lawyers maintained that in conducting their own, undisciplined diplomacy, interlopers endangered the very foundations of English trade and indeed the persons and souls of Englishmen. Their logic echoed many of the other concerns about ungoverned interlopers in Asia, but its theory rested in a centuries-old dilemma rooted in the medieval scholastic tradition, its articulation in early modern Protestant writings on the laws of nations, and even its mirror image in the Koranic concept of *jihad*. Christendom, they argued, was in a natural and eternal state of war (*perpetuus inimicus*) with infidels. Since commerce required traffic, and traffic required peace, commerce with non-Christians was prohibited by natural law. Of course, to facilitate the possibility of trade, many canon and civil lawyers had concluded that such a state of war could be relieved through a temporary, and temporal, treaty of peace. This, however, could not be effected by individuals on their own accord, who lacked the necessary wisdom and circumspection for so weighty a charge. Such a treaty could only legitimately be prosecuted by a Christian prince on his subjects' behalf.[56]

Company advocates had drawn on this argument before. A few years earlier when advising the Privy Council on the subject of interloping more broadly, Robert Sawyer had essentially argued that an individual subject cannot "trade or traffique with any Infidell Country not in Amity" with the king without special license.[57] Exton deployed a similar position against Sandys, insisting it was "dangerous for Subjects to trade with Infidells without license from his Majesty."[58] In the King's Bench case, the lawyers elaborated the point, citing a long history of English law and practice to insist that even if there was a common law right to free trade and traffic, it was hardly absolute. Instruments like the Navigation Acts showed such a right had routinely been refined, rolled back, and even contradicted by both statute and prerogative. The far higher principle was an English monarch's right and responsibility to regulate intercourse with strangers and infidels. Both Finch and Sawyer cited the legal status of Jews in England, including their expulsion in 1290, as precedent, while Holt offered several examples from other overseas charters, including Sir Walter Raleigh's charge "to discover new countries that were heathenish and under infidels."[59] Sawyer insisted, to maintain that infidels were not natural enemies would be "a difficult task, in rowing against the stream of the laws of all christian countries."[60]

From this followed the lawyers' most critical move. As many had argued in the printed defenses of the Company, there was no "League of Peace or commerce" between Asian princes and the English king. The treaties of peace that did exist were made by the Company by virtue of its chartered authority but in its name and pertaining only to those belonging to those under its government. Since Company not Crown diplomacy ensured the East India trade, only those under the Company's auspices could claim to be relieved of the state of war. "All other Subjects," it followed, "are merely precarious and have no pretence of takeing any advantage of any peace made by the Company. So as to them the Indians remain to all purposes Alien enemies."[61] This was a serious position, one that rendered interlopers neither as thieves and smugglers nor violators of a patent but, more fundamentally, "disorderly persons."[62] Holt could not have made this any more explicit than when he argued:

> This Company is incorporated and made to have the government of this trade; they being christians, no question, are to take care of the christian religion; and to take care that their agents and factors that trade under this constitution, keep up to that religion they profess; but certainly it is quite another thing when people trade of their own head; there they converse only with infidels, they cannot have divine offices.[63]

Such a position further implied that the *Sandys* case could not be decided on the basis of common law alone but, as the chief justice acknowledged in his decision, had to take account of "such other Laws also as be common to other Nations as well as ours, . . . namely the General Law of Nations, the Law-Merchant, the Imperial or Civil Law."[64] Interloping, if defined as unauthorized intercourse with infidels, was not only a violation of the monarch's charter but of natural law itself.

Predictably, Sandys's lawyers would have none of this. George Treby insisted it was absurd to imagine "the king is or can be in amity with [Asian princes], as to one part of his subjects (namely the Company) and in enmity with them, as to the other of his subjects."[65] Feigning shock at hearing "so much divinity in the argument," he indicted the entire idea as "a conceit absurd, monkish, fantastical and fanatical."[66] A later pamphleteer dismissed the argument as "a meer Chimera of Popish Original."[67] He was not far off. By turning to civil and canon law and the law of nations, Sawyer—who ironically had himself recently accused Treby's defense of London in the *quo warranto* case of employing arguments from the "Jesuits' school"[68]—and the others echoed the same position the Iberians had taken in previous centuries in excluding other Europeans, including the English, from the Atlantic and Asia. Scholars like Seraphim de Freitas had argued that the Portuguese exclusive jurisdiction in the East rested in rights to tend to Christian souls, by virtue of their late fifteenth-century papal bulls and the subsequent Treaty of Tordesillas that had divided that responsibility with the Spanish. Not only did English overseas charters in themselves share common legal lineages, languages, purposes, and even sacral foundations with those papal bulls.[69] In citing European precedents and drawing on concepts clearly rooted in canon law and the European law of nations, the Company seemed to be figuring its role with respect to other English subjects similarly to that which the Iberians claimed for all of Christendom, replacing (as the English Reformation had) the pope with the monarch and endorsing the principle that an English overseas charter, like the bull, could dispense such an authority over contact with infidels to some of his subjects on behalf of all of them.[70]

Further evidence that this case was replaying a version of European debates over the East India trade could be found in the fact that Sandys's lawyers turned for their evidence to some of the Iberians' principal interlocutors. Both Treby and William Williams cited the Dutch theorist Hugo Grotius, and particularly his defense of Dutch incursions into the Portuguese East Indies, *Mare Liberum* (as well as Grotius's Scottish critic William Welwod), to show that "trade is as free to all men as the air, that the seas are like the highways, free and open to all passengers." Williams ridiculed Sawyer's argument about the expulsion of the Jews, insisting that the fact that "Jews were used thus in England, is no argument that the East-India Company may use English subjects like Jews abroad in other countries."[71] If he deliberately convoluted this point, Williams clearly intuited the profound implications of the Company's more general argument. If the Crown had indeed created a grant that rendered the Company something other than a direct agent or ambassador for the monarch, it could never be withdrawn. The Company was in essence "arguing the king by his prerogative out of his prerogative."[72] Henry Pollexfen reinforced the point by posing a series of rhetorical questions: "Can this then be a good grant? Can the king grant from himself his kingly care, and the trust in him reposed for the care of religion to you, to manage it as you will, and that he will not use it himself without your consent? Surely, you cannot say so."[73]

The response to the notion of the Company's holding a "divine office" also raised a familiar critique of the dilemmas implicit in its constitutional form and a lingering discomfort with the very idea of the joint-stock company. As a corporation, the Company was a perpetual body but its members were mortal; given this, they argued, even if the present committees meant well, there was no assurance its leadership would continue to be faithful to religion in the future.[74] Moreover, a company could not as an institution be trusted with such an awesome charge since it did not really exist. Apostrophizing the Company, Pollexfen insisted that "Dealing with you is a kind of dealing with Spirits, an Invisible Body subsisting only *in intelligentia legis*."[75] His view echoed those of other opponents, including Pollexfen's younger brother John, who argued that the East India Company could not reliably be possessed of property, rights, or debts, since no one person could ever be held responsible for its actions.[76]

Such arguments were on the one hand thinly veiled attempts to recall common indictments of the untrustworthiness and corruption of the Company's present leadership. On the other hand, they repeated the position held by those, such as Levant Company advocates, who would have seen the East India Company reformed as a "regulated" trade. The Levant Company and other such regulated companies were guild-like institutions, in which each member traded on his own account. Meanwhile, the company controlled access, policed standards, and pooled resources, such as exclusive trading privileges, consular stations, factories, and other common rights; in the case of the Levant Company, it also helped maintain a Crown-appointed ambassador in the Ottoman Empire.[77] Investment for trade was thus raised from trade and managed only by those prosecuting that trade.[78] To its advocates, this model was "open and comprehensive," since trade was left to the experts in that trade alone; the joint-stock company conversely, in which capital and government came from shareholders, many of whom had never been to India or even engaged directly in the trade in England, was unnatural and pernicious.[79]

It was not a far leap from the notion that the Company was an illegitimate way to organize trade to the position that it was an illegitimate form of government.

Williams somehow managed to suspect the Company of both popery, in its connections to Iberian theory and practice, and republicanism, resembling as it did
models of trade in places like Hamburg and Amsterdam. Ironically, in defending
London and other urban corporations against the *quo warranto* writs brought by
the Crown, Williams, Treby, and Pollexfen had all insisted that municipal corporations were immortal and thus inviolable, an argument the court rejected as
tending to make corporations "independent of the Crown and in defiance to it,
whenever they thought convenient."[80] Now Williams—who would reverse tack
again when accepting an appointment as James II's solicitor-general in late
1687—seemed to be recycling the position of his *quo warranto* interlocutors,
insisting in *Sandys* that "without any check or controul from his majesty or the
government," the East India Company would "alter the constitution of England,"
since it would be "independent from the government" and "without appeal." To
accept the Company's arguments would be, he insisted in a pregnant phrase, to
accept "a sort of republic for the management of trade."[81] In many ways, this captured indeed what the Company had been arguing.

There was still one remaining, seemingly mundane point of law that had to be
settled: whether the Company even had the right to bring the suit against Sandys
in the first place. For a litigant to have standing to sue, he had to show that he had
been directly harmed by the action in question. Even if Sandys had made his
voyage, would the Company, Pollexfen asked, actually have been at all damaged
by it?

> Did he buy so much of the merchandize of the country, as not to leave
> there sufficient for you to furnish your ships withal, so that they came
> home empty?.... Did he hence export to sell there so much merchan-
> dize, as not sufficient left for you here to buy? Or, did he bring home
> here so much as that there were not buyers sufficient for his goods and
> yours also?[82]

In the end, the only thing with which Thomas Sandys interfered, his lawyer
jabbed, was the Company's ability to engross. If anyone had been harmed, it was
the king, since it was his charter that had been allegedly violated, but since the
Crown did not actually bring suit, the point was moot. This position resonated
with a broader free-trade critique of the Company, which insisted it failed to
exploit the trade to its fullest, something, in fact, no one company with a limited
stock could.[83] As one Levant Company pamphleteer complained, the Company's grant "is near two third Parts of the trading World," but "no Trade at all is
driven to many of them, as *Persia, Japan, Arrachan, Achein, St. Laurence, Sumatra,
Pegu, Madagascar, Mosambique, Sosals, Melinde, Borneo, Zeiloan,* and many
oathers, and yet while they Trade not thither themselves, they violently keep out

others who would Trade."[84] A decade later, Roger Coke noted the objection that the Company's charter granted it more "than half the circumference of the Globe of the Earth." Recalling the 1657 charter under Oliver Cromwell that reinstated the Company as an exclusive trade and permanent joint stock, he raised the explicit connection Sandys's lawyers had made between the Company and both republicanism and popery: "the Pope and [Cromwell] were *Simeon* and *Levy*; but herein the Pope and he differed: The Pope would have all his own Tribe to Partake of his Blessings; whereas *Oliver*, by this Patent, excluded all the rest of the *English* Nation in this Trade."[85]

Once again, Sandys's position bore an uncanny and ironic resemblance to arguments that the Company itself had once made, against both the Portuguese and subsequently the Dutch, in its own early attempts to access the East India trade. The English position in the very early seventeenth century had been that no one could restrict travel, in the words of the colonial promoter and chronicler Richard Hakluyt, in "the vaste, wyde & infinitely open ocean sea." In a brief intended to convince Queen Elizabeth to issue a charter to the Company, Hakluyt—who also translated Grotius's *Mare Liberum* into English, possibly for the Company's use in its negotiations with the VOC in the 1610s—had made the familiar argument in the law of nations that true ownership and sovereignty could not lie in passive grants or first discovery but had to be maintained through the use, occupation, possession, or improvement of the jurisdiction in question.[86] The *Estado da India* could not claim sovereignty over the entire Eastern Hemisphere, Hakluyt argued, since the actual parts of it they controlled were infinitesimal when compared with the "infinit" number of places "out of theire power, Jurisdiction or comaunde & therefore free for anie other Princes and people of the world to repair unto."[87]

The Company's counsel never attempted to show that Sandys had caused any financial damage by his illegal trade; in fact, in the Chancery suit they had even waived rights to his forfeited goods.[88] Finch dismissed the notion that this was even a proper legal question in this context. As he insisted, the Company "are a corporation under stipulations and leagues with other countries for the carrying on of their trade; and so are in the nature almost of foreign plantations, under a regulated and Christian government within themselves, whereby those mischiefs are prevented"; any other "considerations," such as "whether this trade be driven to the full extent of it, or may be more advantageous to be enlarged" was immaterial and not a matter to be decided by this court. Keeping with the general principle that interloping was more an offense against jurisdiction than commerce, Company advocates maintained that Sandys's crime was not his trade per se but his intent in the first place to traffic into the East Indies without the Company's permission to do so.[89] In this view, it did not matter in the least whether the Company exploited all of the trade of Asia, or if Sandys affected its profits. A rightful jurisdiction existed, the Company's argument implied, echoing previous Dutch and Portuguese positions, because it used, occupied, and improved its grant by the very fact that it established contact with Asia, protected the passageways to it, and maintained the infrastructure of both trade and government.[90] As Philopatris had observed, the Company simply had "no more in their Charter, than all the *East-India* Companies in Christendom" and to argue otherwise would have been to insist that "all Christendom, except those few gentlemen that complain, are mistaken in their Politicks."[91]

After almost a year of trial and deliberations, and four hours delivering their opinions, in January 1685 the justices of the Court of King's Bench sided unanimously and emphatically with the Company.[92] In their decisions, Richard Holloway and Francis Wythens stressed the argument that as a public good, the Company could not be a monopoly; moreover, its age was in itself significant, since "possession will in time give a right."[93] George Jeffreys, the chief justice, concurred in a lengthy discussion, noting that while at English law "such a length of time does not obtain the Credit of a Prescription; yet by the Law of Nations and the practices of all other Countries which are only adapted for this purpose, it is otherwise."[94] The Court of Committees found this aspect of the decision particularly pleasing, noting to the Madras council that "the Judges. . . . were pleased to observe that this Company had been in possession of this trade for above 100 years past and that in all time none ever durst presume to call the right of the Crown in question till now."[95]

The judges' arguments, particularly those made by Jeffreys, need to be seen not as a confirmation of the Company's position but as introducing a third side, the Crown, into the debate. Jeffreys rejected the very notion presented by his longtime political and personal rival William Williams that "this Grant hath made the Plaintiffs a mere Republick, and thereby has altered the constitution of *England* in the management of Trade by Common-wealths, by placing it in Companies, who (were they Independent upon the Crown) are truly so called." The Crown simply neither had done nor would do any such thing. Turning the polemic around, Jeffreys suggested that if anyone were to be labeled as a republican, it would have been Sandys for so boldly questioning the monarch's prerogative and a century-old grant.[96] Jeffreys also offered a slightly different definition of monopoly. Monopolies for private individuals, he admitted, were illegal, but exclusive companies established by the prince and for the public good were a very large exception to that rule. He agreed with the Company's lawyers that free trade was hardly an absolute right, but here offered his own account of the very origins of the commonwealth. Calling upon arguments that resembled those offered in *Mare Clausum*, John Selden's refutation of Grotius first published in 1635, amongst other places, Jeffreys described the world in its original state as one in which all property was held in common. This being found "inconvenient," by common consent people created private property and then government to keep order and administer over those things to which no one could claim ownership: waste and uninhabited lands, wild animals, and the like. For this reason, the king was responsible for governing foreign trade and could even claim sovereignty over plantations discovered and occupied by an individual subject. If *Mare Liberum* (which actually implied a similar view of the state of nature) had a point about the freedom of the seas, Jeffreys insisted, somewhat misconstruing Grotius's argument, it was meant to apply at most among nations not to the individuals within them.[97]

In one way, this supported the Company's position, especially in its argument that the case needed to be judged against European practice and the law of nations, not the English common law alone. However, in his strong interpretation of the king's prerogative, Jeffreys's argument diverged from the ones made by Holt and Sawyer in a number of important ways. His arguments confirming the Company's standing returned to a vision of the Company as possessing a patent; its right to bring action, he insisted, was like that of an inventor or the "grantee of a fair, market, or any other franchise." To him, the Company was like any corporation, which held its exclusive powers at the pleasure of the king and as long as it served a public interest.[98] Moreover, one could not read the charter to have abrogated the king's rights either to make treaties in the Indies or to void the charter at his will; he even asserted that since corporate charters existed by virtue of the king's prerogative, he was not even bound any restrictions within them—in this case the clauses preventing the king from chartering or licensing others to trade or traffic in Asia. Jeffreys thus presented a significantly different interpretation of the Company's diplomacy in Asia. He rejected the arguments about trade with infidels as superfluous; the king, he argued, would have had the prerogative to restrict trade and movement out of the realm even if Asia was filled with Christians. To Jeffreys, as a diplomatic agent, the Company was simply an extension of the Crown; in his words, "the King by his Charter makes the Plaintiffs as it were his Embassadours to concert a Peace and Mr *Sands* murmurs because he is not one of them."[99]

The decision for the Company had ostensibly rescued both the Crown's prerogative and the Company's exclusive privilege, but in fact, on its elements, it did little to resolve the ideological dilemma at the core of the relationship between the two: namely, as Pollexfen dismissively characterized it, that in its "politick Capacity" the Company possessed a permanent and inviolable right to "have, use and enjoy" all the English trade and traffic in the East.[100] It hardly deterred interlopers, who remained obstinately convinced that the Company's grant was illegal and that "they might lawfully Trade to the *Indies*, notwithstanding the same."[101] The case did at least reassure the Company's committees that they could expect the political support of the Crown and its courts in their battle against interloping.[102] Immediately following the case's conclusion, the Court of Committees debated strategies on how capitalize upon it, considering the matter so critical that the governor took the unusual step of swearing everyone involved to secrecy.[103] One obvious approach was to continue to pursue interlopers in English courts; just a few months later, suits were pending in the Court of King's Bench against twenty-five ships' proprietors or their alleged accomplices, and the Court of Committees had drawn up a list of sixty-five persons against whom it was encouraging the Crown to pursue its own criminal prosecution.[104] Their confidence was only further bolstered a few days later by the accession of the Duke of York to the English, Scottish, and Irish thrones. James II, the committees were convinced, could be counted on to continue his brother's policy and "vouchsafe us all possible encouragement in the carrying on our trade," especially as he was an "Adventurer in the present joynt stock."[105] Not only had James purchased £3,000 of stock in 1684; he was given an additional £7,000 stock from the committees in 1687 as a deliberate substitute for (and reduction of) the annual 10,000 guineas the Company had been giving to Charles II "since the interloping times."[106] Several patents confirming and expanding the Company's powers in India, particularly against interlopers, followed.

Company leadership and their lawyers also believed that it was necessary to be able to prosecute interlopers directly in India; in some sense, this was preferable since this would keep the matter in Company courts rather than in England, where "we are under another Law."[107] Reflecting its arguments in *Sandys* about the exclusive nature of its diplomacy, the committees reminded their subordinates that all *farmans* and other such instruments be granted in the name of the Company, not the English nation broadly, and now insisted that any agreement in Asia explicitly require that "all his Majesty's Subjects English, Scotch, or Irish, that may dwell or reside in any of their dominions, be delivered up on demand with what belonging to them."[108] To underscore this aggressive strategy, the committees sought to expand the Company's ability to condemn interloping prize in India. In April 1686, James II explicitly confirmed the clauses of a 1683 charter from Charles II that had given the Company "full power and Authority" to enter any "Ship, Vessel, House, Shop, Cellar or Warehouse" within its limits, and "attack, arrest, take and seize" any ships or goods in violation of that jurisdiction, the booty to be split between Company and Crown. To facilitate this, both charters had empowered the Company to erect courts in any place within its jurisdiction, the only strictures being that the courts be on the coast, that they be staffed by one judge "learned in the Civill Laws" and two merchants, and that they decide cases according to equity and the *lex mercatoria*. They could hear all cases of forfeiture and seizure, disputes over contracts, and any "Trespasses, Injuries and Wrongs, done or committed upon the High Sea" or within the bounds of the Company's charter.[109] Despite the broad brief, the committees

understood these courts as primarily "designed for proceeding against all Interlopers and private Ships, and persons Trading in the East Indies, or to or from
the East Indies."[110]

Although not formally named as such in the charter, these were widely understood as the Company's "Admiralty Courts," yet while sharing some commonal-
ities with Vice-Admiralty Courts in the Atlantic, they were quite different
institutions. There was no line of appeal or administrative connection to the
English High Court of Admiralty, the Royal Navy, or the Admiralty. They oper-
ated with both royal and Company commissions, but were established where
and how the Company saw fit. Their judges were chosen by the Company, which
was empowered to remove them at will. Even the courts within the Company's
system functioned somewhat differently from one another. At Bombay, whose
first judge was the well-connected civil lawyer Dr. John St. John, the court was
subordinated to the judicature court and its business largely confined to condemnations. Yet, the Madras court came, at least for a time, to deal broadly
with "Navall & Martiall business," including disputes among merchants, the
enforcement of shipping passes, and at points even adjudicating intestate debts
and taking in the city's revenue and the land customs.[111]

While in practice these Admiralty Courts did not function for very long, they
reflected quite clearly the broader implications of the Company's project to exert
its discipline, authority, and jurisdiction in the East Indies, particularly over
English subjects, in close alliance with but clearly distinct from the Crown and
the English state. As the committees lectured Surat a few years later, the courts'
goal was to

> make all Persons know, that there is an English Politicall Government
> in India and that English men, having the same authority from their
> Sovereign as the Dutch have from their Sovereigns, know as well how to
> govern in India with Coersive Lawes, and a strict execution of those
> Laws, as the Dutch doe.

"Untill you come to that," they continued, "you are not a settled Nation in India,
exercising Sovereaign authority, but a few Scattered English Merchants, destitute
of Wisdome Conduct or Order, not fitt to keep the dominion you have already
in India much less to encrease it."[112]

3

"A Politie of Civill and Military Power"

Diplomacy, War, and Expansion

Just a few years following *East India Company v. Sandys*, the Court of Committees seemed more convinced than ever that it was the Company's role "to defend or offend or enlarge the English Dominion and unite the Strength of our Nation under one intire & absolute command subject to us as we are and ever shall be most dutifull to our owne Soveraigne."[1] This was easier said than done. As the judges handed down their decision in the case, the Company had only three functioning plantations, each of which was experiencing remarkable growing pains, from food shortages to outright rebellion. Mortality was high, garrisons unruly, settlers uncooperative. Most of its factories remained vulnerable to local politics in India, Indonesia, and Persia, where diplomacy was frustrating and exceedingly expensive. Other Europeans, particularly the Portuguese and the Dutch but increasingly the French and the Danes, did not make matters easier. And, of course, there were still interlopers.

The 1680s proved to be a crucial moment in the creation of the Company's regime abroad as it faced and responded to unprecedented challenges with an aggressive policy oriented toward protecting the Company's jurisdiction, reputation, and rights in both Europe and Asia. Its efforts were clearly aided by an increasingly close alliance with an expansive English monarchy but were inspired most directly by the affronts that arose from its Asian, European, and English rivals to its newly aggressive posture. Out of these trials emerged a new commitment to protecting that system as well as new projects for diplomacy, expansion, settlement, and even war. While not entirely successful, the results—some short term, others slower in the making—reflected a deepening and increasingly forward commitment within the Company to the protection and expansion of its government in Asia.

The stress on the Company's jurisdiction and authority was particularly acute at Bombay, where it was tested by neighbors and rivals from the very start. Officials at nearby Portuguese Goa and Bassein had been extremely reluctant to cede authority to the English Crown in the first place and continued to claim jurisdiction over parts of the archipelago and extraterritorial authority over the island's Catholics. The dispute came down in some sense to the meaning of the phrase "Portus et Insula Bombay" in the marriage treaty, which Goa insisted referred to Bombay island alone, arguably one of its least productive and salubrious sites. This diplomatic battle over the islands and people on them was in turn fought out over rights to waterways. Portuguese officials punitively required that ships from Company Bombay carry their *cartazes* and pay exorbitant customs in order to pass by Thana and Karanja (Uran Island) en route to the mainland. The Bombay council regarded these as hostile acts and a violation of the Portuguese grant which in its interpretation had transferred not only "right of dominion over all the Islands therein" but "allso over those small streights and passages which make it."[2]

Meanwhile, decades of warfare between the Mughal and Maratha empires had taken a toll on the Company's establishment in western India. The conflict had left much of the region around Surat "in greate disturbance," something felt keenly by the Company's factors there.[3] It also had extended onto the waters, where Maratha forces and its allies confronted the Sidi costal polity, led by a Mughal *mansabdar* and *jagirdar* known to the English simply as "the Sidi," that served as the Mughal tributary navy along the coasts of Gujarat and adjacent areas.[4] What had been a general threat and disruption began to affect Bombay directly when in August 1679, in order to gain better position on the Sidi, a Maratha fleet occupied and fortified the tiny, rocky island of Underi at the mouth of Bombay harbor. Bombay's council had left the island unpeopled and undefended but still regarded it as falling under its jurisdiction. Neither pleas nor threats were effective. A feeble blockade of Underi left the commander of the small flotilla of three ships dead and fifteen of its crew captive. A slightly larger squadron, commanded by Richard Keigwin—a former deputy governor of St. Helena who had recently immigrated to Bombay and was serving as a justice of the peace and captain of the island's cavalry regiment—was vastly outmatched. Sent only to communicate a transparently empty ultimatum, Keigwin had been forbidden to engage. The Bombay council also refused to dispatch the two European ships that were in its harbor, citing its fears that it might not be legitimate to employ them in such a capacity because they were not owned by the Company itself. This seemed odd to Keigwin, as it later did to the Court of Committees, which pointed out that although the Company did not own most of its European shipping, captains' commissions and charterparty contracts with proprietors expressly required them to serve the Company either "in Trade or Warrfare."[5]

What Keigwin saw as timidity, Thomas Rolt, the president of Surat (and thus *ex officio* governor of Bombay), and Bombay's deputy governor John Child (its chief resident official) understood as part of Bombay's long-standing policy to "[keep] faire with both" the Marathas and the Sidis.[6] Gerald Aungier had initiated treaty negotiations with the Maratha Emperor Sivaji as early as 1671 and sent a rather high-level diplomatic mission to his court in 1674.[7] The Company similarly made constant overtures to the government at Surat for the sake of its factory there; they had even helped defend the town against Sivaji's invasion in 1670, which evidently earned Aungier a token appointment as a *mansabdar* with territorial affiliation in an area south of Bombay.[8] More recently, the Bombay Council had been attempting to curry favor with Mughal officials by reluctantly allowing the Sidi to winter his fleet at Bombay.

The Company's martial establishment seemed premised on defense, Cato's "good old Addage Non minus est virtus quam querere parte tueri"—it is no less virtuous to defend than to acquire—being a favorite one with Company committees.[9] Thus, while London resolved to send one hundred soldiers to help recover Underi, they also reminded their subordinates that the wisdom of Dutch policy was to occasionally wage limited campaigns at sea but always to avoid entanglements "upon the Maine land"; merchants, they insisted, should always favor peace over war.[10] The policy in this case had not met expectations. John Child and the Bombay council had with "great paines and industry" concluded a treaty with Sivaji's forces but could not persuade them to leave.[11] The Sidi meanwhile had positioned his fleet—by one report, 22 large ships, 110 galleys, and about 12,000 men—at Khanderi, another small, abandoned rock of an island near Underi and which Bombay also claimed as part of its jurisdiction.[12] From there, he began to demand that ships take his passes, presuming, the Surat council complained to London, "to give Laws in all that Bay (solely your Honors royalty)."[13]

All of this posturing had made two things clear: the East India Company government regarded itself as having, in principle, a legitimate and inviolable jurisdiction over the entire Bombay archipelago and its waterways and the extent and nature of that jurisdiction were, in practice, constantly tested and shaped by local circumstances. By early 1682 John Child had succeeded Rolt as governor, and Company officials in western India had become convinced that their rule at Bombay required a more forward policy to remove the Maratha and Mughal naval forces and bring the Portuguese "to some better tearms and friendly behaviour towards us."[14] Making matters worse, the wider Mughal-Maratha conflicts in western Asia had begun to take their toll on Bombay indirectly, creating serious scarcities and driving up the price of food, supplies, and labor. Following London's orders to retrench military charges was impossible, putting even greater pressure on the garrison and militia to stand watch and to complete construction on the island's defensive works, particularly the fort's bastions.[15] The Sidi's sailors, who commonly came ashore at Bombay, strained already dear provisions and were resented by many inhabitants, especially in the garrison. Informal scuffles between them and English soldiers were common. In May 1683, one such encounter in the bazaar left one Company soldier, Robert Clarke, injured, and another, Edward Harper, dead. The Bombay council's inability to get the Sidi to extradite his attacker "highly inraged the rest" of the garrison and led several soldiers to retaliate on their own by taking a small boat and foolishly attempting to board the Sidi's ship. Vastly outnumbered, all three quickly leapt overboard after firing off eleven, somewhat randomly aimed shots from their ship's guns.[16]

This incident revealed and exacerbated yet another stress on Company government, namely, growing tensions within its own garrison. Attempts to reduce military expenses, including disbanding Keigwin's cavalry unit, had created friction with officers while declining real pay for the soldiers, owing in part to the Company's failure to account for depreciating exchange rates during the continental war, spread dissention amongst the rank-and-file. Bombay had also begun to crack down on dead musters, the common practice of informally providing subventions for officers' pay by failing to remove deceased soldiers from muster rolls.[17] Despite having recently received a vote of confidence from London in the form of a commission as a member of council and as captain lieutenant of the garrison and the militia, with a particular charge to lead any further attempts at Underi, Keigwin seemed particularly resentful over what he considered Rolt and Child's cowardice with regard to the Maratha forces a few years earlier.[18] His friendship with John Petit, Bombay's dismissed deputy governor turned interloper at Surat, only amplified the situation, as they and their allies began to spread rumors of corruption and abuse of power against Child and his brother-in-law and new deputy, Charles Ward.[19]

By December 1683 Keigwin and the cohort surrounding him had become convinced that the current Company government was irredeemable. During a routine mustering on 27 December, Lieutenant Henry Fletcher and Ensign John Thorbourne seized the fort on Keigwin's behalf, imprisoning Ward, his family, and John Church, the island's appropriately-named minister, proclaiming a new government at Bombay in the name of Charles II.[20] The rebellion was clearly the result of careful planning. Keigwin reportedly had his proclamation and commissions already drafted on the evening of the rebellion, while Thorbourne's wife had been heard complaining for weeks that he was always suspiciously "taken up with writeing."[21] Keigwin immediately sent a letter to Charles II justifying his actions. Among the Company's many supposed failures and inadequacies were its inability to exact justice for the attack on English soldiers, oppressive taxes on land and arrack, and ignoring the complaints of soldiers and inhabitants "like Proud Pharoh with the poore Isralites." He indicted Ward and others as Sabbath breakers and apostates for tolerating Hinduism and Islam on the island. He even implied the Company's leaders were Satanists, citing a laundry list of scriptural and common law precedents for why they should not only be turned out of power but burned at the stake.[22]

As in many rebellions against colonial rule, such as Nathaniel Bacon's recent uprising in 1676 against the government of Virginia, Keigwin and the other rebels insisted that they remained loyal to the king, and that their rebellion was justified because the Company had failed in its primary charge *in loco regis* to protect the island and preserve the security of its inhabitants.[23] In other words, Keigwin claimed to be saving the island from the Company on the king's behalf. He sent a soldier, Thomas Wilkins, with sixty men to seize the Company's ship *Return* and rechristen it the *Royal Return*. He commissioned Stephen Adderton as captain and admiral, with general instructions to inspect ships for passes, seize pirates, and "Oppose all his Majesties Enemies whatever that shall attempt to Oppose you." Adderton was directed to ride with a royal jack and pennant flying in Surat harbor, presumably to tempt Child or others into attempting a boarding.[24]

In articulating this right of rebellion, Keigwin was fundamentally disputing the Company's vision of English subjecthood in Asia as subordinate to its rule as a substitute for rather than a representative of Crown authority. Like Bacon and many others, he embraced the language of English subjecthood in resistance to local colonial authority. His language was also replete with tropes common to the interlopers' critique of the Company as an arbitrary, despotic, and illegitimate government. The rebels focused their attention not only on Ward, but also on both John Child and Josiah Child, the Company's governor in London; the coincidence of their names—which in fact led numerous later historians to assume erroneously that they were related, even brothers—made it easy to brand one the Company's "emperor" at home, the other executing his "Arbitrary" power abroad. Petit complained that "Child at home scatters the Guinnys there as the Other Child does the Rupees here."[25] Keigwin even quipped in his letter to Charles II that his ultimate hope was to restore government to its state when "such perverse Children were not amongst them."[26]

For Keigwin and his compatriots, Ward and the two "Children" had conspired to create nothing short of "irregular Government, continued in malice, avarice, oppression, Extortion, & other Intellerabel Insolencies irregular Actions tending to the ruine of his Island & Garrison & his Majestys Subjects thereon."[27] Keigwin's rhetoric thus echoed that of interlopers in India and Company critics back home. Yet, the potential dilemma in rebelling against the king on the king's behalf revealed fissures in the rebels' ideological position. Interlopers, like Sandys, Petit, and Bowcher, had long questioned the Company's rights as being "only by the King's charter," maintaining they were invalid or at least imperfect without Parliamentary consent.[28] Keigwin himself insisted in one drunken outburst that "his Majesty's Proclamation [to the Company] was of no Vallidity it being made without the Parliament," yet his compatriot Thorburn took exception, exhorting him not to "meddle with the Kings Prerogative."[29] It was also clear that there was simply an element of brute force and personal retribution behind the rebellion. When Wilkins was challenged by the first mate of the *Return* to produce a commission or any authority for his seizure, he allegedly brandished his musket and retorted bluntly, "This is my commission."[30]

As much as Keigwin and his allies rejected Company government, the one they established in its stead did not in fact look all that different. Upon taking control, Keigwin's first order of business was to form a governing council. Just as under Aungier a decade earlier, the new government was proclaimed in a ceremony in the bazaar, complete with trumpeters, "Country Musick," and a parade of soldiers.[31] Keigwin pledged to give an audience every Wednesday and Friday to any inhabitant who wished to issue a complaint about some injustice done them by the previous government, as the Company had done after taking Bombay's reins from the Crown.[32] He sent two men as an embassy to Sambhaji, who had now succeeded his father, Sivaji, to negotiate a truce with the Marathas.[33] He drafted "Articles of Agreement" with the island's inhabitants, pledging to do all the things the Company's government had promised but in his estimation failed to do, such as maintain justice, ensure free trade, and the secure the island's defenses and public infrastructure. The agreement also proclaimed the right to organize inhabitants into a militia and, while accusing Ward and Child of apostasy and diabolism for tolerating Hinduism and Islam, Keigwin pledged to maintain the fundamental freedom of religious worship on the island.[34] His government also began to issue shipping passes, proclaiming the Company's to be invalid.[35]

To Company officials, Keigwin's actions amounted to sedition. London severely upbraided the council at Surat for even referring to it as a "revolution," which, the committees reminded them, "is not English for a traitorous rebellion."[36] It was also taken as a symptom of the spread of interloping, which was the root epidemic of rebellion against proper English government in Asia. Keigwin's close relationship and correspondence with Petit and Bowcher only reinforced the connection. He had invited both men to come to live at Bombay and had given Adderton and others instructions to take guidance from them; meanwhile, George's wife, Ann, was hardly shy in reporting throughout Surat how elated she was by the coup.[37] The rebellion was also not an isolated incident. There had been minor incidents within Bombay's garrison and among Madras's inhabitants in the 1670s, not to mention three much more serious uprisings of soldiers and planters at St. Helena—one of which had been ironically directed at its deputy governor, Richard Keigwin—and another soon to come in October 1684.[38]

The Company's response to rebellion was thus inseparable from its response to interloping more generally. The committees were convinced now there could be no stability in Asia without first subduing the "naughtinesse of our own Countrymen," which meant swiftly and severely punishing offenders.[39] They were not hesitant to call on the Company's royal authority to do so. The Court of Committees had already solicited Charles II for license to exercise martial law over civilian English subjects, particularly at St. Helena, which he granted in 1683.[40] The Company also commissioned a seventy-two gun man-of-war, commanded by Sir Thomas Grantham, to take any ships in "the Sea of India or in any of the Rivers" in order to "end that Interloping Itch of Rebellion for this age at least." Though the committees did not yet know of Keigwin's uprising, Grantham turned out to be a prescient choice, as he had been specifically recommended to the Company by Charles II for his earlier efforts putting down Bacon's rebellion in Virginia.[41]

Grantham also brought with him Dr. John St. John, the first Admiralty judge appointed for Bombay. Upon his arrival, the Surat council published St. John's royal commission but not his Company one, "thinking it for [the Company's] service, that he should be looked on as immediately from his Majesty . . . [to] clap some terrour in the heads of the Mutineers on Bombay" and "the Interlopers men"; Child also lent St. John two of his guard, to add greater pomp to his retinue.[42] St. John in turn lavished praise on Child, recommending to Charles II that he offer him the title Lord Admiral of India.[43] The committees secured an arrest warrant from the king specifically naming four of the most troublesome interlopers in India—Bowcher, Petit, Simon Cracroft, and Edward Littleton—"as persons engaged in Endeavours to subvert the Company's Credit in India, Encouragers of Interlopers, and Advisers of the late Rebellion at Bombay."[44]

In November 1684, Keigwin finally capitulated but only after lengthy negotiations with Grantham, a fair amount of drinking, and the promise of a full pardon for himself and his loyalists, for which Grantham had been empowered by John Child and his council at Surat, "although Sore against our Wills."[45] Grantham took control of the island, delivering its government to Charles Zinzan, who had come on Child's behalf, and "the chair of justice" to St. John, who since his arrival had been holding a makeshift court at the English warehouse just outside Surat, taking depositions on the rebels as well as interlopers there. Like Aungier and Keigwin before him, Grantham also ordered a general amnesty for prisoners, except those convicted of murder and debt, and invited anyone with complaints to present them to him and St. John.[46] For his part, Keigwin returned to England and lived to fight another day; in 1689, he was appointed a ship captain for the West Indies, where he was killed leading an assault on St. Kitts.[47]

As much as the Company was willing to employ its royal authority, there remained serious limits to its willingness to defer to it entirely. There was in fact a long-standing tension in the relationship between the Crown and Company in India, particularly at Bombay. In its brief time under Crown rule, Bombay clashed with Surat over a number of issues, including rights to issue shipping passes; one Crown governor, Gervase Lucas, even warned the king that the "English as others in these parts are taught to believe they are a body apart from your Majestie's Authority or Government."[48] The committees had made it clear to John Child that St. John served at their pleasure, and that he was empowered to dismiss and replace the judge if he saw fit.[49] The happy relationship between the two did not last long. Child appointed John Vauxe, a member of the Bombay council, as chief judge of the island's high judicature court, which enraged St. John, who imagined his station as a royally commissioned judge trumped that of a Company employee. He was soon accused of conspiring with none other than George Bowcher, who allegedly helped him send his letters of complaint illicitly back to England. In retrospect, the charges seem suspiciously convenient; Bombay's attorney general began secretly to draw up an indictment against him, though Child had him sent back to England before they could be exhibited.[50]

In short, these events, and the rampage of interloping more generally, only reinforced the conclusion that no affront to the Company's authority could go unanswered, even if it came with a royal commission. Ship captains now had standing orders to help "reduce" any rebellion they might encounter and ships' charterparty obligations were extended by six months, measures more "for the security of Bombay, then ever was used heretofore."[51] Surat was advised to be wary of the pardoned rebels, as "His Majesty hath intrusted us not only with the trade, but the government of the English in India." While "as meer Merchants we might incline to a Womanish pity," the Company maintained "the political government of the English Colonies in India"; this required above all "the wisdom of Statesmen as not to trust a Traytour or treacherous person, tho' we may pardon him."[52] They reminded St. Helena in the wake of its own rebellion in 1685 of "the verity of that old Vulgar proverb too much pity spoiles a Citty," and that the "speedy execution of Justice upon such notorious offenders" was "the only known way to keep any people in peace, and subjection to good Lawes" and to allow obedient subjects to "live quietly upon lands and Stocks given them by our selves."[53] When Madras faced minor unrest in its "black" town, London, citing St. Helena as an example, insisted it treat such incidents swiftly and severely: "Till that be done, we must expect no good Government nor anything like the face of Sovereigne Authority among the English in India."[54]

Unfortunately, refractory Englishmen and disgruntled settlers were not the only threat to that "sovereigne authority." In addition to tensions with the Portuguese in western India, the Company had grown deeply apprehensive about the Dutch, particularly in Indonesia. In May 1682 the Company welcomed two ambassadors, Keay Nabee Naia-Wi-Praia (Ghiyahi Nghabiyah Nay-Viparay) and Keay Nabee "Jack" Sedana (Ghiyahi Nghabiyah Day-Sadan), from the Javanese sultanate of Banten to London. The men were entertained in lavish style, receiving a gun salute from Tower Hill, several audiences with Charles II, and knighthoods; one had his portrait drawn and a medal struck in his honor, and the entire party even attended the wedding of Josiah Child's daughter Rebecca the following month.[55]

"Keay Nabee Naia-wi-praia, principall Ambassador from Sultan Abdulcahar Abulnazar King of Surosoan, formerly called Bantam, to his Matie of Great Britain &c," 1682. © The Trustees of the British Museum.

Though the ambassadors came bearing presents as well as a flattering letter to Charles II, Child entreated the Privy Council to instruct the ambassadors to conduct their negotiations solely with the Company, "to whom his Majesty leaves all Affaires in that nature."[56] The Court of Committees desperately wanted to forge an alliance to secure its presence in Banten, which had in recent years come to be an entrepôt for spice island commerce. Their main concern was to establish a relationship there to serve as a bulwark against the Dutch, who the committees argued sought "Empire of all those Countries, to the enslaving of many noble & ancient Princes."[57]

Company officials were frustrated when they found the ambassadors had actually come with "no power to treate of any matters much less to conclude." They were nonetheless undeterred. The committees wrote to Abd al-Kahar—also known as Sultan Hajji—the son of the aging Sultan Abu'l Fatah Ageng and who had been left by his father largely in charge of Banten's government. They sought "firm particular & certain Articles of alliance, peace, & Commerce that might have endured as long as the Sun & Moone between your Majesty your Royall heires & Our Selves and Our Successors" and even drew up such a treaty to be sent back with the ambassadors and planned their own embassy to Java.[58] The alliance, however, was not to be. Alarmed by his son's apparent closeness with the Dutch and suspecting he had been behind the murder of his mentor and chief advisor, Sultan Ageng returned from retirement to try to retake power. The "young" king was only rescued from certain defeat by a Dutch invasion. The VOC occupied the port, and all other European and Asian traders were expelled. Within a month, the only sign of the English that remained was the flag the factors had left flying over the factory in protest, which was itself lowered soon after and, as rumor had it, torn asunder to make scarves for the Dutch soldiers.[59]

Recalling arguments Grotius had employed to defend Dutch incursions on the Portuguese in the early seventeenth century, the VOC justified their intervention on the grounds that they were permitted, even obligated, by the law of nations to defend their allies. The invasion was a "Work of Charity and Love" not an act of universal empire. In fact, one VOC advocate wryly noted that even the English Company clearly recognized the "young" Abd al-Kahar as the lawful king, since it had just recently been in negotiations with his delegates; in supporting his father, it was the English factory that had encouraged rebellion and had to be expelled.[60] Predictably, the committees saw the matter quite differently: the uprising was a Dutch conspiracy, the "young" king a rebel and a VOC puppet, and their expulsion an act of war.[61] They requested the king and his Privy Council lend them five or six frigates, humbling themselves that "this Nationall Gangreene needs speedyer & stronger remedyes then can be applied by any private Merchants."[62] Though the royal fleet was never sent, Charles II did offer joint commissions for Company ship captains.[63] Meanwhile, the committees proposed an alliance with Abu'l Fatah, to help restore him to the throne.[64] Unable ultimately to raise a large enough force to confront the Dutch, the Company turned to diplomacy. The committees sent their agent, Jean Chardin, and the king's ambassador to the Netherlands, Thomas Chudleigh, as envoys to demand reparations. The Dutch ambassador in London made polite visits both to the English Court and the Court of Committees, but the negotiations that followed were largely unproductive.[65] Five years later, the Company was still petitioning for redress for the Dutch "injustice and violence."[66]

Banten hardened English Company attitudes toward the Dutch, whose system they simultaneously vilified and emulated. The incident derailed already tenuous negotiations for a mutual alliance against European interlopers and conversely reinforced suspicions that the VOC contrived to encourage them.[67] It stoked general anti-Dutch sentiment in English politics, easily recalling as it did the torture and execution of Company officials and their alleged Japanese co-conspirators at Amboina in 1623. That incident, which had been resurrected as propaganda during the most recent Anglo-Dutch war, embodied for the English the unlimited potential of Dutch rapacity.[68] To the Company, Banten was simply one step in an insidious Dutch plan to obtain universal empire in Asia. Their "injurious and Subtill practices if not timely prevented," the committees protested, would leave the VOC masters of the Indonesian pepper trade. From there, they would proceed to control the Bay of Bengal, the Ganges, all of Bengal and its saltpeter, and ultimately even all the trade of Surat and western India, leaving the VOC "absolute Lords of these seas" able to give "absolute Laws at Sea to all Nations throughout the world."[69] To reinforce the point to their subordinates, a few years later, the court of committees sent various stations in India copies of Samuel Purchas's *Hakluytus Posthumus*, considered by many at the time to contain the authoritative English account of the Amboina massacre, as "a booke very necessary for you thoroughly to peruse at all leisure tymes."[70]

If the rebellions at Bombay and elsewhere were symbols of the devastating consequences of *not* stemming the tide of disobedience and disloyalty, Banten was taken to reveal the critical importance of aggressively defending respect for the Company's authority from its neighbors. Continuing confrontations with the Dutch in Persia and in Golkonda, where VOC forces subsequently seized Masulipatam and ejected the Company's factory "after the same manner they did at Bantam," only proved the point.[71] Together, Keigwin's rebellion and Banten became rallying cries for a more forward and aggressive attitude toward the Company's establishment in Asia. They also prompted some important institutional changes. It was in this context that the Company first established its "secret" committee, with broad powers to manage sensitive political business.[72] It also led to a greater centralization of the Company's system in Asia. John Child had been elevated to the post of "admiral" and "captain general" during Bombay's rebellion, and was restyled in 1686 as "general," with command over all the Company's affairs in Asia and attended by a permanent grenadier guard of thirty English soldiers.[73]

Company leaders were also determined to invest in Bombay's defense and infrastructure.[74] Since first obtaining the island, the committees had hoped to move the Company's western presidency there from Surat; by the mid-1680s, they were ready to do it, considering such a move "convenient & consistent with the growth of the English Government & Colony at Bombay, which is the best seat of warr in all India." When it finally happened in 1687, Bombay was briefly restyled a "regency," in self-conscious imitation of the Dutch at Batavia and Colombo, though the moniker never took.[75] The committees also committed to sending more troops from Europe, and ordered Surat and Bombay to recruit Protestant European sailors out of Company ships as well to create two additional native companies, consisting mostly of Rajput soldiers with no ties to other European powers.[76] "That Island put in a right posture," they noted a bit later, employing what would become in future centuries an iconic metaphor for British India more generally, "is a Jewell, that we will allwaies endeavour to make as Strong and Secure as money & art can provide."[77]

Though clearly conceived of as the Company's "footing" against European, Asian, and English rivals alike, Bombay was hardly the only settlement to receive such attention.[78] In 1687 St. Helena was sent a war chest, "not to be broak open, but in the case of some exigency of a rebellion or an invasion, as the Romans [did] formerly, after they had been so frequently invaded by the Gauls."[79] London urgently ordered Madras to wall in and fortify its black town, as well as expand its boundaries.[80] The committees also began to recommend that subordinate factories, such as Karwar and Tellicherry in southwestern India, add ordnance and soldiery, even though they did not expect to make much profit on the pepper trade there.[81] In 1687 Bombay was instructed to negotiate with Sambhaji for a *farman* to expand their territorial jurisdiction around the fort at Tellicherry, to set the Company "upon as thriving a foundation in point of revenue and Subjects" as the Dutch at Cochin and the Portuguese at Goa.[82]

By the mid-1680s, the Court of Committees' project had explicitly become to defend vigilantly what they had by actively acquiring a firm, preferably fortified presence "in every Princes Dominion with whose Subjects we trade."[83] The goal of such a policy was to strengthen a network of enclaved, independent, urban settlements like Bombay and Madras from which to project naval power, protect the Company's rights and reputation, impede Dutch universal empire, and enhance the Company's authority over those it considered its subjects.[84] Its ultimate purpose, in the committees' words, was to "defend our Priviledges in all places." While certainly ambitious, this was hardly a dream of a vast territorial empire. The Madras council began to contemplate a garrisoned fortification in the Maratha-dominated territory of Jinji, to its south, which could serve as another prophylaxis for interloping, exert pressure on Golkonda, which had been encroaching on Madras and the Company's revenues on the coast, and "balance one Princes interest by the others, which is good Policy" and a "provision for futurity."[85] On the other side of the world, ship captains had standing orders to explore, settle, and fortify any islands near St. Helena that, in their judgments, might prove convenient for plantation. The committees were particularly hopeful about Tristan da Cunha, an island to the southwest of St. Helena. In April 1684 John Gayer, commander of the *Society*, was given a report from a mate on a previous year's ship as well as instructions to sail there on his outbound voyage to India, to survey it and the islands near it, judge their harbors and potential for provisioning ships, and catalog their plants and animals. He was instructed to leave three pigs and a letter in a bottle to mark a claim to any island he considered habitable.[86] Captain Robert Knox, who had received similar instructions from the Company, similarly surveyed the flora, fortifications, and inhabitants of the Cape Verde islands, which he later detailed in his *Historical Relation of Ceylon*.[87]

Company leadership was also committed to recovering its position in southeast Asia. It kept up its Indonesian pepper trade, though not terribly profitable, "not so much for the gaine we expect by them as to keep up our intelligence & knowledge of those people & places till we have time and see cause to make a fortified settlement."[88] In fact, Thomas Grantham had been sent out with instructions to make such a settlement. Before arriving at Bombay, on 12 May 1684, he landed at Hippins Island in the Straits of Sunda, which he claimed "in his Majesties name & for the use of the Honourable East India Compa[ny]," planting a royal flag and restyling the island Carelus Secundus.[89] The committees soon ordered the island abandoned, as better prospects had come along at "some small Island or the Mayn of Sumatra" under the jurisdiction of Aceh. They wrote to Aceh's Sultana, Zaqiyat-ud-din Inayat Shah, in terms almost identical to those employed with the sultans of Banten a few years earlier. The Company desired a perpetual grant like those of Bombay or Madras, emphasizing the role such a fortification could play in preventing the encroachment of Dutch power. They specifically cited the earlier events at Banten as evidence of the consequences for Aceh should the sultana not permit it.[90] The committees also instructed Madras that should she or the *orang kaya*, the powerful merchant oligarchy at Aceh, not agree to a settlement, it should pursue one on some uninhabited island, claiming it "by the best right pretended to by any people, Viz. prime of occupancy."[91] After making an agreement for the west Sumatran territory of Pariaman, Madras instead accepted an offer to settle at nearby Bengkulu ("Bencoolen"). In 1685 Ralph Ord, a former soldier and schoolmaster at Madras, led a party to conclude negotiations for a grant, which included land for a fortification, York Fort, and declaration of the Company as the "onely Lords & Sole Proprietors" of all the land within reach of its cannons.[92]

Life was by no means easy at Bengkulu. The fort and town were particularly vulnerable to earthquakes, severe weather, and disease. The European mortality rate was so high that council members Benjamin Bloome and Joshua Charlton complained ironically (and morbidly) that so many Englishmen had died they did not even have enough people left to dig graves.[93] The circumnavigator William Dampier, who visited Sumatra a bit later, called York Fort the "most irregular piece I ever saw."[94] Labor and materials for building were in short supply and extremely expensive, Company officials being extremely dismissive of the Malay population as "a lassie sort of people, that will not work, how poor soever they are."[95] Despite such challenges, Company leadership at all levels approached the project with their typical utopian enthusiasm. The committees were convinced the Sumatran settlement would in time "lay the foundation of our new habitation, Defence, and busyness there" and "become as considerable and formidable as any place this Company hath in India."[96] London sent soldiers, treatises on both martial and civil law, a printed book of the Company's rules and orders, and a commission for Ord (who had actually already died) to serve as Admiralty judge. They also designated several men in England to inspect the royal blockhouses at Gravesend, in order to devise a model for their Sumatran barracks.[97]

As with its other Asian colonies, Company ambitions to populate Bengkulu with European volunteers, especially from St. Helena, soon gave way to plans to attract Indo-Portuguese and particularly East Asian immigrants, who were thought to be experienced merchants, planters, and sugar cultivators.[98] As at Bombay, Madras, and St. Helena, the council was instructed to attend to city planning, making sure "their Buildings range the more regularly," especially by "lay[ing] out the streets and divisions by Lines."[99] Places were to be set aside for a bazaar, church, hospital, prison, and custom and warehouses. Immigration was to be encouraged by offering lower taxes than the Dutch at Batavia and by permitting a free private pepper trade with India and China, the customs on which were to offset the settlement's growth and infrastructure.[100] The council encouraged the building of two English and two Chinese "publick Houses," and a decade later London authorized giving land and up to £1,000 in loans to encourage the opening of Chinese-owned taverns, sugar refineries, indigo farms, cotton mills, gardens, "or any other busyness" that would encourage them to come and stay.[101]

They also addressed the labor problem in Sumatra by turning to slaves, imported from Madagascar or other Company settlements, to serve as soldiers, blacksmiths, builders, carpenters, and shipwrights. The model for slavery at

Bengkulu, unlike at St. Helena, mixed certain features of a European Atlantic model with southern and southeastern Asian practice, which tended to treat slaves as neither free nor chattel but as a form of encumbered laboring caste.[102] On the one hand, there was a clear recognition of such slaves as "humane Creatures," who required "fitting Lodgings Clothing and Dyet"; Company officials were forbidden to use them as personal servants, gardeners, grooms, or for "other such like menial Services."[103] On the other hand, they were understood as property and to some extent an investment. Slaves were encouraged to marry, "that they may encrease," and their wives given small plots to plant their own gardens "as is done in Barbados."[104] Discipline could also be extremely harsh; in 1709, a slave convicted of murdering a Portuguese garrison soldier was sentenced to be hanged, drawn, quartered, and burned, his heart to be displayed in the *bazaar* and the temple and his head and quarters "set upon Poles," in five different places, "for a Terrour to all villainous Rogues."[105]

Despite Bengkulu's hardships, by 1686 the Madras council reported triumphantly that the Company had "the Sole Government of that place," while the Court of Committees remained stalwart that it "may in time become a famous & well governed English Colony" and "a great City."[106] London meanwhile contemplated new factories in Japan and Mindanao, in the Philippines, which would, like the Sumatran settlement, give "protection to Chineses & all other trading Nations of India" while preventing the "arts & contrivances" of the Dutch.[107] A proposal was also floated to secretly invite an envoy from the king of Jahore to Madras, who they imagined would inevitably be so impressed with it that he would invite the Company to make a similar plantation in his territory.[108]

Company policy by the mid-1680s now seemed firmly fixated on securing its establishment through plantation and fortification, the better to confront "all Others that may abuse you in your Interest at any time."[109] This included not just European rivals but Asian powers as well, especially those Mughal officials in Bengal, Surat, and elsewhere who had suborned English interloping. The Company had also grown extremely impatient with Persian officials, who continued to resist the Company's efforts to collect on its half-century old rights to the share of the customs at Gombroon. As John Child and the Surat Council boldly pronounced, "The Moors grow mighty insolent & its high time they were taken down."[110] London agreed, reminding its subordinates that war was not an end in itself, but both force and the appearance of force were simply a means to a firm settlement of the Company's reputation, rights, and autonomy. Bombay was to maintain its stores and exercise its soldiers, since, as the committees wrote, "when your Emulators see you in such a posture they will not be so apt to affront you as they have been for tho' the Old Maxim was, Pax queritar Bello, Peace may as well be preserved and obtained by being in a formidable and strong posture of Warr and Defence as by Warr it self."[111] Still, while officials in western India remained reasonably reluctant in the aftermath of the Bombay rebellion to confront both Mughal and Persian forces at the same time—"it is not good or safe to have too many Irons in the fire at once," they noted—London countered with its own cliché, insisting that it was "possible and adviseable to kill two birds with one Stone."[112]

Soon, the Company decided to throw its first stone, but when it did it was not in the western Indian Ocean but in the Bay of Bengal, at Siam. Like Banten, Siam's capital Ayudhya and chief trading port of Mergui had become in recent decades international commercial centers; among European private traders, it had a reputation as both a financial and sexual paradise. Siam's King Narai offered numerous incentives for the Company to keep its business and its ships there to counter Dutch and French ambitions in the region and significant opportunities for private European traders to profit from important positions in his government. A former Company employee, the Greek-born Constantine Phaulkon had risen to the position of *phrakhlang,* or minister of the royal treasury and foreign trade, while his former patrons, the Englishmen Samuel White and Richard Burnaby, who had headed the Company's factory there, took up the prestigious and lucrative positions of *shahbandar* and governor at Mergui, respectively. Burnaby became particularly active in shaping Siam's foreign policy and leading it into war with Golkonda, where another former Company employee, Thomas Ivatt, was serving as Narai's ambassador, and thus Phaulkon's agent, at Masulipatam.[113]

Siam thus presented a number of interrelated problems for the Company. In offering these powerful positions to Englishmen, it became a haven for interlopers, something the Madras council expressed, succinctly but exasperatedly, in early 1685 with the words, "Wish Sir Thomas Grantham was there."[114] Company officials had come to regard Phaulkon as a "very naughty man," especially as he drifted from the English interest to the French, converting to Catholicism and arranging for two envoys to be sent from Siam to Versailles in 1684 and 1686 as well as welcoming an embassy and fleet from Louis XIV to Siam.[115] Although James II and Louis XIV had famously close ties—the Siamese embassy to France actually stopped in England and offered presents to the king, who sent a letter of gratitude in return—for the Company, a Siam within a French sphere of influence would have been catastrophic. The Siam factory had by now become completely dysfunctional, split into factions between one party in alliance with Phaulkon and another backing its chief, Samuel Potts. When the factory itself burned down, the English suspected foul play. Matters only became more tense when Potts was seized and put in stocks on Phaulkon's orders. John Child sent Samuel Lake, captain of the Company's ship *Prudent Mary,* to withdraw the factory and exact reprisals on Siamese shipping, but Lake too was apprehended and died in prison.[116] A couple of years later, several Burmese merchants at Madras complained that they had been seized at sea, imprisoned, and robbed by Samuel White at Siam; they petitioned the council to seek redress, "seeing they are inhabitants and assistants of this fort under the Honourable English Company's flagg."[117]

Especially in the wake of Banten and Bombay, London was unwilling to allow such affronts to go unanswered. By its account, the king of Siam owed it upwards of £35,000 for all of these "injuryes, wrongs, and debts." Lake's "murther" also became a rallying cry for retaliation, even though he had been a constant thorn in the Company's side during his life, bordering on an interloper himself.[118] Before they knew of Lake's capture, however, the newly formed secret committee had already decided to pursue an "open war" against Siam. Officials in India were instructed to employ their new powers of martial law and the Admiralty courts to seize Siamese ships in the Bay of Bengal and other Indian ports, especially those owned or piloted by Englishmen. In July 1686 the Company secured a general proclamation from James II recalling all English subjects from the service of "foreign princes," not just in Siam but throughout Mughal, Maratha, and Aceh territories as well.[119] When the proclamation reached Madras, it was sent to Siam with a fleet under the command of Captain Anthony Weltden; it was also proclaimed with great ceremony at Madras, read before the entire English population, translated into six languages, and posted at all the city gates "that itt may bee publisht to all persons & Nations in India."[120] The Madras Council gave ship captains orders to board any foreign ship, seize any English subject without a pass, and bring them for condemnation into the Admiralty Court.[121]

The Company's decision to go to war in the mid-1680s has generally been regarded as the moment when it turned away from its necessarily peaceful commercial objectives toward a misguided attempt at territorial dominion, either at the behest of a particularly small and bellicose junta among Company committees led by Josiah Child or as an extension of the wider territorial and imperial ambitions of James II.[122] Yet, when seen in the context of the manifold stresses on the Company's system that had been building over the decade, the conflict at Siam seems less a revolution than an evolutionary, if particularly hawkish, outgrowth of the Company's commitment to protect the integrity and authority of its government in India. The problem with Siam was the way in which it had become both a potential base for a European rival and "great friends to the Nest of Naughtiness, Interlopers"; to win this war was thus to root out one such haven and reduce the English there to obedience to Company governance and Company laws in Asia.[123] King Narai and Phaulkon's reciprocal declaration of war in 1687 only confirmed this position, distinguishing as it did between its enemies the "Company & their Servants" and "all freemen, that are English," who were exempted.[124] Phaulkon also taunted the Madras council for even considering its authority as equal to his, "similiseing merchantile authority and power with those of a monarch."[125] Men like Samuel White—later known in imperial lore as "Siamese White"—exemplified this problem as an interloper who had "made himself a Subject as well as a servant of the King of Siam."[126] It was, the committees insisted, "a Silly thing" for the Company to be considered the English government in India if it could not control, at the very least, the English in India.[127]

Despite all this bombastic rhetoric, the committees nonetheless held out hope that the Englishmen of Siam could still be brought into the fold. Privately, they believed the proclamation from James II could serve as a ploy to provide a "plausible & Justifyable excuse" for Englishmen to safely and legitimately abscond from Siamese service. A second letter from James II specifically directed at White and Burnaby made this point explicitly, assuring them of his personal recommendation for employment at Madras should they comply.[128] Regaining control over White, Burnaby, and the rest was critical to reducing them to obedience to the English king as well as the Company, which had been "appointed not only to advise but to bear rule & exercise sovereign power in India over their persons & estates." Obedience to government followed not from human nature but only from good and effective laws; the proclamation, the committees insisted to their subordinates, was thus "A regula[ti]on of most indispensable necessity, if you ever think to make the English Nation in India look like a political governing State in India."[129]

This use of royal instruments and the royal name to discipline Englishmen in India was nothing new, though admittedly it was of a different order this time. The Company had been extremely successful in persuading James II of the dangers, in particular, of Dutch universal empire, and it seemed to be able to ally its own ambitions with James's desires for expanding the "English dominion" abroad, exemplified for example in his creation of the Dominion of New England.[130] The Company certainly capitalized on his sympathy to the project. The war at Siam was prosecuted in the king's name and during its course, the Company had the Union flag hoisted over Fort St. George with great ceremony and revelry: prisoners were freed, alms given to the poor, and the soldiers, the council reported, were "as merry as Punch could make them."[131]

Yet, if the Company's war profited from its alliance to James II and his imperial aspirations, it was not always clear who was manipulating whom. There were also subtle but striking moments of divergence. Though prosecuted with the king's backing, it was the Company, not England, that was at war with Siam. The war also raised an interesting dilemma as to whether someone like White should be treated as an English subject, and thus an interloper, or a Siamese official, and thus an enemy of war. In 1687 Bombay's newly arrived deputy governor and judge of its Admiralty Court, John Wyborne, complained that he was being pressured by John Child to treat such ships not as English interloper but as war prize—in which case, as spoils of war, only one-tenth rather than one-half of the booty would be owed to the Crown. Wyborne, who like St. John before him had both a royal and Company commission, clearly imagined his power from the king had rendered him superior to those in the Company's government. He actually spent almost his entire outbound voyage quarreling with the ship's commander, Joseph Eaton, over precedence, reportedly almost leading the crew to mutiny.[132] Now, he insisted that to condemn the ships as enemies rather than interlopers would be an affront to the monarch. The issue was ultimately unresolved as Wyborne died from a "violent fever" soon after, and more pressing events at Bombay prevented the continuation of the proceedings.[133] Still, the experiences with both Wyborne and St. John led Josiah Child and a number of other committees to insist to James II by 1687 that "no person in India should be imployed by immediate Commission from his Majestie," lest "the Wind of extraordinary honour in their heads would probably make them so haughty & over bearing that in a little time we Should be forced to remove them."[134]

If the war in Siam was an opportunity for expansion, it fit within the Company's greater strategy of securing a limited network of enclaves to support its maritime power and protect and expand its commercial and jurisdictional rights. The Company had for some years investigated the possibility of an agreement for an independent, fortified settlement at Siam or nearby. In early 1684 the committees observed to Bombay that "if Wee can once secure our selves, and the Country be our owne, Wee doubt not, but Wee shall dayly grow stronger."[135] Although there was no hope of a "great Trade" from there, Mergui seemed nonetheless to be a key strategic point for harboring ships and a potential fallback should the Company ever be expelled from Bengal; the committees even imagined enticing Bengalis to settle there and "fabricate many Sorts of those Manufactures" currently bought dearly at Kassimbazar.[136]

Once at war, it now seemed possible simply to seize Mergui. With their recent experience at Sumatra in mind, the committees believed the conflict would prove a just pretense for acquiring a fortified settlement "by agreement, surrender or free."[137] They were only encouraged by George White—Samuel's brother, a former Company servant, private trader, one of Phaulkon's early patrons, and quasi-agent for Narai in London—who advised (either misguidedly or maliciously) the Court of Committees that it would take only a small force to seize Mergui, as it was supposedly undefended and populated by a "Sheepish cowardly people, like your Gentues." George's apparent assistance only reinforced the hope among Company leadership that Samuel could be returned to the flock; the committees even promised him appointment as second of council of the new settlement should he suborn their plan.[138] When rumors began to spread in London in early 1688 that Narai had died and that Phaulkon had been executed, the committees saw it as "a brave & just opportunity for you to seize & fortifie Tenassaree (flagrante instante bello)," and to obtain a peace, with a grant of "sovereignty & customes [etc.] of that place for ever to his Majestie for the Company's use, with some convenient Territory thereunto," which again was crucial not in itself but for its ability to "support of a navall force on that side of India."[139]

Unfortunately, the news had been slightly premature and the project far too optimistic. Narai did fall fatally ill but not until the summer of 1688, after which Phaulkon was indeed executed—publicly beheaded and left in pieces for vultures.[140] However, it turned out the opportunity had already been lost. The arrival of Anthony Weltden's fleet at Mergui and his publication of the royal proclamation had led to a devastating uprising against the English there; one of his ships was captured and burned and a number of people were killed.[141] Meanwhile, the French embassy and fleet had arrived, and Pondicherry, the French settlement south of Madras, began to offer sailors and passes to Siamese shipping. All of this ultimately dashed hopes of a conquest. The Company had acquired Negrais, just off the Burmese coast, which Weltden claimed by burning some huts and planting a royal flag, a plate, and a piece of wood "carved with Siam characters."[142] However, the Company never made anything of it and further attempts at Siam were to no avail. The war itself simply fizzled out after Phaulkon's death. The new *phrakhlang* declared himself more well disposed to the English but took Siam into greater isolation from all the Europeans.[143] Meanwhile, though ostensibly agreeing to return to Madras with Weltden, Samuel White managed to abscond to Pondicherry and then on to London, where he remained a vociferous Company opponent until his death in 1689.[144]

The interest in a Siamese settlement was not an isolated affair nor was it considered the only possible solution to the Company's problems in the Bay of Bengal. Madras was instructed in August 1688 to pursue negotiations with its Burmese allies at Rangoon (Yangon), which in their estimation was perhaps not as useful as Siam, but far preferable to the bird-in-hand of Negrais. None these options, however, compared to their first choice: "application to [Aurangzeb] for a fortified place for our Shipping in Bengall."[145] While their stated preference was for an island off the mainland like Bombay, the court of committees instructed the factory at Hugli to pursue a *farman* for any adequate settlement with a harbor to protect its shipping and "ground enough to cultivate" for a settler population, again modeled on Dutch Batavia. The council was given leave to spend upwards of 30,000 rupees for securing a "perpetuall inheritance" in Bengal, the committees "not doubting but that our Charter & this Company is longer lived than the youngest of our Grandchildren."[146]

Like Siam, the committees had contemplated a permanent, fortified, and populous Company settlement in Bengal for quite some time. Its presence in the province dated to the 1640s but was, as at Surat, constantly at the mercy of local and regional politics. An independent colony would give the Company a much firmer footing from which to exert authority over interloping Englishmen in the province as well as project maritime power outward into the Bay of Bengal. Fortification also seemed crucial as a bulwark against the declining but lingering influence of the Portuguese and, far more importantly, the Dutch, who in recent years had conspired with local officials against the Company not only at Banten but Persia and Masulipatam as well.[147] The Bengal and Madras councils insisted to Mughal authorities, as they had argued in Sumatra, that a Company presence was the only way to protect Bengal from the Dutch, though it was clear a fortification was less to secure the Mughal province from the Dutch than the Company from both Dutch and Mughal power. As London wrote, "we look upon the Mogulls Governours, but as Instruments, which we hope to compell by fair means, or foul, to use us better hereafter."[148] In particular, an English fort and garrison in Bengal would have given the Company far greater leverage against the growing impositions of Bengal's *nawab*, Shaista Khan, who in 1680 had imposed a new 3.5 percent duty on exports and an even larger tax on the Company's imported bullion. As William Hedges, the Company's previous chief in Bengal had argued, no amount of diplomacy could arrest the *nawab's* ambitions; only a fortified settlement would do this, which in turn could only be acquired if the Company were to "resolve to quarrel with these people."[149]

Keeping true to their sense that it was best to kill two birds with one stone, the Court of Committees saw the war at Siam as a present opportunity to confront the *nawab* of Bengal. The Siam fleet sent from London came bearing the Company's formal declaration of war on the *nawab* and was to be joined by detachments from Sumatra and Madras to assist in prosecuting that war.[150] The Company meanwhile pursued secret treaties of alliance against the *nawab* with both the Marathas and Burma.[151] By October, hostilities had broken out. Early minor victories further convinced Job Charnock, agent in Bengal, and his second, Francis Ellis, that "It's time wee had an absolute conquest & might have made the Towne our owne."[152] Lacking sufficient men, money, and ammunition to effect such a plan, however, Charnock was ultimately forced to abandon his orders to attack Mughal shipping and invade Chittagong. Instead, he moved about twenty miles downriver, where he initiated negotiations with the *faujdar*, via Dutch intermediaries, for a peace.

Fighting continued intermittently at various places, which made clear just how crucial a maritime establishment was to underscoring claims on land. The Company captured seven Mughal ships in the Bay of Bengal, which, along with other prize taken in the Siamese war, were valued by the Bengal Admiralty Court, held shipboard, at over 104,000 rupees.[153] Given the recent Mughal conquest of Golkonda, the Madras government also set about reinforcing its own defenses, ordering new gun platforms erected, constant watches within the city walls and at its gates, a tank built to store water in case of a siege, a new lodging house for the soldiers, and the hiring of a few ships to ride in the harbor for protection. By year's end, its council had also voted to pursue a diplomatic engagement as well, and to continue to seek a *farman* for the "firm & lasting Settlement & enjoyment of the English Interest & trade in India."[154]

Back in Bengal, by September, a truce had been negotiated with the *nawab*'s representatives. While hardly an outright military victory—Charnock ultimately had to retreat to Madras—the war in Bengal, unlike Siam, had achieved its main purpose. Despite the *nawab*'s obfuscations, by 1690 Charnock was able to return to Bengal to begin to plant a settlement in the very place to which he had first escaped: the towns of Sutanuti, Govindpur, and Kalikata on the Hughli river, which together soon came to be known, as one early nineteenth-century historian stated, "by the more pompous and comprehensive name of Calcutta."[155] By 1698 the Company was in firm possession of a *zamindari*, a Mughal office and title of land-holdership and revenue administration, over the towns and had begun to build its Fort William; the council there was instructed from London to call upon as many soldiers and sailors they could get to do this as quickly as possible, "for until a City or an army be intrenched, out of danger of the Enemy," the committee opined, "no man ought thinke himself too good, to give his helping hand."[156]

4

"Politicall Science and Martiall Prudence"

Political Thought and Political Economy

In September 1687, the East India Company Court of Committees promoted Nathaniel Higginson to second of the Fort St. George council. Higginson was an odd choice for a group of merchants, but not for a company-state in the midst of a three-front war with the *nawab* of Bengal, the king of Siam, and a bevy of English interlopers on both sides of the world. The third generation of a family of New England clerics, Higginson was a graduate of Harvard and a former tutor and apprentice at the London Mint. With less than five years at Madras, he had far less experience as a merchant or in India than anyone else on the council and even some factors. The Court of Committees insisted nonetheless that Higginson's appointment to such a critical post was "for the publick good." He was "a man of learning," well versed in Greek, Latin, and history, and it was only a "good stock of naturall parts" such as this that "can render a man fit for government and politicall Science Martiall prudence & other requisites to rule over a great city," including making of treaties "of peace or war or commerce with foreign Princes." While "little other science was necessary when we wee [were] in the State of mere trading Merchants," times had changed "since his Majestie has been pleased by his Royall Charters & during his Royall Will & Pleasure to forme us into the condition of a sovereigne State in India."[1]

The Company's ambitions had certainly been bolstered by the support of James II, but such sentiments were hardly new. In claiming the right and responsibility to govern English subjects in Asia and colonial proprietorships over European and Asian subjects of its own, the East India Company had ceased to be, if it had ever been, simply a commercial body; over a decade earlier, Gerald Aungier had reflected with a bit of ironic and feigned surprise that in "his calling is as a Merchant," he had never expected he would come into such a charge as Bombay and thus have to become "a souldier, Lawer, Philosopher, Statesman;

and much lesse a Governour."[2] A decade and some later, the committees now seemed convinced that the Company had lost its way, "the want of this politicall science" only encouraging the myriad of challenges to its authority from rivals at home and abroad.[3] They thus turned not only to a project of defensive expansion but were committed to grounding the government of that system in its first principles, guided by a variety of historical and contemporary examples from Venice to Virginia, from Roman books to the book of Romans. Many of the ideas they had about effective governance reflected their understanding of the Dutch, who, as Josiah Child had put it, were "the wisest *People* now extant." Echoing the ambivalence about the Dutch found in much late seventeenth-century English political and economic writing, the Company envied their commercial and political success in both Europe and Asia but desperately sought to avoid what the committees regarded as their "inhumane Crueltys and injustice, which we abhor."[4] Seeking "the same end by contrary & gentler means," Company leadership in this period believed they could arrive at a "golden mean," finding "a middle way between our abused simple weak lenity & their too great extreme rigour."[5] The result was a synthesis of political ideas and political economy that balanced universal principles with local practices, paternalist political authority with commercial and political liberty, and the obligations of rulers to provide the conditions for their subjects' security and prosperity and those subjects' reciprocal duty to contribute to the protection and well-being of their city, colony, and civil society.

At the root of this Company political thought was an almost obsessive concern with the correlation between population and strength, particularly economic strength, a notion with firm roots in Restoration economic thought.[6] Josiah Child had argued that "whatever tends to the populating of a Kingdom, tends to the Improvement of it," and the best way to effect this was through the establishment of "good Laws."[7] The basic principle behind the Company's project of peopling its colonies was to ensure a freedom of trade and security in property to inhabitants and foreigners.[8] Unencumbered commerce would encourage people to choose to settle in Company plantations, attract wealth, and increase navigation, all of which contribute to the strength of a polity; in turn, settlers should be encouraged to cultivate land, placing great importance on the Company's role in providing a legal apparatus to ensure due process in matters such as probate, land transfers, property disputes, and confiscation. Despite the emphasis on plantation, this was a vision of economic and political strength that was commercial and maritime in its basic conception. "There is no possibility," the committees advised to the "young" Sultan of Banten and his advisors in 1682, "for a small City or Country to hold out against a great & mighty people, especially great in Navall power, but by making such small Cities or Countries the place of a great trade & Commerce." This required granting merchants special privileges, unrestricted movement, relief from excessive taxation, and protection. Although it might seem counterintuitive, evidence for the wisdom of such a policy could be found all over the world and in "the histories of former times, which We frequently do in Europe, by which we discover the Rise as well as the decay of great Cities, Princes, and States." Indeed, the committees boasted, one did not have to look very far for a modern example: it was "by like meanes" that Madras had developed "from a small village . . . to a great city, of above 100000 Inhabitants, in less than 30 years time."[9]

If this emphasis on freedom of trade seemed odd for the supposed standard-bearer of monopoly mercantilism, it is because those "mercantilist" arguments were hardly as black-and-white as often caricatured. As had been reflected in the *Sandys* case, even the most strident advocates of "monopoly" and the royal prerogative did not see monopolies as an unmitigated good. Where trade was already safe, secure, and governed or where monopolies allowed for private gain over public good, they were unnecessary, damaging, and possibly even illegal. Where there was reliable government, restrictions on movement and commerce inhibited immigration, the generation of wealth, and navigation, all of which were crucial for the security and prosperity of a nation, city, or plantation. The counterexample of the mercantile Italian city-states or Amsterdam testified to this fact. Thus, while the East India Company insisted that European trade with Asia required exclusive corporate government, within Asia, once governed, trade had to be allowed to flow "as free there as water does run in the Rivers." People and investment would flock to such a settlement, they believed, "as naturally as Crowes resort to carrion," and a place like Bombay harbor could become the Thames of British India or at least what some like Child wanted the Thames to be.[10]

Such policy was not simply a rationalization of the Company's inability in practice to control such trade.[11] It fit squarely with a political economy, which one could also see evidenced in defenses of the Company in England, that emphasized the importance of a vibrant overseas commerce as the key to generating wealth, encouraging productive immigration, and increasing navigation, which in turn provided both greater security and a nursery for seamen.[12] Free trade, however, was not uncontrolled or ungoverned trade. Such liberty did not extend to the point that it impinged upon the Company's jurisdiction or authority, and Company councils frequently restricted certain forms of local economic activity when it was necessary to secure some perceived common good. For example, in the colony's early years, Bombay seized a number of fishing vessels from nearby Portuguese settlements, which had continued to claim a customary right to fish near the island, in order to "dispute their said priviledges and secure your right."[13] Around the same time, it also forbid buckshawing—that is, fertilizing the ground, especially coconut trees, with small, dried "buckshaw" fish, likely bummalo—which tended to a "corrupting [of] the air with a noysome smell"; the Company's government insisted it would "prefer the health of our people more than the profit that would arise to us."[14] In the late 1680s, Madras began registering slaves for export in the choultry in an attempt to stop the exportation of children, eventually outlawing the practice entirely.[15] In 1683 the Company forbid any trade in or out of St. Helena that was not on Company or Company-licensed ships, in a sort of Company Navigation Law for the South Atlantic.[16] The Company was also not categorically hostile to the idea of pursuing regional monopolies and exclusive agreements with local sovereigns, like the Dutch; it just seemed not to be, under normal circumstances, a wise path to follow.[17]

The thought behind all this was that inhabitants desired first to be secure in their persons, trade, and property; once this could be assured, they would inevitably flock with their families and their wealth to a city. More people brought more wealth; more wealth, in turn, brought revenue, "the Soul and life of all the rest."[18] The goal of raising revenue on customs, excise, and land revenues, shipping passes, and court and licensing fees on taverns and liquor sales was to create a self-sustaining, autonomous system, which, as Aungier had put it, could make "the publique Revenue . . . answere the publique charge."[19] It was crucial, however, not to confuse revenue with profit; as the Court of Committees later argued, a strong and flourishing English presence in Asia could not be fulfilled "by the form and with the methods of trading Merchants, without the politicall skill of making all fortified places repay their full charge and expences."[20] The committees cited the Dutch frequently on this score in particular, though local revenue was also clearly crucial to supporting many other powers in Asia, including the Portuguese.[21] They were convinced local revenue made the VOC "settlements in India impregnable," allowing them to "conquer all other European Nations," and "to secure by great expences and Forts their soveraigne state in India, Enlarge their Dominion as well as their Trade, and to be alwaies in a condition to revenge any affronts that are offered them."[22] The committees even envied Dutch correspondence, which, they noted to Bombay in 1689, had one paragraph about trade for every ten about "their government, their civill & military policy, warfare, and the increase of their revenue. . . . 'tis that must make us a nation in India, without that we are but as a great number of Interlopers, united by his Majesties Royall Charter, fit onely to trade."[23]

Revenue was what separated the "meer Merchant" from a public authority with a sound "Politicall Basis."[24] It was its lifeblood, "as absolutely & indispensably necessary to support the English dominion in India, as Armes, Powder & Shott."[25] People paid taxes, and taxes made possible both a civil and military infrastructure. This perspective resonated in many ways with the reciprocal and mutually reinforcing relationship between power and plenty in some early modern European economic thought and foreign policy.[26] Extracting revenue was also a claim to jurisdiction in itself, a corollary to the notion, which informed both sides in the Sandys case, that possession lay not just in occupation but improvement of one's property.[27] Peopling a settlement and cultivating it was a signal claim to dominion, far more important in many ways than its particular foundation. Collecting revenue and investing it in the colony represented an ongoing claim to legitimacy as a government over it, its people, and their commerce; in turn, as the committees wrote to Madras in 1687, "It is only the trade and populousness of the place that gives opportunity to the Governours to create a revenue, and not the manner of their first entrance, whether by Conquest or Compact or treachery."[28]

If there was a tension between the belief that revenue was absolutely critical to sustaining a settlement and its population, but that keeping taxes "mild" was the only way to attract people there in the first place, the Court of Committees did not accept it. The "experience of all ages & all places of the Universe," and certainly at places like Amsterdam, Livorno, and Madras, taught them that attracting immigrants, permitting free trade, and maintaining low customs were "infallible" means by which "to make a little Citty a great One, and a Small Territory able to defend it self against Princes of Vast Dominions."[29] The number of immigrants and volume of trade flocking to a wisely run colony would offset the losses from lowered customs and rents, while people should be quite willing to pay some taxes for the security in their person, property, and trade they could expect in return. "It is not paying a few moderate dutyes to the Government that discourages the Population of any Colony," the committees wrote Bombay in 1692; it was "the preservation of liberty and property to the Inhabitants and the just and equall distribution of justice [that] will encrease the riches and numbers of any Colony." On this, the Bible offered useful instruction: "In righteousness all governments as well as the thrones of Kings are established as we find it in the old Scripture."[30]

Not everyone of course thought the Company's taxes were all that moderate. Councils in India consistently proved more reticent than their London superiors over the implementation of new tax schemes. They had good reason to be cautious: Keigwin's rebellion in 1683, the subsequent rebellion at St. Helena, a 1686 general strike in the black town of Madras, and many other routine and less dramatic political struggles were, in whole or in part, tax revolts.[31] Such resistance either from subjects or subordinates clearly frustrated the London committees but hardly surprised them. As Company lawyers had argued in Sandys, one had to expect private individuals to pursue their own goals, without a clear vision of the common good or even their own true interest. This was precisely why one had government. Councils not only taxed but, ideally if not always in practice, tried to control exchange rates, supervise creditor-debtor relationships,

and regulate and record land transfers to prevent unnecessary conflict and litiga-
tion. Thus, the committees insisted a cap on interest rates, which many including
Child had lobbied for in England, would prove the key "to the making of any
place great, rich, populous and consequently powerful, though it may run
counter to the private Interest of some particular persons, who being but a
handful with respect to the multitude are not to be regarded in the making of
Lawes."[32] This unwavering belief in their role as the wise governing council,
removed from the peculation of private concerns, also seemed to lead to a bit
of comforting, if slightly circular, logic: if a colony failed to yield an adequate
revenue and persuade its inhabitants of the virtue of taxation and other restrictions, it was not because the expectation was unreasonable but because "public
national and honourable ends" must have been diverted by corruption, waste, or
"private ends."[33]

Through good order and good husbandry, one could also educate and persuade subjects and inhabitants to see their own interest and duty in the common
good. They simply had to be reminded that taxation "is a security to their Lives,
Houses, Wives and children and all that belongs to them."[34] This could not be
done too harshly but rather according to "one Maxim, Suaviter in Modo fortiter
in Re"—that is, to be gentle in manner, but strong in deed—and to "please the
Commonality where fairly you can in the Method of raising Revenues, and in
everything that will contribute to, at least not hinder their better Advancement."[35] Anticipating the unpopularity of a 1685 tax for building city walls at
Madras, the committees insisted the council simply explain to inhabitants that
such bulwarks would not only secure but increase the value of residents' property in the long run. "Wee shall doe them good against their Wills," London
insisted, "which when they are older and wiser, they will thanke us for."[36] As if
with a copy of Hobbes's *Leviathan* in hand, the committees vented to the council
at St. Helena on the subject of planters' objections to taxes:

> It hath been our Care and our Cost, to nurse them up to what they are
> now, as it shall be to raise them to a better Condition, But whether they
> are willing or not, they must be reduced to Such a Form of civil Govern-
> ment and Expense for their Protection & preservation as is necessary to
> all Societies of Mankind and without Which the world would returne
> to its first Chaos.[37]

Without revenue there could be no government, and without government there
was only anarchy. Given the general view of human nature as inherently self-
interested, evidenced as well in the Company's arguments against interlopers in
the *Sandys* case, government had to be both coercive and persuasive, a paternalism that was critical since the multitude had neither the maturity nor the

perspective to see beyond their particular interest to the common good; such paternalism also quite literally extended to the Company's slaves, who, if bought directly in East Africa and taught English would "know neither Father nor Mother nor Countrey of their owne, but the English East India Company."[38]

This sense that Company government was responsible for the protection and improvement of its subjects was further reflected in its policies directed toward regulating and governing individuals' behavior within society and in the market-place. Like other early modern governments in Europe and the Atlantic, Com-pany councils, in theory, monitored and set maximum prices on essentials, such as meat and bread, and luxuries, like wine and even slaves. Letter after letter from London vilified engrossing, usury, and litigiousness. Councils, at times, pro-vided for orphans and widows and facilitated collections and other stopgap measures, such as abating taxes, during time of dearth and famine. In 1688 the committees recommended Bombay appoint a few "Fathers of the Poor" to supervise the raising of a charitable fund, modeled on the Dutch in Europe and Asia, since "in all Colonies be a necessity sometimes to relieve distressed poor."[39] Even liquor licenses, while a potential source of revenue—the committees esti-mated licensing brought the English state revenue amounting to a million pounds a year—were at Madras set at progressive rates: forty pagodas a year to the most profitable and busy European tavern, twenty to the second, ten to the third, and five to the rest; native public houses were rated similarly, though the fees ranged from four pagodas to one.[40]

The goal of all these policies was not simply to protect but to improve and even remake colonial subjects. Company leadership seemed constantly engaged in a vigilant, if Sisyphean, struggle against villainy and for the cultivation of the "hearty vigorous & active spirit" of those under their command; this sort of vir-tue was the first and last defense against interloping and disorder.[41] Much of this anxiety concentrated on soldiers, who were hardly the "sober" or "plain honest Country" people for which Company leadership might hope. Acknowledging that the Surat Council had been displeased with the character of some soldiers recently sent from London, the Court of Committees explained that their hands were tied:

> We cannot imagine you should hope that We can send you onely Such, or pick and choose, or know here a drunken mutinous Knave from an honest man. Comonly the worst of men when they seek employments shew the fairest outside. It is not our Choice of Souldiers here, but your Strict Military discipline & Martiall law must make Bombay a sober Garrison, if it were not for that, all armies in the world would be as intolerably wicked as Thievs & Highway men; Murders, Rapes nor any kind of abominations could be prevented.[42]

Such discipline was particularly necessary in Asia, "so remote and in a place of so much luxury."[43] Indeed, disobedience and dissoluteness went hand in hand. Thus, Richard Keigwin was not just a rebel but "debauched"; Company servants who failed to do their duty were "corrupt and depraved." Preventing this condition was critically important, as "a person once inhabituated to and contaminated with Infidelity Sloth or Luxury," the committees wrote in 1682, "will never mend to that degree as is fit for us to trust him again."[44]

In this sense, the relationship drawn amongst discipline, the active spirit, and virtue resembled in its broadest outlines humanist languages about the role of virtue and public life in shaping good citizens. Luxury and sloth, seen as endemic in Asia, were anathema to order and could only be confronted with frugality and the extirpation of private interest and corruption.[45] One arrived at this in garrisons through strict martial discipline and amongst employees via strict hierarchy enforced by contracts, sureties, and constant exchange of writing. For settlers and inhabitants, the signal virtue was to be found in service, particularly in the active support and defense of own land and city. The Company emphasized in particular the importance maintaining the militia in all of its settlements.[46] As in the English Atlantic, a well-regulated and trained militia was not just a means to get defense on the cheap but was in fact an integral part of the social and political life of a colony.[47] As such, it certainly was a cornerstone of the Company's vision for its one Atlantic colony. Militia service and training in arms was one of the terms upon which St. Helena's first planters were given their initial twenty acres of freehold tenure.[48] Each planter was required to "keep Watch and Ward" once a week or to pay forty shillings a year for every twenty acres owned, while every free person on the island "able to bear Arms" was to be quartered during emergencies and regularly mustered and trained. As in other plantation societies in the English Atlantic, such as Barbados and Virginia, the Company imagined that out of this would evolve a coherent political class that could maintain order, hierarchy, and even become a genteel model on a barbaric frontier.[49] The Court of Committees imagined these planters acting as English gentlemen, importing English goods, enclosing their lands, and becoming "the first Occupants and Gentlemen Freeholders of that Island . . . [with] Estates sufficient to maintain the dignity of that Title, and defend their Country on horsback."[50]

The Company did not imagine the inhabitants of Asian plantations as potential English gentlemen, but its policies there emphasized similar values in the relationship among duty, service, virtue, and subjecthood. This was what made paying taxes such a serious moral responsibility. It was an ironclad, universal rule that "all Mankind," the committees noted in one way or another on many occasions, "must & doe defray the charge of their protection & preservation in all parts of the World wherever the Sun or Moon shynes."[51] Good subjects, especially those whose property and liberty was secure, paid their taxes. Even to voice objection was to fail in one's civic responsibility. Thus, an English interloper who refused to make his home in a Company settlement was noxious not only because he resisted proper authority, but because in so doing he failed to pay taxes or contribute to the upkeep and defense of the English establishment in India.[52]

Yet, as was the case throughout the English Atlantic as well as Dutch and Portuguese Asia, free inhabitants and especially landholders in particular were expected not just to pay for their own defense but to provide it.[53] The earliest instructions for Bombay advised "that the Inhabitants bee put into Armes and reduced into Companies to keep watches." Despite some initial resistance, within its first decade Bombay announced its militia had been "perfected," with about six hundred men at Bombay, Mahim, Syon, and Mazagon serving as night watchmen, civil law enforcement, and for the island's defense.[54] Bombay's government seemed to have had such confidence in the idea of the militia that in 1683 officials in India argued to London that the Company could avoid hiring another two standing Rajput garrison companies, since there were already "on your Island" well-trained Muslim inhabitants "who watch by turnes," a number of Hindu residents who "constantly do duty and [are] always ready," and Indo-Portuguese "that are of the Militia with the Moores that are indifferent good free men."[55] The militia was such a crucial foundation for both defense and civil society that even Richard Keigwin included it as a term in the agreement with the island's inhabitants, which was announced immediately following his seizure of power at Bombay.[56] In 1676, the Madras council defended its decision to allow its Indo-Portuguese inhabitants to live rent free in the white town partly because they did "the duty of trained bands in watching & warding in times of trouble."[57] A decade later, London ordered all members of its council as well as Jews and other merchants "of any Considerable Estate and busyness" to keep a personal horse and arms so that the city might have a supply for the militia in times of need.[58]

If owning land and profiting from commerce in Company settlements implied an obligation to protect that settlement, failure to serve was seen as a supreme failure of civic responsibility and raised critical issues about the Company's civil government and authority. The earliest test of this came in 1673 when under rumors of an impending Dutch attack almost all of Bombay's four thousand Portuguese residents fled the island. Their "timorousness and disloyalty" prompted the Company to reshape both the militia and the garrison, and in particular to rely for the future on a far greater proportion of *bhandari*, Muslim, and Rajput soldiers.[59] The council, which had ironically just begun the process of investigating titles and restoring lands taken under the Crown governorship of Gervase Lucas, now set about making its own confiscations. It was particularly concerned to make a "publique example" of the Fidalgo Alvaro Perez de Tavora, whose "crime of desertion" was all the more appalling because he recently had been made captain of the militia on the island of Mazagon. Perez was convicted of treason by a jury of English and Portuguese inhabitants; his lobbying of Portuguese and French officials in India and Europe, the English Lords for Trade and Plantations, and even Charles II for redress came to no avail. Only when Perez changed tack and rested his case on pleas for the Company's "tenderness and compassion" did the Court of Committees intervene. It ordered Bombay to restore his lands but gently reminded him that it did so only out of pity, since the lands had been seized justly, not for any "Sinister respect, but for maintaining the honor & upholding their Government on the said Island."[60] When Perez then boldly demanded that he also be given rights over the *kolis*—that is, laborers and servants—on his land, Bombay's council strenuously objected, citing both its responsibility to protect its poorer inhabitants and the fact that the claim itself was a "considerable privilege of sovereignty," which should not be devolved "to a subject as Alvaro Perez is." If the right to control people were not retained under the Company's "own power and authority," it would prove "only under an empty name to extend no farther than the walls of your Fort."[61] The committees agreed that under no circumstances was Perez's restitution intended to "divest ourselves of any Royalty or Priviledge belonging to us."[62]

Demonstrations of service and loyalty within Company plantations were not reserved to the militia. A 1678 petition from some of the Indo-Portuguese inhabitants of Madras cited as proof of their rights as subjects the facts that they not only assisted as both garrison and unpaid militia soldiers but that they had been generally obedient to the Company, built houses, planted land, and "serve[d] according to their quallitys & merits all the Honourable imployments of the Republike."[63] Planters at St. Helena annually elected amongst themselves highway overseers and church wardens and played other informal roles, such serving as executors for orphans' estates; all others, including slaves, were to dedicate at least one day a year repairing highways.[64] In 1688, the Madras council established a law providing for the appointment of two people in each street of the black town as overseers to facilitate the collecting taxes as well as for "keeping the Streets in repair & good order."[65] Inhabitants in all of the Company's settlements served on juries, while some administered justice directly, in Madras's choultry, Bombay's lower court and *panchayats*, caste councils, and other forms of community arbitration. As the original instructions for Bombay insisted, it was "a great encouragement to the Banian in severall places that they have a little power for the ordering of themselves and for the hearing of small controversies that arise from amongst them."[66]

Perhaps the most important office available, after the militia, was that of tax farmer. As elsewhere in Asia, Europe, and the Atlantic, taxes in the Company's

Asian plantations—including customs, liquor and tavern license fees, and excise on a range of consumables, such as betel nut and tobacco—were typically not collected directly by the government. Instead, the rights to collect those taxes were rented, or farmed, for an annual fee to the highest bidder. Admittedly, the market for such farms was volatile in these early years, given fluctuations in prices, tax policy, and the integrity of commercial and military infrastructure. While the Company could generally count on customs and tobacco farms selling, others, like cotton and oil rents or arrack licenses at Bombay could easily go out for bid without any takers and eventually sell at significantly at lower rates than the initial asking. Still, Company leadership was convinced that offering farms served a variety of purposes: easing its administrative burdens and providing a reliable source of revenue, investing its holders in the life and success of the colony, and attracting the growth of an indigenous moneyed class, the kinds of "portfolio capitalists" who could generate wealth for both the island and its government, in turn attracting others to immigrate there.[67] In early 1685, the Surat council suggested that Bombay might encourage the return of a number of *bhandaris* who had fled during Keigwin's rebellion specifically by encouraging them to take on farms.[68]

Service solved the dilemma at the core of a nonliberal polity that expected its inhabitants to participate in civic life and shoulder its burdens yet refused, for the most part, to allow the populace to govern itself directly.[69] Places like Bombay, Madras, and St. Helena did not have the sorts of elected assemblies or legislatures found in some Atlantic plantations. The Company did, however, undertake one significant experiment with urban representative self-government. In December 1687, a few committees approached James II and the Privy Council with an idea for "incorporating Fort St. George into a Body Politique consisting of Mayor Aldermen & Burgesses," established with Crown consent but under the Company's charter and control.[70] The Court of Committees drafted a charter modeled on that of Portsmouth, England, where Josiah Child had once been mayor and John Biggs, Madras's new judge advocate, had served as town recorder. It constituted Madras as a corporation with a mayor, twelve aldermen, and (ideally) between sixty and one hundred and twenty burgesses. The mayor— Nathaniel Higginson was appointed to serve as its first, in addition to his other duties, but the position was to be elected thereafter—was empowered to convene a mayor's court and serve as a justice of the peace "within the Precincts of the said Corporation and without the Walls of Our said Fort."[71]

With a stroke of the pen, the old Vijayanagar town of Madraspatnam was thus converted into an English-style incorporated municipality. When it was received at Madras the next year, the charter was proclaimed with all "due sollemnitye" and all the trappings of state. The governor, Elihu Yale, gathered at the fort with Biggs, Higginson, and the aldermen—three members of council, one

French trader, two Portuguese residents, three Jewish residents, and three Hindu residents—all robed in scarlet. After the charter was read and the officials sworn, the group, led by three maces and a silver oar that the committees had sent from London, marched to the town hall where they feasted to the sounds of music and cannon fire.[72] The mayor and aldermen were afforded the right to have umbrellas carried before them and "decently furnished" horses, just like the Lord Mayor and aldermen of London.[73] A few years later, the committees also recommended increasing the number of burgesses "for more generall Satisfaction & the better appearance of our Corporation on any Solemn day."[74]

In incorporating Madras, the Company followed a model that was a mainstay of European urban life, and which could also be found in Dutch cities in Asia as well as in Tangier and the English Atlantic; the blanket right to incorporate was included in the Fundamental Constitutions of Carolina, and just a couple of years later, William Penn would issue a similar charter for the incorporation of Philadelphia. Like the company-corporation, urban corporations were critical spaces for the exercise of politics, governance, and the articulation of a political culture.[75] The Madras corporation was designed to invest inhabitants directly in administering petty justice as well as facilitating self-taxation. The corporation had the authority to collect money for city walls and a school to teach English as well as "Arethmetick and Merchants' Accompts," which many political economists in England including Child argued was how the Dutch cultivated reason, thrift, and a love of commerce in their people. The committees hoped the corporation would also attend to a range "Publick Good works," "stately Buildings" such as a guildhall, jail, courthouse, town hall, "or such other publick Structures as are made for common Use and Ornament in most of the Incorporated Cityes and Townes in Europe." The committees even offered to donate a post and insurance office to facilitate its development.[76]

The corporation was supposed to be a broadly representative institution, one of those freedoms in liberty and property that would inspire immigration, settlement, and investment in the city. That anyone at Madras could serve as an alderman or a burgess was critical to the success of the experiment.[77] Thus, when the Madras council soon attempted to assert undue influence over the corporation and the English residents came to dominate its leadership and juries, the committees sharply reproached the governor, Elihu Yale. They instructed him to correct the problem immediately, by "gentleness and perswasion," and to be sure that for the future aldermen include a broad sampling of Armenians, Jews, Portuguese, Hindus, and Muslims among their ranks. Only a "Corporation consisting of the Heads of all Casts and representing them in a Subordinate manner" would prove legitimate and effective. Though the corporation never did live up to its expectations, its basic institutions, particularly the mayor's court, did come to shape civic and social life in the town and became a critical avenue through which subjecthood in early British India would be articulated.[78] It also served as a model for future Company colonies; as early as January 1688, London recommended Bombay's council consider whether incorporation would be appropriate there as well.[79]

The corporation experiment further revealed the extent to which projects born in London also had to be negotiated through particular circumstances, such as Company councils, regional institutions and traditions, and the expectations and demands of a cosmopolitan body of inhabitants.[80] Many institutions, like the mayor's court, though English in form, were in practice shaped by local practices, customs, and law.[81] Well before incorporation, the Company had relied for its rule on alliances with caste heads, influential members of communities, and commercial and political magnates, perhaps most notably the entrepreneurial Kasi Viranna in Madras in the 1670s. Viranna was first tied to the Company as its chief agent for purchasing goods in Southern India, but soon, as with many chief merchants in Dutch settlements, this blended with significant civic immunities and responsibilities.[82] Viranna eventually became a major landowner in both the white and black towns, and served at points as a revenue farmer and a choultry judge. In 1678, the council granted him a personal right to pay only half customs on goods at Madras, a privilege he also received from the *nawab* of Golkonda, whom he simultaneously served as a revenue farmer.[83] He was saluted with nine guns upon his appointment as chief merchant and with thirty guns at his death in 1680 (Streynsham Master also claimed to have prevented his wife from becoming *sati* by burning herself on his funeral pyre).[84] A figure like Viranna was thus integrated into Company governance through service, and in turn served as an intermediary between the Company's council and its subjects, such as in 1678 when he was asked to help negotiate an end to the resistance to a new census and poll tax in the black town, intended to subsidize street sweeping and other measures for "keeping the Towne cleane after the manner in England."[85] Yet, his independent political and financial power also revealed the volatility of such an arrangement. One critic of William Langhorne, a Madras governor in the early 1670s, put it thus: "Sir William governs within the Fort and Verrona without."[86]

The composite politics of Company government and legal administration were perhaps no clearer than at Sumatra, where abstract English principles of equity merged with Company understandings and interpretations of local practices. A Malaysian inhabitant found guilty of attempted murder in 1700, for example, was enslaved and deported to a nearby ruler, which was the council's understanding of "the Custome among the Mallays."[87] Bengkulu administered the environs and diplomacy of York Fort by calling local rulers to "publick bitchars" (*bichara* or *bitjara*), local deliberative assemblies and legal proceedings that served alternatively as diplomatic audiences with other regional powers as well as courts of justice, interpreting the *adat*, or Malay customary, law. The word was even turned into a verb: "to bitchar," meaning to consult or negotiate with local officials. These were serious and important affairs, often involving "as handsom a retinue" as possible, including displays of guards, gun salutes, well-provided feasts, and even careful attention to seating order and placement for the deputy governor and his guests. Just how English and local law would inter-mix was not consistent, and depended on circumstances that varied over time. Some Company governors attempted vigilantly to impose their sense of English law; others, like Joseph Collet, proclaimed himself in 1714 uncomfortable judging "Civill Affairs among the Malays whose Laws I do not know," preferring instead to erect himself as "mediator" in disputes among Malay inhabitants while also hoping to "instruct them in the Nature of Our Laws."[88]

The Company's regime was far bolder and assertive in Sumatra than in Mughal India and in some general ways in fact foreshadowed behaviors that would follow from the expansion of Company power in India in later centuries. *Bichara*, like later imperial *darbars*, served not only to administer justice but as diplomatic spectacle, which incorporated inhabitants of Bengkulu as well as local rulers into the Company's sphere of influence. Self-consciously imitating the Dutch at Banten and the Portuguese formerly at Hormuz, the committees observed that

> The way to govern those people, is to govern them by petty Kings of their own, whom you must honour before the people and make them your Instruments to keep the people in subjection while you governe them and keep them in dependance upon you that is, the antient and true Method for Europeans to maintain their Dominion in those Countryes.[89]

The Company attempted to woo these "petty Kings" with gifts, like swords and medals. There was at one point a proposal to provide the king of Sillebar with a "Lifeguard" of eight grenadiers and another to make a few "principall natives" titular members of the Bengkulu council and to "now and then pretend to call them to consultation."[90]

Efforts to incorporate populations into governance were clearly conditional, and as in all other cases, limited by the ultimate goal of preserving Company authority and the integrity of its rule. Bombay's minor courts were to be toler-ated as long as they did not "clash with our government." Muslim populations were to be watched closely lest they "carry any sort of Sway or be form'd into a subordinate Government in that City." The mayor and aldermen of Madras were a "wise Councill," but unequivocally under the Company's "supreme authority." In 1699 the committees even rejected a proposal from the Madras governor to convert the town's outer neighborhoods into wards and create a city common council, fearing that "by advancing any of those People to a heigth beyond their usuall wont, they become giddy with the honour, and set up for heads of factions and mutuinous disorders."[91]

Company government in Asia was thus riddled with dilemmas: among hierarchy, consultation, and civic participation; between service as a path toward civic virtue and omnipresent anxieties about a subject's inherent corruptibility, especially in Asia; between an understanding of society as divided into self-governing "castes"—a term bluntly used not just for Hindus but for Muslims, Jews, Armenians, African slaves, even other Europeans and English—and fearing the potential power of those groups to organize and resist Company power.[92] Committees and councils needed to manage risk by keeping those forces in equilibrium. For example, the Company's boldest experiment in representative government, the incorporation of Madras, was accompanied by orders to take a census "of all your severall casts whatsoever," recording their religions, occupations, and other details.[93] Such a desire to know the city was of course a practical necessity, facilitating taxation, law enforcement, militia mustering, and the like; a similar survey of St. Helena's estates was initiated a few years later. It was also an articulation, if a fairly crude one, of an understanding of the connection between governance and demography in the age of the "political arithmetic" of political economists like William Petty, Gregory King, and Charles Davenant.[94] Like a premature, urban version of censuses in British India centuries later, such a survey could serve as a technique of control and surveillance and a means of defining communities as much as accounting for them.[95] Thus, while the committees ostensibly ordered the Madras census to satisfy the king's curiosity, who had requested some information on Madras's population (James was himself deeply interested in political arithmetic), they also clearly understood it as absolutely crucial to better "comport our government by ballancing of the Severall Powers or Numbers under your government."[96]

This notion that "Ballancing of Powers is the truest Art of Government"—among rivals, between imports and exports, the obligations of ruler and ruled, jurisdictional authority and a political economy of free trade, paternalistic and absolute (or "despotic") authority and the administration of justice among self-participating subjects, and the interests of subjects—typified this emergent Company political science. It was a common trope throughout English political economy and political thought, derived from ancient understandings both of civil society as well as the importance of anatomical and physiological balance of the humors.[97] This notion, again, of a golden mean was embodied and articulated in the very structure of Company sovereignty and government, premised as it was on a critical, if at times precarious, balance among various sources and forms of authority from Europe, Asia, and the products of its own political behavior and institutions, especially the great importance placed on government by counsel.

As a value and a policy, balance was a means of assuaging the anxieties of corruption and rebellion which were inevitable in such a geographically dispersed and multi-ethnic polity.[98] In 1676, for example, the Madras council dismissed London's fears that there were too many Portuguese inhabitants in the town by observing that the population was "not of any single nation," but divided among "Topasses, Mestizos, &c: Converts."[99] In 1685 the committees ordered the Bombay council to distribute militia posts so "that you may not have too many of any one Cast; but that the power of the Island may be so equally balanced, that the whole may be the easier governed."[100] In the early 1690s, the committees recommended to Bengkulu that they enlist Macassars and Bugis, from the Celebes (Sulawesi)—whom they compared to Ottoman Janissaries— as the lifeguard for the king of Sillebar, but to mix them with Indo-Portuguese soldiers, to make them more "respective and obedient"; the council also soon after began recruiting Bugis in the hope that it would keep the garrison balanced and apolitical. The garrison also included slaves, for the very same reason: "the wisdome of Government in such a place is, wisely to ballance the Power of the Sword under severall and different Casts and Nations, that no one Cast, not the English Soldiers themselves may be able to give the least disturbance to our Government." Without such wisdom, the committees continued, the Company might as well "build Castles in the Air as in India."[101]

Perhaps the most crucial balance, or tension, at the core of Company political theory was in the persistent negotiation between universalism and localism. On the one hand, sovereignty and the law were particular to time and place; "All Christians," the committees wrote in 1696, "are to be governed by the Laws of the place where they inhabit, as if a Dutch man resides in London, the Laws of England and not of Amsterdam are to be his rule and his direction."[102] Law had to accommodate local practices and expectations; more broadly, there were also clear historical differences between Europe and Asia, and one could find traces of typical European rhetoric about Asiatic despotism within Company discourse.[103] Yet, on the other hand, the very nature of the Company's system assumed that, like people and plants, political principles were transportable and transplantable around the world and even throughout history. Underneath Company policy were catholic principles about the obligations of sovereigns and subjects and of a natural law, or, in Gerald Aungier's words, "the Laws of God and all Nations."[104] Colonial government was rooted in what seemed to be a universal conception of human and political nature, which held that individuals were naturally inclined to pursue their own private interest, that they would often mistake the true nature of that interest, and, as a result, one could not expect obedience out of "the good nature of mankind, but must be compelled by coercive laws & power to put those Laws in execution."[105] If human nature was consistent, then so too should be the law that governed it; as London opined to Bengkulu in 1714, "Men are rational Creatures be they of what Countrey soever they have all the same general notions of right and wrong of Mildness and Tyranny of Truth and Falshood of Good Nature & Cruelty."[106] Its governor Joseph Collet seemed to agree, but for different reasons. He wrote a friend a couple of years earlier that his experience in Asia had convinced him that human nature was universal, not because all "men were reasonable Creatures, and capable of being Influenced by Principles of Reason, Justice and Gratitude" but because "English, French, Portugueze, Brasilians, Africans, Dutch, Moores, Indians of many Sorts are (almost) all alike" in their potential for corruption. "This Experience," he concluded, "has entirely alter'd my schemes of Government. I try first to oblige, and when that fails, I make all under me know that I will be obey'd. I gradually work on the several affections, Gratitude, Hope and Fear, and find Springs to move them all."[107]

Whether bringing into harmony different "castes" in the garrison or collecting and deploying a variety of sources for its political establishment, Company government by the end of the seventeenth century had become a legal and political regime supported by clear and somewhat consistent principles designed to cultivate safe, populous, thriving, productive, and even virtuous colonies and colonists. That polity expected its subjects in turn to return the favor through loyalty, duty, and service. Attention to such virtues of service and obligation ensured not only material but moral improvement. This was the core charge of government, one which the Company took extremely seriously and which found its most vibrant expression in the most typical early modern language of government there was, religion.

5

"The Most Sure and Profitable Sort of Merchandice"

Protestantism and Piety

By the later seventeenth century, establishing effective, productive, and just government over settlements and subjects abroad had become a guiding preoccupation within the East India Company. In doing this, they faced no deeper problem than religion. In the early modern period, religion was intertwined with almost every aspect of lived experience, and most certainly politics; ecclesiastical institutions, ritual behaviors, and political theology underscored the practices and ideologies of statecraft, and sovereignty went hand in hand with the responsibility for the soul.[1] As John Holt had insisted in *East India Company v. Sandys*, care for religion was the "prime and original end" of government, and in Asia, the English government *was* the English East India Company.[2]

Though plagued with an enduring reputation as either commercial agnostics or godless apostates, rulers over an emergent polity so deeply concerned with the integrity of its jurisdiction and authority over places and people could not help but have religion front and center in their minds.[3] Attitudes toward religion in the Company-State mirrored the tension between liberty and authority that informed its political and economic ideology, balancing the toleration of freedom of religious practice incumbent upon a commercial and cosmopolitan colonial society with the prerogatives and demands of jurisdiction and sovereignty. Like elsewhere in the early modern world, Company officials seemed to take providence, piety, and biblical thinking quite seriously.[4]

In a world only just beginning to come to grips with the concept of probability, so risky and dangerous a venture as a transhemispheric commercial and political operation could not help but call upon some degree of faith.[5] All the

Company's sophisticated mechanisms for predicting markets and regulating politics—or, as Bombay called them in 1687, "the most wisest and prudent heads"—could not obviate the commercial, physical, and emotional anxieties wrought by war, accident, disease, weather, high mortality, and simple contingency and uncertainty in a system that extended across the seas, halfway across the globe, and into a world imagined by many as perilous.[6] Such ordeals were infused with providential significance, which offered comfort in times of calamity and encouragement in times of triumph.[7] Bombay's "raines" and "pestilence" were thus evidence of the "afflicting rod of divine providence," while news of an interloper's shipwreck in 1683 was received by the committees as "a just Judgment of God upon their disloyal and unjust proceedings."[8] The key to success in the East Indies, one pamphleteer noted, was simply to live a pious life, "take the most probable ways of Security, and leave the rest to Divine Providence."[9] This was the message one took from the Company's seal itself, emblazoned as it was with the twin mottos *"deus indicat"* (God reveals) and *"deo ducente nil nocet"* (guided by God, nothing is harmed).

Such abstract sentiments were borne out in policy and behavior. Among Gerald Aungier's first acts in arriving at Bombay in 1672 was to declare a "publique fast and humiliation for God's blessing," and to issue a proclamation "against the breach of the sabboth, profanness, drunkenness, and uncleanness." As George Wilcox reported, "this rejoyct us al, hoping when God was in the beginning, a blessing would be in the conclusion."[10] In his speech to the island's inhabitants, Aungier likened the delivery of Company rule to Bombay to the Mosaic Lawgiving itself. Paraphrasing Deuteronomy 4:6 and 4:8, he proclaimed that:

Plaster cast of East India Company seal, 1675. National Maritime Museum, SEC0264. © National Maritime Museum, Greenwich, London.

Formerly the name of the English nation was knowne to these parts only by the honesty of their Traffiq but now I trust In God, through the just Execution of these Laws, that our Neighbor nations wil have cause to say of us . . . Surely this great nation is a wise & an understanding people, for what nation is there soe great which hath statutes & judgments soe Righteous as all these Laws which I set before you this day.[11]

If Aungier, whose maternal grandfather had been archbishop of Dublin, was particularly zealous, he was not unique. Biblical examples peppered Company instructions, policies, orders, and rhetoric. For Aungier, Bombay was a "Plant watered by Divine Providence,"[12] but Madras, the committees hoped, would develop into a "Mart for Nations," which was "the means to which God almighty of old promis'd to make Jerusalem great."[13]

Yet, if Madras and Bombay were to be new Jerusalems, they were also supposed to be new Amsterdams and Livornos as well. Josiah Child had argued that while Dutch and Italian commercial success lay in its toleration of Jews and other strangers to trade and have the freedom of their commercial and urban corporations, and the Spanish empire suffered under the weight of its supposedly uncompromising Catholicism, the English followed a confused middle ground, "vainly endeavour[ing] to arrive at a Uniformity of Religion at home, yet we allow an Amsterdam Liberty in our Plantations."[14] The Company unsurprisingly aspired to this sort of "Amsterdam Liberty" in its settlements. The original laws for Bombay were emphatic that "none be molested for their Religion," including the "free exercise" of Roman Catholicism, which was in any event required both by the Anglo-Portuguese marriage treaty and the patents transferring the island to the Company. Given the great number of Catholics on the island and the delicate diplomacy with *Estado* officials in western India, it would have been impractical to forbid popery even had the council there wanted to.[15] Although Madras was under no such treaty obligations, it not only tolerated Catholicism but offered incentives to attract Catholic settlers. The town had a "Portuguese" (i.e. Roman Catholic) church and priests decades before it had an Anglican one; the committees also later offered land at Madras for an Armenian church for "the worship and service of God in their own way."[16]

Toleration was not reserved for Christians alone. "Be always most kind & indulgent to the Inhabitants that observe our Laws," London instructed Madras in 1686, "and protect them in the same uninterrupted liberty of their several Religions in which they were born & bred, as you doe those of our own Church & Nation."[17] Within Madras's first decade, Beri Timmanna, one of the town's wealthiest merchants, had already built two Hindu temples, one for Visnu and another for Siva, collectively known to the English as the "Town Pagoda."[18] At Bombay, one faced a month's imprisonment and a fine equivalent to about 50 shillings simply for any "unbeseeming irreverent and contemptuous words of the Religion of any other."[19] It was surely not from a lack of familiarity with the Pentateuch that Aungier's speech to Bombay's inhabitants skipped over Deuteronomy 4:7, with its much more starkly monotheistic overtones.[20] In 1671 the Bombay government sanctioned the annual Muslim pilgrimage to the tomb and shrine of Makhdum Fakih 'Ali Paru at Mahim.[21] The committees similarly instructed the council in Bengal not to "suffer any prejudice to be done to Churches, Mosques, Pagodaes, or other publick Places, where God is worshipped, or pretended to be worshipped."[22]

Such instructions and practices regarding the freedom of religion grew out of a more general approach to questions of politics and political economy.[23] "Libertie in religion" was, like liberty in trade and property, a comparative advantage in drawing settlers, particularly Hindus, whom the English assumed would flock to such a colony from the supposed persecution of Muslim regimes in Mughal India as well as Portuguese territory, where Goa had been prosecuting an inquisition for over a century.[24] Even the rebellious Richard Keigwin, though indicting Bombay's government as "worse Heathens then the Heathens" for allowing free Hindu worship on the island, made one of his first acts in charge to guarantee "the Inhabitants the liberty of Exerciseing their Respective Religion."[25] Some Company leaders expressed fascination and admiration for the religions they encountered in Asia. Streynsham Master, a factor at Surat and later governor of Madras, regarded the Hindu and Muslim rigor in religious practice and observance as a model for Christian piety.[26] By the 1710s, there was also an "English Lodge" on the island of Salsette, as the pagoda there had become a fairly popular tourist attraction.[27]

Given all of this, it is unsurprising that the Company's attitudes toward religion have long been characterized as ranging from agnostic to "cautious and tolerant."[28] Yet, "toleration" was hardly the same as acceptance. Etymologically, culturally, and politically, to tolerate something was not to consent to it but to bear it, to suffer its existence or practice despite distaste, disapproval, and the desire to alter it. Attitudes toward religion in the early modern world were defined by the problematic but frequent coexistence of toleration, persecution, and confessional zeal, especially overseas and even for the Company's prime exemplar, the Dutch.[29] Moreover, freedom of religion, again like trade or property, was hardly absolute and could never to be suffered to trump the Company's rights to jurisdiction or sovereignty. Company councils in India clearly understood the control and command of the institutions, finances, and public practice of religion to be a critical mark of political power. Freedom of Hindu worship did not stop the Madras council from attempting to intervene in the management and patronage of temples, and in particular seeking to control taxes levied for their support.[30] Bombay insisted pilgrims to its Muslim shrine be disarmed and even at one point issued vague restrictions on the volume of the noise made during prayer.[31] A later minister at St. Helena accused the governor there, "who is Supream Magistrate here in Civil Affairs," of claiming the right "to direct in all Ecclesiasticall matters."[32] As governor of Madras, Joseph Collet similarly boasted in 1718 that "while I have the Civill power I will also be Head of the Church."[33]

The tension between toleration and authority could be seen most clearly in policies toward Catholics. Portuguese officials in India, on the basis of the late fifteenth-century papal bulls and their elaboration over subsequent centuries, considered themselves to be the pope's delegates in Asia and thus claimed the "jus Padroada" over all "the churches in India." Portuguese governors and Jesuit priests insisted that the 1661 Anglo-Portuguese treaty ensured their continuing extraterritorial "spiritual jurisdiction" over all Catholics on the island.[34] For the English Company, none of this was up for debate.[35] When the Portuguese bishop at St. Thomé, which had been a bishopric seat since the early seventeenth century, appointed Paulo de Saa as vicar of the Company's new southern Indian settlement at Cuddalore in 1694, the Madras council rejected him, "first because wee must not owne his Episcopall authority in the English Government . . . within the Limitts of their Jurisdiction," and only second, because they objected to the choice in particular. The council reminded the Portuguese cleric that he was not "Governor nor Bishop of Cuddulore no more than of Madrass."[36] In 1704 the Madras council similarly refused one priest permission to heed a call by the patriarch of Antioch to leave the town to return to Pondicherry, since "we could not allow of no Persons to have Authority over the Priests . . . that lives under our Government" and "within our walls."[37]

Company leaders, like many English Protestants, suspected Jesuits particularly of being instruments of Portuguese "power and interest."[38] One strategy they pursued was to dilute their influence by inviting other monastic orders into their colonies, though these priests' positions were only moderately more secure. Madras invited in Capuchin monks, whom one later governor claimed to have made his "spyes" and "secret Intelligencers,"[39] but later fearing growing French influence replaced them with Italian Theatines, who in turn were expelled, briefly, soon after.[40] Bombay, where the potential spiritual and political influence of Goa was greatest, at one point encouraged the settlement of an Italian Carmelite mission.[41] When the Portuguese protested these efforts, the Company made it clear that it understood its responsibility at Bombay to provide for free "exercise" of Catholicism; how and by whom it would be practiced was inevitably up to government.[42]

One serious limit to this freedom of religion was conversion. Priests who proselytized Protestants "or any way attempt to Inveigle or intice them away from the protestant faith" were treated as enemies of the state.[43] In 1678 the Madras council ordered the investigation of two Catholic priests, one rumored to have converted a Protestant slave, who was also a drummer in the garrison, and the other for supposedly conducting private marriages.[44] A decade later, the Bombay council charged a Jesuit with high treason for agreeing to convert an Anglican, Nathaniel Thorpe, to the "Romish religion."[45] Equally threatening was the possibility of Company servants converting to Islam.[46] After all, the Company had argued in *Sandys* that one of its prime responsibilities in Asia was "to take care that there is not an infection, by correspondence with infidels."[47] If interlopers who simply took service as ship pilots, soldiers, and officeholders under Asian polities were regarded as "a greate disgrace to our Nation & Religion,"[48] to actually become a Muslim was synonymous with political desertion. Certainly interlopers and others clearly understood the power the threat of conversion possessed as a form of challenge to Company government. Quite a few, including John Petit, taunted Company leaders with declarations of intentions to "renounce his Religion & turne Moore."[49] In 1696 one group of drunken English sailors who had assaulted a group of merchants at Surat managed to evade reprimand by threatening to convert if punished for their deeds.[50]

The impulse to protect and preserve Protestants and Protestantism arose from a much broader sense that order and prosperity in Asia was bound up with maintaining and preserving "Christian" lives among those under their charge. Like most overseas English ventures, the Company had long established procedures and regulations for sending preachers overseas and aboard ships.[51] The Court of Committees appointed a general chaplain for its Indian factories in 1658 to "instruct and teach the people that shall be committed to his Charge, in building them up in the knowledge of GOD and faith in JESUS CHRIST."[52] By the 1670s there were chaplains at Bombay, St. Helena, Surat, Madras, Bengal, and Banten.[53] Chaplains could make upwards of £100 a year; in mid-1680s Madras, only the governor was paid more.[54] These chaplains were also chosen with some care. The committees solicited recommendations and endorsements and, from time to time, required audition sermons at St. Andrew Undershaft, the Company's parish church, just across Leadenhall Street from the India House.[55] Clergy sometimes sat on council and participated in governance. Ministers and churchwardens collected money for poor relief and care of orphans and, in theory, policed attendance at prayers as well as keeping eyes out for "drunkenness, swearing, uncleanness and other Debaucheries."[56] They also ran schools so that children might be "taught and instructed in those things that may be usefull to them as Men and Christians."[57] On at least one occasion, the chaplain at Madras dispensed benefit of clergy to an English convict, allowing him to avoid prosecution in exchange for a branding.[58]

The committees regarded the ministries in their colonies and on their ships much as they did city walls, garrisons, and other public institutions. While the Company might contribute and direct the religious establishment, it was ultimately the community's responsibility to support it, as "in all Parts of the known World and among all sorts of Religions the Inhabitants after they are once settled do pay something towards the charge of a Minister."[59] The Company's "church" was not formally part of the Anglican episcopacy. Clergy were Company employees but, as far as the Court of Committees was concerned, in a settlement, they would ideally be supported by contributions and taxation from the populace at large. The same was true of the Protestant churches themselves. Building a church at Bombay was Gerald Aungier's pet project, as important to him as reinforcing the fortifications and establishing the colony's legal system. He imagined a grand Anglican cathedral, suitable for more than a thousand congregants in the "forme proportionable to our usuall Churches in England," funded entirely by subscription (Aungier himself left 5,000 rupees toward the church in his will).[60] Though he would not live to 1718 to see his project completed, the first Anglican church in India was erected not long after, at Madras. English Protestants there had worshipped in a makeshift chapel in the Fort until, under Governor Streynsham Master in the late 1670s, the council helped to raise 805 pagodas for a permanent structure. Ground was broken for St. Mary's church on Easter Monday, 1678, and the church was dedicated and opened in October 1680; it registered its first marriage—between Elihu Yale and Catherine Hinmers—the following month.[61] Within its first decade, Calcutta set about building a church as well, a project, the minister there reported in 1704, to which ship captains, Company servants, and "other Inhabitants of the Place, have contributed freely and cheerfully." It opened in 1709.[62]

It would be easy, though misleading, to confuse the Company's insistence on churches funded by local revenue for a hesitation or reluctance to support these settlements' religious establishments. For decades, London complained about delays in the Bombay church as a "scandal to our Nation, that your Church should remain so many years unfinished." They even offered in 1689 to pay the balance of what could not be raised by subscription "rather than it Shall remain such a shamefull spectacle of our Sloth, or want of zeal in our Religion."[63] Though this plan was derailed, the Company did contribute in a variety of ways. As early as 1677, the committees had granted 4,000 rupees toward the Bombay church out of the Company's cash.[64] While "of great charge and without precedent," they approved the following year of sending goods for the "ornament" of the Madras church; a decade later the council donated an organ and ordered another steeple built, for which the committees donated six new bells.[65] In 1708 London subscribed one thousand rupees to the Calcutta church, as well as providing iron for its windows; a few years later, the Fort William council donated a clock.[66]

The Court of Committees also frequently sent books. In 1659 Surat and Madras received a six-volume, multilanguage edition of the Old and New

Testaments, probably Brian Walton's *Biblia Sacra Polyglotta*, donated to the Company by one Thomas Rich, "hoping it may be a meanes to propagate and spread the Gospell in those parts, which is his, and our earnest desire by all meanes possible to advance and further." At various points, London sent printed sermons, including some preached to the Court of Committees. Among other books sent out were Augustine's *City of God*, Foxe's *Book of Martyrs*, and Purchas's *Pilgrims*, which famously promoted the notion of a providential English mission overseas.[67] In 1678 the committees ordered £5 worth of primers, psalters, and testaments to be sent for Madras's schoolmaster Ralph Ord, to assist him in "teaching the children and youth to read English, write and cipher, and instructing them, by catechizing, in the principles of the Protestant religion."[68] By the early eighteenth century, visitors to Madras noted that its "publick library" consisted "chiefly in books of divinity," estimated to be worth a little under £450.[69] Likewise, in 1679 the committees sent a hundred books "containing the Principalls of Christian Religion" to Bombay, and "a great Bible" and two Books of Common Prayer for Banten's library, which at the time of the Company's expulsion three years later contained upwards of 165 books, mostly works on theology, religion, and history.[70] Benjamin Adams, appointed chaplain for Calcutta in 1699, also came out bearing a "handsom Collection of modern books as an Addition to the Library" donated by William Hewer, a member of the Court of Committees.[71]

The impulse on behalf of both individuals and the institution to support and expand the Protestant ecclesiastical establishment in India, at sea and on land, fit within the Company's broader project to support civic and political life in its settlements and among those subject to its authority. The structures of religious life reinforced the authority of government. Madras's mayor had his own reserved seat in a pew in Madras's St. Mary's, with a conspicuous spot for his mace. As one onlooker noted, the church had a fine organ "with which, as one observes, they salute God and Governor."[72] Several years later, Joseph Collet reported that he "is always attended with a Guard, but appears with the greatest pomp when he goes to Church."[73] Conversely, a religious life was an orderly life; as the committees put it to Surat in 1669, all who "live, as in the feare of God, soe in eace and quieties with one another."[74] It was thus the prime duty of a governor, George Oxinden's 1661 commission and instructions noted, to make it his "cheifest care to promote his service and worship," setting a good example and checking "all things that may be scandalous to our christian profession."[75] Streynsham Master reported that the captain of the ship on which he took on his initial voyage from London required strict attendance at daily prayers, services on Sundays as "in the Churches," communion, prayers read for the sick, and proper burials at sea, all to maintain "Civill Government."[76] The same attitudes could be seen in Company settlements, where many clearly believed it was the responsibility of government to encourage piety and punish "profaneness and vice," in order to produce "a Civill and well governed man."[77]

Regulating "private" life—worship, marriage, sexuality, sobriety, and morality—ensured both salvation in the next world and a proper compliance with law, hierarchy, authority, the norms of civil society, and state power in this one.[78] Company plantations sought to inoculate their subjects from disorder by promoting virtue, and in turn refashion them as subjects. While particularly important for Protestants, this attitude applied widely to all. Thus, the committees responded to the governor of Bengkulu's complaints that the early Chinese immigrants there were "loose extravagant idle debaucht fellows" by observing that this was the cross all colonial governments, throughout history, had to bear:

> We would have all Men sober and vertuous if it were in our Power, but must take notice, that the beginnings of all Plantations, and the greatest Cityes that ever appear'd in the world have been from such loose and wicked People at first, So it was in Rome Naples, and in most our English Plantations, especially Virginia, Jamaica and Barbadoes, New England indeed had another beginning, but very few other Places in the world rose originally from any other Sort of Men.[79]

Like service and discipline, piety and morality, always vaguely and subjectively defined, served to refashion settlers into obedient and productive subjects; in turn, "debauchery or prophaneness," the Surat council wrote in 1671, was "the root of all disorder." Reissuing decades later its ten basic rules for governing behavior (which came to be known, perhaps cheekily, as the "Company's Commandments"[80]), the council at Surat observed that "he that leads a debauched life in Swearing drunkenness or whoredome or is Refractory to his Superiors and disobedient to the above Rules was to be dismissed."[81] Streynsham Master, who was in the Surat factory when the "commandments" were first issued, implemented an adapted set for Madras when he became governor there. Both the civil and military sections first and foremost "Christianly admonish[ed] every one imployed in the service of the Hon'ble English East India Company to abandon lying, swearing, curseing, drunkenness, uncleanliness, prophanation of the Lord's-day, and all other sinfull practices," establishing a series of fines and penalties for offenders.[82] Though these regulations applied only to Company servants, in 1678 the Madras council also attempted to ban gaming houses in the black town, and later forbid cards, dice, and cockfighting at Bengkulu.[83] It issued regulations on the sale and service of liquor and the offering of accommodations, citing the king's charter to the Company and the Company's commission to them as their authority, and the 1660 Act of Parliament governing the sale, adulteration, and price of wine in England as their precedent.[84]

The St. Helena council was similarly instructed to encourage "Vertue and Piety" and discountenance "Vice and Immoralityes by which means you may expect the Divine blessing and favour."[85] The original commission for the island's government even specified that the governor and council were to see that the Sabbath was kept, establishing a "convenient place" for worship and banning all forms of secular labor and "unlawful sports & Pastimes" on it. The council was also to "take care that all Prophane swearing and taking the Name of God in Vaine, be carefully avoided, together with all Intemperance, Fornication and uncleanness."[86] Its more formal laws and orders of 1681 included a section "touching Religion & the Worship of God," empowering the governor and council to punish "Crimes, Sinn and Wickedness."[87] The island's government also issued a table of fines and punishments in response to "very scandalous Reports of loose Women goeing on board our Ships."[88] Bombay's original civil code, written in London principally by Thomas Papillon and the Company's solicitor William Moses, likewise extensively addressed issues of "religion and the worship and service of God." As in the other settlements, it criminalized Sabbath breaking, swearing, taking God's name in vain, public drunkenness, and "all Fornication Uncleaness and Adultery."[89] The first section in the island's martial laws similarly detailed duties to God and morality.[90] More specific regulations followed, governing gaming, taverns, and prostitution.[91] Two decades later, the Bombay council also forbid the playing of "Country Musick" on the Christian Sabbath.[92]

There were also prosecutions. As early as December 1672, Bombay's judicature court ordered a few resident's houses taken down for selling drink and allowing gambling on the Sabbath, as well as in general for "debauchery," "wickedness" and "lewd women." Several residents were also tried for spending Sunday in the tavern rather than the church "to the Scandall of our Christian Religion and Contempt of Government."[93] Gerald Aungier and George Wilcox seemed proud of their court for having, in their estimation, dramatically reduced profanity and licentiousness.[94] Both Aungier and John Child presided over witchcraft trials at Bombay; one in 1671, of a "noted wizard," resulted in a jury conviction and burning at the stake.[95] In 1682 Madras sentenced one Thomas Burret, for "having most impiously in his cups drank a health to the Devil," to run the gauntlet and ultimately deportation "to deter others from committing crimes soe hellishly wicked."[96]

St. Helena seemed particularly rife with such anxieties, a good deal of which appeared to focus on the behavior of women. If English female settlers were supposed to be the potential saviors of the civilization of a settlement, disorder among them was easily understood as the greatest threat to it; as elsewhere, criminalizing or ostracizing the "scold" and other dominant women was a key strategy in maintaining a patriarchal social and political order.[97] Punishment could be harsh but typical of the early modern English world. In 1676 a married woman named Elizabeth Starling was publicly ducked for "being private [with] A gentleman Man," including "prostitut[ing] her selfe . . . to the said Stranger Amongst the physick nutt Trees."[98] That same year, Ann Cannady was sentenced to five lashes in the face for having "detained" some sailors and then assailing their captain "with many Horride and bitter Curses," only to be given a reprieve as she was pregnant.[99]

Cannady frequently found herself in court under accusations of fornication, adultery, and generally disruptive behavior. Her various cases revealed just how much the patrol and punishment of moral and religious offenses served to underscore concerns with civic discipline; at the same time, it was clear in these and many other cases that inhabitants recognized the authority of the Company's court, if even just as a tool for community regulation and accusations of sexual or moral misconduct as a weapon to use against one's neighbors.[100] In 1682 the indictment of Cannady for "keeping Company together a whole night" with a soldier, Richard Alexander, set off several rounds of accusations and a parade of witnesses offering vivid and salacious testimony. While a few described their sexual encounters in excruciating detail, even more damning evidence seemed to focus on her character. One witness in a subsequent trial simply insisted she must be guilty because she had called his mother-in-law a "Bawd" and his wife a "Whore," and mocked him for having a "rotten pocky Legg." Meanwhile, a garrison officer testified that she had verbally abused the Company itself, referring to the governor and council as "Turks, and Blood suckers."[101]

Concerns over religion and morality were clearly heightened at St. Helena, where the vast majority of the population were English Protestants. Unlike in India, where the committees were often silent on issues of theology, St. Helena was enjoined to a more orthodox Anglicanism. Its services were to include a prayer for the king and for the Company as well as the recitation of the long and complex Athanasian Creed, reinforcing the doctrine of the Trinity.[102] In 1705 the chaplain at St. Helena reported that "No body professes any other here than the Church of England, observing the same rites and Ceremonys as are observ'd in England."[103] While some, even quite prominent governors, in India aspired to an Anglican conformity, their efforts were generally idiosyncratic and short lived. No doubt with the Interregnum fresh in mind, Gerald Aungier was particularly insistent, he and his council believing that "nothing hath proved more fatall to Commonwealths than confusion in matters of religion." They even boldly accused their superiors in London of violating Bombay's very principles of freedom of conscience by choosing two nonconformist ministers for the island, whose "principles of religion" differed so much from most of the Company's servants there. Streynsham Master at Madras agreed that allowing both Anglican and dissenting governors and chaplains led to "confusion amongst ourselves" and undermined attempts to spread Protestantism in Asia; "this New Straine of opinion and learning are not at all fitt to plant the Gospell here," he insisted, adding that "the humour of these People, nay I thinke the air of these Climates, doth much incline the old orthodox Doctrine and episcopall government."[104]

Still, there was ultimately little consistency on these issues. William Hedges, the agent in Bengal until 1684, was by his own account a fairly "rigid" Presbyterian.[105] Joseph Collet, a Baptist whose religious beliefs bordered on Unitarianism, forbid the reading of the Athanasian Creed at Madras's church services, as he had "no more regard to St. Athanasius than to the Council of Trent or Synod of Dort" and did not "love to hear myself damn'd by the whole congregation"; it was his belief that the governor was the "head of the Church" that emboldened him to do so.[106] Despite insisting on certain church practices, Collet ultimately exhibited little interest in confessional disputes among Protestants. He looked upon the High Church Tory revival and measures like the Schism Act with great disdain, and in fact likened the controversy between High Church and Low Church in England to the Investiture Conflict. He even once observed that Britons could learn a thing or two from the experience in India of subordinating religious conflict to political authority. "In my Dominions are a great many Religions but no disputes as to the Civill Affairs," he insisted. "Every man must do what I command, and let me tell you, a Whigg in Power will be as absolute as any Tory."[107] He also seemed to develop a friendship with the Theatine priest John Baptist Milton, reporting on lively debates in which "the Punch bole commonly decided the controversy."[108]

Even the official conformity at St. Helena ran up against many unorthodox common practices, such as the performance of baptisms in peoples' homes, marriages outside of church, and private burials; unlike in India, there was in these early days no consecrated church or cemetery on the island.[109] Aungier too seemed to be resigned to the diversity; before the objectionable clergy had arrived at Bombay, he and the council came to understand that the "difference between us is not in fundamentals but in outward Ceremony only," and that they could embrace them with "armes of brotherly love . . . under one body of Christian congregation."[110] After meeting them, he determined them to be "godly and worthy," and insisted any disagreements among them be would be a strength not a weakness, and "like the dispute between St. Paul and Barnabas, be instumentall to the greater propagation of the Gospell and flourishing of religion and virtue in this Island."[111]

Inevitably, the Company's concern was with promoting a very broad concept of both Protestantism and piety, constructed against equally broad notions of Roman Catholicism, Islam, Hinduism, and other Asian religions, all designed in the first instance to support Company political authority and sound civil society.

These goals, however, could not be achieved simply by making Protestants into better Protestants. While officially tolerant of religious practice, there was a lingering sense among those at the Company's helm that it would be far better if as many of its subjects as possible were, in fact, Protestants. Slaves and "black servants" at St. Helena and Bombay could be manumitted and given status as freemen if they were baptized and exhibited good lives and Christian conversation for a set period of time (seven years at St. Helena; three at Bombay).[112] The first group of English women sent to Bombay were forbidden to marry non-Protestants, and the financial incentives offered for unions between English soldiers and native women were to be paid to the women only after the Protestant baptism of a first child.[113] In the late 1670s, the Madras council began offering two pagodas for any male child of an English-Portuguese union who could say the catechism from memory in church; nine such rewards were given out 1678, rising to sixteen the following year.[114]

While it was never as preoccupying a goal as taxation or defense, the early East India Company was clearly sympathetic to a program, as the general minister sent out in 1657 was instructed, "to endeavour the advance and spreading of the gospell in India."[115] As the Company had maintained in *Sandys*, commerce, traffic, and religion were inseparably intertwined, especially in the extra-European world; the publisher's preface to a 1689 printing of George Jeffreys' decision in that case explicitly insisted that among the Company's contributions to the nation was that "they Convert Infidels, or at least civilize them and make them more humane by their Correspondencies."[116] If overly optimistic, this raised an important and specific point. Unlike the more forward missionizing found among Portuguese Jesuits in Asia, the English tended to regard the very act of "traffick" as a form of proselytizing in itself and the spread of the Gospel most effective through the inspiration of the "godly example" of a serious preacher, an effective church, and a well-ordered and morally unassailable Protestant society. Its efforts to maintain "Christian" observance and morality among Protestants was also crucial to seeing that "its Precepts" might be "admired by the Heathen among whom you dwell."[117] As Aungier observed, "wee must first reforme ourselves before wee hope to convert others to our beleife."[118] In turn, Collet noted, "the Propagation of the Gospell among the Indians" was a key to removing the constant temptation of Protestants in India, something "now more necessary than they were for its first Establishment amongst the Jews, Greeks and Romans."[119]

This belief in the infectious power of Protestant profession and example reconciled the apparent dilemma between toleration and the active promotion of Protestantism. The original code of laws at Bombay made it clear that toleration was a means to the end of stable government and, ironically, even conversion:

Though we could and do heartily pray and wish that all people were brought to the full knowledge of the Truth and especially that all Christians were of One heart and one Way, that the Lord might be one and his name One in all the Earth yet forasmuch as for the present it is otherwise, We do strictly enjoin that none be troubled or molested for their Religion, Civil Laws and Constitutions of the place [but all] be permitted to enjoy the liberty in their Houses, and that Life and Conversation be only used to draw people to a Love and embracing of the true Religion but that no force or constraint be put on any in Religious matters.[120]

Aungier and the Bombay council envisioned the Protestant church itself as a way for "natives & Strangers" to "observe the gravity and purity of our devotions." They even rejected an early proposal to build the church out at Mendams Point, since, though in many ways a better situation, they deemed it too remote to "answere our main designe" of inviting Bombay's non-Protestant residents to attend to be convinced of the error of their ways and lead them to salvation.[121] Master also envisioned the new Anglican church in Madras as a means "of the English having Proselytes in India."[122] While the Company was fairly ecumenical in its approach to such proselytizing—in 1690 Surat even helped smuggle one Muslim man "desirous of turning Christian" to Bombay—its leadership seemed particularly eager about attracting Catholic converts.[123] In 1705 the Madras council made an exception to its prohibition on Catholic garrison officers in the sanguine hope that one Sergeant Dixon's "preferment may make him return to the Protestant religion," adding that he would prove "a valuable convert."[124] At one point, the Madras council even briefly entertained the quixotic hope that their minister could be so effective as to persuade the French and Portuguese *priests* in the town of the "error in their Way."[125]

Like many Company projects in this period, such efforts rarely met expectations. Governors like Aungier and Master frequently complained about their chaplains' ineffectiveness while a number of ministers, like Benjamin Adams at Calcutta, protested about the shackles allegedly put on them by the "opposition of the chiefs."[126] Even if such "affective" proselytizing was not always effective proselytizing, however, it could prove as earnest and aggressive as the more invasive labors of the Company's Portuguese contemporaries or later English evangelicals in British India.[127] Moreover, a good many in London, both in and out of the Company, were eager to support an even more forceful expansion of English Protestantism in India, especially as Dutch claims to have converted forty thousand souls and tales of mass infant baptisms had reached as far as New England.[128] In the early 1680s John Fell, the bishop of Oxford, complained to the natural philosopher Robert Boyle, who served on the Court of Committees in the 1670s, of "the shame that lay upon us, who had so great opportunities by our commerce in the East, that we had attempted nothing towards the conversion of the Natives, when not only the papists, but even the Hollanders, had laboured therein."[129] A decade earlier, Boyle had himself raised the issue of "makeing Proselytes to the Christian religion" and reportedly received "a very favourable hearing" from other Company officials. For its part, the Court of Committees studied the issue, and by 1677 something seemed to be underfoot.[130] George Berkeley, soon after the first Earl of Berkeley, raised a motion to raise money for the project.[131] Boyle and Fell lobbied other committee officials, including Robert Thompson and Daniel Sheldon, all of whom responded favorably.[132] In 1679 Berkeley, Josiah Child, and a few others were formally assigned to come up with a plan.[133]

Boyle's project of "inlargeing the Pale of the Christian Church" in India was modeled on Dutch efforts as well as the New England Company's strategies of "Gospelizing (as they phrase it) the Natives of New England"; it also resembled designs Boyle had for Ireland and, to a lesser extent, the Ottoman Empire. Its main focus was translation: rendering key Protestant texts and training of Englishmen in Asian languages while educating children in "the English Tongue & European Learning."[134] Such approaches were of course nothing new. They obviously fit within a more general Protestant emphasis on vernacular texts and preaching, and, more specifically, as early as 1670, the committees had offered to pay a subvention to the assistant minister at Bombay if he would learn and deliver sermons in Portuguese.[135] Master had also argued that converts would not come by teaching English "to as many as will learn it" but by the English learning native languages and customs. As he wrote,

> I have lived above 20 years in India, and have known a great many Chaplains, but never any one who set himself to learn the languages of the Country, or to humour the people a little to gain them; but they are generally so well pleased with their own school-learning and manners that they undervalue all others, which is not according to St. Pauls rule, nor has it proved so; for I never knew any one converted to Christianity by any of our Chaplains, who are extreamly out in their methods, and I despair of ever converting them to understand their own errors, unless they were bread up in their countries from children, by which they might more perfectly come to the knowledge of the Manners, Coustumes, and Humours of the Natives.[136]

Boyle himself had earlier sponsored, with the Company's blessing, Edward Pococke's Arabic translation of Grotius's *De Veritate Religionis Christianae*.[137] He now suggested to Thompson, a member as well of the New England

Company, the publication of "a solid, but civilly pennd" refutation of "Authentick" Hindu texts.[138] Meanwhile, Fell and the theologian Gilbert Burnet approached the Court of Committees with the proposal for a fund to be raised by subscription from "several persons of quality & pious disposition" for the education at Oxford of at least four individuals in "Eastern languages & in divinity," who could serve as chaplains and set up schools in India. Boyle pledged £100.[139]

The committees decided in the end not to establish the fund, but their arguments for refusing were telling. The Court had no problem in principle with the project, nor with accepting the advice and assent from the current managers of the donor fund, including Burnet, Fell, the archbishop of Canterbury, and the deans of Canterbury and St. Paul's. What they feared were the constitutional implications of accepting the fund as a perpetual endowment. These objections went to the heart of their prime concern for maintaining the Company's corporate autonomy above all else. "Considering all persons are mortal; and that Companies and Bodies politick have a kind of perpetuity by their constitution," the Court of Committees argued that they could not allow an external board to determine how their successors approached government, even over these "charitable and pious works." They did, however, pledge to take it on themselves.[140] In February 1682, the Court assigned another group of committees "for propagating the Christian Religion in the East Indies"; their report, issued a few months later, recommended that the Company follow the donors' proposals but raise the money from stockholders rather than from those outside the Company.[141]

By the end of the decade, a few committees, and particularly Josiah Child, seemed still committed to the project. In 1690 the Court procured for Bengkulu a copy of a Malay New Testament, most likely Thomas Hyde's translation of the *Jang Ampat Evangelica.*[142] In 1691 the committees also suggested to Madras's governor Elihu Yale that a separate Portuguese-language church be erected "for the Protestant black people & Portuguez & the Slaves which serve them, who have now no place to hear the word of God preached in a language they understand & therefore are necessitated to go to the Popish Churches." The committees offered to solicit donations in England for adorning the church, to send out a Portuguese-speaking minister and a deacon, and to have the Book of Common Prayer translated into the dialect of Portuguese commonly spoken in India.[143] Until such a church was built, London instructed that Portuguese prayers and sermons should be read at least once a week at St. Mary's.[144]

Yale was deposed soon after as governor, dedicating part of his East Indian fortune, mostly in books, to a different colonial ecclesiastical establishment: the college recently founded by Congregationalist dissenters at New Haven, Connecticut, that would soon after bear his name.[145] This did not, however, arrest the project. Child continued to correspond with Hyde on the matter, who in turn reported to Boyle that he "perceive[d] the good inclinations of the Company to do something for the service of God and Religion," and continued to urge the Company to educate their chaplains in Malay.[146] Though in relatively poor health and infrequently attending meetings, Child continued through the 1690s to take a special interest in the project.[147] The Company funded the Portuguese studies of two ministers recommended by Hyde and sent them to Madras in early 1692.[148] George Lewis acquired remarkably good Persian while there and became a crucial advisor to the Company both in India and upon his ultimate return to England. Jethro Brideoake, on the other hand, evidently behaved "himself so ill" that he was sent back on the same ship that brought him and was branded by the committees as "an Enemy to the Company."[149]

Plans for the Portuguese Protestant church stalled, but the committees remained committed to the Portuguese translation of the Book of Common Prayer. They commissioned Dr. Benjamin Woodroffe of Gloucester Hall, Oxford, to oversee the project.[150] Over one thousand copies of the translation were ultimately printed and leather bound, and a hundred immediately sent to Madras, Surat, Bombay, and Bengal "so the Gospell and the Protestant Religion may be made known to those and ignorant Natives in their own Language to the honour of God and the Glory of our Church." Three hundred more were sent out a few years later.[151] By 1710 Woodroffe had begun to supervise a project for an edition of a Portuguese-language New Testament as well.[152]

Not everyone was content with the Company's progress. In 1695 Henry Prideaux, the canon and later dean of Norwich, recalled Boyle's plan and complained to the archbishop of Canterbury that the Company, though "having for a great number of souls by their own confession under their Government they have done nothing to instruct them in the means wereby they may be sav'd."[153] Prideaux noted that there were "a Million of Souls" under Company government "by vertue of their Charter," but while there were Mosques, Synagogues, Pagodas, and Catholic Churches, there was only one Anglican church in India. In his estimation, the Company had failed "to propagate the Gospell among the Natives although it be their secular interest as will as their Spirituall to make as many of their Subjects as they can of their owne Religion." He claimed, misleadingly, that the Company did not allow a minister at St. Helena, and accepted the complaints of some that they treated their ministers in India "soe badly" that they could do nothing effective. Moreover, the Company's toleration for nonconformists corrupted any efforts they might make; Nathaniel Higginson was particularly blameworthy, "who had his birth and education in New England and is deeply begotted to the Religion of that Country, it is expected that it will not be long er[e] the Church of England Chaplain be found to yield up his church & pulpit to the Independent practice." Prideaux compared the Company to the Dutch, who, he insisted, maintained schools, a university, and sufficient ministers to preach, catechize, administer sacraments, and "Converting of these poor Infidells under their Dominions."[154]

While he offered some particularly novel suggestions—including bringing South Asian children to be raised in England so that they could return to India to preach without danger of being corrupted by the climate, and establishing a seminary in England to train ministers and missionaries—Prideaux's ultimate recommendations were essentially what some in the Company had been proposing for some time: churches and schools to teach in the vernacular, "men of piety & prudence" to be found to serve as "the first planters of the Gospell," and, of course, in all things learning from the Dutch experience in India, or what the English thought the Dutch experience in India was. In fact, despite Prideaux's characterization, Boyle's project was still somewhat alive within the Company. Josiah Woodward, the Company's minister at its hospital and almshouse at Poplar in East London and the committees' principal spiritual counselor, exhorted them to revive his proposals. It was, he maintained, the Company's duty and in its best interests to pursue souls in India, "the most sure and profitable sort of Merchandice."[155] Meanwhile, the Bombay government proposed increasing native soldiers' pay if they turned Protestant, which in turn would encourage their children to attend the English schools there.[156] Madras's governor discussed with George Lewis strategies for how the town "might be brought to consist of all Protestants." Lewis in turn recommended solutions uncannily similar to those of Boyle, Master, Aungier, and many before him. First, the Company must successfully proselytize "at home," that is within its plantations. He also advised building two schools, one for boys and one for girls.[157] London endorsed the plan, pointing out that such a project was in the service of the state. Not only were they losing many soldiers to Catholicism—"whether by the Perswasion of their Indian Wives or Landladys or for what other reason"—but that, being mostly Hindu or Catholic, south Indians could also not fully be trusted in "time of danger." Until "the Natives were Educated in the Protestant Religion," Madras would never reach its full potential, and they "should be glad to hear of any good method to bring about so noble a design . . . [and] would not grudge to be at some charge to effect it."[158]

Company officials meanwhile began to develop a close relationship with the Society for the Propagation of Christian Knowledge (SPCK), whose mostly German missionaries in India were based out of nearby Danish Tranquebar. Madras solicited them to establish a Portuguese school in its white town, and "Mallabar Schools" in its black town, both of which were thought would "serve for many useful purposes in subordination to that greatest of all the enlarging the Kingdom of our Lord and Saviour."[159] The society sent books to furnish libraries both at Madras and Bombay, whose minister also solicited its assistance in establishing a charity school, in imitation of the one at Madras.[160] In return, through the 1710s and 1720s, the committees often provided freight for the SPCK, including a printing press, Bibles and other books, specie, and other provisions, including globes, a clock, a telescope, and English beer.[161] In 1715 the governor of Madras, Edward Harrison, declared to the SPCK he would be "always happy if in the discharge of my affairs, I can by any means promote your pious and laudable endeavors for propagating the Gospel of Christ."[162] In 1728 SPCK missionaries were formally invited into Madras and, nine years later, to Fort St. David. In return, the society formally thanked the Company for its efforts on several occasions, including in a sermon preached in 1736.[163]

As late as 1752, the Company had authorized the governor of Madras to give money to support SPCK projects, and well into the 1790s evidenced little objection to the idea of Protestant missions or missionaries in India. Their protests followed only from the demands of evangelicals, like William Wilberforce, that any English schoolmaster and missionary who wanted to go to India be allowed to do so freely. In the vicious debate that followed, up to and through the 1813 charter that finally opened India to all missionaries, the Company was branded as a commercial apostate.[164] Yet, even then, the core problem was not with missionaries per se but with those missionaries' demands to have free, unfettered, and ungoverned access to the East Indies. In short, the question for the East India Company remained not only about Protestantism and profit but rather, as it had been for centuries, jurisdiction and sovereignty.

PART TWO

TRANSFORMATIONS

"Great Warrs Leave Behind them Long Tales"

Crisis and Response in Asia after 1688

In October 1687 the Company's general, John Child, sent a letter containing thirty-five complaints to Mahmet Khan, the *mutasaddi* of Surat. Chiefly, he demanded a settlement to the conflict in Bengal and that the Company finally receive its long-desired *farman* from the Mughal court, confirming its relief from certain customs and other commercial impositions and requiring Mughal governors to turn over any English interlopers found within their jurisdictions.[1] Child was also insistent to restore the Company's reputation in India, and he was willing to make a show of force to achieve it. In August 1688 the Court of Committees endorsed his approach, simply advising the Bombay council that if they did find the need to start a war on their side of India, they should "pursue it stoutly & resolutely at the first while good purchase is to be had."[2]

By the final decade of the seventeenth century, the East India Company had become committed as an institution to a defensive expansion of its rights, jurisdiction, and government throughout Asia, particularly to exert its authority over the English "nation" and a growing network of colonial enclaves. Tensions in western India were running particularly high, especially following the conflict in Bengal and the Company's removal of its western Presidency, and thus the center of its trade, from Surat to Bombay. Yet, even at its height, such aggressive posturing was never unbridled. Even now, amid two ongoing conflicts and rising tensions in western India, the secret committee in London worried that the Company "are Merchants & must live by trade & not by a long War."[3] Though he had stationed ships at the mouth of Surat's harbor, John Child protested to the *mutasaddi* that his "business in this part of the world is wholly trade."[4] Meanwhile, the committees insisted to Aurangzeb that violence was "very much against the naturall bent of our minds, which hath always been to pursue our Commerce innocently & peaceably without affecting Dominion, increase of Territory or the oppression of other Princes Subjects," unlike the Dutch or the Portuguese.[5]

Clearly there were times when being able to claim to be a "mere merchant" was an extremely useful rhetorical position, one to which the Company often took recourse. Still, there was a kernel of truth in such claims. The Company seemed to seek violence neither for its own sake nor for territorial aggrandizement. The conflicts in Siam and Bengal aimed not at war but peace, which could confirm Company rights and authority and obtain independent, garrisoned colonies from which those rights could be protected, power particularly over maritime space projected, and the Company's jurisdiction over settlers and English subjects secured.[6] In short, the Company was undoubtedly a merchant but, like its European rivals, committed to no longer being considered a *mere* merchant. As the committees wrote Surat in March 1686:

> the Governor [i.e., *mutasaddi*] there looks upon you now but as private Merchants, and therefore it is high tyme, that We should now make him (and officers that have abused you) know, that We are a government and have as much sense of honor, as the vindication of our rights and priviledges, as any other European Nation.[7]

A few months later Madras was similarly reminded of "what a mighty charge we are at to advance the English Interest and make this Company a formidable martiall Government in India which formerly the Dutch despised as a parcel of mere trading Merchants or Pedlars."[8]

It was in this context that John Child announced in early 1687 that if the Mughal government would not come to a reasonable terms in Bengal, "then it will become us to Seize what we cann & draw the English Sword, as well on this Side of India as the other." Only by such a "quarrell" did he believe the Company could finally "gaine a New Settlement and defeat the Dutches hopes," though in this case by "settlement" he meant not a new colony but a newly settled and expanded *farman*.[9] Aurangzeb's conquest of Bijapur and Gulkonda, and advances against both the Marathas and the Portuguese, had rendered the security of the Company's "footing on this side his Dominions" as well as an enclave in Bengal ever more critical, even if they had to "Venture a good bloody nose" to do it.[10] This was not, however, their only reason for assuming a warlike posture. Doing so, London believed, would also compel the Portuguese to cease their claims over parts of the Bombay archipelago, particularly the island of Salsette, which had been in dispute since Bombay's first transfer.[11] A breach with the Mughal empire in Bombay's environs would also present ample excuse to seek "a strict amity" and "a close confederacy" with the Marathas, though these aspirations dissolved with the Mughal defeat and capture of Sambhaji in early 1689.[12] In all, any war, Child insisted, would be prosecuted with a "true Zeale for the publick Interest," and "noe regard to particular Interest that soe little is in our thoughts that it stands not att all in Computition with the publick."[13]

The only possible impediment to this plan Child could imagine was the Sidi Yaqut Khan, but he was convinced that Company naval strength was ample enough to "pay the Siddies sides handsomely and give him and his People their bellys full of sea fighting."[14] This turned out to be a sad miscalculation. On 15 February 1689, Yaqut Khan launched a preemptive attack on Bombay, landing at Sewri on the eastern shore of Bombay island. The infantry lieutenant Child sent to "beate the enemy off the Island" soon returned, having discovered that the Sidi had arrived not with four hundred troops, as Child expected, but six thousand.[15] It turned out that far from the Company giving the Sidi a bellyful of fighting, the Mughal forces, as a later English visitor to India put it, arrived with "men enough to have eaten up all the Company's servants for breakfast."[16] The troops easily ensconced themselves on the island, burning houses and Company buildings, and set about a protracted siege of the fort that would last for more than a year.

That Bombay should fall so easily to occupation should have been unsurprising. Its military and civil establishment was barely two decades old. The fort was still under construction. There were too few European ships available, and war in Europe, of which the council was unaware, prevented reinforcements from arriving. Heavy rains rendered what firepower the soldiery and militia had relatively ineffective and also likely contributed to a high incidence of mortality among the troops. The Company's army also bled from desertions: 63 in the first month alone, and 116 before the entire affair was over, some even absconding to the Sidi's employ. As when Bombay was under threat of Dutch invasion in the 1670s, a number of civilian inhabitants including particularly the Indo-Portuguese militia fled. "Hardly one," the council complained, "struck a stroak in the Defence of the Island."[17]

After a few months, Bombay had agreed in principle with officials at Surat on peace talks to be held on neutral ground at the Portuguese colony of Damão. Yet, even with his island under occupation, Child would not cede ground. He refused to attend the talks in person, neither trusting the new *mutasaddi* Mukhtiar Khan nor believing it appropriate to his own status to attend; "it may be argued that the Nabob [i.e., the *mutasaddi*] is but Governor of the Towne," he insisted, "whereas the English Generall represents the whole Nation."[18] When Bombay finally sent an embassy the following month, it consisted of three relatively low-level representatives: George Weldon, Abraham Navarro, and Barker Hibbins. Mukhtiar Khan also sent surrogates: Qazi Ibrahim, Mir Nizam, and some Surat merchants "with ample power to conclude peace." By September they had reached a tentative agreement. Yaqut Khan would withdraw from Bombay, Company money and goods seized at Surat (valued at 73,000 rupees) would be restored, and the Company would also get its long-anticipated *farman* accommodating Child's thirty-five demands, including the Company's exclusive trade and jurisdiction over English subjects in Mughal dominions. In return, the Company would restore the prizes that East India ships had taken, resume trade at Surat, and make a *peskash* of 25,000 rupees to the *mutasaddi* and 500,000 for Aurangzeb.[19] To confirm the deal, Weldon and Navarro set out in late November for Bijapur to catch up with Aurangzeb's court, where they found favor from Asad Khan, his chief *wazir*, or minister.[20]

There was one catch. Asad Khan and others at Aurangzeb's court insisted that John Child come in person to Surat to receive the *farman*. Even if he had been willing to do this, the question was mooted by Child's death in early February. Yet, as the inscription on his tomb insisted, "Death to Empire will not grant reprieve."[21] John Vauxe, the chief judge and Child's acting successor, would go in his stead. Both Vauxe and his council acknowledged the risks, but they had few options; they also seemed to think the prisoners they had captured during the occupation would serve as adequate collateral to ensure his safe return. On 28 February, Vauxe left the island's government in George Cooke's hands and departed under a twenty-gun salute, all fired in the direction of the Sidi's soldiers.[22]

Vauxe arrived at the Surat River several days later but did not come ashore until 4 April, by which time Surat had yet another new *mutasaddi*, I'timad Khan. Mughal officials at Surat were routinely rotated out fairly quickly, which of course only added (likely intentionally) to the uncertainty of Company politics there. More favorably inclined to the Company than his predecessor, he released the council from imprisonment. The *farman* and gifts were exchanged with great ceremony the next day. Meanwhile, Cooke engaged in talks for a cease fire with the Sidi, who withdrew his last troops in June.[23] Everything seemed to be working out, that is, until Vauxe and the others had the *farman* translated. What they discovered was a "disgracefull thing," and "a worse sham story then the Phirmaund that came down in Mucteer Cauns time."[24] Essentially, the *farman* laid all the blame for the conflict on the Company and insisted that "Mr Child who did the disgrace be turned out & expelled."[25]

Vauxe and the Surat council rejected the *farman* as incommensurate with the terms they thought they had negotiated. Mughal officials in turn refused to allow Vauxe to leave Surat until the Company complied with its demands. Thus, while hostilities had ended, the peace remained technically unresolved. Meanwhile, Bombay was in shambles. More than a hundred Company soldiers and Bombay inhabitants had died, another 125 had been wounded, and untold damage had been done to the island's civic, martial, and commercial infrastructure.[26] The Bombay council reported that the island bore "the Marks of ruine & destruction soe deeply engraven as wee believe may require a good competency of time to wear out." Lamenting that "it is a common proverb in the World that one misfortune is a step to an other," the council also noted that the Sidi's withdrawal was met not only with the monsoon but also an epidemic outbreak, which either killed or drove off the island a number of those who remained.[27] Bombay complained of a desperate need of fresh soldiers and officers from England; five years after, most European soldiers were still not healthy enough to promote, and there were in fact "very few fit to carry a Musket."[28] The island's infrastructure had been devastated. The value of the revenue farms was severely depressed. In 1694 the customs were put up for sale twice, with no bidders either time.[29] Though these did eventually recover, the war delayed many of the Company's great projects; a decade later, there was still no courthouse (or judge) and no church (or minister), "all which," the Bombay council noted, "renders us little in the esteame of our Neighbours & strangers."[30] As the president of the Surat factory, Bartholomew Harris, lamented in 1691, "great Warrs leave behind them long Tales and such as are more Sharpe and Seveeer, doeing more harm to the publick then all their Swords and bullets."[31]

The Court of Committees remained nonetheless sanguine. Admitting neither the conflicts in Bengal nor Bombay had been "to the height of our Expectations," London was convinced the effort had been honorable and effective, having "confounded all our adversarys and is wonder'd at by forreign Europeans that know the Power and greatness of the Mogull." Though not yet aware of the nature of the actual text of the *farman*, London noted that

> We know the attempt in making warr upon that Great Monarch the Mogull was very dangerous but it was just because it was necessary, Bonum quiq unicum, it was wise because there was no other way to save the English Interest in India from being ruined by the Interloping English and the Extorting moors Governors who were instigated by them, to deprive Us of all our ancient Priviledges.[32]

The war had been intended as preemptive, to assert the Company's rights over refractory Englishmen and to protect its reputation against the threat posed by the seemingly intractable expansion of universal empire, whether it be Mughal, Portuguese, or Dutch. The war, by the committees' estimation, had not been one of aggression but defense. In this sense, it had been just.[33] The goal had always been the diplomatic settlement that would follow.[34] On the day of Yaqut Khan's invasion, half a world away, the committees wrote to remind Bombay again that "the end of all just Warr is Peace," and that they should be eager—but not too eager—for a truce.[35] Officials in India believed this was in fact what they had achieved. The Surat council dismissed much of the language of the *farman* as pro forma "Vanity": "the high and haughty expressions and uncouth as unheard off Phrases in any of our Christian Courts that are in all their Phirmaunds and writeings."[36] In fact, Bombay insisted that the Company had pulled off a victory. While in Europe one would have expected such a return to *status quo ante bellum*, they argued, a full withdrawal and restoration of the island was unprecedented in India, where triumphant Mughal armies tended either to conquer or raze territories they invaded.[37] According to this logic, that the Company had not suffered *more* was itself a signal mark of success, not to mention "God Almighties providence (who would not suffer us to be Swallowed up)."[38]

The Bombay government set immediately about the task of restoring the island's martial and civic infrastructure. The lesson that seemed to be learned from the occupation was not to be less aggressive but that they had not been aggressive enough in making Bombay capable of supporting such ambitions. Though "the burnt Child dreads the fire this makes him very cautious," the Bombay council observed, no time could be lost in restoring and expanding the island's defenses.[39] It had in fact been a "great evill" that it was not done earlier.[40] Some native soldiers were assigned to build a new ten-gun platform against the bay to ward off any further invasion by sea.[41] In October 1690 the committees designed to send over one hundred additional soldiers to Bombay "that you may appear formidable amongst those People."[42] They retained the wartime position of general, once more insisting he be appointed by the Company not the Crown.[43] After briefly considering elevating Elihu Yale to the post, the Company sent out Sir John Goldsborough, a former Company ship captain, with the official title of "Supervisor Commissary General and Chief Governour in East India." He was charged with the task of subjecting the Company's settlements and factories to his "Ocular Inspection," to "settle the Companyes Revenue and all Our affairs."[44] For all intents and purposes, Goldsborough was John Child's successor, but the Company withheld the higher rank until it was decided where his permanent residence would be.[45] When he took up Madras as his base of operations in April 1693, a commission as "Captain General" followed. The committees also created a new position, naming Nathaniel Higginson, the governor of Madras, and John Gayer, the former ship captain now Bombay's governor, as lieutenants general.[46] Goldsborough died before his formal commission reached India, leaving Gayer to take up the post, which he would hold for more than a decade and from which he would greatly influence Company policy in India, despite multiple private pleas to London to relieve him and allow him and his wife to come home.[47]

One of Gayer's first orders of business at Bombay was to deal with restoring the lands occupied during the invasion. His predecessor, George Cooke, had confiscated much of the island's private property, with the intent of publicly reinstating those who "had bin faithful" and for those who had fled to serve as an "Example to be degraded & loose theirs."[48] The issues at stake were the same as with the threatened Dutch attack two decades earlier: settlers' and inhabitants' rights to property were not absolute but dependent on their willingness to defend that land and the colony. Cooke had also not yet restored the lands because he was committed to doing so through some form of due process, but not only were there too few healthy men available to make up juries but the island's only remaining experienced judge, John Vauxe, was unable to leave Surat.[49] Though agreeing in principle that a judge should ideally oversee the process, Gayer was far more concerned that the unoccupied lands were quickly giving over to waste, and becoming both unproductive and unattractive for settlers. The punctilios of law, he essentially argued, were meaningless if one did not have any inhabitants to observe them. Restoring the property to ownership was the only way to begin to rebuild the island's population and tax revenue.

This was also an opportunity to reshape Bombay's civil society by encouraging landholding over tenancy, and a security in property that would naturally set landowners "heartily about improving there estates & making them true to [the Company's] interest."[50] The council quickly set about restoring all small holdings that yielded under two hundred Xeraphins per year (roughly £15), on the condition that one quarter of the annual produce of the land be paid back in rent to the Bombay government, as an "Expedient or Remedy . . . inclined to favour the said poorer sort of Inhabitants in their Estates."[51] More generally, though, it was loyalty to government that became the benchmark for a restitution and reward following the invasion. Several residents came in with petitions emphasizing their past and present service. Rama Comotin, a *saraf* whose family had owned the tobacco farm of Bombay from 1686 and suffered great losses in the occupation (not the least of which was a leg injury sustained by friendly fire from a company mortar[52]) emphasized his loyalty as well as his family's contract "with the Right Honourable Companys Ministers." His lands were restored, along with title to rice fields on the southern tip of the island, which had formerly belonged to Muslims accused of aiding the Sidi. He was also offered two lucrative positions for his service in the "late Warrs": overseer of the Company's revenues as well as muster master general of native outguard soldiers. His brother Lolla remained chief *saraf* of the treasury.[53] The cash-strapped council suggested that they might offer their loyal "Gentue" garrison soldiers land to cultivate in lieu of pay. Gayer further lobbied with the committees in London not to disband the Rajput soldiers as they "have sworne themselves to your Honors for ever, & by promises they have rec[eive]d from the Government to be continued, have rejected many offers from Rajahs of their owne Nation & Call'd all their families hither."[54] In their petition, the inhabitants of Mahim similarly stressed that they should be secured in their titles because they had remained on the island and fought as "people humble vassals Subjects & obedient to the most Honorable Company & to the General."[55]

Despite their eagerness to return land to productivity as soon as possible, Gayer and his council were not prepared to offer a blanket amnesty. As they noted, the "Inhabitants of Bombay Island & formed into the Meletia thereof were as all good Subjects are engaged to defend their Countrey and Estates as well as the Garrison Souldiers"; failure to do so was a "great Crime."[56] While some Portuguese inhabitants petitioned for redress, pleading for the Company's mercy on their "miserable" situations,[57] those who remained recalcitrant and continued to insist on the reinstatement of their lands as a matter of right were far less successful. The council was particularly critical of the island's Jesuits, accusing them of encouraging the Sidi and abetting the Portuguese residents who fled. Like Alvaro Perez decades earlier, the priests appealed to officials in Goa, Lisbon, and London; also like Perez, their efforts were unsuccessful.[58]

In turning attention to Bombay's security on land, Gayer also inevitably looked to the sea. His government made reinstating and enforcing Bombay's sea passes a priority.[59] He also sought to expand the authority of governors in India over European shipping. The committees had already in 1690 delegated to their subordinates the power to negotiate extensions to charterparty contracts but there was still no way to compel a captain of a privately owned ship to agree; this was something Gayer understood firsthand, as he was actually the first ship captain whose contract had been continued in India under this power.[60] He now noted to London that

> the little power and Command wee have of the Ships in your Service, who after their time is out are ungovernable . . . Renders us very weake and unless care be taken thereof for the future 'tis unreasonable to expect you should ever attaine any Soverainty in these parts worth the takeing notice off.

The Dutch, he observed, had such authority, without which "they had undeniably been as low in India as wee are now but they too well saw that a Controuling power was indispencibly necessary for the Raiseing a Dominion."[61]

In essence, the trials at Bombay had not turned Company leaders from their fundamental political science but back to its first principles: building population and prosperity through defense, maritime power, and security of trade, property, and civil society. Elsewhere in Asia, the Company continued to strengthen and expand its system. Madras—though experiencing some setbacks, including a famine raging throughout southern India and an unexpected three-day tempest, which destroyed over thirty ships in the harbor—was even able to find some advantage in the dislocations wrought by Mughal expansion.[62]

The council reinforced the settlement's defenses, undertaking a large project in 1692 to dig trenches and build bulwarks in the black town, "at the charge of the Inhabitants for whose defence they are made onely."[63] Even the interloper Alexander Hamilton was forced to admit that Aurangzeb's advancing armies in the Deccan "made Fort St. *George* put on a better Dress than he wore before," as the settlement was able to advertise itself as a safe haven for merchants fleeing devastation inland.[64] Its government also forged productive diplomatic ties with its new neighboring Mughal officials. Following the conquest of Golkonda, Zulfiqar Khan, son of Aurangzeb's *wazir* Asad Khan, reissued the Company's grants for Madras and Masulipatam, relieving the city of its tribute obligations entirely, confirming its rights of mintage, and also offering the Company three more villages, which were in turn farmed out for an annual revenue amounting to about 1,200 pagodas.[65]

In Bengal, Company officials spent much of the 1690s attempting to actually take up the promised *zamindari* grant for Sutanuti, Govindpur, and Kalikata. Both the current revenue farmer and Bengal's *nawab* tried to obfuscate and delay; the former was particularly eager to have the grant made to a Bengali proxy rather than the Company directly, since otherwise, the Calcutta council intuited, he feared "the place will be wholly lost to him."[66] None of this seemed to stop the Company from planning as if the grant had been settled. In 1693 London ordered the establishment of a permanent Admiralty and Judicature court for Calcutta. The council began to farm out the revenue, which was estimated to be worth about 2,000–2,500 rupees a year, regarding the very act as a claim to de facto sovereignty, "consistent with our own Methods & Rules of Government & . . . the only means wee can think of till wee can procure a grant for our firm settlement."[67] It was also crucial, the committees insisted, to begin to make "the place bear its own charge, without which it is a vain thing to imagine the Company can ever attain to any lasting Dominion in India."[68] In 1698 the council managed to reach a settlement with the *nawab*, Azimu-sh-Shab. In exchange for a payment of 1,300 rupees, any other *zamindars* would immediately "make over their Right and title to the English," which the Company would hold at the same rates.[69]

The Company understood its *zamindari* at Calcutta as akin to its English proprietorships over Bombay or St. Helena or its agreements for settlement in Madras and Bengkulu: that is, as a perpetual grant for a sovereign but tributary jurisdiction over a fortified, independent settlement. Against all evidence to the contrary, the committees envisioned Calcutta as "the most flourishing Spott of Ground in Bengall," which would, history proved, only flourish more under Company stewardship:

> It was our Trade and Government made Fort St. George from being a
> Chinapataum or a small Diminitive Town, as it was called become the

most flourishing City between Cape Comorine and the Bay of Bengall, It was our Trade raised Cassumbuzar from a small Inconsiderable Town for the silk Production to be the great Mart for Raw Silk and Taffatyes in Bengall, And we can see no reason why Culcutta should not resemble, if not Vie with either of these in a series of years, but the foundations must be first laid, And we are desirous the Glory of that at least should be your due.[70]

Made independent from Madras in February 1697, Calcutta was elevated to the status of a presidency, equal to Bombay and Madras, just before the turn of the century.[71]

If ultimately the most famous and successful, Calcutta was actually only one of a number of such projects for new settlement. In 1689 the committees considered using the European war with France as pretext for both luring French soldiers to Company service as well as for seizing the French town of Pondicherry, particularly given the recent French attack on Montserrat in the West Indies.[72] Though prescient—the Company would indeed use war with France as a pretext for attacking Pondicherry, but not until 1748 and then finally in 1793—nothing was in fact made of it, perhaps because by the late 1680s the Company had already acquired another nearby settlement, on grants from Raja Ram in Jinji: the towns of Cuddalore and Thevnapatam, soon known more formally as Fort St. David. With Madras as a model, the Company immediately set about fortifying and building there. By 1691 the Madras council reported that the fort and town "flourish bravely, daily encreasing in revenues Strength Trade and Inhabitants & bears the best aspect for a future greatness & improvement of any new Europe Settlement in India."[73] John Goldsborough visited the town in July 1693, ordering further improvements, including city walls, stronger fortifications, cultivation of lands, and new procedures for the collection of rents, customs, and other fees.[74] In 1696 John Berlu, the Madras council's secretary, arrived—accompanied by a garrison officer, eight halberd bearers, a flag, the governor's palanquin, and musicians—to "proclaime" a stamp for a new pagoda coin, featuring a Hindu deity on the obverse, surrounded by an outline of the Company's balemark and the town's name.[75]

Goldsborough also appointed the first judges to the town's choultry. As at Bombay and Madras, justice at Fort St. David served a number of purposes indelibly imbued with political significance: keeping order, establishing the authority and respect for government, and representing the Company's jurisdiction, both within and without its bounds. Punishments ranged from chastisement to transportation, corporal and capital punishment; one man found to have come from Jinji with the intent to steal horses from the Company had his ears and one hand amputated.[76] In 1696 a *banian* working for the Dutch, found guilty of a crime only noted as "of a very henious nature," possibly an adulterous relationship with the wife of a goldsmith from Jinji, was ordered to death by a caste tribunal, only to have his sentence commuted by the council to public humiliation: he was to be mounted backwards on an ass, marched through the streets, and then deported, forbidden to return on penalty of having his ears cut off and being enslaved by the Company.[77]

This particular incident also revealed a great deal about the Company's understanding of the relationship between jurisprudence and jurisdiction. Before the sentence could be executed, the convict had managed to abscond into Dutch custody. The VOC promptly claimed he fell under its jurisdiction and thus was subject to its justice. Fort St. David's superiors at Madras demanded Laurens Pit, the Dutch chief on the Coromandel Coast, return him immediately, "the English Company being lords proprietors within the bounds of Tegnapatam purchased of Ramaraja they have the Sole Dominion and Right of Judicature within the said bounds." They also dismissed VOC officials' claim that they also held *kauls* from Rama Raja, since, unlike the English, the Dutch grants "both in the intention of the Giver, and Receiver Relates onely to the Management of Trade, as Merchants . . . [and] there doth not appear the [least] Ground for claiming a Right of Judicature over the Native Inhabitants, in Criminall cases which Extend to forfeiture of life or Estate." Thus, according to Madras, "impeding the Execution & detaining and protecting of the Criminall from Justice, is a violation of the English Company's right of Government which wee cannot Recede from but are oblidged to claime."[78]

Meanwhile the Company continued to pursue its ambitions for another fortification in southern India, across the continent on the pepper-rich Malabar coast. For decades, English officials had been in intermittent negotiations with the Rani of Attingal, in the present-day state of Kerala, about the possibility of such a settlement.[79] In 1676, the Surat Council proposed the Company find some suitable fortification at Karunagappally, offering, as usual, the promise of protection from the VOC, "which is the string on which all those petty Mallabar Rajahs have harped since their Yoake under the Dutch."[80] Despite further overtures, nothing came of the proposal.[81] Ten years later, Surat still remained "bent in a settlement."[82] In 1687, having been sent down the west coast on various business, Captains John Shaxton and Richard Clifton were instructed to revive the negotiations.[83] London imagined "with good Words or money" they might acquire a settlement, much like Madras, with rights to revenue and a garrison "sufficient to maintain the Place, as well in Warr as in Peace."[84]

That plan stalled, owing in part to some jurisdictional confusion between Madras and Bombay at John Child's death, when there was no general with clear authority.[85] However, by 1693, with Goldsborough firmly in charge, two more emissaries, Daniel Acworth and John Brabourn, resumed negotiations, with full credentials as diplomatic representatives of the Company. As their predecessors had, they stressed to the Rani the "danger she is in of the Dutch becoming lords over her people at Sea & land." The two men were instructed to insist on nothing short of a sovereign enclave, with "a phirmand for to hold the place Limitts & privildges thereof for ever as long as the Sun & moone indures in the name of the Right Honorable English East India Company as a free possession of theirs for ever." They were to acquire rights to free customs, to administer justice, to mint coin, and, crucially, "that her Highnesses Rajadores or Governors shall have no Jurisdiction in our limmitts nor in noe part thereof, but that we shall be absolutely free to be Governed with in our selves by such laws as we shall thinck fitt to make."[86] In July 1694, ostensibly on these terms, the Rani finally gave her *ola* for a Company settlement at the coastal town of Anjengo as well as a monopoly over Attingal's pepper exports.[87]

Anjengo was, as John Gayer observed, neither as "healthful" nor as well stationed for the pepper trade as other possible locales; its true advantage was its strategic situation to project power over both land and sea, and particularly to protect navigation in and out of Kerala from Dutch aggression.[88] This hardly pleased the Dutch, who claimed the very settlement violated their sovereign rights in southeastern India; once again recalling the arguments Grotius had made on their behalf almost a century earlier, the VOC insisted that it had acquired firm authority in the region by virtue of both conquest, of south Indian as well as Portuguese territory, and the "firme and authentick Contracts" they maintained with local powers.[89] The VOC officials threatened to invade Attingal. They also punitively refused to allow their doctor to assist any ailing English at Anjengo.[90] To Company leadership, such claims served only to confirm the necessity of such a settlement and further evidence of Dutch desire to obtain a "sovereignty of the Sea" and to make "the whole World . . . their Tributaries."[91]

Even by the Company's standards, the early days of the Anjengo settlement were extremely trying. Troubles in the Deccan and up the west coast rendered provisions and workers, such as carpenters, stonecutters, and lead workers, in short supply and extremely expensive. As at Bengkulu, prejudices and complaints about the laziness and extortions of the local workforce abounded. Brabourne noted a shortage of food, since there was neither room to graze beef cattle nor would it have been politically savvy to do so in the largely Hindu area.[92] The settlement still had no English doctor, and with venereal disease running particularly rampant among the European soldiers, many deserted to Dutch service "where they have the Conveniency of Physitians."[93] To make matters more complicated, in early 1695 the Danish East India Company sent a well-apportioned embassy with the goal of stealing away the exclusive arrangement from both the English and Dutch.[94]

Despite these hardships, by mid-1696 construction was underway on a stone fort, and two years later all four bastions, ramparts, and curtains were complete.[95] Meanwhile, the Company pursued other, less successful projects. In 1692 two emissaries went to Calicut to try to negotiate for a settlement, now using the agreement with Attingal as a model.[96] The Company reordered its Persian affairs, shifting priority away from Gombroon toward its revived factory at Isfahan, in part to underscore the Company's growing relationship with the Armenians there and its ambitions to redirect the silk trade from the Levant Company.[97] In 1698 Bombay also hosted an "ambassador" from Ethiopia, whose "errand is to desire a trade and good correspondence with the English";[98] even though the ambassador may have been a fraud, the committees' enthusiasm for the mission "from Prester John's Country" revealed latent aspirations for a coffee trade and possibly even settlement in northeastern Africa.[99] Perhaps the most far-flung enterprise came in 1696, after a few Company committees had been seduced by tales from one Frederick von Werlinhoff, a German military officer formerly in VOC service at the Cape of Good Hope, of a large, lucrative, and mysterious spice island somewhere in the South Seas, which, given the description of the route he offered, seemed conspicuously to be somewhere in the vicinity of New Guinea. According to Werlinhoff, the Dutch purposely kept the island off of maps and plans, but were unable to colonize it themselves, it "being so large half as big as England." He provided extremely detailed navigational directions to this unmarked "great Island of Nutmegs," where "the People wear long black hair and some of them speak Portugueeze." Tantalized by his information, London sent Werlinhoff to Madras with an appointment as "Engineer & Miner General."[100] He also was given a set of top secret instructions—only he, Madras's governor Nathaniel Higginson, and the ship captain were to have knowledge of the expedition—to sail to this island, "build a small Paggar in the Nature of a little fort & a house for our People to dwell in," plant an English flag, and obtain "a Paper under the Rajahs or Orunkeys hands . . . that they doe Surrender the said Island and the Trade thereof unto his Majesty the King of England and the English East India Company."[101]

Many of these projects were ultimately fool's errands, but they revealed something critical about the continuity between the projects of the 1680s and those that followed. The wars at Bengal, Siam, and Bombay were seen to be unfortunate necessities not anomalies; discovery, negotiation, or purchase of rights and grants remained as useful as, if not preferable to, armed conflict. Bombay was reminded in 1699:

> not to put everything to the extremity & revenge every affront, as if our busyness was nothing but Conquest, Noe, it is much more convenient for us to patch up a Breach with a small piscash sometimes which will

not cost the Twentyeth part of the charge, as repelling force by force, especially if to do with a formidable Enemy, In which Case an Ounce of Discretion will go further than a pound of force & Money together.[102]

The 1690s witnessed a continuation of the same policy as before: diplomacy when possible, force when necessary.[103] Attempts to build military and naval strength were largely designed as intimidation ideally to avoid rather than foment conflict. Fortification and demonstrations of power also ironically made possible new diplomatic alliances, especially between English and Mughal interests.[104] Both Madras and Bengal curried favor with Mughal forces by providing munitions, food, safe haven, and in some cases even soldiers; the Calcutta council acquired a great deal of political capital, and ultimately the permission to build Fort William, after it denied two rebel *zamindars*, Sobha Singh and Rahim Shah, passage and protection, and watched as Mughal forces killed twenty-six of their soldiers within reach of the factory's guns.[105] When in 1694 the governor of Madras wrote in a letter that "my study is to serve the King & [I] doe humbly hope it will be So accept[ed] by him," he was writing not to a Privy Councilor of William III but to Asad Khan, Aurangzeb's chief *wazir*.[106]

Unfortunately, despite such overtures, serious tensions with Mughal powers persisted on both sides of India and in fact were exacerbated by the appearance in the 1690s of what seemed like an infestation of Anglo-American "pirates" in the Red Sea and the Indian Ocean. This reached a climax in 1695, when the English Captain Henry Avery (or Every) famously seized two Mughal ships in the Red Sea, including one, the *Ganj-i-Sawa'i*, which was said to have belonged to Aurangzeb and which was transporting hajji returning from the pilgrimage to Mecca not to mention a great deal of money. Many at Surat, including government officials, traders, clergy, and the crowd, held the Company, along with the Dutch and the French, responsible. All European trade was stopped out of the port. Clerics and merchants, particularly the shipping magnate and mullah, Abd al-Ghafur, who had lost a good deal of shipping during the hostilities with Bombay, demanded the English factors' execution, proclaiming the "towne . . . so defiled that no prayer can be offered up acceptable to God til Justice is done."[107] I'timad Khan, the *mutasaddi*, had the Company's employees in the town arrested and confined in irons, as Gayer put it, "like a Company of Doggs," ostensibly to save them from "the Rabble," who, possibly instigated by al-Ghafur and others, had laid siege to the factory.[108] The Company's council was deprived of "the libertye of a Penn and Ink," and what correspondence did get out was clearly being intercepted, since Samuel Annesley, the factory's president, developed secret code to indicate when a letter had been written under duress, that it was intended as misinformation, or that its content should for some reason be disregarded.[109] Soon after, the English, Dutch, and French were all forbidden from traveling in *palanquins*, carrying arms, or flying flags, and sounding trumpets in the town.[110]

It is hard to imagine many at Surat truly believed that the Company was responsible for or capable of controlling the pirates; as the Surat council observed, even it could not "determine wether the severity of the Mores to us proced from a real belief of the Charge brought against us or from polliticall causes."[111] The incident was certainly not unprecedented. As early as 1628, Company officials at Surat had been importuned on the account of pirates or others in the Indies flying English colors, and similar incidents were among the reasons the Company had been so eager to relocate the center of its western Indian government to Bombay.[112] Moreover, Avery was, after all, an Englishman; since the Company had been protesting vigorously to be recognized for some time as the only government over the English in Asia, it as not unreasonable to assume it should be held liable for the actions of its subjects. That Bombay continued to reject the *farman* and as such had not yet made its promised restitution for seizures made during the wars at Bengal and Bombay did not help matters, many at Surat failing—or choosing to fail—to make the same fine distinction as the Company between a licit act of war prize and an illegal act of piracy. Tensions were only further exacerbated by the fact that in 1692 Bombay had begun to mint a rupee coin, with the names of William and Mary transliterated into Persian characters; such a coin with "the name of their impure King" had reportedly incensed Aurangzeb, who considered such rights to be a prerogative of his sovereignty. There was a rumor of another invasion of Bombay and possibly one of Madras as well, until word came from the *mutasaddi* that "to coin as formerly with the RHCs arms & an inscription in English would not be taken notice of." The Persian coin was abandoned the next year.[113]

The piracy "crisis" thus became an opportunity to test the Company's incipient but growing claims to independence and power in the region. The *mutasaddi* and others began to pressure the Company to recommit to trading from Surat. Merchants took the opportunity to force the Company to pay its war reparations; repercussions reached as far as the Arabian coastal states, where the brother of the Surat trader Hassan Amudan managed to have about 310,000 rupees seized from the Company at Jidda, and its two factors there imprisoned.[114] Mughal officials, including some at Aurangzeb's court, used the moment in fact to expand their naval security, demanding the Company, along with the Dutch and the French, protect its Arabian trade, the hajj route out of Surat, and Mughal coastal interests by providing shipping convoys in the Indian Ocean and Red Sea. It soon became clear that their definition of a "pirate" included not just the Anglo-Americans, but Gujarati, Malabar, Maratha, and Portuguese rivals as well. In Annesley's words, "I suppose they take [piracy] to be a Comprehensive name including any one that may attack them."[115]

Bombay rupee, 1692, inscribed with names of William and Mary in Persian characters. © The Trustees of the British Museum.

The piracy issue laid bare the great potential for conflict among the European companies as well. Dutch and French officials reportedly fed the rumor that the English Company had backed the pirates. The VOC tried to offer its own convoys to Arabia in exchange for special privileges and when the English attempted to do the same, the Dutch director at Surat secretly underbid them and alleged that the Company's offer was a ruse to lure Mughal shipping to a fleet in the Red Sea, poised to avenge the situation in Surat.[116] The French Company, conversely, refused convoy demands, threatening war on behalf of Louis XIV should they be compelled into such an arrangement.[117] Fearing the possibility of English and Dutch convoys of Mughal shipping, the Portuguese—who did not even have a presence at Surat and were not subjected to the reprisals there—took the opportunity to renew complaints in London that English Company shipping passes violated their sovereignty, undercutting *cartazes* and authorizing the smuggling and violence of "Infidells Vessells."[118] The English, for their part, attempted to lay blame for the piracies—even those of Captain William Kidd, the infamous New York privateer—on the Danes.[119] Bombay also offered up some captured French and Dutch sailors to the *mutasaddi* at Surat as pirates, Gayer evidently overcoming his ostensible reservations about turning over Christians to the infidel.[120]

It seemed the only threat the pirates did not pose to the Company was to its shipping. If this was a crisis, it was a political one, and as such it presented political opportunities. To fight piracy was to claim to be able to draw fundamental distinctions between just and unjust violence, public and private right, and honorable and dishonorable behavior at sea.[121] It was also to assert the right to enforce those distinctions and exercise a certain form of *imperium* over the sea lanes. Practically speaking, a war against piracy allowed the Company to insist upon the efficacy of its ships, passes, and law across oceanic space.[122] Gayer attempted to turn Mughal demands back against the Surat government, refusing passes for the town's shipping until Company factors were freed; he even insinuated ironically that without passes Mughal merchants just might be mistaken for pirates and sunk.[123] He ultimately agreed to the convoys but on certain terms. First, there would be no convoys without a final settlement of an acceptable *farman*. In failing to provide the *farman* before, he argued, the Mughal government had effectively invited the piracy crisis by failing to support the Company's authority over refractory Englishmen, a point his predecessor Goldsborough had also made to the *subahdar* and *diwan* in Bengal.[124] Piracy was simply an extreme form of interloping and as such could be eradicated only if Mughal officials would acknowledge the Company's authority over all Englishmen in India and recognize its extraterritorial claim over them throughout Asia.[125] In turn, the convoys themselves became leverage against Mughal impositions. When some more pirates appeared a few years later, Bombay threatened it would cease protecting Mughal ships if its employees at Surat were imprisoned or mistreated; not only did the ultimatum work, but it even rallied as stalwart an English enemy as al-Ghafur now to lobby on the Company's behalf.[126]

Samuel Annesley at Surat had even bigger ideas. He insisted any convoy agreement should include permanent immunities for the English at Surat, including the right to fly the flag and have it carried before Company officials "according to their former Custom."[127] In return, he proposed, far more ambitiously, that the Company should not just offer protection but actively pursue the pirates to "discover the place of their Rendezvous."[128] In doing this, he suggested to Gayer that they should pursue a position for the Company to serve as a "Salt water" *faujdar*: that is, a tributary military and police force for the high seas "to secure the Navigation of his Subjects from Pyracy." Modeling his idea after the role the Sidi played in the western Indian littoral, Annesley predicted such an office would bring the Company a *jagir*, assignment of revenue, of 400,000 rupees, increase Bombay's naval power, provide leverage against the Sidi, and better the Company's position with Mughal authorities on land.[129]

The idea that the Company could serve as a tributary Mughal officer was far from inconceivable, but it was impracticable. A *faujdari* for the high seas was a contrivance, which Aurangzeb and his advisors were unlikely to have accepted. Gayer was not persuaded either, though his objections were not ideological: the Company had neither the shipping nor the requisite orders from London to embark on such a massive undertaking.[130] By the following year, Annesley had abandoned the notion of assuming a Mughal office for an even more capacious vision of the convoys as an extension of Company sovereignty in its own right. Convoy ships, he now argued, need to be seen as "in Nature of Castles and those under our Command as in our harbours [which] the Lawes of Nature and hospitality obliges us to defend."[131] According to Annesley, ships were floating forts, which carried sovereignty with them along the sea lanes and, thus, according to natural law were responsible to provide "hospitality," that is protection, to subjects or strangers within the limits of one's sovereign and physical power.[132]

Even if Annesley's furtive imagination was stimulated by the fact that he was being held a virtual prisoner at Surat, it nonetheless revealed a conception of Company authority that drew both on structures of Mughal sovereignty and its own political behavior, akin to arguments that had for centuries informed Portuguese claims about the *imperium* to be found in maintaining and controlling the Eurasian sea route, including suppressing piracy.[133] It was not surprising that the entire project for joint Anglo-Dutch convoys almost stalled over which flag the fleet would fly.[134] The situation meanwhile created an opportunity to press for expanded powers in London. The Company's Admiralty Courts had been primarily conceived a decade earlier to combat interloping, not piracy; their main ambit was to condemn prize, not confer punishment. John Gayer thus insisted the committees pursue a new commission "to try & Execute some of those bold audacious Malefactors in India."[135] The committees of course saw the piracy crisis as a prime argument for even further expanding its power over English subjects as well, since "the experience all mankind" was "that Interloping not only ruins Trade but never fails to turn into Piracy at last." The Anglo-American pirates' appearance in India they hoped "will prove a good effect of an ill cause, because all persons in authority here which could not see the evill consequences in the Theory or Root must of necessity [discern] them in the practick & the branches which have grown from such a poisonous root."[136]

The Company began a forward political assault. Bombay, Surat, and other Company settlements, factories, and ships detained, confined, interrogated, deposed, and often sent back as informants any deserters from pirate ships. Some even subsequently made careers with the Company, such as Philip Middleton, who as a young boy escaped to inform on Avery and was subsequently given a reward, a year of schooling, and appointed a junior factor for Bengal, ultimately rising to the rank of a chief supercargo.[137] The Company formed an ad hoc committee dedicated to investigating Avery specifically and a month later petitioned the Lords Justices for action.[138] A £500 reward for his capture was added into later drafts of the Privy Council's proclamation against him after the East India Company secretly agreed to pay for it.[139] The Company ordered a hundred copies of this proclamation sent to India on the next shipping and drew up its own commission promising an additional 4,000 rupees as a reward if Avery's crew were captured in India.[140] In August, £50 was offered for the capture of any of his crew, again to be paid by the East India Company.[141] Robert Blackborne, the Company's secretary, also wrote to various parts of England and Ireland upon intelligence that some of Avery's men might be headed there.[142] Crewmen were ultimately detained in the West Country, Liverpool,

Dublin, and Newcastle. The Company disbursed over £130 for their transportation to London for trial, in addition to gratuities to various state officials who helped.[143] In the six months following the first proclamation, the committees paid out at least £350 in rewards, but were spared the £500 as Avery himself was never apprehended.[144]

Aside from its own direct efforts, officers and committees of the Company also began to discipline the resources of the English state, convincing its officials of their common cause.[145] Blackborne culled information out of correspondence from India, redacted and repackaged it for the Privy Council and the Board of Trade.[146] The Company's solicitor was sent to consult with the Lords Justices "for the more effectuall prosecution of the said Pyrates," and many petitions on the subject followed.[147] Pardons to repentant crew were not uncommon in these situations but, while a source of seamen for the English navy, such a tactic did not serve the Company's purposes.[148] Several committees were assigned the task of lobbying the Admiralty to keep these to a minimum, or at the very least to bar pardoned mariners from the East Indies; when such a pardon was ultimately issued for the Atlantic in 1701, the Company had successfully had the East Indies excepted from it.[149] The committees also pressed for instructions to be sent to the governors in the West Indies to stop the pirates at their source; the king eventually issued letters to each of the American colonies.[150] One of the committees also began to communicate directly with Edward Randolph, the surveyor general of the customs in the American colonies.[151]

The Company's coup de grâce came toward the end of 1697, when Blackborne alerted the English Board of Trade that a pirate haven had been definitively discovered on a small island off Madagascar: a "Government of Robbers" with perhaps forty to fifty guns, fifteen hundred men, and seventeen ships, supplied from across New York, New England, and the West Indies, all under a pirate king named Baldridge who "has made himself the Head of a disorderly Rabble of Europeans, and of many Natives also."[152] The paradox alone—by definition, governments could not rob, and robbers could not govern—helped make the Company's case for assistance, as did its offer to help pay for royal squadrons to patrol the Indian seas and support the Indian Ocean convoys.[153] The Company also continued to forward digested intelligence on others, like James Gilliam and, perhaps most notoriously, William Kidd of New York. Kidd's public hanging at Execution Dock in 1701 was itself designed to make its case as much in India as England; among the spectators was a merchant from Surat brought to London so he could report back in India that pirates "will find here noe maner of Mercy, his Majesty being resolved totally to extirpate that Hellish Crew."[154]

Kidd represented the culmination of the Company's efforts not only to convince the English state that the Indian Ocean was infested with pirates, but that

these pirates found succor, shelter, and supplies from the English American colonies.[155] Making the "pirate" not just a threat to the Company's authority in
India but the Crown's in the Atlantic, the Court of Committees had stumbled
upon a critical argument for its power both as piracy fighter in India as well as a
counselor to the state and an intelligence entrepôt in England. If Parliament
in particular could not be persuaded that interlopers were criminals, surely
pirates—the enemies of all humanity—were unequivocally so. English state
authority over Atlantic trade, colonists, and (especially proprietary) colonial
officials had been an anxiety as much under William III as James II; the issue had
occasioned, for example, both the renewal of the Navigation Acts and the creation of the Board of Trade in 1696.[156] In the ways in which it was suborned by
local governments and communities, piracy represented a struggle between
local power and the authority claimed from London. If to the Company piracy
was a form of interloping, to Crown officials like Edward Randolph, it was a
version of corruption and customs evasion; it was no coincidence that his report
on Red Sea pirates in Carolina was included with a list of Scottish Pennsylva-
nians involved in smuggling tobacco.[157] Bombay seemed to perceive and play
upon this anxiety when, in a letter to the committees which was eventually
passed along to the Board of Trade, it likened the bribes pirates routinely offered
the governor of New York as akin to the much-maligned *peshkash* tributary payments so common in India.[158]

   The East India Company's complaints set in motion claims from a variety of
competing agents of the English state and empire abroad for expanded resources, jurisdiction, and power.[159] Randolph now pushed for an attorney general and Vice-Admiralty judge for each colony, increased naval patrols, the
direct appointment of colonial governors, and the annexation of proprietary
colonies.[160] The House of Lords began to consider a bill that would have forced
the surrender of all such charters to the Crown.[161] Customs commissioners
pressed for a colonial court of Exchequer.[162] The Royal African Company and
the governor of New York began to request men of war to patrol for pirates.[163]
The controversy even became a battleground in England between the civil and
common law, as its respective advocates debated which courts, and thus which
system of law, had jurisdiction over English pirates on the seas.[164] Ultimately,
the piracy issue offered a key opportunity for the Crown to claim much greater
control over the fragmented Atlantic empire. An act "for the more Easy Conviction of Traytors & Pirates" finally passed Parliament in 1700, affirming the jurisdiction of the Admiralty over piracy and authorizing trials and executions
abroad. By March 1701, New York's chief justice and attorney general were
given double-duty as Admiralty judge and advocate general, "with particular
regard to Pirates and Irregular Traders."[165] Not coincidentally, the envoy sent to
hand deliver the act and the 1701 pardon to each governor was also instructed

to undertake some surveillance and issue a report on the general state of the colonies.[166]

The East India Company had successfully attempted to discipline English state resources to its purposes by persuading many quarters of the English state that piracy was as real a threat to their proper authority as the committees believed interloping to be to theirs. In so doing, even as the Company faced increasing opposition in Parliament, it had found a way to assert its power and importance. It could press for closer control over the Thames, demanding inspection of eastward-bound interlopers, many now styled pirate-suppliers.[167] Using such a strategy was ultimately to wield a double-edged sword. Calling upon the Crown and Parliament for help meant compromising some of the Company's long-held autonomy from state oversight and even inviting them into a share of Asian governance, in the form of commissions and naval support; the Company even proposed a Vice-Admiralty for India to replace its largely defunct, ineffective, but independent Admiralty courts.[168] By the middle of 1698, the Company had persuaded the English Board of Trade and the Admiralty to send a squadron to the Indian Ocean to hunt pirates and "reduce" the pirate haven of St. Mary's.[169] It was a fairly desperate move that invited the English state, in the form of its growing naval power, into Asia. Some on the Board of Trade even entertained the possibility that the fleet's captain, Thomas Warren, might take the opportunity to evaluate the prospects of replacing the pirate kingdom at Madagascar with an English Crown colony.[170] Such a role for the English state in Asia would have been unthinkable just a decade earlier.

The piracy problem reflected a vibrant articulation of the issues with which the Company had been dealing for decades: maintaining the integrity and security of its settlements, particularly Bombay; the volatility of its unfortified stations within others' territory, like Surat; competition and rivalry with other Europeans in Asia; and the complex relationship among its English, Asian, and autonomous sources of jurisdiction and power. If fighting pirates ultimately buttressed such claims to authority in Asia, eliciting and mobilizing the English state in its service had potentially significant ramifications for its autonomy in Europe. This became particularly crucial, as the 1690s confronted the Company with a reinvigorated political assault from rivals in Britain. Interlopers in India—a group which now counted among its ranks John Vauxe, who had since been dismissed acrimoniously from Company service—even had begun to insist that largely because of the piracy, King William III had decreed that a new Company should take its place.[171] Company leadership in Asia vehemently denied these as baseless lies. Unfortunately for them, this time the rumors were not without merit.

"Auspicio Regis et Senatus Angliae"

Crisis and Response in Britain after 1688

On 28 May 1690, the ship *Benjamin* arrived in Bombay harbor bearing news. It appeared that the apparently pernicious and improbable rumors VOC officials had been circulating around India for some months—that King James II had been deposed and that the Dutch William of Orange and his wife, Mary, James's daughter, now occupied the English, Scottish, and Irish thrones—were in fact true.[1] On the surface, the "Glorious Revolution" of 1688–89 should have effected a sea change in the East India Company's affairs in Asia, bringing as it did both the end of a half-century of conflict in Europe with the Company's biggest European rival, the Dutch, and the start of a decade and in some ways a century of war with its newest rising competitor, the French. Were these simply national ventures, one would at the very least have expected détente between the English and Dutch companies and perhaps even a revival of projects, floated time and again from the 1610s to the 1680s, to "unite their power to our wealth."[2]

However, Company policy in Asia had never mapped neatly onto English foreign policy. While the 1690s brought war between the Dutch and French to Asia, for the English it seemed mainly to mean great shortages of its own shipping and soldiers from Europe.[3] The language of Anglo-Dutch Protestant brotherhood now had new purchase, but in Asia it seemed much less a New Testament Christian universalism than an Old Testament sibling rivalry. If a sermon preached in the wake of the Amboina massacre likened the English Company to Joseph betrayed and sold into slavery by his Protestant brothers, John Gayer now recalled a different sort of fraternal jealousy.[4] The VOC, he complained, "retaine their old Edomitish principles and rejoice to have Jacob laid so low as never to Rise again."[5] For their part, the Dutch did not seem to change tack; they even allegedly explained the revolution to some in Asia as a conquest, having made the king of England a vassal of the Netherlands and thus the

English Company subordinate to the VOC.[6] Thus, even in the heady days of 1689, the committees cautioned their subordinates to regard the Dutch as "an emulous and ambitious neighbour" who still aimed at nothing less than "dominion of all Seas."[7] A decade later, the political economist and Company advisor Charles Davenant warned "Whatsoever Nation can work England out of the Indies either by Craft or Power will give Us the Law at Sea, & we must Trade to most Parts of the World under their Banners & by their Permission. The Principall Rivalls in this fair Mistress are, the English and Dutch."[8]

While affairs in Asia continued apace, the Glorious Revolution did fundamentally transform the East India Company's position within British politics. The newfound pride of place for both the English and Scottish Parliaments signaled danger for a corporation that was constitutionally rooted in royal grants at home and prerogative abroad. The East India Company's attempts over the previous decade to curry favor with Stuart monarchs by displacing prominent Whigs from its ranks proved even more problematic than the relationship of many of its leadership (like Josiah Child) with the Republic had at the Restoration. Ideologically and rhetorically, Parliament had long figured as an outlet for dissent against monopolies and, now especially, against the monarchical power that theoretically constituted them. Unsurprisingly, old rivals appeared from every corner, while new ones emerged. What followed was what the early nineteenth-century Company historiographer John Bruce called a "warfare for rights," not just in England but in a pan-British context, the result of which was to erode the Company's constitutional autonomy and create the political possibility for its incorporation into the expanding British state and empire through the next century.[9]

This battle was doubtless in part fueled by a conflict over practical interests, which also hit upon long-standing disputes over the proper organization of trade and the nature of wealth.[10] Yet, as in the 1680s, there were multiple sides to the debate; the ideological dispute was neither clearly bipolar—say, between free traders and monopolists, or between royalist and liberal—nor was it confined to economic concerns alone. As a corporate, overseas body politic, the East India Company raised serious but familiar problems of sovereignty and empire for a rising Parliamentary state. The assault on the Company that followed through the 1690s was thus essentially a critique of the nature of its government, both in London and Asia. Its principal languages were the typically protean ones of absolutism and despotism, popery and arbitrary government, liberty and order. While the Company's advocates persisted in their belief in the importance and inviolability of its corporate power, its enemies branded it as a form of tyranny, situating their critiques within the familiar condemnations of both Stuart and Asiatic despotism. It also called upon long-standing criticism of its administration and its leadership, particularly Josiah Child, who as Macaulay later observed, was likened to every villain imaginable—Oliver Cromwell, Louis XIV, Goliath, Satan—and tarred as the "despot of Leadenhall Street."[11] In the process, these debates shaped both the historiographical reputation of the early Company as a creature of the Stuart regime as well as, in the long run, the very structure and nature of the British Empire in India.

Certainly, one political problem for the Company in the wake of James's ouster was the great support it had received from him.[12] James himself was invested in the Company, to the tune of £10,000 in stock, a fact that then and since seemed to be damning evidence of his close ties to the Company. Yet, while the Company's alliance with James II was indisputable, it was in itself no Jacobite nor was it, like the Royal African Company, institutionally tied to the Crown. In fact, £7,000 of James's stock had been given to him as a form of lobbying, in lieu of the much larger gift the Company had begun to offer Charles II in the early 1680s to solicit his support against interloping. Moreover, the Company was also equally committed to investing his successors similarly in their fate. Not only did the committees give William and Mary the same amount of stock in the Company; they gave them the very same stock. Though James was able to sell off his £3,000 personal share in the Company as he fled the realm, in 1691 the Court of Committees simply transferred the £7,000 from his account to the new monarchs.[13]

In the end, the problem for the Company was not its ties to any one monarch in particular, but its constitutional and institutional ties to monarchy in general. Parliament, eager in its own way to establish its authority with respect to the monarchy, became a natural venue in the years following 1688 for the Company's enemies to air their long-standing complaints.[14] A bevy of petitioners, the committees noted, "filled the ears of the house of Commons by scurrilous papers."[15] Petitions for redress covered a range of issues, from sailors' widows seeking compensation for their husbands' service in the war in Bengal to weavers, silk merchants, linen drapers, haberdashers, clothiers, druggists, upholsterers, calenderers, feltmakers, and hatters, all of whom believed their livelihoods had been irreparably damaged by the Company's trade.[16] Interlopers also saw present opportunity to press old cases. Thomas Skinner, who had been for almost half a century seeking restitution for a ship stopped in 1657, filed one such petition, as did Thomas Sandys.[17] State agencies also made new demands. The Treasury and Ordnance insisted the Company provide more saltpeter at lower prices, even below cost, while the customs commissioners issued a new requirement that the court of committees provide personal securities as collateral for payment, where the Company's seal had always sufficed.[18]

If there seemed to be a universal chorus against the Company in the 1690s, it was, as in earlier decades, sung in a range of disharmonious keys. Some clamored for a completely free trade and insisted the Revolution itself had made it legal to trade to the East Indies "till there was an Act of Parliament to the contrary."[19] For many others, the call for "free trade" was simply a demand to be able to buy shares in the Company.[20] Some lobbied for expanding its capital stock to new investment and thus potentially to new leadership. Others, like John Pollexfen, pushed for refashioning the East India Company as a regulated company.[21] There were also some, particularly disaffected, dismissed employees, whose opposition seemed more personal than practical or political, and that coterie of investors surrounding Thomas Papillon that had split from the Company a decade earlier, whom the committees regarded as "a combination of Interlopers, Malecontent quondam Committee men, and some Adventurers that have sold their stocks at high rates, & would fair come in again at low Rates, or procure a New Company that they might rule the Roast."[22]

Company leadership saw nothing particularly threatening or unique in all this. To them, it was simply history repeating: "A lightness and vanity which [interlopers] have always abounded in, especially upon every Change of the Government or lesser Changes of Ministers of State or favourites." History also showed there should be nothing to worry about: "their Boastings have alwayes come to nought, and so they will now, all Governments being wiser than to be swayed by such irregular disorderly vain men."[23] While the Company had long maintained that neither Parliament nor its statutes applied in its plantations, it had not been hostile to the idea of a Parliamentary foundation; the committees made periodic attempts, in 1661 and again in the 1680s, to lobby for a legislative confirmation of its charter, thinking it would underscore its battle against interlopers.[24]

In their confidence, however, they failed to appreciate the tectonic shifts in politics and political language that had occurred, not to mention the ways in which the Company's particularly aggressive behavior abroad in the previous decade could become a focal point for controversy. Politics in this new experimental regime were an open battleground, and the anxious aspirations of the new monarchs, the House of Commons, and a variety of state agencies and corporate communities to establish their authority at home and abroad gave a newly powerful voice to an old argument: namely, that the Company's constitution and actions threatened not just the trade but British (particularly Parliamentary) sovereignty over subjects abroad. Moreover, the 1690s offered novel material conditions for political debate, which meant that this war over the Company would be waged in an unprecedentedly concerted if diffuse battle in print, via petitions, pamphlets, books, and broadsides.[25]

All of this conspired to ensure that the opening blows against the Company would come as an attack on its politics. Even before the arrival in London in late 1689 of news of the invasion and occupation of Bombay "raised the Spirits & Wings of our old adversaries," those enemies had already begun their assault on two other, closely related issues: the war against Siam and the uses of martial law and capital punishment to suppress rebellion at St. Helena.[26] Siam was largely brought into English political discourse by the brothers Samuel and George White. Their particular complaint centered around the Bombay Admiralty Court's condemnation of Samuel's ship *Satisfaction* as "Goods of publique Enemies."[27] In this pursuit, however, the Whites argued far more broadly that the seizure had been unfounded because both the war and the Company itself were illegitimate. They insisted that John Child in particular had handled the war cruelly and ineptly in employing "so despicable a Force for so considerable an Attempt"—overlooking the fact that George was the one who had convinced the committees in the first place that they would need no more than one ship and fifty soldiers to prevail.[28] Samuel further indicted the Admiralty Court as an illegal institution, insisting that it had violated its charter because none of its judges were in his estimation "learned in the civil law." As far as he was concerned, the Company's entire government in the East was illegal and arbitrary, John Child specifically having declared "he has DESPOTICK POWER AND SOVEREIGN AUTHORITY *in his breast.*"[29]

The Company never denied that its power abroad was despotic, meaning not tyrannical but, in its early modern sense, the absolute power a monarch or a proprietor had over colonial possessions.[30] Francis Davenport, another former servant in Siam, insisted in the Company's defense that White was a deserter and a traitor, and the wars were both justified and necessary to defend the rights of the English in India. In fact, he argued, were it not for interlopers like White, who attacked the Company's reputation and credit and promoted defection and even rebellion among the English in India, war would not have been necessary.[31] George White, who took up his brother's mantle at his death in 1689, countered that it was the war, not his brother, that had ruined the English reputation in India. As evidence, he cited testimony he claimed to have received from a South Asian merchant, who, in "the *Banyan's* way of talking broken *English,*" insisted that:

> When Honor have her, *English-man* very Good-man have, buy Good, Pay Money; *Banian* put Life in *English-man* hand: Now this 'LENCY [i.e., "His Excellency," John Child] come, DEVIL *thing come,* buy Good, run away, no pay Money, then War make, take Ship, take Good, kill Man, Devil think this 'LENCY, this 'LENCY, DEVIL *thing have.*[32]

White's account further emphasized the tension in India between English sovereignty and the Company's claims to its political jurisdiction, juridical authority, and its rights to wage war, convene courts, and exercise government over English affairs. He insisted that an eminent lawyer had advised him that John Child was guilty of "little less than *High Treason*." He also observed that Davenport had referred to the Company's servants as the "Company's Subjects under the King, which is another *bold Stroke*," adding that he hoped "*True Sovereign Authority* shou'd be at length provok'd to Convince him of his *Error*.[33] Worse yet, the Company had insulted Parliament with its very arguments, employing the sort of "Sophistry as would be Ridiculous amongst *School-Boys*, framing Disguises for his *Evil Actions* by most *fallacious Arguments and Inferences*."[34] Though the Company claimed to serve the public, it was in fact both "the *Voice* of *private Interest*" and an arbitrary government that had been for a decade "made subservient to the boundless Ambition and Avarice of *One Aspiring Person*," that is, Josiah Child. The best evidence for this, he asserted unsurprisingly, was the war against Siam.[35]

Despite these efforts, the Commons neither intervened in the Whites' affairs nor took up the Siam issue directly, and by May 1690, George seems to have indicated some willingness to come to a private settlement with the Company.[36] It was another issue, one that White mentioned only in passing, that ultimately captured the Parliament's attention: the petitions and publications of a number of widows, mothers, and children of men punished or executed under martial law in the aftermath of the most recent rebellion at St. Helena.[37] As these allegations surfaced, the Court of Committees remained confident that the Commons understood how crucial it was "to preserve the peace of Such remote places," but simply wanted to make its point that such a power had to come from Parliament rather than the Crown.[38] The Company's critics, however, again depicted the use of martial law and capital punishment as a conspiracy against both king and Parliament. Alluding once more to the offstage figure of Josiah Child, White insisted obliquely that St. Helena's Deputy Governor "had been order'd by SOME-BODY to begin the setting up a *New Sovereignty* there in the Name of the *Company*; telling the Inhabitants they were no more the *King's, but the Company's Subjects*."[39] This assertion of sovereignty over English subjects seemed to have far more rhetorical power than alleged atrocities against the Siamese or Bengalis. On the back of the various accusations and petitions it received, in June 1689 the House voted 159 to 138 to exempt anyone who procured or executed the commission for martial law at St. Helena from the Bill of Indemnity, thus keeping alive the possibility of prosecuting them for political crimes later.[40] In November that same year the Parliament convened its first ever committee of inquiry into the East India Company, with the St. Helena issue front and center.[41]

The Court of Committees remained sanguine, if a bit incredulous. On advice of counsel, the governor and deputy governor refused the committee's request for the commission for exercising martial law as well as to answer any questions about it; when they did produce documentation months later, it was a packet of prepared and selectively edited documents.[42] The governor, Benjamin Bathurst, also introduced a bold response to the General Court of stockholders, which approved it unanimously. The petition defended the administration abroad, recalling that "according to the ancient usage of their Predecessors," the Company had been empowered to "manage their trade & establish & govern Colonies Forts & Garrisons of their property within the Limits of their respective Charters . . . & never found cause to doubt of their proceedings therein till they apprehended the Sens of this honorable house to be otherwayes."[43] The Company's defenders also continued to maintain that colonies abroad, even if under the king's direct control, were not properly part of England, its statute or common law, any more than English law became Norman law with the conquests of William I or Dutch with those of William III.[44]

A new Parliament was called in February, which gave the committees confidence that they had "great reason to hope we may live to See this Company better settled by Law as well as by arms and fortifications than ever it was in any former age."[45] They were confident it would confirm its charter, as it had done for the Hudson's Bay Company and seemed ready to do for the Royal African Company.[46] This was not to be the case. A year later, that group of interlopers and former Company committees and servants had begun to meet formally about strategies to solicit Parliament for a "new nationall joynt stock." Citing the "manifold abuses and unlawful Practices of the present *East*-India *Company*, both at home and abroad," they drafted their first petition to the Commons on 23 October, and it was introduced five days later.[47] The day after, the Commons resolved that a new exclusive joint-stock trade to the East Indies should "be established by Act of Parliament."[48] In November it issued a list of complaints against the Company, built on the testimony of a parade of familiar witnesses, including the interlopers Thomas Pitt and Jeremy Bonnell, the dismissed Admiralty judge John St. John, and, of course, George White. They offered testimony on subjects ranging from the debts the Company had contracted in India to its wars with the Mughal Empire. Several witnesses accused the Company of abusing its power, especially toward its South Asian allies and subjects. Among the most damning evidence were letters John Vauxe had sent to his brother and his father after having been taken captive at Surat, which painted an extremely dim picture of the Sidi's invasion of Bombay. Vauxe was summarily dismissed from service, not only for the tenor of his letters but for having sent them back outside the Company's approved system of correspondence in the first place (For his part, Vauxe flippantly dismissed his dismissal, imagining the committees were simply "angery with me for writing to my friends"; while he claimed not to remember what he had written, he was sure he meant no harm).[49]

In the end, the Company was subjected to range of remarkable but familiar accusations. It had borrowed money with no intent to repay. It pirated Mughal ships, disregarding even its own passes. It erected an "arbitrary Admiralty court" that illegally seized the property of English subjects. The execution of capital punishment at St. Helena was in fact "Murther." It had prosecuted an "unwarrantable war" in which:

"1. Many outrages and Violences were committed upon the Innocent Natives on Shoare
2. Many of them Killed
3. Their dwelling houses, warehouses & goods burnt & destroyed Their ships at Sea seized & made prize."

There were even charges made about the Company's "arbitrary" confiscation of lands from Bombay's Jesuits after the Sidi's invasion. At home, the chief committees and largest stockholders had become an oligarchy that mixed the worst characteristics of commercial excess and arbitrary government, "engross[ing] to themselves the Government as well as the Advantages of the trade." It was even alleged that its declaration of large dividend payments was "openly used as an Argument in their Committee . . . [as] the only way to keep them out of the Power of the Parliament."[50] On the strength of such evidence, in February the Commons formally requested the king dissolve the present East India Company in order to constitute the new one.[51]

All of the issues raised in Parliament were echoed in print, where the Company was pilloried as "the most wicked, tyrannical, and injurious Usurpations over other Men, and the greatest violations of the law of nature, than any other."[52] A number of writers, including White, popularized a particularly humiliating account of the Bombay war, which stressed the text of the *farman* that had ordered John Child posthumously expelled from India.[53] Some in London even echoed the slanders popular among interlopers in India that the Company had directly aided Avery, Kidd, and other Indian Ocean pirates; when the Company threatened legal action against one such author in 1698, he claimed he could not be guilty of libel as the Company's guilt "was the common discourse of the Coffee House."[54] In general, the message was that the Company's "constitution" was "calculated for the Advancement of *Arbitrary Power*," its leadership "a Particular Interest" not a "Publick" one, and commercial and municipal corporations by their very nature "oppressive Oligarchies."[55] Foreshadowing the critique of nabobs in the following century, its ill-begotten Asiatic riches also threatened the English constitution, being enough for "2 or 3 particular Men to make them as great as Dukes."[56]

For its part, the Company continued to defend its actions, insisting East India affairs had to be kept on "the Old Foundation," rights and privileges that were not only commensurate with all other European practice but, as had been argued in the *Sandys* trial, "refined to the present System by the wisdom of Severall Ages." (The chief justice's decision in that case was itself printed in 1689). Its wars had been just, lawful, and designed to "vindicate the *English Nation* from the insults and injuries of the *Indians*," which Company leadership insisted they had done successfully.[57] If anyone should be held accountable, they countered, it was the interlopers, who "were, really, the Original cause of the War."[58] The Company was simply a victim of the "violent prosecution" by Parliament and the "violent persecution of Interlopers and Others their Adherents," whose accusations were "as vile and odious as Malice itself can invent, or a Pen dipt in the very gall of Asps can depaint."[59]

Remarkably, by 1692 the committees remained confident that such arguments would prevail and that they would be a "Company hundreds of Years Or if any Change ever will be like the Change of the Moon, the same again little Alteration of the Persons or Conduct more than what happens by deaths or buying and Selling."[60] Josiah Child echoed these sentiments just a few months later, adding that all this clamor "will serve none of the ends of our furious brainsick adversarys."[61] Even if it came to a confirmation by Parliament, "all their huffing & struggling" would only entail some "triviall alterations" to the Company's affairs.[62] The first attempt at such alterations came in the form of thirty-two propositions from the Earl of Nottingham, one of the secretaries of state, in mid-1692. The proposals, however, were far from "triviall." Foremost among them was a doubling of the capital stock to allow for new subscriptions as well as greater limitations on the voting rights of large stockholders and their ability to split stocks—a clear attempt to placate those who wanted access to the East India trade as well as to dilute the power of the current leadership, essentially making a new East India Company without confronting the thorny constitutional, political, and practical issues having to withdraw the charter of the old one.

To the committees, these "remarkable" proposals reflected again the typical agitation of ungoverned interlopers, which it had come to regard as "a worse Kind of civil Broil" than either of its wars in India or Siam. The limitation on individual holdings was to them outrageous economic policy, since to restrict the flow of capital—which "is a free Agent, and must not be limited or bounded"—would be disastrous; not even the radical egalitarian Levellers, they insisted polemically, had ever proposed limiting personal estates in anything other than land. The core of their argument, however, rested in a full-throated defense of the Company's government. The committees dismissed outright the very premise that a small, committed, and experienced leadership amounted to oligarchy or arbitrary government. Governments and companies alike could function only under the supervision of a wise council, which in turn needed to be guided by strong leaders. "The Company, nor peradventure, any great

Business in the World," they argued, "did ever thrive where some or two Men or very few did not Arrive to soe much reputation (as Machiavell calls itt) as to be able to Moderate the Councells of the Commonwealth or Society." Such a change to the Company's constitution would furthermore be seen in India as a sign of weakness to be exploited by the Mughals. A clause forbidding the Company from licensing ships on private account was "unreasonable," since private and leased shipping was critical to the Company's naval power, had been indispensable in its wars, and was of great use "in settling of new Plantations, which the Company best know when and how to effect." A requirement that the Company's charter be limited to a twenty-one-year period struck at the heart of the very idea of a corporate body politic. It would be, they argued, "ridiculous all the World over" to expect someone to plant an orchard, build an estate, or found a city "upon such Terms," and it was "a most impolitick Notion, that any Company can thrive by frequent Change of Conduct and Council, any more than a Nation, by often changing the fundamental Laws." In this view, Company government was comparable to that of a manorial lord, a municipal corporation, and even a monarchy or republic. Yet, this was no mere analogy; the East India Company, they observed, was itself in the business of founding towns. They offered the example of Bengkulu, which had been founded a decade earlier though it would be decades "before it can be made a compleat, secure, (and morally speaking) an impregnable *Asylum* to the *English* Nation."[63]

All of these arguments stressed some recognizable points: the Company not only should be a government in Asia but it *was* one; it was best governed by a small council of committed and leadership wisely suspicious of the private interest of the multitude; its age and nature as a corporation, its experience, and its physical and diplomatic infrastructure in Asia essentially rendered it immortal and largely immune from regulation and supervision. Needless to say, the Privy Council found the Company's refusal to acquiesce to any of these "material Particulars" frustrating. In November 1692 the king sought a legal opinion on the extent of his power to dissolve the Company's charter, and discovered he could do so, on the condition he gave the Company three years' notice and did not charter anyone else "in the meantime." He returned to the Commons, essentially directing Parliament prepare an East India bill.[64] On 25 February 1693 the Commons resolved again to have the king give this notice and presented it formally to him a week later.[65]

The next month, this profound debate over the constitution of imperial sovereignty abroad was interrupted by a seemingly trivial mistake. The Company paid its taxes a day late. This technically violated the terms of its charter and rendered it forfeit. Neither of the committees' official explanations made much sense. Their claim that they had forgotten seemed implausible, and their insistence that the Exchequer was closed for a holiday turned out to be untrue (one member of the Commons evidently went to the trouble to check).[66] It was possible this was in fact a carefully calculated move. It was fairly common to contrive a forfeiture of a charter as a perfunctory aspect of being granted a new one upon change of regime; this was essentially what the Company had done at the Restoration, but without nearly as much drama.[67] Ironically, Parliament could not regulate or revoke a charter that did not exist. By forcing a new charter, the Company put the East India issue back entirely before the monarchs, where it had always been more comfortable, and issued a de facto ultimatum, in the implicit threat that the absence of any chartered East India Company would ruin both trade and government in Asia irreparably, as had in fact happened the last time the Company's exclusive rights were suspended under the Protectorate. Mary II appointed her chief lawyers to look into the matter and heard arguments from various merchants for and against reissuing the charter.[68]

In the end, the gambit worked. In October a new East India Company charter passed, which took note of the "Disorders and Inconveniencies which would befall the said Company and other Persons concerned and employed in their Trade and Adventures, especially in the Remote Parts of the World, if We should take Advantage of the Forfeiture." It recited the Company's previous charters dating back to Charles II and confirmed all of its previous rights and privileges. Importantly, it also formally rendered to legal oblivion the failure to pay the tax, eliminating any possible legal break in the Company's constitutional history.[69] There was, however, a catch. The charter was a hasty piece of work, but buried in it was a novel proviso requiring the Company to "submit and conform" to any regulations of its affairs the monarchs and the Privy Council "think fit to make, insert, limit, direct, appoint, or express" before the end of September 1694; failure to do so would render the charter void.[70] The very next month, such a "charter of regulations" was issued, ostensibly aimed at making the "Trade and Traffick to the *East-Indies* . . . more national, general and extensive than hitherto it hath been." The Company was compelled to increase its stock by £744,000 in new subscriptions, essentially what had been demanded in the original Nottingham proposals. The more stringent restrictions on stockholding and voting were absent, but the regulations did prohibit the issuing of private licenses to traders and required the Company to sell the Ordnance five hundred tons of saltpeter. Most importantly, the monarchs had capitulated to the demands of merchants and woolen manufacturers; the Company was now compelled to export £100,000 of English goods annually to the East Indies.[71]

For the first time, the Company's governance at home and abroad had been subjected to a formal institutionalized review by the Privy Council, and potentially the Parliament. This put new political pressures on it for greater transparency with the "public" in its affairs and made possible a potential overthrow of the current leadership by diluting their stock and thus voting power.[72] And there certainly was demand. When the Company opened its books to take in the new stock, it received subscriptions exceeding £1,219,000, forcing a refund of about 25 percent on each subscribed amount (Never failing to spin gold out of straw, the Court of Committees claimed to be pleased; after all, more stockholders pledged to the Company meant fewer interlopers).[73] The requirement to sell English woolens in India and Persia was imposed whether there was demand abroad, shipping, or even woolens available at home; the Company had to request an extension on its very first deadline, complaining that the textiles could not be dyed in the appropriate colors in the damp of London's winter.[74] The statutory obligation to import saltpeter imposed no like obligation on the Ordnance to buy or pay promptly. Higher taxes and restrictions on imports through newly promulgated sumptuary laws put more pressure on the Company's revenues. Still none of this satiated the popular odium incited by critics' continuing propaganda. The devastated public image of the Company combined with the depressed domestic weaving, linen, and dying industries to prompt a "rabble of Weavers" to besiege the East India House in protest on 21 January 1697.[75]

By now, this conflict had begun to take its toll in India, undermining the Company's reputation and emboldening interlopers and other rivals; after all, it was not very long ago that a "rabble" at Surat had surrounded the Company's factory there as well. The Bombay council marveled at "how farr the actions of some of that Cast in England have Contributed hereunto by declaiming against all acts of justice done in India against Malefactors, [styling] all in authority either Murtherers, or arbitrary."[76] The Nine Years' War in Europe severely limited available shipping and soldiers, which in turn undermined the Company's efforts to rebuild and defend Bombay as well as its anti-piracy convoys.[77] It had also made what shipping the Company could send extremely expensive. Insurance during wartime alone could amount to as much as 20 percent of the cargo's value; in 1691, the Company's freight charges had doubled from just a half-decade earlier.[78] Delays waiting for naval convoys or diverting ships for security via Ireland or Scotland added extra costs, and even with such precautions, several well-laden Company ships were lost to French privateers in March 1693, October 1694, and August and September 1695. All told, the Company reflected in 1698 that for the duration of the war, it had paid over £85,443 in taxes on its stock and almost £295,030 that year alone in customs, without being able to pay out any dividends. It lost twelve ships and took out loans in the form of bonds from its own stockholders just to stay liquid. In short, the committees insisted to the Commons that their rivals had it backwards: the state was benefiting from the trade, but the Company was not.[79]

The Company had also become far more reliant on that state. It was forced continually to solicit the Admiralty for permissions to sail and for convoys for ships that sailed home from India via the Caribbean.[80] Company sailors were impressed in England, Atlantic ports, or even neutral outposts en route to India, like the Dutch Cape of Good Hope; each occasion sent the committees before the Admiralty and Privy Council to plea for safeguards for its seamen, and the situation became so bad that the Company inserted a penalty into its charter-party contracts of £10 per ton for any Company ship that stopped at Barbados on its homeward journey.[81] Even potential Company vessels were not safe. One "great new ship" building at Blackwall, which had already been partly rigged and which was designed to carry a large shipment of broadcloth that had already been baled, was bought out from under the Company by the Crown.[82] Further-more, a wartime prohibition on the export of bullion in 1695 led to greater com-petition for silver with the newly created Bank of England, forcing the Company to purchase more specie on the Continent, which was both expensive and sub-jected its activities to the review of yet another English state agency: the Council (soon after Board) of Trade.[83]

As if all of this were not bad enough, the House of Commons had not given up its assault. Two significant interventions followed. The first came in a lengthy dispute over the legality of a Company seizure of an interloper. Unlike *Sandys*, this case was tried not in the Court of King's Bench but before Parliament, and its verdict in January 1694 reversed the core principle of that earlier decision. The Company and the judges in *Sandys* had maintained that the Asian seas were closed to English subjects until opened by the king or the Company. In finding for the interloper, the Commons now explicitly declared that by law the East India trade was open to all English subjects unless specifically prohibited by Par-liament.[84] The second crisis followed soon after. The Company, along with other bodies including the corporation of London, found itself under investigation for rumors of extraordinary sums of "special service money" spent in securing its new charter—£170,000 in 1693 alone—as well as offers to lend members of the Commons money to buy stock in the Company and even to buy it back if they were not satisfied with the returns.[85] Insisting "an universal corruption had over-spread the nation; that court, camp, city, nay and the Parliament it self were infected," nine House members convened as a committee of inquiry, charged with inspecting the Company's books and investigating allegations of bribery.[86]

Many, at the time and since, have taken for granted that the Commons inves-tigation indeed "revealed practices . . . which were rightly regarded as objection-able if not fraudulent."[87] Yet, "corruption" here was not a self-evident crime but a political and ideological position. For Company critics, that it had to resort to "secret" money only confirmed that the Company had no reasonable or lawful public claim to maintain its charter and powers.[88] The scandal also underscored accusations of Company despotism, recalling not only the Stuarts but tropes of Asiatic luxury and corruption of the sort that brought down Sparta and Rome.[89] At stake here was also an attempt by the Commons to discipline its own members' loyalty and to assert the primacy of their allegiance to Parliament over other corporate and political communities in the realm. Five of the committees implicated were members of the Commons and the controversy ultimately brought down the Speaker.[90] One of these members, the Company's deputy governor Sir Thomas Cooke, had been serving as governor when the alleged "bribes" were distributed. He was confined for a time to the Tower of London, through what Cooke called the "very new and extraordinary measure" of a House bill compelling him to reveal what Company monies were disbursed on the account, without offering him the opportunity to defend himself.[91] After some wrangling, he was promised indemnity from criminal prosecution if he would provide the requested information.[92] Cooke admitted disbursing over £67,000 to several leading members of the Company and about £90,000 in stock, in pursuit of confirmation of the Company's charter.[93]

For its part, the Court of Committees failed to see what was so shameful or clandestine about their actions. It was hardly uncommon for merchants or corporations to spend private money in the pursuit of charters, access, and privileges, and to avoid costlier public legal proceedings; the VOC made similar presents, as did other English overseas companies, like the Hudson's Bay Company.[94] Tribute, loans, and presents were certainly the Company's stock-in-trade. Between 1660 and 1684, it had made over £324,000 in "gifts" and "loans" to Charles II, including 10,000 ounces of silver plate at the Restoration intended to persuade Charles II to favor the Company at his accession and to overlook the relationship it had developed with the late Commonwealth. The Company also maintained an extensive tipping regime, routinely offering gratuities in cash and kind to courtiers, customs and post officials, dockworkers, authors, informers, and many, many others on whom it relied for its smooth operation.[95] Tea, for example, found its way directly into England at first only in fairly small quantities as "presents . . . to our great friends at Court."[96]

Furthermore, if the committees had regarded this money as particularly secret, they did a terrible job of hiding it. Expenses "in their Affairs towards granting a new Charter" were openly discussed in court minutes in 1693, which recorded the governor's reimbursement for such expenditures and "Thanks for his great care pains and trouble in their Service."[97] The largest of Cooke's cash disbursements was £10,000 given to Francis Tysson, which Cooke testified was intended as the "Customary Present" to the monarch, which the committees had evidently decided to offer again in cash to William and Mary in 1692.[98] Another £10,000 went to Richard Acton to defray what the Company considered to be lobbying expenses.[99] Even the Commons could not in the end find a crime that had been committed. But times clearly had changed. When one member of the House asked rhetorically "By what law it was a crime to take money at Court?" he was told not only that it was against the law of God but "if there was not a law, it was time there should be a law to prevent it . . . and that there were Parliaments to punish such crimes." On 2 May 1694 the Commons finally made it its law.[100]

Though dodging this bullet, the Court of Committees now recognized there would be no settling their affairs without placating the Commons. Charles Nowes, the Company's solicitor, began to spend a great deal of time at the Commons and even at the homes of several of its members, for which he was offered a bonus in excess of £300 over his annual retainer of £50.[101] One committee, Nathaniel Tenche, even insisted somewhat implausibly that the Company had always preferred a Parliamentary settlement but that "the temper of the Princes of the last two Reigns, how tender they were upon all the points of their Prerogative" made doing so "next door to an impossibility."[102] By March 1697 it appeared a compromise was reached. For a loan of £400,000, Parliament would confirm the Company's charter. The Court of Committees announced itself begrudgingly "Satisfyed" with this solution to its "Severe troubles & Suffereings."[103] Yet, before the ink had dried, the Company's rivals had redoubled their efforts. Even though the Court of Committees defensively almost doubled its offer, those former Company committees, servants, and interlopers who in 1691 had resolved to pursue a new East India Company staged a staggering counteroffer: a loan of £2 million, though at double the interest.[104] Before the month was out, the Commons had authorized, by a vote of 126 to 99, the creation of a General Society of investors to take in subscriptions.[105]

The Company appointed a super council of fifty-two people to advise with its lawyers as to proper next steps.[106] The General Court resolved to try to raise its own £2 million by devaluing current stock, taking in more subscriptions, and raising a £200,000 down payment out of voluntary contributions from current stockholders.[107] The Court of Committees was bewildered, however, when the Commons rejected this proposal, protesting that the Company that already existed should at the very least be allowed the opportunity for a fair counterbid as "has been the common practice, in farms, bargains, and offers of the like nature."[108] Seeking "remedy" from the House of Lords proved futile.[109] In July, an act "to authorize & appoint any number of persons to take & receive all such voluntary subscriptions . . . by or for any person or persons, Natives or Foreigners, Bodies Politick or Corporate" passed, and the king sent formal notice that the "old" Company was to cease within in three years.[110]

The £2 Million Act, as it was colloquially known, essentially paved the way for the creation of another overseas trading company to traffic in the East Indies. As an Act of Parliament, rather than a royal charter, it was unprecedented.[111] Though calling itself the Governor and Company of Merchants of *England*, rather than "London," to stress its more "national" foundations, subscriptions poured in predictably mostly from London: £10,000 from William III himself and more than £2,000 from former committees like Thomas Papillon, a former governor of

Madras, Streynsham Master, and former Company servants-turned-interlopers like Edward Littleton and George White, who had in the meantime already made another private voyage to Surat. Master and Papillon's houses were proposed as possible initial meeting places for the new Company.[112]

Yet again, the "old" Company's committees remained unfazed and obstinately optimistic. To them this was simply

> a tryall of Skill, you may call it, if you please a civill Battle between Us and the New company, and two or three years strife must end the Controversy, for the Old or the New must give way. Our Joynts are too stiff to yield to our Juniours. We are Veterane Souldiers in this Warfare, and if our Servants abroad in other Places do their parts as well . . . We don't doubt of the Victory.[113]

They solicited Parliament for a license to continue as a corporate body, with or without the exclusive trade, beyond the three years. Then, the committee of fifty-two was empowered to subscribe £315,000 to the new fund, making it the largest single stockholder in its rival. This meant that the old Company could not be abolished because its more than 1,200 stockholders now had a property right in the new Company, which could be secured only if the old Company continued as a corporate body.[114] The new Company's directors clearly took the move as a serious threat and petitioned the Commons against it.[115] This was, on the one hand, a stroke of strategic genius.[116] On the other, the fact that the old Company had to resort to such a tactic was indicative of a desperation and revealed just how far and quickly it had allowed its constitutional foundations to erode.

Still, it was not the only argument at the committees' disposal. Drawing on its composite constitution, the Company now argued that to dissolve its charter would be to also divest the Company of its other "possessions": the "perpetual inheritance" of St. Helena and Bombay from the king; Madras, Fort St. David, Bengkulu, Anjengo, and Calcutta held on "purchase and Grants, from Indian Princes, and Others"; and the grant in perpetuity of customs from the port of Gombroone. These "Grants Phirmaunds and mutuall Stipulations," the Company insisted, were "not onely beyond any other Nations trading thither but even beyond the Natives themselves," but brought revenues "which arise from Customes, Rents, Quitt Rents, & Ground Rents, Farms and Other Incomes," estimated at over £40,000 per year.[117] To divest the Company of its English charter was furthermore to jeopardize the "100,000 Inhabitants in India [who] pay them rent" as well as all the grants made by Asian powers to the English, "by which they meane the Company for they know no other English Nation."[118] In March 1700, the Court of Committees sent a letter to the king, indicating that there was no "prospect of securing their Estates, or preserving to England, the great benefit of their Priviledges, Possessions, and Revenues, in India" if they were not to be "continued a Corporation," adding that the Company "in their Publick, as Private Capacityes" had suffered great losses during the war assisting the king and the nation. Only once "they shall have a Legall Existence" could the Company "be ready, to enter into any Treaty, which his Majesty in his Royall Wisdom shall think to be for the Good of the Kingdom."[119]

The "new" Company proprietors did not counter this argument so much as ridicule it. "The two Chief forts are Bombay and Fort St. George," they responded, "the one they have from the Crown and the other by Lease from the King of Golcandah [sic]; the first is a good Harbour the other a Wild open Road, Neither of them Well seated for Trade. The Revennue are noe other than what they Extort from the poor Inhabitants, yet all will not by far maintain the Charge of them."[120] They also set about establishing their own factories in India and China, and sought royal commissions for its presidents as "Consuls for the English Nation," allegedly so they might better combat piracy.[121] This new Company also proposed a Royal Ambassador be sent to the Mughal court. The king agreed. Sir William Norris, knighted for the occasion, was commissioned on 1 January 1699 and set sail three weeks later, the first such envoy from England since James I and the Company had sent Thomas Roe to the court of Jehangir more than eight decades earlier.[122]

After remaining stalwart for so long, the prospect of a new Company and royal ambassador in India finally seemed to convince the committees that they were under dire threat. In a petition to the king, they again stressed the "divers Forts Lands Inheritances Revenues Phirmaunds Grants & priviledges acquired & purchased in [Asia]." They appended a list of all of their *farmans* to illustrate the point.[123] Both companies requested pirate commissions for their officials in India.[124] In the summer of 1697, the committees also hastily attempted to organize an embassy of their own. They selected none other than Charles Davenant, a leading member of Parliament, former Excise commissioner, prominent civil and common lawyer, one of England's leading economic theorists, and most recently a Company advocate lobbying against the £2 million act. Davenant, who despite his prominence was largely impoverished, accepted the post at the extraordinary salary of £1,500 up front plus £1,000 a year for three years, if "he shall so long live."[125] Perhaps owing to this ominous reminder of his mortality, Davenant suddenly withdrew just as all preparations were in place in May 1700, and no old Company embassy ever sailed.[126] He did, however, continue to serve the Company's affairs with his pen, remaining a key figure in ongoing negotiations between the two Companies. Davenant fully recognized that "if a Company be Erected by Authority of Parliament it will become a part of the State." However, this was absolutely necessary to give the Company "a better figure a broad & be able to Contend with our Rivalls the Dutch & Enable Us to Defeat the Scotch Act."[127]

The "Scotch Act" to which Davenant referred was the final piece of this puzzle, one that revealed the extent to which the political dislocations of the Glorious Revolution had ensured that the East India issue would become not just an English but a British problem. Scotland and England shared a sovereign, as they had since 1603, but they were not one nation. The Glorious Revolution had perhaps emboldened the Scottish Parliament even more than its English counterpart to establish its power with respect to the royal prerogative, as its anxieties were compounded by efforts to assert its independence from its wealthier southern neighbor and the ambiguities of state and empire in a composite monarchy that had now clearly been brought to the fore.

One such effort was the 1693 Scottish Act for Foreign Trade and the subsequent 1695 Parliamentary act chartering a "Company of Scotland Trading to Africa and the Indies." The Scottish Company is perhaps best known for the spectacular failure of its one major colonial adventure, the "Darien" plantation of New Caledonia on the isthmus of Panama, and its role in shaping not only the impending Anglo-Scottish union but also Anglo-Spanish diplomacy and colonial policy in the Americas.[128] Yet, before this Company could become an Atlantic or a British issue, it was a "Scotch East India Company," and the 1695 act seen by many contemporaries as an "East India act."[129] Its earliest proposals for projects included a fort and factory in southwestern India, a would-be deal with a group of wealthy Armenian merchants to carry goods on freight to Surat, and an African colony near the Cape that would serve, like St. Helena, as a Scottish entrepôt between East and West.[130] The first voyage it considered, in December 1695, was to be to India.[131] Even the Panamanian plantation was designed not simply to bottleneck Spanish silver and insert Scotland in the European Atlantic but, like the canal that would follow centuries later, as base for a more efficient route to the East, which could undermine the English and Dutch and serve as a free port that could attract the world's commercial wealth.[132] It was, as its principal projector William Paterson famously remarked, to be Scotland's "Door of the Seas and the key of the universe [which] with any thing of a Reasonable management will of Course enable its proprietors to give Laws to both Oceans."[133]

An odd coalition emerged in opposition to these Scottish efforts, which ultimately included both English Companies, the Royal African Company, the Hamburgh Company, and Jamaican proprietors, each pressing English politicians for outcomes that would enhance its particular agenda and needs.[134] The "old" East India Company, which had often made claims over Scottish and Irish subjects in Asia, regarded this Company (like its "new" English rivals) as another interloper. The Court of Committees even added a special oath for its stockholders, specifically forbidding investment in the Scottish venture.[135] In January 1696, it pressed the king to stop the ship *Antelope* in the Thames, insisting it was "as an Interloper in the Service of the Scotch East India Company," even though no one was certain who its proprietor was and the Scottish Company's subscription books did not open for another month.[136]

Despite its own troubles, the Company also approached the English Parliament, where it found a favorable hearing.[137] The House of Lords petitioned William III on the issue, who famously declared that he had been "ill-served in Scotland."[138] The Commons opened a committee of inquiry into the Scottish "East India Company" affairs in early 1696, ultimately indicting all of its directors and its secretary, Roderick Mackenzie, for the high crimes and misdemeanors of taking an *oath de fideli*, attempting to raise funds for an East India company within England, and for suppressing evidence. Mackenzie absconded safely to Scotland, prompting the English Privy Council to issue a warrant for his arrest. He later described the entire situation with "a Phrase, which I heard was once us'd by a certain Lady upon another Occasion: *That it was a hard thing to be call'd a Wh[or]e, and yet to have none of the pleasure.*"[139] Out of options in London, the Scottish Company directors turned to the Continent.[140] There, however, the Company had enlisted the help of the VOC in Amsterdam and Paul Rycaut, the English resident at Hamburg, to shut down their efforts.[141] At this point, the only capital the Scottish Company could legitimately raise was to be found Scotland; this in turn radicalized the rhetoric surrounding the project, now tied to a more chauvinistic nationalism fueled by "the unaccountable evil Treatments of our said Neighbours."[142]

For the committees, there could be no better evidence than "the Scotch Act" of the need for a Parliamentary act settling the question over their Company once and for all. As they had argued about the pirates, the Scottish Company had been the ill consequence of humoring interlopers; its global ambition only offered further evidence of the need for expanding the Company's powers.[143] Some Company critics predictably argued that the way to defeat the Scottish Company was again to remodel the English commerce to India as a regulated trade, which according to their economic logic would bring down the price of goods and kill the Scottish venture via the marketplace. Such arguments involved some very peculiar feats of logic, including in one case an odd analogy to a presumably fictional conversation with a Hindu merchant over the effects of vegetarianism on the price of chicken.[144] The conflict itself also arose from the inherent ambiguities of the British multiple monarchy at the dawn of a Parliamentary age. Both English Companies comprehended the Scottish venture not as another European competitor but as an interloping British subject. Meanwhile, the proprietors, investors, and politicians behind the Scottish Company had come, almost by necessity, to regard their Company almost exclusively as a national venture, designed specifically to compete with the English among others. This, ironically, served as an argument for allowing it to seek investment in London. As a published broadside asked rhetorically after London investment in the Company was shut down, "'Tis sufficiently known that the *English* are concern'd in the *Dutch-East-India*-Company, and the *Dutch* and *Scots* in the *English*; and why should it be esteemed a Crime for the *English* to be concern'd in the *Scots*."[145] The tensions reached a fever pitch in 1704, when the Scottish Company retaliated for seizures of its ships in London by arresting a new Company ship, the *Worcester*, in Leith Harbor, while it waited for a convoy to London. Its captain, Thomas Green, was charged with violations of "the Law of Nations and . . . the municipal law of both kingdoms," for allegedly possessing a counterfeit Scottish Company seal, selling East India goods in Scotland, and of having been a pirate. Green and a few others were convicted in a Scottish court and executed, in what many considered to be a politicized exercise in judicial murder.[146]

Alternatively operatic and comedic, the crisis that had emerged among the three British East India Companies laid bare the serious and complicated issues about the nature of politics, authority, and sovereignty at the heart of East India affairs and colonial ventures more generally that had been forced by the Glorious Revolution. The Scottish Company clearly regarded an affront from the English no differently than that of any realm in amity with the Crown; that England and Scotland shared a king was in this sense immaterial. In his defense, Green stressed that the means of reprisal under the law of nations in such a situation fell to the Sovereign, not a Company; exercising of such authority, in turn, would be tantamount to *imperium in imperio*, and therefore impossible and illegal.[147] The Scottish Company, and ultimately the judge of the Scottish High Court of Admiralty, disagreed. Company directors maintained it did not need to convict Green of piracy to take reprisal on him and his ship, but had such a right *prima facie* through the expansive corporate powers found in its Parliamentary charter, which like its "old" English neighbor, derived from the need "by force of arms to defend their Trade and Navigation, Collonies, Cities, Towns, Forts and Plantations, and other their effects whatsoever; as also to make Reprisals, and to seek and take reparation of Damage done by Sea, or by Land."[148] Although it might be customary to receive letters of marque from the monarch, the 1695 act had made such a request superfluous.[149] In essence, the Scottish Company maintained that its Parliamentary charter and its existence as a corporation rendered it irrelevant that its reprisals were taken against subjects of England or that they shared a monarch. Moreover, the behavior of the English toward the Scottish Company had justified such actions. As one of its lawyers insisted, "the iniquity committed in England by the influence of such a Powerfull Society as is the East India Company will appear as palpable as it is evident that the Thames is on this side the Cape of Good Hope or that a Scots Act of Parliament cannot be reversed in England." It was an "unjustice . . . so manifest" that "nothing but Machiavell or Hobe's principles . . . can give any countenance to it."[150]

Back in London, the Scottish controversy had highlighted the absurdity of coincident English Companies. As early as the autumn of 1698, Thomas

Papillon initiated discussions about a union between the two; by the opening months of 1699 both had appointed designates with power to "treat" with one another for some kind of accommodation, which may have been what really arrested the Davenant embassy.[151] Almost everyone seemed to agree that "The East India Company in any Nation can be but one Body Politick Two or more are like two Earthen Vessells, if they knock they Break." As the committees informed Madras, "it seems to us their Principall Relyance is upon a new fashion'd word now in Vogue in all publick Places, They call it Coalition, by which We think They mean that our Stock should be joyned to theirs."[152] After significant delays and prevarications, by early 1700 William III offered to arbitrate a treaty between them.[153] Following William's death, negotiations continued under his successor Anne. In 1702 the old Company agreed to surrender its charter to the Crown, beginning a process that resulted first in the creation of a joint interim Court of Managers and then, finally, a single, joint Company in 1709, implemented in a tripartite agreement between both companies and the Crown, and an instrument known as Godolphin's Award, after the Lord High Treasurer who coordinated the affair.[154] While some Scottish directors continued to hold out hope their Company would ultimately be absorbed into this new one, the English companies would hear nothing of it.[155] The Company of Scotland was instead a casualty of another impending union, dissolved in article fifteen of the Anglo-Scottish treaties of 1706 and 1707 that created Great Britain.

The conflict between "old" and "new" Companies had been, in Macaulay's words, "as serious an impediment to the course of true love in London as the feud of the Capulets and Montagues had been at Verona."[156] And, in the end, there was a plague upon both their houses. The "new" Company's projectors had essentially followed a strategy that had become common in other forms of corporation, inviting in the Crown, and in the 1690s Parliament, as a tool to try to gain advantage over one's rivals and even reform corporations in the hands of new government. In so doing, however, they unwittingly suborned growing claims to power of the English, soon British, state.[157] The new Company made very little effort to distance itself from the authority of Crown and Parliament, allowing, even seeking, novel regulations on its domestic and foreign affairs, the presence of royally credentialed officials in India, and the requirement that the bishop of London approve all of their future chaplains abroad.[158] In this context, the debate over which offered the most "national" trade diminished significantly the premise reflected in *Sandys* that the Company might have represented and served the English nation but it was not an extension of its state.[159] In the course of debate, the old Company had given ground on this previously nonnegotiable point, by drawing in the state to help battle the pirates and the Scots and by increasingly articulating its exclusive privilege in terms of property right as much as a fundamental charge of government.

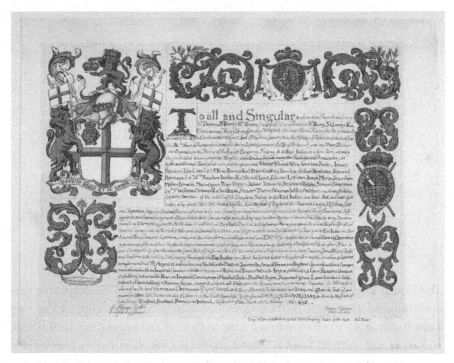

Grant of Arms to "new" East India Company, 1698. © The British Library Board, Asia, Pacific, and Africa Collections, WD 2901.

The politics of the 1690s and especially the £2 million act effectively allowed both the Crown and the English House of Commons to establish limited precedent for overseeing and regulating English overseas activity in Asia. Others attempted to take advantage as well; the corporation of London, for instance, attempted unsuccessfully to have the charter for the new United Company require its directors be freemen of the city.[160] There were now new strictures on the taking and giving of gifts, which even new Company directors seemed to believe were impossible to follow in Asia or England.[161] Godolphin's Award permanently grafted the Company's capital stock into the national debt, literally making it, as Davenant had predicted, a part of the state.[162] The United Company's charter was now limited to eighteen years, making it inevitable that the charter would be periodically reviewed.[163] It also got a new flag—the Union Jack replaced the Cross of St. George in the canton—and a new coat of arms and motto, modeled on the armorial grants given the new Company in 1698. Where the old Company's *"deo ducente nil nocet"* invoked the authority and protection of God, this new one acknowledged more worldly guardians. The United Company was now *"auspicio regis et senatus angliae"*—that is, under the command and protection of the monarch and Parliament of England.

"The Day of Small Things"

Civic Governance in the New Century

The United English East India Company that emerged in 1709, despite its new constitutional footing in Britain, would ultimately have to confront the very same issues in Asia as its forebears: how to defend and expand the jurisdiction and authority derived from a mixed corporate constitution; encourage the population, prosperity, and power of its settlements; and increase its revenue in support of a self-sustaining political system in Asia. First, however, there was the no small matter of uniting these two Companies, and if the conflict between the two in London reminded Macaulay of *Romeo and Juliet*, the struggle that ensued in India seemed more like something out of *Richard III*.

Ironically, when the Admiralty-appointed, pirate-hunting squadron for which the old Company had lobbied so strenuously finally arrived at Surat in 1699, it came carrying Ambassador William Norris, the presidents for the new Company's three planned factories in India, and their entourages. Norris and the other new Company officials immediately sought to assert their authority over all the English in India, as the old Company's factors at Surat put it, by any means "that they could invent with the assistance of hell."[1] "Whether projected from Wanstead, Leadenhall Street, Over the Channell, or evilly agitated by unthinking Fools," the new Company's representatives regarded the "undigested politicks of the Old Companys factors" with a virulent contempt reminiscent of the language of interlopers, indicting them of offenses ranging from private interest and corruption to apostasy, Jacobitism and treason.[2] To many in the old Company's leadership, such language only confirmed that the ambassador and others were simply pompous interlopers. In a somewhat literal sense, they had a point. Edward Littleton, the president and consul destined for the new factory at Hugli in Bengal, was the same Edward Littleton who a decade earlier had been recalled from India in an arrest warrant from Charles II. John Pitt, the consul for southeastern India, was another dismissed factor, as well as the cousin of the infamous interloper Thomas Pitt, who ironically had reconciled with the old Company and was now governor of Madras. The man sent to head the new factory at Surat, Nicholas Waite, was a former Company factor at Banten and, according to John Gayer, a "great man Sunk with his Overtburthen of powers," a "goatish monster" who, among other sins, was said to be engaged in a bigamous relationship with a woman he called he suspiciously referred to as his niece.[3]

In one sense, Norris's mission reflected the fundamentally different relationship between corporation and state the new Company had introduced. Norris was the first royally credentialed English ambassador in almost a century, accompanied by the three new Company chiefs bearing royal consular commissions. The old Company's advocates had insisted that diplomacy in the East Indies was categorically different from that conducted by the Crown or other English overseas companies and proprietors, especially the Levant Company. Norris instead was specifically instructed to model his efforts on agreements between England and the Ottoman empire. He even carried with him copies of those treaties as models.[4]

However different its relationship with English authorities, in India the new Company's representatives expressed their claims to this power in strikingly similar terms to their rivals, fighting battles over some very familiar issues. Upon arriving at Masulipatnam, John Pitt began minting a series of low-value coins, bearing the new Company's balemark. He also refused to salute or acknowledge as legitimate the royal standard flying on Fort St. George.[5] Littleton declared the old Company's shipping passes in Bengal invalid and began to issue new ones in the name of William III, not "merely for the fees Sake" but since "it will be expected that such Vessells belonging to the English and receiving passes from us be under our protection and Jurisdiction and not that of the Enemy."[6] Waite demanded that he be allowed to have trumpets and that the *mutasaddi* should compel the old Company to strike its flag as he passed.[7] He also ordered John Gayer to stop issuing passes and administering justice at Bombay, claiming his status as "Publick Minister & Consull Generall" gave him sole authority to do both.[8] Most important to Norris, Waite, and Littleton (who mounted his own legation to the *nawab* of Bengal) was acquiring a *farman* confirming their Company's rights throughout Mughal India. They insisted it had been the new Company that had secured Warren's pirate-hunting squadron, and Waite promised the *mutasaddi*, Dianat Khan, even more ships from England to hunt pirates and an extraordinarily large *peshkash* if he would only eject the old Company from Surat and facilitate an agreement. Waite even allegedly produced a Persian "translation" of the £2 million act that cited the old Company's complicity in the piracies as cause for their dissolution.[9]

Like their superiors in London, this "old" Company in India had not yet given up the fight.[10] Thomas Pitt warned his cousin John not to come to Madras with drums, flags, or trumpets, "for there shall be but one Governor whilst I am here." He snidely proposed that his cousin take up "reading and practiseing" a number of Aesop's fables, including the "fable of the Froggs," in which an ungoverned community of frogs request a king from Jupiter only to reject a series of mild governments until they end up under the tyranny of a stork or a crane. In its appended "Reflexion," the recent, popular version by the Tory royalist Roger L'Estrange had taken the fable to reinforce the divine right of kings but also to warn of the "madness" of fecklessly rejecting proper government. Thomas wrote John that he hoped "the morall and reflexion will make Such impression on you Soe as to prevent your having the fate of the frogs," who in most versions are devoured by their avian overlord.[11] Meanwhile, on the other side of India, Gayer rejected Waite's claims that his status as consul gave him any authority over the old Company's servants, Bombay, or its inhabitants. The Surat council staunchly dismissed his demands that it strike the flag on the warehouse, notably justifying their refusal by virtue of "our indubitable rights and priviledges by the Divers phirmaunds of the present Mogul, as likewise by them of his Ancestors and predecessors . . . enjoyed time out of mind."[12]

There was no fundamental ideological rift in the old and new Companies' approach to authority and governance in India. Both were exclusive companies and both claimed to be the sole English government in India. The question was simply over which one should and could exercise that power. In any event, the point was soon moot. Having spent remarkable sums of money, Norris left India without any agreement, much less a *farman*, and died en route home. Soon after, in May 1704, a second royal pirate squadron, commanded by Captain Robert Harland, appeared at Surat bearing letters from the newly constituted Court of Managers, ordering their subordinates to "lay aside and utterly forgett those unhappy animosities which have been between them" and form one government in Asia.[13] The United Company's core presidencies would be at the old Company's centers of Bombay, Madras, and Calcutta, while it continued to support the other established settlements and pursue new projects. The new Company's directors also formally had their representatives' status as consuls revoked.[14]

To proclaim a union was one thing, to implement it was another. Even the debates among the managers in London as to how to coordinate it had, according to one observer, occasioned "such plots and warm debates . . . that has brought them almost to daggers drawing."[15] Predictably, the union was most problematic at Bombay and Surat, where tensions and tempers had run hottest. Here, the two Companies' councils were to be merged, John Gayer appointed as general and governor of Bombay, Nicholas Waite subordinate to him as the president of Surat, and from there on down the line, alternating old and new

Company factors through the hierarchy.[16] There remained a problem, however. A couple of years earlier, Gayer himself had gone to Surat in an attempt to counter Waite's agitations and settle a new broil that had arisen on account of the seizure of a Surat merchant's ship by pirates while under English convoy. Gayer, like John Vauxe before him, had been seized upon his landing; though releasing him to the factory, the *mutasaddi* refused to allow him to leave the town. Aware of this, the managers had preemptively specified that if Gayer were not free within three months, Waite would assume his post. If they both remained at Surat, the post would fall to John Burniston, Bombay's deputy governor.

Burniston wrote to the *mutasaddi* and to Abd al-Ghafur to explain the situation and to lobby for Gayer's release.[17] On May 25 both Waite and Gayer agreed they would each send a representative to explain the arrangement, even though the new Company's *vakil*, or agent, had already gone to the *mutasaddi* to machinate against Gayer's release.[18] Gayer's two emissaries, William Mildmay and John Brangwin, reported that the two new Company representatives, Jeremy Bonnell and Edmund Crowe, had insinuated that Gayer was to be fired if he did not pay all the old Company's debts in three months, all the while brandishing copies of the new Company's seal and the tripartite indenture. In response to Gayer's ultimatum that he would suspend the pirate convoys unless given his freedom, Waite promised his own convoys as well as 500,000 rupees collateral if he would be allowed to go while Gayer and the others remained in the town.[19] Both sides began to intercept one another's correspondence and the old Company was convinced Waite had even ordered an assault on one of its messengers.[20] Meanwhile, a merchant named Mahmud Ali—possibly connected to Waite, but whose identity seemed to perplex even the Surat merchants like al-Ghafur—through his *vakil* at the Mughal Court, insisted the old Company had stolen ten million rupees from him, killed hajji en route to Mecca, and insulted "Persons of quality" by disrobing them. His connection to Waite seemed all the more likely as he also evidently encouraged the story the old Company had been dissolved for committing such "outrages." By late summer, Asad Khan had ordered the *mutasaddi* to keep Gayer in the city, while on 7 November 1704 Waite, after offering his security for convoys both to Mokha and the South Seas and a *peshkash* of 35,000 rupees, was allowed to go to Bombay, escorted by a guard of ten horsemen and twenty armed soldiers.[21]

Arriving at Bombay only to discover that Burniston had died a few days earlier, Waite claimed the posts of general, governor of Bombay, as well as president of Surat, and thus *ex officio* deputy governor of Bombay. Suddenly, the "goatish monster," who had spent the last five years cavorting with interlopers and attempting to have old Company officials arrested, imprisoned, or worse, had assumed almost complete authority over Company affairs in western Asia. On the morning of 20 November, a proclamation to this effect was issued at Bombay

"in the usual and Accustomed Places."[22] This hardly settled matters. Gayer continued to claim to be general, establishing a sort of shadow council-in-exile at Surat
and maintaining correspondence with Madras, Bengal, Persia, and Calicut; he
also continued to issue shipping passes.[23] John Brabourne refused a commission
as second at Bombay, citing his inability to serve under Waite; the following year
Thomas Pitt reported he had "hearde severall say that they had rather be a private
Centenell in Fort St. George then to serve as Second under Sr. Nicholas."[24]

Waite, however, now had a pulpit from which to preach. His criticism of Gayer
struck a number of familiar notes. He had been a bad governor, who attempted
to exercise "unlimitted power." Moreover, he "act[ed] with or without advise of
the apointed Councill" and dismissed those advisors "at pleasure," which
amounted to "an unintelligible management against the interest of all Comuni-
tys."[25] The Bombay council, largely purged of Gayer's allies, echoed these words,
almost verbatim. They blamed him for "Sleeping in his Watch," and of "mistaken
Polliticks" for having allowed himself to become the *mutasaddi's* hostage. His
failure to consult with his council and arbitrarily dismissing subordinates was
"repugnant to the Interest of every Comunity, clouding the Rationall part of
Man, precipitately seweing in very untoward darkness."[26] Waite prevented
Ephraim Bendall, the old Company factor who was next in line to head the factory at Surat, from taking his post because he was too driven by "private Interest,"
and soon suspended all correspondence with the Surat factory altogether, insisting it had become a "Corrupt perverse Councill."[27] Ironically, Waite also accused
Gayer and the others of corresponding with interlopers.[28]

Waite and his new council did not just speak like their predecessors but acted
like them as well. No sooner had this royal consul and "publick" minister taken
command at Bombay than he fell out with Robert Harland, the commander of
the royal fleet, over a variety of issues. Waite objected to Harland's threats to
seize Mughal shipping in reprisal for Gayer's continued confinement. The two
had disputes over allotments for Harland's victuals and his refusal to convoy
Company shipping to Anjengo to defend against a French fleet in the area. Harland also had impressed English sailors out of a Company ship that had been
patrolling the island's shores to protect fishing boats.[29]

Particulars aside, the core problem recalled what by now was a familiar
tension between royal and Company authority in India. Harland presumed to
have precedence at Bombay, since in his estimation his status as a Crown-
commissioned commodore trumped a "Government of this Island belonging to
a Company of Merchants."[30] His ships engaged in a halfhearted blockade of the
harbor and, under the cover of darkness, had another seven sailors impressed
from Bombay's hospital. He evidently also challenged Deputy Governor William Aislabie to a fight.[31] Warning him "not to concern himself in these Affairs
out of his Sphere," Waite countered that Harland had no more rights on the

island than would be extended to any English subject, "this Castle and Island being out of her Majesties aboundant Grace & free will, transferred under certain Limittations by her Royal Charter under the great seale of England." The council objected particularly to his impressing its inhabitants as leading to the "weakening this Depopulated Island or bringing the Government *as he calls it* belonging to a Company of Merchants to reproach among the severall Princes round."[32] Waite issued a new shipping pass, which specifically required any English subject "whether Commanding any Ships of her Royall Navy or others in Service of said Company" to obey them.[33] The Bombay government then posted soldiers along the shore to guard against his taking anyone else off the island. Harland, the Bombay council suggested with exasperation to its superiors in London, "does you more Prejudice then Service against the Pirates."[34]

Despite the drama, the managers, Waite, and the council all seemed to be eager to return Bombay to some state of normalcy. Waite's government set about restoring Bombay's diplomacy in the region. He continued negotiations Burniston had begun with the Portuguese, while insisting, as John Child had, to discuss serious matters only with the viceroy at Goa, whom he considered to be of equal status.[35] In 1707 Bombay entertained an envoy from Persia. Waite appointed a *banyan*, Girdhardas Rupaji, to write to a number of Mughal officials to obtain "such Grants as shall hereafter be d[elivere]d him in charge for benefit of this Island," including coining of rupees, in order to "Increase this Collony in wealth and Trade free from those Tyranical oppressions of the Moores Government."[36]

The Bombay government turned its attention to defense. A general survey of the island's stores, armaments, forts, houses, warehouses, and vessels ordered in October 1705 revealed that the guns on the fort were inadequate and awkwardly placed to repel another assault. Many of the small arms were in disrepair, a warehouse had fallen in a recent storm, and a number of Company buildings burned down during the 1688 invasion had yet to be repaired or rebuilt. The Council also suggested enlarging Bombay Fort and extending its walls to the back bay "to inclose the Towne, for Secureing the Merchants and other Inhabitants." A small fort, later called Fort George, at Dongari—the site just along the eastern coast of the island, north of the fort, where the Sidi had managed to ensconce himself during the siege—was judged inadequate and in need of renovation. They also recommended replacing the dilapidated fort at Worli with a new armed bulwark and building a new fort at Sion, to secure the Mahim river, which "if well fortified, will render it all most impregnable" from the north, or "Portuguese," side of the island—something John Gayer had proposed just a few years earlier.[37]

A survey of the "Millitary state of the Severall Companys and Casts of People" similarly led to a complete overhaul of the garrison. The soldiers appeared "ragged." Half of the 502 "Gentue" outguards were not armed appropriately. Some, it appeared, were teenagers. The solution was to appoint four companies of eighty men each for Bombay Fort, while a new company of sixty men was required for the "Marrine Service," particularly to convoy merchant ships in and out of the harbor. Mahim and Worli, on the north side of Bombay island, required additional companies while more men were to be placed at outposts at Sion, Dongari, and Sewri. Waite ultimately called for increasing the native soldiery by more than two hundred, all required to do exercises every month under the command of an English commissioned officer.[38] The council later ordered that half of each company was to stand at ready guard while the other half were deployed on fortification and other construction projects.[39] The managers approved of expanding the garrison with western Indian soldiers, as long as the council remembered the old wisdom: "the more Casts the better," necessary to "keep the whole in an equall balance."[40]

This ultimate purchase of this security regime was to encourage immigration and again make Bombay "the Seat of our trade as well as power."[41] According to one estimate, the population had dropped from its high of about 60,000 in the 1670s to around 16,000.[42] While the numbers are not entirely reliable—Waite observed only that "hundreds" had fled over the previous decade—it was clear that others would not come until Bombay could be made demonstrably secure from assault and its infrastructure rebuilt. The council appointed four "head Masters"—a shipwright, carpenter, stonecutter, and bricklayer—at an annual salary, all reporting to the Company's chief engineer and charged with recruiting workers "to come with their familys and be inhabitants Subject to the Government thereof." It also regularized the pay for laborers, so as to compete with wages offered in Portuguese, Mughal, and Maratha territories.[43]

As in its early days, Bombay relieved customs duties and issued orders against engrossing and monopolizing of grain and other necessities to prevent "depopulating and destroying this Collony." Its patrol ships were instructed to treat "all Persons . . . Civilly," while never diminishing "the Right of said Jurisdiction, Port, or River."[44] The council removed taxes on iron work and the sale of ships, "as if no such duty had bin heretofore Collected."[45] A few months later, the council ordered a general survey of the island, its streets, the bazaar, and the population, "as ought to have bin done soon after the Towne was destroyed by the Siddee Warr."[46] It also rented out land at encouraging rates; one Khwaja Marcora, for example, was given a twenty-one-year lease on some land near the custom house and a residence "for his dwelling" at a five rupees annually, "as an Acknowledgement to the Lords proprietors of this Island."[47]

At the core of the project of reviving the island was still to convince "the Natives . . . of the great difference between the Moors despotick and the English Mild Government," particularly by maintaining free trade and the "impartial" and "equal" administration of law, "lest Justice be turned into Wormwood." The judicature court was restored, albeit in a fairly rudimentary form. Juries were summoned to try both civil and criminal cases. By 1719 the Court of Directors, as the committees had been restyled under the United Company, approved the fairly high salary of 500 rupees per year for the chief justice. Of course, as usual, the outcomes of that justice were fairly uneven. Six sailors from Sidi Yakub Khan's fleet were arrested in April 1705 for coming armed to Bombay, wounding some people in a scuffle, and even killing one, but they were ultimately returned to the Sidi "in honour to the Great Mogull and Respect and friendship."[48] The next month, a jury of five Englishmen and seven Portuguese men ordered a thirty-five-year-old, single Portuguese native of Bombay, known as Dominga, transported to St. Helena to serve the Company for seven years for murdering her infant.[49] Both Cudde Zaun, a Muslim woman, guilty of the same offence, and Bimjee Gufsajee, convicted of murdering his wife, simply had their property confiscated "for the use and benefit of the Soveraign of this Island."[50]

In these efforts to repopulate and sustain the island, Waite and his council turned their attention to a remarkable range of seemingly mundane but absolutely crucial aspects of governing the island's daily life, particularly issues pertaining to public health. They established regulations on the cleaning of the island's wells and committed to enforcing the ban on the "Nautious Corruption" of buckshawing near the fort and town, first instated by Gerald Aungier and reissued as recently as 1699, to prevent polluting the island's water and air, spreading illness, and "greatly discouraging allmost any Nation resideing in this part of the Island" (The practice was also blamed for giving the island's poultry and pork a "fishy" taste that rendered them virtually inedible, contributing to a shortage of provisions).[51] Three months later, thirteen fishermen were fined for violating a new order that forbade laden fishing boats from docking at Dongari too long "till their fish stinkes and Poisons the Air."[52] The council also prohibited the fermenting of coconuts in pits—part of the process of producing coir—within a two-mile radius of the town, blaming it again for producing a "poisonous smell."[53] The government continued to pursue its predecessors' reclamation projects, including draining of marshes, recovery of waste, and damming of the breaches at the northern end of the island.[54] The managers in London insisted the island take steps to stop the spread of dysentery, including adding of chalk into the water "to qualify the Cold Laxative quality of the Nitre with which the Water is impregnated."[55] Such attempts to stave off disease by managing specific local practices reflected a belief that colonial climate and health could and must be managed through sound policy, even if it was at the short-term expense of commercial and agricultural productivity or the Company's coffers.[56] As London observed to Captain Charles Richards, outbound to Bombay in 1703, "although we are willing to save all the mony we can, yet we would not grudge any tollerable Charge to render [Bombay] healthfull to the Inhabitants and form[id]able to the Natives of India."[57]

Waite's critics accused him of exaggerating the chaos and disrepair "to reduce all into method" and to "hide his own Crimes," such as using Company money to cover the costs of his release from Surat, machinating to prevent Gayer's release, and displacing his old allies, like Rama Comatin—whose estates perhaps not coincidentally were disproportionately affected by the prohibition on buckshawing—so that his favorites might take on lucrative offices like the tobacco and coconut farms.[58] Only when Waite was finally dismissed from the Company's service did the island's government, under William Aislabie, earnestly set about trying to secure Gayer's release.[59] Although Aislabie had been prepared to recommend a show of force, Gayer was finally set free in 1710 without incident though died at Bombay soon after. Some in London suspected he could have in fact been freed earlier, had he been willing not to insist on his authority as general but to go "Privately, and not with Drums beating and Colours flying." This was a condescension to which he evidently would not submit.[60] Despite the great differences that emerged with Waite on matters of government, Aislabie and his successors over the next several decades followed in his steps in pursuing work which had begun in many ways in the 1670s. Within the next couple of decades, the town was walled in, the fort restored, and the naval establishment significantly expanded. On Christmas 1718, the cathedral opened with great fanfare and much drinking. By at least one report, the prohibitions on buckshawing and the stopping of the breaches had also reduced disease and mortality significantly.[61]

Bombay was not unique. At all of their settlements, the Managers and then the Directors seemed to understand that this new United Company's establishment in India was built upon seventeenth-century constitutional and institutional foundations. In 1708, St. Helena was specifically enjoined to adhere to the old Company's "orders and Directions . . . and the old standing Constitutions"—in the very same language used twenty-five years earlier—as if they "were the Magna Charta of the Island."[62] A decade later, the directors reminded John Smith, the island's newly appointed governor, of "the standing Law from the first Peopling the Island," that every white settler be given twenty acres and in return serve the island's militia.[63] At Madras, the new Company's representatives to the Court of Managers had proposed to rotate Thomas and John Pitt in and out of the governorship, but the old Company's delegates successfully resisted, insisting, as Thomas had earlier told John, that "there can be but one Gover[nor] at the fort."[64] (John Pitt was given a consolation appointment as head of Fort St. David, the news of which would almost certainly have killed him had he not died of "an Appoplexy" before it could reach India.[65]) The Madras corporation also continued upon the same constitutional foundations and conditions, as the directors put it in 1717, on which "we that is to say our Ancestors granted that Charter."[66] At Calcutta, the managers in fact tried a rotating chairmanship, but the dismal exercise lasted only until 1710, when the Company restored "the Ancient Method of Management in the Bay under a Presidency," appointing Anthony Weltden, the veteran captain of the Siam war, as president and governor.[67]

If the location and style of government persisted, so too did many of its core principles and languages. "Easy government," "Religious & Civil Libertys," and the "impartiall administration of Justice" remained keys to the increase of population and thus security and prosperity.[68] The Madras council insisted its population continued to grow because it was "applauded in the Countrey far and near for their Justice and Regular Government."[69] "Let the Cause be always tried but the Person never," London reminded Bombay in 1719, and "always religious perform that Maxim in Magna Charta, Nulli Vendemus, Nulli Defermus, Nulli Negabimus Justicam."[70] "Let justice be impartially dispenced," the managers had insisted to Madras, recalling "the Scripture Rule to regard neither Rich nor poor in Judgment but only the Cause" and "the Wisemans Remark will be found to be eternally true That the Throne can only be Establisht in righteousness."[71]

Justice, while impartial, still had to be firm; any hint of rebellion or disorder was to be dealt with swiftly and decisively because, in 1708 just as in the 1680s, "too much Pity spoils a City."[72] Despite its new Parliamentary charter and shifting constitutional foundations in London, the Company also held fast to the notion that its law, and not English statute law, was supreme abroad. As its predecessors had been instructed many times before, in 1704 and again fifteen years later, the St. Helena council was reminded to use English law books for its reference but not to "have your heads troubled with Nice points of the Common Law of England." Cases were to be judged according to equity, as

> strictly speaking our English laws reach no further than in England (now Great Britain) Wales & Berwick many of them do not affect Ireland & none of them (if not particularly provided for) any of the Plantations. These are the Laws of the Lords Proprietors or if they are immediately the Kings, then by the Laws of the Privy Council or those made by the People on the Place . . . as We are by Charter under the Broad Seal constituted absolute Lords Proprietors of St. Helena & have power to make what laws We shall judge reasonable and proper for the good Government of the whole Island.

Laws might not be repugnant to those in Britain, but they could not hardly be expected to be uniform. After all, they observed, customs and legal principles differed by county and city even within England.[73]

Above all, the directors remained deeply concerned, like their forebears, on revenue, still regarding as a model the Dutch and even the waning Portuguese, who, the directors marveled in 1714, made their settlements "bear their own charges . . . tho their general Character is pride & Laziness & boasting themselves of selling but empty Titles."[74] London approved of a policy at Bombay of applying fines levied by its court toward the building of a Town Hall and its proposal to establish a bank to encourage inhabitants' commerce. "Though this is indeed taking so much Money out of our Pocket, for We are Lords Proprietors, yet We are not against it," they wrote, with the caveat that all fines be for the "publick benefit" and proportional to both the crime and the means of the criminal, again citing both Magna Carta and the procedures of Madras's mayor's court as precedent.[75]

The managers and directors were also as impatient as the committees had been with those who saw taxation as a burden rather than a duty. Madras was reminded in 1706, as it had been seven years earlier, to "remember the Old adage Suaviter in modo fortiter in re," that is, to be gentle in manner and strong in deed.[76] When Bombay's new levies on water for ships, quitrents on houses, and duties on cows were "complained of as a heavy Tax," London was unmoved, since without a self-sufficient garrison and settlement "our Trade will infallibly fall into a consumption by the yearly draining away so much of its Vital Blood."[77] That a settlement's infrastructure was primarily for its inhabitants' use and defense and thus its responsibility to maintain was a principle agreed upon "by the common consent of all Mankind," not to mention one enshrined in the "English constitution."[78] Even the poor had little cause to complain, since, as in London, high taxes were far outweighed by the "Conveniencys" of living in the city.[79] Objections to a road tax at Madras in the late 1710s met again with comparisons to England: "We apprehend the mending that highway was for the common benefit of all the Inhabitants," the directors wrote, so "We can see no reason why they should not contribute to & pay the charge as is the practice here of Highways belonging to every Parish." Only in this way would revenue "again flourish & revive as in times past," which was the duty of those "who have the executive Authority in their hands."[80]

The nature of Madras's "executive authority" was exemplified in its role in mediating the ongoing disputes between two rival Tamil caste groups, the *valangai* and *idengai*, otherwise known as "right-" and "left-" hand castes. The conflict between the two was rooted in the mythical past but presently sparked in 1707 when the right-hand castes reacted violently to a left-hand wedding procession crossing into their parts of the black town.[81] Rather than allowing the inhabitants to arbitrate the problem themselves, the council had a number of the principal "Ring leaders" jailed and attempted to ameliorate the situation through mediation and even city planning. The council ordered a survey of the black town, demarcating right- and left-hand quarters with boundary stones and attempting to relocate people from one side to the other. Though this seemed to rankle everyone involved, what was clear was that the Company was to all involved an apparently legitimate and effective government empowered in some way to resolve the dispute, becoming a sort of south Indian "little king" capable of negotiating and mediating social conflict.[82] A large group from the right-hand castes came to the fort in August with a formal petition and protest: "from the beginning of the World," they insisted, "it was never knowne that any Government did take away your Petitioners streets and give them to the left hand Casts people." A menacing note was posted on the boundary stones, noting similarly that "since the foundation of this City no such thing has been knowne." Thomas Pitt convened a summit in the fort's consultation room, inviting twelve representatives of both castes; he offered a general pardon for all parties if they would take "oaths of friendship," which they reportedly did.[83] A number of the right-hand castes had fled in protest to protection at St. Thomé; to get them to return, the Company offered carrots and sticks, sending a delegation of Armenian, Persian, and Pashtun residents of Madras, another formal pardon, and a Brahmin, a Mullah, and a Catholic priest to negotiate as well threaten an attack on St. Thomé if they did not return.[84]

The inhabitants came back by October, and in 1710 the council overconfidently reported that the "casts" were in "perfect peace" and that, in fact, all "foreign nations who live at Madras" were evidently "in love with the Government."[85] In turn, the directors regarded the successful segregation of the black town's neighborhoods alone as "an honour to the Government there."[86] Of course, this did not settle matters. Tensions flared periodically, several subsequent governors entertaining complaints about the violation of the "Ancient Priviledges" of one side or another.[87] When Joseph Collet arrived as governor in 1717, he found among one of his earliest tasks was to arbitrate a rift between the left-hand caste Beri Chettis and the right-hand caste Komatis, ostensibly over the latter's performance of religious ceremony in front of a Pillaiyar (Ganesh) temple within the former's district. As under Pitt, the Madras council first tried to mediate a settlement and then issued a set of regulations concerning worship and ceremonial rights. The Komatis would be permitted to perform the ceremony in front of the temple but all inhabitants now had to seek permission from the council before building new temples, and only the Company's flag or the flag of St. George could be flown in ceremonial processions.[88] Personally, Collet had little patience for such "religious controversies," which he likened, unfavorably, to the contemporary row in Britain between High Church and Low Church Anglicanism: "tho' they both worship the same God and the same Devil, yet they differ about some certain Ceremonies which being misterious are hard to explain." For Collet the solution to both was strong government: "I interposed as head of the Church, establish'd Liberty of Conscience and oblig'd the Deserters to return, so that now we also are in perfect peace and upon a better Establishment than ever we were before," he wrote a friend back home, adding snidely that he wished "good King George had the same power in England."[89]

Responses to challenges from without similarly revealed the nature of Company government in early eighteenth-century southern India. Mughal expansion in Madras's environs had prompted a several-months' siege in 1702 by the *fauj-dar* of Karnataka, Da'ud Khan Panni. The settlement's ability to withstand the attack, in the words of the Mughal historian John Richards, essentially "sealed the autonomy of what had become a city-state."[90] It set its diplomacy with its neighbors, particularly Da'ud, on a much stronger footing, while spurring a number of long-awaited infrastructural improvements, such as a cannon platform to protect the harbor, a guard house near Egmore walled in with a sixteen-foot ditch, and turnpikes on the roads into Madras, to "secure the Villages against the insolencys of the Moors horse."[91] Fort St. David similarly stocked up on provisions, enhanced the fort, enlarged the garrison, and built walls around both its towns to both prepare for a possible attack as well as to encourage "trading people" to "inhabitt there and raise the Revenues."[92]

A serious test came in 1710, when Sarup Singh, the *qilidar* at Jinji, used the occasion of a debtor who had fled to protection in Cuddalore to forward a series of claims to rights of jurisdiction over the town's waterways and to its rents. He insisted this fell under his *jagir*, but the council would have none of it, insisting their grants from Rama Raja predated the Mughal conquest of the region and were "the Company's propper inheritance," having had been "ratified & confirm'd by sundry Perwannas, Phirumaunds & Cowles" from Mughal officers as well.[93] Singh besieged the city nonetheless; though he was never able to breach its defenses, the attack drove up grain prices, led many inhabitants to flee, and even prompted an attempted mutiny in one garrison company.[94] One Company garrison officer went on a vengeful rampage, burning and pillaging the countryside, which, the governor of Madras, reported somewhat proudly "exasperated the Enemy beyond reconciliation." Eventually Fort St. David and Madras began to sue for peace, though "with Sword in hand," insisting whatever money they had to give be exchanged for territory or some other "Equivalent," so "that it might look like a Purchase not a Peace offering."[95] With the mediation of the French governor of Pondicherry, a settlement to this "tedious expensive war" was finally achieved in June 1712.[96] By the next year, Madras insisted that "all remembrances of the blood Shed at St. David seems to be forgot": revenues were increasing, inhabitants retuning, and Sarup Singh placated by the confiscation on his behalf of good portions of the debtor's estate.[97]

The directors in London acknowledged that the conflict had been expensive but did not seem fundamentally disturbed by it. "Good will at least ensue," they wrote in words that recalled attitudes following the siege of Bombay two decades earlier, as "the Natives there and elsewhere in India who have or shall hear of it will have a due Impression made upon their minds of the English Courage and Conduct that were able to maintain a War against so Potent a Prince as the Rajah of Chingee." The directors ordered the further strengthening of the fort, its barracks, prison, lodgings, and other buildings in the town. They even contemplated tearing down the factory and rebuilding a "proper Fortification" at Cuddalore, which, again citing the walls at Madras, was to be paid for by its inhabitants.[98]

The Court of Managers ordered a formal survey of Anjengo, but the report they were sent in 1704 was not encouraging. Needed improvements to the fort were estimated at upwards of £3,000. It also desperately required soldiers, as the council felt the Portuguese in their employ were far too vulnerable to manipulation from the Jesuits and officials in nearby Goa.[99] The nadir of the Company's fortunes there came in 1721 when Anjengo's chief, William Gyfford, fell into dispute over the pepper prices with some local inhabitants and was ambushed and killed on his way to negotiate matters with the Rani; rumors circulating at the time held that he had been brutalized, tied to a board, his tongue cut out and nailed to his chest, and floated down the river past the English fort.[100] Still, something came of the tragedy. The fort successfully managed to withstand attack, and within the next decade, the council's fortunes were recovering. It even received grants from both the raja of Travancore and the rani of Attingal expanding the Company's jurisdiction, supposedly as compensation for Gyfford's murder.[101]

A few years later, the Court of Directors appointed a special subcommittee to look into the "state of Bencoolen" as well. Growth there had also been slow, due to infighting on the council, disease and natural disaster, and shortage of supplies and people, owing partly to disruptions in Europe from the war of Spanish Succession. The York Fort council was convinced that there were three main factors keeping settlers away: climate and health, the "severity" of some previous governors, and the "weakness of our Fort & Garrison."[102] The councils in Madras and Bengal set about proactive measures to address all three. They continued to try to get inhabitants and soldiers from other Company settlements to emigrate to Sumatra.[103] At the council's urging, the Court of Managers had already agreed to allow free passage for the wife of any English Company servant to Sumatra, as it would "tend to the good of the place in fixing their aboad here."[104] Some came freely from St. Helena, such as one Catherine Vandenand and her daughter who left for Bengkulu in 1716; others were sent as slaves and transported convicts, particularly crucial after a 1708 smallpox epidemic wiped out a good number of the African slaves at the settlement.[105] London and Bengkulu still envisioned the settlement's salvation as resting in Asian settlers, particularly from eastern India and China.[106] They believed that with the right population, the colony could easily cultivate a variety of agricultural industries, including sugar plantations more profitable than Java; in 1703 Bengkulu requested gardeners, farmers, and, like St. Helena, some "vigneroons" to capitalize on "this fertile soil."[107] Strategies for attracting these immigrants mirrored earlier ones, at Sumatra and elsewhere, and ranged from attention to public health—such as finding cleaner water upstream from the fort to reduce disease and mortality "for the sake of common humanity as well as our benefitt"[108]—to the construction of a Catholic chapel and efforts to find a "Portugueze Padre" to draw South Asian Indo-Portuguese families to the colony.[109] Most important was as usual to appear "mild" in govern-ment, particularly "to encourage the Chineeses who are an industrious ingenious useful sort of People" to settle.[110]

Addressing the "severity" of particular governors, and maintaining stable relations with Bengkulu's neighbors, also seemed to become a priority. Deputy Governor Robert Skingle was cited by his successors as a chief impediment to the settlement's security and growth; they singled out as particularly problem-atic his suspension of the practice of using Malay judges and *bichara*, and the insults to Malay soldiers by insisting they disarm before entering the fort. Joseph Collet, who came to head Bengkulu soon after in 1712, set out self-consciously to repair the damage. He was particularly concerned to increase Chinese immi-grants to the colony, who he reported in 1713 had started to flock "hither in considerable Numbers," and to "establish a good correspondance with the Mallays."[111] The directors had become convinced that Bengkulu's troubles came from its overextention into local politics: "We would not have our People set up to judge of the right of Government," they wrote Collet, reminding him that "Trade is our business as you well observe and if fully pursued will take up the time of our Councils at all places . . . without indulging their ambition in setting up one petty Prince or putting down another."[112] Officially, Collet seemed intent on keeping these orders. He insisted to the sultan of Manduta that "all the Busi-ness I will have to do with any of the Natives" was to "give you Dollars for your Pepper."[113]

In a way foreshadowing processes that would repeat in later centuries in India, despite these sentiments, the logic of settlement seemed to mean Bengkulu could not avoid such intervention for long. Collet observed to his sister that to maintain government at Bengkulu he had to treat Malay rulers "as a Wise man shou'd his Wife . . . very complaisant in trifles, but immoveable in matters of importance."[114] He was somewhat more direct to his brother:

> Their Kings and Princes obey my commands with as great readiness as if I were their natural Sovereign, so that without assuming the title I am really an Absolute Prince with respect to the Malays. The Buggese [*bugis*] and Chinese who live here are properly subjects to the Com-pany and consequently under my immediate government. And as for the English we make up one great Family of which I am the head and

common Father, to whom all pay the Reverence, Respect, and Obedience of Children.[115]

Collet had come to regard his authority as a "Great King" in Sumatra as crucial to maintaining authority over his own subjects, and in effecting his pet project of a "reformation of manners" among Bengkulu's inhabitants, especially the English, "both by Authority and Example."[116]

There was another, more obvious reason for intervening in local politics: to keep stability. Henry White, head of the Bantal factory subordinate to Bengkulu, soon found himself spearheading the Company's direct involvement in a complicated and drawn-out struggle amongst the Sumatran sultanates of Moko Moko, Manjuta, and Indrapoora, which had disrupted security in the region while also driving up the price of pepper.[117] White believed it would only take a small force to "get possession of Manduta and Moco Moco and then prescribe Laws to both partys." Officially, Collet responded to White that he did not have the troops to spare but secretly sent two ships and twenty soldiers to support White's efforts to reinstate the Company's ally Sultan Gulemat to his "Government but restrain'd from a tyrannical exercise of his power." Anyone who interfered Collet reckoned "an Enemy to the Company" to be "proceeded against accordingly"—but he cautioned White to always "remember the Motto 'Pax quaerit in Bello,'" that is, again, the ultimate point of war was not the war itself, but the peace. The Company successfully restored the sultan to his "regal authority" over Moko Moko and Manjuta; in return he guaranteed the Company rights of settlement at either place, should it ever choose to do so.[118]

Despite the forward policy, there was still much work to be done to secure the establishment at Bengkulu. York Fort in particular had proven a crowning debacle. It was built in a particularly unhealthy and inconvenient spot, leaving its inhabitants susceptible to disease and its foundation literally vulnerable to earthquakes. In 1708, the council hired James Clarke, an engineer off a Company ship, to design improvements; he was able to make some modifications, but all seemed agreed that its fundamental structure was "crazy and crack'd thro." The council recommended building new low, brick structures "as the Dutch doe," though warned that it would be remarkably expensive to repair fully "such a fortification, if may deserve that name."[119] On coming into power, Collet and his council decided to cut their losses and abandon it entirely. An entirely new fortification was constructed about two miles away, christened Fort Marlborough, after John Churchill, the first Duke of Marlborough—"a name," Collet wrote wistfully to his brother, "which I endeavour to perpetuate in India because it seems to be forgot in England."[120]

By the time he left Sumatra to take up the governorship of Madras, Collet boasted that he had "layd the strongest Fortification in India and have rais'd a

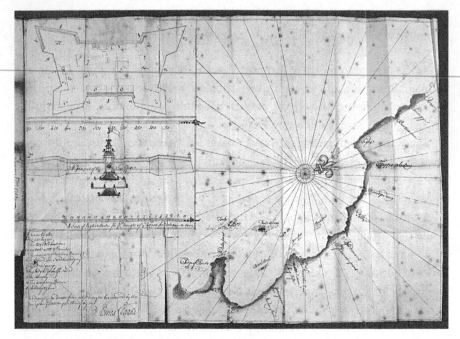

James Clarke's plans for repairs to York Fort, Sumatra, c. 1708/09. © The British Library Board, Asia, Pacific & Africa Collections, IOR G/35/6 no. 85.

populous town adjoyning call'd by the same name."[121] He had "baffled" the Malays, and "gone through two successfull Wars without the loss of one man, and yet have perform'd what the whole country believ'd impossible and at the same time have gain'd the Love of the people I have conquer'd."[122] It was not long before this supposed "love" transformed into something else. Gulemat's hold on power was tenuous, and in 1717 he was again deposed by his enemies. Now the Company too was attacked. Bantal was burned and in 1719 the new gem of Fort Marlborough was besieged and subsequently lost to the "natives of the country."[123] The entire affair had distinct echoes of Banten, and the directors were unequivocal that it was "absolutely necessary to recover if possible the Settlement." The subcommittee for correspondence recommended sending two 450-ton ships "with as many Souldiers and Such Ammunition and Stores they can conveniently carry."[124] Yet when the fort was finally recovered three years later, it was more through negotiation than force of arms; even by the late 1720s, the Madras council was reporting that many would "rather choose to be dismiss'd their service than go to that Settlement."[125] Still, slowly and steadily, the garrison was increased, a new gunroom crew appointed, and work on the fort continued; there were also new projects hatched, such as plans for a coffee plantation.[126] Through the eighteenth century, Chinese merchants and migrants did eventually come, taking up revenue farms, and dominating a number of the domestic industries, such as sugar production, brick making, and lead- and iron-working trades; some opened tea shops and others engaged in small-scale cash crop agriculture.[127]

Though perhaps excruciatingly slow in the making, Bengkulu was held up by the Company, like Madras, as a model and encouragement for new expansion. In 1701 the council reported that growing discontent with Dutch "tyranny" in northern Sumatra might present an opportunity to establish a settlement there. Three years later Madras opened negotiations at Aceh to allow English factors to return, though by the following year all of the English had been again driven out, one killed and another wounded.[128] In the late 1690s Thomas Bowrey, a former Company ship captain-turned-colonial projector, offered a number of proposals for new settlements, including one at Mozambique, where he imagined culti-vating a Jamaican-style sugar plantation, and another on a small island near Sukadana, off the west coast of Borneo, an ideal place in his estimation for settle-ment in the East Indies, offering a "convenient harbour," proper soil, and well situated as a fortification for protecting both Company shipping, Chinese and other immigrants, and a "Free Port for all Trade."[129]

The managers were not persuaded about east Africa but did pursue a sta-tion at Banjarmasin, on the southern coast of Borneo. The new Company had designed a factory for there, hoping to access both the China and southeast Asian trade. Company servants, however, reported tense relations with inhab-itants, and that Chinese settlers in particular were "impatient for a Fort to pro-tect them."[130] In late 1702 the managers resolved to "settle a strong fortification," and sent out plans by December 1704, authorizing more than £4,100 in ex-penses, including the purchase of one hundred slaves and several ships.[131] A footing at Banjar was made even more urgent when the small fort the new Company had erected at Pulo Condore just three years earlier was devastated in March 1705 by a mutiny of Malay soldiers, who also burned the Company's warehouses and killed a number of English there, including its president Allan Catchpoole.[132] The events at Condore made it only more obvious to some that "nothing but power," as Henry Barre wrote from there, "will make the Place beneficial."[133] This seemed remarkably prescient when, despite reports of pro-gress in 1705 and 1706, the projected Borneo fortification was first delayed by heavy rains and lack of labor, supplies, and inhabitants, who were to have been provided from Condore. In 1707 an uprising of neighboring inhabitants, which Company officials strongly suspected had been instigated by the Dutch, drove the Company out entirely.[134]

Thus, while the managers and the United Company's Court of Directors were at times more hesitant than their predecessors to "encrease our Settlements or Territorys," they did not fail to consider opportunities when they presented themselves, especially if it would help protect what they already had.[135] The Banjar council, in exile at Batavia, recommended retaking the settlement and even settling at nearby Tomborneo, at the mouth of the river, "with familys," but a couple of more attempts ultimately came to naught.[136] A few years later, the directors approved of the Madras council's projects to obtain a footing at Divi Island, at the mouth of the Kistna river, which was only abandoned because of the "unsettled condition of the Countrey Government," and to purchase St. Thomé, to "populate it with the Manufacturers of Goods proper for Europe," and thus remove the Company even farther from its investments at Vizagapatam.[137]

None of these efforts, however, compared to the rapid growth and investment in the Company's newest fortification in India, at Calcutta. Much like at Madras, St. Helena, and Bombay, the council set about planning the city, improving the fort, and growing the garrison and its "reputation."[138] A strong Fort William, the directors wrote in 1718, was in itself a claim to sovereignty: "our three towns being within our own jurisdiction and as it were under the reach of our own Guns are to be defended by Power."[139] "An impartiall administration of Justice to all your Inhabitants" remained the key to establishing "the difference between the mild English Government and the Arbitrary tyranny of the Moors."[140] London was particularly concerned that the president and council make "Publick Examples" of anyone who used their position to their private advantage, which "will always prove as so many Worms at the root of our Revenues." Still, government needed to be persuasive not dogmatic, recalling that "excellent Rule of our Saviour which even the Heathens could not but admire To do as you would be done unto."[141] Accordingly, the council boasted that justice at Calcutta "pleases" its inhabitants and was envied by its fellow neighboring *zamindars*.[142] London ordered Calcutta to make a "Common Seal or Chop" for public business, particularly for sealing its *dastaks*, as well as its passes for "all Ships under the Company's protection."[143] *Dastaks*, commercial passes that extended to its holders the Company's immunities under its *farmans* such as relief from customs impositions, were seen as particularly critical "to propogate the future Interest of our Nation in India," ensuring that private trade could flourish but always under the watchful eye and jurisdiction of Company government.[144]

Like Bombay before it, Calcutta also turned its eye to encouraging immigration, particularly by suspending customs charges until they "have had [the towns] in quiet possession some time longer and the Government better settled."[145] At the same time, the managers urged Calcutta to "Cultivate every Branch" of taxation they could manage, investigating "the Country method" of collecting revenue in neighboring towns, and imitating them, except in one critical way: they were to try to make those duties lighter and thus "satisfy the People under you that the great charge you are yearly at a great part of it is for the Protection of the Inhabitants in the free enjoyment of their libertyes and

Propertyes under the Mild English." In the end, as at other Company settlements, it was "nothing else" but revenue that "can be sufficient for us to trans-
mitt the English Interest in India down to posterity any thing Considerable."
The Court of Managers cited two familiar examples: "the wise Dutch" and
Madras.[146]

In fact, previous Company experience in India was constantly held up to
Calcutta as an exemplar. The murage duties in Madras's black town were a precedent for insisting inhabitants contribute to infrastructural and defensive works,
such as digging a ditch around the city and a new quay within sight of the fort.[147]
A strong fortification, Calcutta was reminded, would lead "the richer Natives to
inhabit there," as it did at Madras.[148] The division of Calcutta into "white" and
"black" towns itself mirrored Madras, and Calcutta administered justice,
collected revenue, and tended to public works in the black town in its role as
zamindar.[149] Efforts to design a more regular layout for the city, for both order
and public safety, resembled earlier approaches to urban design at most other
Company settlements.[150] Its garrison was reminded to follow the model of its
predecessors in balancing the soldiery among its various nations, especially the
Europeans.[151] Much like Bombay, the Calcutta council set about draining the
city's grounds, as "the Standing Water thereabouts contributes to the unhealthy-
ness of the place and Subjects People to Agues feavers and fluxes," the managers
likening the problem to similar issues found in the English marshlands.[152] And,
as elsewhere throughout the Company's system, London insisted it "would not
grudge any reasonable Charge to make our Territory there safe defensible and
healthy."[153]

Very soon, Calcutta reported its fortifications were strong enough to resist an
attack and its garrison growing.[154] Inland bastions were added, a new wharf built,
and various sanitation measures taken, particularly to attempt to stave off the
high mortality and incidence of malaria.[155] Trees and bamboo were cleared and
a four-mile walk out to the lake cleared, for public health.[156] Calcutta's population swelled from around 15,000 in 1704, leveling to about 120,000 between the
1720s and 1750s, and spiking to about 200,000 in 1780; some extravagant contemporary accounts hold the number to be as high as 400,000 by mid-century.[157]
The cities also expanded their boundaries.[158] More people and land meant more
revenue. In 1707, the government of Fort William reported collecting 5,756
rupees in revenue more than they did the previous year, mostly in monthly rents
but also in pass and license fees and other small duties.[159] By some estimates,
between 1708 and 1747, Calcutta's revenues increased by a factor of six.
Spending, however, grew dramatically as a proportion of that income.[160] Military
charges at Calcutta rose from just under 30,000 rupees in 1709 to a little more
than 45,947 by 1722, although this was still only a fraction of the garrison
charges at Bombay, which were almost three times that amount.[161] In the end,

the Court of Directors reflected the very same patient vigilance as their predecessors, understanding that flourishing colonial settlements took time, and their
efforts were "not so much for our present benefitt as for the sake of our successors."[162] As they put it more poetically to Anthony Weltden in 1709, "we must
not despise the day of small things," implying, of course, their hope that larger
things were soon to follow.[163]

9

"A Sword in One Hand & Money in the Other"

Old Patterns, New Rivals

In 1707 the ninety-three-year-old Aurangzeb died, bringing his half-century reign to an end and setting in motion a process by which "the Mogols Kingdom," as Nathaniel Higginson had predicted a decade earlier, would be "Cantell'd out into severall Sovereignties."[1] The so-called successor states that seemed to emerge in the eighteenth century had, of course, been there all along, but now the overlapping networks of fragmented and layered forms of local and regional political power South Asia were increasingly laid bare. It was a situation for which the East India Company, as a corporate and hybrid body politic adept at drawing on various sources of legitimacy to buttress its own power and authority, was well-suited. Many of the Company's objectives, to protect and expand that authority, remained the same. The early eighteenth-century Company was still preoccupied with obtaining its long-desired "comprehensive" *farman* and continued to battle familiar enemies.

Yet while the categories in which Company leadership understood the world remained stable, their content shifted with context. Thus, the Company continued to expand its pirate-fighting regime, but it was now reoriented from battling Anglo-American to Asian and Arabian maritime power. The interloper remained a universal enemy, but his definition expanded from English subjects to British subjects; increasingly and subtly, it came to include to upstart rivals from elsewhere as well. As the Company became more implicated in the geopolitical strategies of the emerging global British Empire, the French replaced the waning Dutch and Portuguese as the Company's biggest European threat. Finally, changing political context in India and growing Company maritime power allowed for the Company to overcome some of its longstanding adversaries, such as the *mutasaddi* of Surat and the Sidi, while being confronted with newly powerful ones, particularly the *nawabs* of Bengal. In the process, the concerns of the late seventeenth century Company regime, milled through early eighteenth-century circumstances, became a crucial foundation for the political and ideological conditions that made the Company's territorial empire in India conceivable.

One absolutely indispensible, if underappreciated, aspect to the expansion of Company power in eighteenth-century India was the phenomenal growth of its maritime strength and its role in underpinning its eventual claims on land. All of this grew directly out of the Company's seventeenth-century concerns with interlopers in the 1680s and their brethren pirates, "those Vermin, the Common pest of mankind," in the 1690s. The legal and maritime regime established through these conflicts—passes, Admiralty courts, convoys, naval power, and the like—had increasingly and effectively extended Company claims over the sea lanes and its ability to suppress this violence.[2] Even more important was the Company's political success in enlisting the British state in the effort, which in turn had underscored the efforts of the Crown, Parliament, and a host of agents to exert greater control over an Atlantic colonial system. In all, the age of Anglo-American pirates in the Indian Ocean had come largely to an end by the 1720s. As early as 1714, Woodes Rogers, sent on a reconnaissance mission to Madagascar, could find little trace of the once powerful pirate haven of St. Mary's or its famous

Plan of the fortress of Angria, the Pirate, and the Island of Culap [Colabba] on the coast of Concan, by an Italian hand. © The British Library Board, Manuscript Collections, Add.MS 15,505 f. 15.

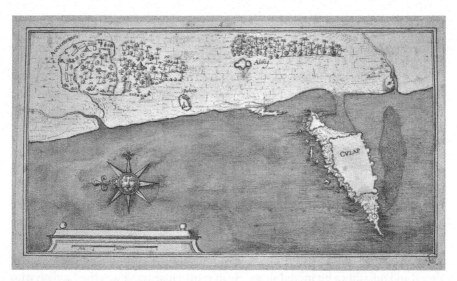

Plan of the fortress of Angria, the Pirate, and the Island of Culap [Colabba] on the coast of Concan, by an Italian hand. © The British Library Board, Manuscript Collections, Add.MS 15,505 f. 14.

pirate king; in fact, many former "pirates" had not left, but on the contrary had become settlers and planters themselves.[3]

By then, however, the Bombay council had already come to train its attention on a very different species of "pirate." In September 1703, it passed a resolution calling for the pursuit of one Kanhoji Angre (or Angria) for "injurious & Pyratical Actions on the Inhabitants of this Island."[4] From its first foundation, Bombay had complained about Malabari and Arabian maritime marauders, but Kanhoji was different.[5] A Rajput by heritage, he served the Marathas at sea somewhat like the Sidi did the Mughals, particularly in the context of the Mughal-Maratha conflict that dominated late-century western India. He was appointed a Maratha *sarkhil*, or military commander, in 1690, for which he received a revenue assignment, a *chauth*.[6] Like most in his position, he was also a rising political power in his own right, conducting diplomacy, establishing treaties, issuing shipping passes, and, from his base in the Konkan, seeking to challenge both Sidi and European naval dominance over the western Indian littoral.

Ostensibly, for the Company, he was the most powerful of a number of "Sevajees," that is Maratha, ships plaguing Bombay's shipping and travel along the western Indian coast.[7] Yet, Bombay's own political language was rife with odd but telling disjunctures and juxtapositions.[8] When Kanhoji sailed into Bombay harbor with seven ships in November 1704, the council indicted him as a "Pirate a Rebell independent of Raja Savajee" yet only permitted reprisals upon him should he violate a treaty he had made with John Gayer to "not comitt any

Act of Hostility upon Boates belonging to the island." The Bombay council ordered William Reynolds to take a few ships and acquaint "said Chief Robber," that attacking any shipping coming to or from the island would be considered a "breach of that Friendship the English Nation has allways had with Raja Savajee and all his Captains." Only if he proved hostile was Reynolds to "absolutely destroy him"; otherwise, he was simply to conclude a written agreement with Kanhoji, and even offer him a gift of scarlet cloth "as Customary."[9]

These instructions productively conflated a number of ostensibly irreconcilable categories. Kanhoji was a rebel to Maratha authority, insofar as Company officials regarded reprisals against him as independent of any breach with the Marathas. He acted as a legitimate political power, insofar as he could make some treaties and be governed by others. He was an enemy, when he broke those agreements. Finally, he was a thief and a pirate, a designation which allowed Bombay's ships to pursue his boats at will. Kanhoji was understandably bewildered and possibly a bit incredulous. He in return insisted it was the English who had "never kept their word with him" and explained that if he did act aggressively it was because four decades of war against the Mughals had forced his people to live "by their Sword." This "pirate" also insisted he had the same right the Company claimed to attack any boat that did not carry his passes.[10]

If one thing was clear, it was that Kanhoji was a problem for the Company, and the "war" against him became an urgent justification for building up Bombay's infrastructure and defenses. He was a far greater threat than the European pirates had ever been to the island's local shipping, and thus its inhabitants' security and trade and the government's revenue. The council there hoped that stopping him would also make an example for others and "strike a Terror and Awe upon the many litle Robers lying between this Place and Rajapore." This was the only way to persuade the island's residents they were "safe in their houses" until Bombay could build up its naval strength to secure "its Inhabitants from the darke assaults of such and other Perverse Enemys."[11] Ship captains and others consulted recommended building fifteen ships of various sizes and strengths, to protect against any "Attempt" on the island. The Council awarded John Van Duuren, the chief engineer and master of the works, a bonus of half his regular salary, fifty pounds, to supervise these projects.[12] The Calicut factory was ordered to have a ship built "intending her for a Cruizer to protect our Merchants Boates belonging to this Island."[13] A few months later, the council issued new regulations concerning the landing and sale of prize vessels at Bombay "by any Nation or People whatsoever," allowing one-third "to the Informer" and the balance to the Company, revenue that was in turn to be dedicated to the various fortification and infrastructure projects Nicholas Waite's government had begun.[14]

Kanhoji was not intimidated. Just six months later, he attacked a few small boats from Bombay, allegedly taking their crews' clothes and tearing up their flags and passes. The event only further convinced Waite that the "Pyraticall Governours"—another strange oxymoron—"are untoward growing Evills that unavoidably must be removed as soon as can be suitably provided with men and Vessells" and ordered more protective patrols, with specific instructions not to harm any ship with a Company pass.[15] Hostilities with Kanhoji and his successors ensued for the next several decades, occasioning the Company to continue to build up its naval strength in western India. The Court of Directors in London remained committed to doing anything necessary to protect the island, though they also continued to insist that money for such improvements be raised locally through taxation. Yet again citing Madras's city walls as precedent, they reminded the council that "People [must] pay the charge of their Protection."[16] In 1715, Charles Boone's first year as Bombay's governor, he ordered four frigates, ranging from sixteen to twenty-four guns, built.[17] A few years later, Bombay instituted a 2 percent duty "on account of the War with Angria" to subsidize convoying residents' trade between Bombay and Surat.[18] In 1719 a subcommittee of the Court of Directors, specifically appointed to review affairs of Bombay, concluded that it needed extra shipping, seamen, and soldiers immediately, "since the War is commenced between the English & Conajee Angria," and also recommended that one of the ships it sent be sold in India, since it also hoped the sailors would stay and settle.[19] The directors offered special incentives to seamen to "excite their Courage in case of being Attackt by an Enemy," providing ship captains with three or four treasure chests to be put on display and "lye ready to be distributed as soon as the Encouragement is over."[20] They also sent three smaller 160-ton galleys. This, they insisted, showed they were "willing to spare no Cost to defend our Countrey Shipping against Angria's attempts in hopes to curb that insolent Pickaroon."[21]

That cost was indeed high. Even at the turn of the century, garrison charges represented Bombay's highest expense.[22] By the 1720s, the conflict with Kanhoji was costing the island around seventy thousand to eighty thousand rupees per year.[23] Moreover, both London and Bombay had become resigned to the fact that the expense must "continue to be Considerable," since peace could never be had with Kanhoji, "on the terme he Expects it which is the dominion of the Sea."[24] Still, as Bombay's naval power expanded, its governors grew more confident. By 1724 Governor William Phipps was refusing to negotiate with Kanhoji, reminding him of his agreements dating back to the days of John Gayer and patronizingly explaining to him that "taking what is anothers is called Pyracy, and those guilty thereof are esteemed enemies to all nations, a character I therefore hope your honor will not be fond of." Phipps demanded he return those Bombay inhabitants he had been holding as hostages and offered a thinly veiled threat: "Any State bordering upon a neighbour that lives on plunder and robs under colour of friendship," Phipps noted, "must necessarily be careful for their defence."[25] Kanhoji again seemed perplexed. As far as he was concerned, the Company was hardly innocent of the "desire of possessing what is anothers" and Bombay was actually holding a number of his people prisoner as well.[26] In fact, a prisoner exchange was arranged in 1725.[27]

Figuring the battle against Kanhoji as a war against piracy allowed for these campaigns to fit into but dramatically expand a legal and martial regime that had been established in the first instance to combat Euro-Atlantic interlopers and pirates, now no longer much of a threat. Bombay soon expanded its patrols to include a number of other rivals in the region, including "Cooley Pyrates" cruising off Cambay (Khambhat), Sangari Rajputs near Sindh, and "Malwan Pyrates" off to the south.[28] Looking westward, Bombay had become concerned with the so-called Muscat Arabs, a group of tribes, most prominently the Qawasim, from the eastern Arabian coast of what is now Oman. Like Kanhoji, the Qawasim acted as coastal polities in their own right as well as tributary naval forces for Omani sultans and, later, Saudi Wahhabi rulers in the Arabian peninsula. For whomever they sailed, the Qawasim had become a formidable naval presence in the Arabian sea and Persian Gulf, a region the British would come to call the "Pirate Coast."[29]

The Company's war against "Muscat" piracy also had late seventeenth-century roots. In 1697 the Isfahan factory had first suggested that the piracy squadrons the Company was seeking from England be instructed to pursue not only European but also Arabian pirates in the Indian Ocean.[30] The Company's failure to discipline pirates at sea had done irreparable damage to the credit and reputation of the *koolah-pushan*, or hat-wearers, as the English and other Europeans were known in Persian slang; it was even reported that Persian merchants jested about how "the English hats were grown thread bare."[31] In early 1702 John Gayer complained to the Imam of Muscat of the "several piratical actions" committed by his subjects for almost a decade.[32] He set the Company's ships on a "posture of defense" and authorized them "not only to defend your Selves . . . but to take 'em for that they have proved them selves pirates."[33] The governor and council at Madras permitted residents to send letters to the Company, the English ambassadors and consul at Constantinople and Cairo, and even to William III, acquainting them with their "misfortunes" on account of seizures made of their Mokha and Jedda shipping.[34] By early 1710 Madras claimed to have thwarted Arab attempts to establish a shipbuilding enterprise as distant as Pegu, eliciting relief from the directors who feared these "perfect Pyrates" were establishing themselves in eastern India.[35]

Once again, the Company in London and Asia saw piracy not just as a threat but an opportunity. The directors argued in 1719 that "one good use" of making peace with "these Pickeroons" would be to compel them to take and honor Company passes, and perhaps even raise their price.[36] In 1725 Bombay reported proudly that it had seized four country ships "that had not our Pass," fining them eight hundred rupees and prompting a number of others to seek passes.[37] Bombay used its ongoing piracy convoys and growing naval power as leverage with Mughal power on land as well.[38] When a ship belonging to Abd al-Ghafur's grandson was seized in the Red Sea, for example, the Bombay council again sent two East Indiamen and a few other ships to threaten a blockade of Surat and to withhold passes if the *mutasaddi* exacted any reprisal on the Company's factors there. Clearly times had changed. Surat officials now capitulated, even committing in writing to the fact that the piracies were not the Company's fault.[39] The Company also boldly demanded compensation from al-Ghafur for protecting his ships in the Red Sea.[40] Meanwhile, the council at Gombroon was directed to use an offer "to destroy all the Muscatters great Ships" to help bring about a settlement to the continuing dispute over the Company's "Ancient Capitulations" of its share of the Gombroon customs. London subsequently authorized Bombay to offer pirate convoys and station two ships in the gulf "for the Protection of the Persians" on the same condition.[41] As Calcutta observed, "Nothing would gain the English So Much favour in Persia as destroying the Muscatters."[42]

The battle with the Qawasim would last into the early nineteenth century, but the Company had decisively subdued the Angre regime by the 1750s. Kanhoji was succeeded at his death in 1729 by several of his sons, most notably Tulaji Angre, who became notorious in Britain as an "arch-pyrate." In 1733 the Bombay government under Robert Cowan entered into a treaty alliance with its once mortal enemy, the Sidi of Janjira, for a "firm & lasting foundation a perpetual alliance and sincere friendship," and a "league against all the enemies of both Governments in India (Europeans, subjects of the Kings of Hindostan, Persia, Arabia, & China excepted) and particularly against Angria, both Governments making a vigorous war by sea & land." The treaty gave the Company rights to build a garrisoned factory and fort in Kolaba, should the territory be conquered from the Marathas.[43] Despite "many expensive, fruitless attempts," in the words of one contemporary Company servant, to root him out of his base at Gheriah, Tulaji kept on until 1756, by which point he had sufficiently alienated the powerful Maratha Peshwa of Poone, Balaji Bajirao, also known as Nana Sahib. It was thus a joint Company-Maratha offensive, led by the British naval admiral Charles Watson and a Company sepoy detachment headed by Robert Clive, that finally subdued the Company's greatest maritime rival in the western Indian littoral.[44]

Both the process and result of the war against the Angres had helped to solidify British supremacy in the Western Indian littoral. It had occasioned a rapid expansion of the Company's naval power in the region, lionized as the Bombay Marine. This security regime bolstered Bombay's status as a colony and its maritime and naval economy; immigrants followed, such as the renowned Surat shipwright Lowjee Nusserwanjee who came in 1736, along with almost a dozen other Parsi carpenters, laying the foundations for a commercial ship-building empire later known as the Vadias.[45] Bombay continued to use its passes to define its jurisdictional authority at sea.[46] The fear of attack also led Stephen Law's government in 1742 to dramatically increase the number of troops on the island and to order a survey of all the inhabitants, length of residency, their "characters," and their weapons "as it is the undoubted and fundamental maxim of all States to pursue such cautionary measures as may be best calculated for the prevention of any design whether attempted from open and public force or secret treachery."[47]

Finally, this power turned on the very place where the Company's presence in western India had been first established a century and a half earlier. In 1759 John Spencer, on behalf of Bombay's government, seized control of Surat's fort. Writing to the Mughal emperor Alamgir II, Spencer, perhaps unwittingly, recalled words John Child had written to his namesake Aurangzeb (also known as Alamgir, or world-seizer) almost a half-century earlier, insisting that "our Business in those parts of the World is only Trade and Merchandize and we are Not desirous of Taking or governing City's or Countries." The seizure was, as the Company had been arguing for its other fortifications for decades, intended only to protect the inhabitants of Surat, the Company's allies, from their common enemies. He reminded the emperor that Surat was "the only port of Good Mussullmen to the Tomb of your Prophett," and offered all services in his power to defend his city, its inhabitants, and "your Majesty's Authority." He also ousted the Sidi's forces from the city. The Company's "protection" of Surat was acknowledged in September in the form of a *farman* appointing the Company as *qilidar*, or governor of the fort of Surat, and a *husb-ul-hookum* to take on the "the office of Deroga of the Great Fleet." The Company thus assumed both the top military position at Surat *and* the job of patrolling the seas that had been performed for generations by its old enemy and more recent ally, the Sidi, as well as the *tanka*, or assignment of revenue, that office received in exchange.[48]

In taking on the *qilidari*, the Company had in fact achieved something first proposed by George Oxinden, the first Company governor of Bombay, almost a century earlier, while taking charge of the fleet and maritime defense of the western Mughal empire certainly echoed Samuel Annesley's proposal in the 1690s to make the Company a *faujdar* of the high seas.[49] The Bombay council noted in March 1759 that the post "would in a few years answer better to Your Honours than all your possessions on this Coast."[50] In 1760 the Court of Directors ordered that its factors at Surat reside not in the factory but in the castle and maintain a "respectable force," making sure never to "injure or maltreat the inhabitants," and to keep up a good relation with the *mutasaddi*, who increasingly came under the Company's control. They were reminded to "appear the Merchant Advocate and Protector," because "in defending them from Oppressions you establish your own Security, such candid and fair behaviour will unite the Inhabitants in Affection and respect to your government." Once again, Company officials there were reminded to "make no ill use of Power, distribute Justice equally to all."[51]

This power did come at a cost, as the expansion at sea that underpinned it increasingly had come to rely upon the support of the British state. War in Europe continued to compel the directors to solicit the Admiralty for Atlantic convoys and the return of impressed sailors; in December 1710 a press gang even raided the India House in Leadenhall Street, attempting to nab sailors while waiting for their pay.[52] In 1721 the first East Indian Royal Navy squadron explicitly instructed to pursue both Anglo-American and Indian pirates was fitted out for the East Indies. Company ships also received nine separate commissions to seize pirates between 1709 and 1716; in 1715 the directors had resolved that all outward-bound ships carry royal commissions for seizing pirates, and between 1748 and 1755, the Company requested twenty-one of them. The Company found it necessary to have the commissions for trying pirates at Madras and Bombay renewed at the accession of both George I and George II.[53] When in 1739 the Court of Directors asked the king to grant letters of marque for the pursuit of pirates in India, the Crown's lawyers insisted that the Company's Admiralty Courts, which had fallen into disuse, be first reestablished, though now as royal rather than Company courts. The Company also sought direct royal commissions to authorize the governors of Bombay, Madras, and Calcutta to issue letters of marque, "the like Powers as are Given to your Majesty's Governours in the West Indies."[54]

The Company's efforts to involve the British state in piracy suppression ironically did as much to erode its autonomy from that state as it did to expand it in Asia. Still, this change was gradual and efforts to resist it subtle and consistent. The directors, for example, seemed committed to maintaining the long-standing legal distinction between the Company's jurisdiction in the East Indies and the Crown's authority in the Atlantic. In 1708 they successfully lobbied Parliament to have a clause added to the "Act for the Encouragement of the Trade to America" (the "Sixth of Anne") governing privateering and impressment in the Atlantic to restrict the commissioning of privateers to "within the space of One hundred Leagues of any Part of Asia or Africa."[55] In 1715 the Court of Directors sought the opinion of legal counsel as to whether they could license a free trader to Madagascar, even if they had certain knowledge that the person was intending to break English law by smuggling East African slaves to the West Indies. The lawyers noted that while doing so might have political implications, legally speaking the Company's only obligation was to consider what the trader did in the East Indies; what happened thereafter "concerns the Person licenced and not the Company."[56] The Company issued the passes in question, though refused requests in 1721 from both the Royal African Company and the South Sea

Company for similar licenses.[57] That same year, the Privy Council intervened, formally illegalizing trade in East Indian slaves and goods between licensed East India servants and American smugglers, effectively extending the purview of the Navigation Acts in a limited sense into East India affairs for the first time.[58]

The Company continued to need the British state to fight interlopers as well. While many of its old foes had died off or reconciled themselves to its authority, the union of the companies had not settled the problem of illegal Eurasian trading or of British subjects living in Asia without Company permission. In 1705 the Court of Managers drew up a "Declaration of Encouragement for Persons to Discover clandestine Trade" to be published in both England and India, which raised the prize for those who successfully informed on interloping voyages from one-quarter to one-half of the booty.[59] The United Company reconfirmed this declaration in the form of a bylaw, which included a number of additional regulations governing the exporting of goods and bullion to the East Indies.[60] Its charterparty contracts fined ships' proprietors £100 for any person left in or brought home from India (including St. Helena) without permission.[61] It also began to use a new covenant and bond for free traders in India, imposing a security of £2,000 liable to forfeiture should they even have a relationship with interlopers.[62] Early in his term as general at Bombay, Nicholas Waite ordered both the Madras and Calcutta councils to issue passes only to Company servants or inhabitants of the three cities "or other Collonies"; he also expressly forbid issuing them to Mughal-owned ships piloted by English subjects, "preventing all that's possible those many untoward Evills Incourageing their Navigation [and] destruction to the English Nation by permitting her Majesties Subjects sailing over India in their Service."[63] The directors later insisted the councils again clarify to free traders "that by the Laws No Subjects of his Majesty can stay in India without Our leave" and that their right to stay in India was dependent upon their "good behaviour," including not "Assisting Our Enemys, Or openly striking at Our Priviledges, Or refusing to comply with the Rules by Us perscrib'd for the good Government of Our Settlements."[64]

By the 1710s, the Company had also become concerned with what the directors termed "the New Interlopers." In the late seventeenth century, the Company's greatest anxieties were stoked by Englishmen like Samuel White, who took up employment and protection under Asian polities; its attention now shifted to "Subjects to the King of Great Brittain [who] trade to India under Foreign Colours."[65] This was particularly brought into focus by the creation of an East India Company in the Austrian Netherlands, chartered by the Holy Roman Emperor and known more generally as the Ostend Company. Similar to the Scottish Company of the 1690s, this venture had a self-proclaimed global scope, designed to compete with the English, Dutch, French, and Danes in both Indies and Africa. The parallel was not simply metaphorical. While much has been made of the Scots who found their way into English Company service after 1707, many of them continued to travel Scotland's more well-trodden routes to Asia via the Continent, finding employ with the Dutch, Danes, and now the Ostend Company.[66] This would, the directors feared, only encourage more Britons to seek employment and perhaps even privateering commissions "to cruise on all Mahometans Moors Persians or Turks" from elsewhere in Europe, including Russia and Malta, thereby complicating the Company's diplomacy in Western Asia.[67] In themselves, Britons in Ostend service flouted Company authority and were a threat to government. This seemed to be confirmed by the arrival of an Ostender ship at Surat in October 1715, piloted by an Irish captain, most likely the notorious Jacobite Xavier Sarsfield, whose father had fought for James II in Ireland and who had himself just been granted a certificate of *noblesse* from the Stuart Pretender, James III, in exile at St. Germain. Particularly in the context of the Jacobite rebellion in Britain that same year, it was not hard here to draw a very clear link here between interloping and rejection of proper government.[68]

The combination of the growth of Company power on the Indian seas, the firm establishment of its claims to jurisdiction over Britons established by the defeat of the Scottish Company and the union of Great Britain, and the apparently great number of Scots and Irish subjects serving other Europeans allowed for a very subtle shift in the Company's approach to its rivals. Soon, it was not just Britons but "the Ostenders or other such sort of East India Traders" themselves who the directors came to treat as if they had "come to interlope upon Us."[69] Private French traders in the Bay of Bengal were also implausibly counted as amongst the "New Sort of Interlopers."[70] As with its battle against Asian "pirates," this language permitted a far more aggressive approach to confronting these Europeans, not entirely unlike the sorts of claims the Portuguese had made to exclusive jurisdiction in Asia centuries earlier. Company councils and ship captains in Asia and St. Helena were authorized not just to seize interloping British ships but to forcibly remove "any English Scotch or Irish" from any ship in Asia, despite "their pretence of Foreign Commissions whether real or counterfeit or surreptitiously procur'd." The directors also issued instructions to expel any Company servant "Civill Military or Maritime" that offered such a ship assistance.[71]

The Company vigilantly made its case to the British public, through petitions, pamphlets, and even opera, all in the service of soliciting royal and state support for its efforts.[72] Much like the case the committees had made against piracy in the 1690s, the Court of Directors attempted to sell interloping as a challenge to the very foundations of the new Hanoverian dynasty's authority over its British dominions and, in turn, reinforce the Company's control over its own jurisdiction. The argument seemed to work. George I issued a proclamation reaffirming the prohibition on British subjects without Company license to "Visit, Haunt, Frequent, Trade, Traffick, or Adventure into or from the East-Indies," including those serving other Europeans.[73] In 1718 the Company secured a Parliamentary ban on British subjects traveling under the auspices of foreign East India Companies, particularly the Ostend Company. By 1720 the directors reported confidently that "We have law eno[ugh] on our side to make them pay dearly for Coveting after such forbidden fruit."[74] Such legislation was reissued in 1721 and 1723, and in 1725 the attorney general reaffirmed the Company's power to seize any British person "going thither with the intent to make a Settlement whether on the behalf of himself or any other person."[75] Under George II, the Admiralty was given the power to commission East India ships to "take, seize and destroy any foreign Ships, trading from the Austrian Netherlands to the East-Indies."[76] The Company also sued violators in British courts; in 1728, one captain who made two voyages to Bengal was pursued in 1728 for reparations, which the Court of Exchequer granted in the amount of £1,500: £500 for the King and £1,000 for the Company.[77]

Not everyone agreed the Company was on solid ground in its approach to the Ostend Company, but even these objections reinforced a sense of the Company's jurisdiction; for example, the politician Horace Walpole, the brother of the chief minister, felt that its right to make seizures should be "limited to the other side of the line"—that is, in the East Indies rather than Europe or the Atlantic.[78] Ultimately, British diplomats in Europe, together with the Dutch and French governments, took up the cause and under this pressure the Ostend Company was dissolved by 1731. Far from arresting the problem, this simply sent many Scots and Irish elsewhere, such as to Poland, where their efforts were also hindered by British officials.[79] Since around 1717 Irish projectors had also been proposing an East India Company to officials in Sweden, imagining it could somehow capitalize on the increasingly dormant trading networks erected by the Madagascar pirates. While these proposals did not proceed, in the wake of the Ostend Company's demise, the Swedish king Fredrick I did grant a fifteen-year patent for an East India Company, developed largely by Scottish exiles, and financed and crewed by Englishmen and others from the Continent.[80] The very next year, the Company and British diplomats also sounded alarms over proposals in Spain for an "East India Company," which, though ostensibly designed to link Cadiz and the Philippines, many feared would become a base for an independent Spanish East India trade.[81]

The Company's old rivals had begun to fade and give way to new ones. After years of devastating war in western Asia and declining fortunes, the Portuguese were increasingly less of a concern for the Company, despite continued conflicts over Bombay's jurisdiction, which even reached open hostilities, and the *Estado da India*'s brief resurgence in Bengal.[82] The Dutch by the mid-eighteenth century also precipitously declined in power in India; as they did, they transformed for the English from a model of imperial virtue to the prime symbol of decadence and effeminacy, rivaling even the Catholic Portuguese.[83] Meanwhile, the extension of European war to Asia, from the wars of the Spanish (1702–13) and Austrian (1739–48) Succession to the Seven Years' War (1756–63) brought a new sort of rivalry with the French East India Company. In 1703 French forces seized a new Company ship, the *Canterbury*, in the Straits of Malacca.[84] The Madras council began to keep paid spies at French Pondicherry,[85] and even to engage in counterintelligence efforts of its own.[86]

These early-century conflicts remained intermittent and largely maritime, but matters changed as both sides militarized dramatically during the wars that followed.[87] Famously, both companies began to pursue alliances with southern and eastern Indian powers, which served to extend the European conflict into proxy wars in South Asia.[88] Under the leadership of Joseph François Dupleix, the French and their *sepoy* army at Pondicherry had emerged by the middle of the eighteenth century as a serious southern Indian power. French forces briefly occupied Madras in 1746 and Fort St. David in 1756; meanwhile, the English Company followed an unsuccessful siege of Pondicherry during the War of the Austrian Succession with a successful invasion under a decade later.

European war had returned to India, with the Company now fully involved in it. Still, the directors' agenda was not always identical to British geostrategic concerns. There were extended but ultimately unsuccessful negotiations in 1754 to declare both St. Helena and the East Indies—from the Cape of Good Hope to the Canton River—neutral.[89] The Calcutta council was on its own attempting to forge "Simple Neutrality with the French within the Ganges, by Sea and Land" as late as 1757.[90] Once war in India became inevitable, the relationship between Company and British authority in Asia remained unclear. This was put into stark relief as lawyers tried to work out the rights to the spoils of these wars. An opinion offered in July and August of 1757 by the Crown's advocate, attorney, and solicitor generals implied that, legally speaking, there were in fact two wars going on simultaneously. The question, which centered on an interpretation of the statutes governing the division of war plunder, was prompted by the invasion of Calcutta in 1756 by Siraj-ud-daula, the French-allied *nawab* of Bengal. Ultimately, the lawyers decided that the law in question applied only to acts of war with France and had "no concern with the Disputes and Hostilities between the East India Company and the Nabob of Bengal." This raised a further dilemma: if the Company should recover control of Fort William with the assistance of Crown troops or ships, how should the plunder be divided? Their opinion was revealing in its complexity. Anything controlled prior to the invasion, most importantly Calcutta, should revert to the "old Dominion," that is, Company control. Any new territory or movable goods conquered as a result of the conflict were the Crown's by right of conquest, to do with what it pleased. The king could choose to give such property over to the Company, which he did, but he was by no means obligated to do so. The opinion thus made a far more extensive claim to a right to dominion by conquest in the East Indies, independent of the East India Company, than any previous British monarch had. It also did not address the converse question: what of conquests made by Company forces while fighting the French? The directors, noting that they had for generations kept forces in India on behalf of the nation, at great expense and risk, argued they should be able to keep all of the "plunder and booty taken" seized by Company forces "from any of your Majesty's Enemies, or from the Indian Enemies of your Petitioners." Thus, to the directors, the French were the king's enemies while the *nawab* of Bengal's was theirs, but, if its military participated, the Company deserved the spoils of war with both.[91]

The rapid buildup of both British and Company forces in India ultimately also led to some fairly familiar friction on the ground. When the 1721 anti-piracy squadron arrived at Bombay, Governor Charles Boone refused to salute it from shore, despite orders from the directors to do so, since, one contemporary reported, Boone "imagines, as all other great Men in such Stations would, that he was something superior to a Commodore of a Squadron."[92] Decades later, George Pigot, the governor of Madras, complained that Colonel John Aldercron, commander of the Crown infantry regiment that had come out with Admiral Watson on the eve of the Seven Years' War, had proclaimed his rank superior to any of the Company's officers and himself "accountable . . . to none but his Majesty." Pigot wrote his superiors in London that he found "the Powers and Prerogatives claimed by Colonel Aldercron, to bee incompatible with the Nature of your Governments, and contrary to your Interest." He even recommended that the Company figure a way to have the field officers recalled and have the royal soldiers incorporated into the Company's military, even during peacetime "for as I apprehend it would be still necessary, to keep a respectable Force on Foot at your Several Settlements in India."[93]

Such a force was necessary not only to counter the Company's European enemies, but because, the Bengal council put it in 1703, "nothing but a sword in one hand & money in the other will do much with the Moors."[94] It was crucial, especially in this newly fragmented political environment, to be able to "[repel] force by force," but also simply to "to keep up a face of Power." The Company had sought to capitalize on the "interregnum" following Aurangzeb's death in 1707 to reinforce Calcutta's Fort William, which promptly also hired more soldiers and gunmen. In 1722 the directors commended Bengal for having built up its garrison to such a point to intimidate the nearby *faujdar* out of threatening the town. "Tho we are sensible it costs dear," they wrote, "we are content to bear (care being taken there are no false musters or other wrong Charges therein) because We consider you are thereby able To prevent your Towns being plunder'd or other Insults from your Neighbours . . . & also to secure your selves from the Extortions or arbitrary demands of the smaller Branches of the Government." A show of "military force" had the added benefit of keeping security on land, serving as a check to "Insolent" *zamindars*, and enhancing the Company's sea power and the efficacy of its shipping passes.[95]

Equally as important as the "sword," however, was the "money," that is, not just commerce but diplomacy. In March 1704, the newly united council in Bengal appointed a *vakil* to negotiate with the *diwan* of Bengal, Murshid Quli Khan, on a number of points that would have seemed quite familiar to their predecessors: recognition of the new united Company as the exclusive English representative in Bengal; a single annual tribute payment to the Mughal emperor for both the trading privileges and the *zamindari* rents; and a *parwana* for concessions to trade throughout Bengal, Bihar, and Orissa. Talks continued on the subject for several years, frequently stalling on crucial differences of interpretation over previous *farmans*, from Shah Shuja's original grants for the English trade in Bengal to those granted by Aurangzeb. Matters appeared to be reaching a conclusion in 1707, when news of Aurangzeb's death caused the Company to recall its envoys and again put everything on hold.[96]

The United Company was in fact as committed to obtaining a "general" or "comprehensive" *farman* as ever. In early 1709 Bombay was instructed to offer a *peskash* to the *mutasaddi* at Surat, "to encourage him to obtain the Moguls Phirmaund."[97] Calcutta continued to treat with Murshid Quli Khan for his *sanad*, even though he was particularly reticent, refusing even to grant the Company's representatives an audience.[98] The directors recommended attempting to cultivate relationships with his courtiers, remembering that such a strategy had "been practic'd formerly," and had proven particularly useful in finally securing the *zamindari* for Calcutta.[99] London also ordered Bengal to send "handsomely and correctly written" translations of all previous "Grants or Writings in our favour," for the directors' reference.[100]

Like other Europeans in the region, Madras also continued to cultivate close relationships with a number of regional powers, in hopes of furthering this enterprise.[101] The Madras council was resolved to maintain "a good understanding with the Moors Governors near them," through presents and other means, to "preserve what the Company have left and endeavour to get what more they can . . . in the Company's name."[102] In July 1708, Governor Thomas Pitt received the *diwan* Zia-ud-din Khan, in Madras's new, massive garden, known as the Great Walk, "with all Ceremony usual" in order to receive a *husb-ul-hukum* confirming the city's privileges, which potentially paved the way for an expanded *farman* from the new emperor, Shah 'Alam.[103] For a decade since his siege of Madras, Da'ud Khan Panni, the *faujdar* of Karnataka and later *subahdar* of the Deccan, had been courted by Pitt and other Company officials, who offered him gifts of cash, liquor, and "raritys" like bear dogs and swans from England. Thanks to these efforts, Madras acquired the rights to five adjacent villages: Tiruvottiyur, Shattankadu, Kattivakkam, Vyasarpadi, and Numgambakkam. Tiruvottiyur, to the north of the town, was seen as particularly advantageous to counterbalance the increasingly troublesome Mylapor and St. Thomé at the opposite borders of the city. The Company also received forty acres of land nearby, which the council planned to use as a new garden and residence for factors and writers.[104] It also again investigated the possibility of renting or buying St. Thomé, on which the French now had designs, and added more villages to its environs in 1742 and 1749.[105]

The relationship Madras had cultivated with Zia-ud-din Khan became even more useful when in 1710 he became *faujdar* at Hugli in Bengal.[106] With the Portuguese weakening and the Dutch distracted by conflicts with the Mughals in Bengal and at Surat, the Company seemed well positioned for some diplomatic success. Both the Madras and Bengal governments continued to try to send a rather large present to Court, including six elephants, brocades, velvets, and broadcloths, but they complained it was hard to send anything substantial securely to a constantly peripatetic court; the Company regarded offers from other officials at court and in Bengal, like Zia, to have the presents sent through them with suspicion.[107] The councils were also somewhat hesitant to commit to great amounts of money given the instability of Mughal politics and quick rotation of officials, from the emperor on down.[108] Such fears diminished, however, at the accession of the Emperor Farrukhsiyar in 1713. "The New King," Madras informed London, "is about 26 years old is reputed brave prudent Generous is the last of Aurengzebes race. . . . this Seems to be the King who is to have the Company's present."[109] Rupchand, a Company *vakil*, and a couple of Armenian agents began the process of soliciting for protection for the Company's present to travel to court; in January 1714 they also secured an order declaring the Company's trade free throughout Bengal.[110]

The time thus seemed ripe to push for the *farman*.[111] After some debate, Calcutta appointed John Surman of their Patna factory to head an embassy to court. He was to be accompanied by Edward Stephenson, John Pratt (who ultimately did not join), Hugh Barker as secretary, the surgeon William Hamilton, and Kwaja Sarhad, an extremely successful Armenian merchant at Calcutta who had been involved in obtaining and delivering the recent instruments as well as the original *zamindari* grants (Sarhad was also the nephew of Kwaja Kalantar, who had been instrumental in first negotiating with Josiah Child and Jean Chardin for Armenian settlement in Company territories in the late 1680s).[112] Two hundred thousand rupees' worth of presents were sent from Calcutta under the guard of three hundred soldiers. In fact, there were so many gifts that Surman had to rent additional warehouses in Patna to store them.[113] Surman also rented a separate residence for the council not only because the factory was out of space but because the "Awe We are in (as Merch[ants]) from the Government hinders us in our preparations." It was, he argued, crucial "that we appear in a more publick manner than it's possible to doe att present, that we may have the greater respect from the government."[114]

When the group finally departed from Patna in May 1715, they certainly did so in a self-consciously "publick manner." Surman and his council rode in silver palanquins, trailed by one hundred sixty wagons carrying the presents and other stores, fifteen camels, ten carts, twenty-two oxen pulling large guns. They were accompanied by six Company soldiers, a trumpeter, smiths, carpenters, spadesmen, twelve hundred porters, all preceded by two Union flags and an official armed escort from the Mughal Court. The embassy even had with it a clockmaker, whose sole job was to tend to the vast number of clocks it had brought as presents.[115] The Surman embassy also traveled with a sense of its place in history. In anticipation of its departure, Madras had sent Bengal copies of grants dating back to the 1640s and "a full account of our Ancient priviledges, when granted and how confimr'd," including John Child's efforts "to have a Generall Phirmaund from the Mogull." Calcutta made Surman a similar list of grants from former emperors and *nawabs* in Bengal. Bombay's instructions for the embassy meanwhile recalled familiar issues, most notably insisting a *farman* would be unacceptable if it did not prohibit Britons without Company license from residing within Mughal territories. Surman also evidently had with him an account of William Norris's failed embassy to Aurangzeb on behalf of the new Company fifteen years earlier, as well as a description of a more successful Dutch venture in 1711.[116]

On July 5, the embassy entered the town behind a vanguard of drums and trumpets, "flinging" rupee coins into the crowd, in order to "aggrandiz[e] our first appearance." Surman and Surhad met with Farrukhsiyar two days later, as well as his "Prime Ministers," including the *wazir*.[117] Surman's embassy offered its gifts. Ever eager, they even contemplated renaming Calcutta as Farrukhbandar and the three towns together as a *pargana* to be known as Farrukhabad (the present Farrukhabad in Uttar Pradesh had been founded that same year), a proposal tactfully "Laid Aside" when it occurred to them that using the emperor's name as well as the suffix *bandar* (port) could serve as grounds for stationing Mughal officials in Calcutta or levying taxes on it.[118]

Citing as precedence the Company's *farman* from Aurangzeb and other instruments dating back to the early seventeenth century, Surman presented a formal petition requesting nineteen particulars to be covered in the new *farman*.[119] These included trading concessions, such as free passage and customs for Company goods in Mughal dominions, and greater security of goods landed and traveling through the country. Yet, Surman also pressed on a number of long-standing issues concerning the Company's political establishment: immunity from the *farmaish, faujdari,* and *zamindari* demands of other local officials over Calcutta or British subjects; a confirmation of the right to mint rupees at Madras; full and permanent control over the Company's factories at Patna and Surat; an unambiguous and perpetual settlement of the *zamindari* over the towns in the environs of Calcutta, Sutanuti, and Govindpur; the rights to Divi Island near Madras; and a positive order for the protection of Fort St. David from the "Severall Jemidars &ca round that place [that] are troubling & molesting us." He also demanded the return of the five towns Da'ud Khan had granted to Thomas Pitt for Madras, which Da'ud and the *diwan* of Arcot (and later *nawab*), Sa'adatullah Khan, had recently attempted take back.[120] During the inevitable delays and further petitions that followed, Surman amended his request with six more demands, including rights to coin at Bombay and the standing rights to "punish . . . According to law" any Mughal subjects who might commit a crime within the Company's jurisdiction in Bengal.[121]

A year and a half later, the embassy had still not accomplished its goal. In 1717 Surman had almost given up, and was poised to leave Shahjahanabad without his *farman.* As the story goes, the Company's fortunes were reversed by what the London directors called "a very lucky accident": the surgeon William Hamilton had "miraculously" cured the emperor of what was only ambiguously referred to as a "malignant distemper," and which has over the years been assumed to be everything from a tumor to a venereal disease.[122] True or not, the story fit a pattern, as it resonated with the equally potentially apocryphal account of the Company surgeon Gabriel Boughton, whose treatment of Jahanara, the favorite daughter of Shah Jahan, had been long credited for securing the Company its first grants for a factory in Bengal in the 1640s.[123] It also did not hurt matters that the embassy continued to spend a remarkable sum in tribute and presents, while Bombay renewed its threats to stop its trade from Surat and cease its Arabian convoys.[124]

Whatever the cause, Farrukhsiyar finally consented to grant the *farman.* The directors in London, who had become extremely agitated with the time and expense of the embassy—while at Delhi, Surman and his council were disbursing per month more than Calcutta spent on its garrison, including periodic charges for new pillowcases for their *palanquins, nautch* dancers, and a serious stockpile of pickles—now "applaud[ed] the obtaining so many Phirmaunds & Particular favours never granted before by the Mogull to any Nation." They expressed their gratitude to Surman personally in the form of a £5,000 bonus.[125] There was revelry at Calcutta, Madras, and Bombay, including feasting, drinking, gun salutes, bonfires, and parades.[126] The *gurzbardar,* mace bearer, who brought news of the *farman* to Bombay was greeted by a procession of *palanquins* flanked and followed by European and native soldiers, native merchants, flags, trumpets, and "Countrey Musick," all leading to a ceremonial pavilion, lined with perpetuana, an English textile, for walls, carpeting laid out for a floor, and "adorned with other Embelishments" including a "Chair of State" for the president, Charles Boone, who arrived soon after to receive the *sarapa*, the ceremonial dressing and exchange of gifts customary on such an occasion. A few days later, the text of the *farman* itself arrived with Company captain Charles Boddam, and was greeted with equal fanfare. Boone met him at the sea gate in his "Chariott of State," i.e., his *palanquin*, accompanied by fifty grenadiers, the council, a procession of the covenanted servants walking two by two "with their swords drawn," native soldiers marching four abreast "with Colours and Trumpets," four state horses led by liveried attendants, the Company's native servants, island inhabitants, naval officers, pages, *chobdars* (staff-bearers), the marshal, and two masters of ceremony. Boddam presented the *farman* to Boone on a satin-lined silver plate, which was then placed ceremoniously on a velvet stool. Before the *gurzbardar*, a toast was raised to the Mughal Emperor and to the Company, and a gun salute fired from the fort and the ships. Following the recessional, "an Entertainment to all the principall English inhabitants" lasted well into the night.[127]

There was, after all, much to celebrate. The *farman* not only represented the culmination of more than a half-century of efforts by Company officials but, along with the other grants that accompanied it, it far exceeded the expectations of Surman's predecessors and perhaps even Surman himself. The Company had a promise of customs-free trading through Bengal, which Calcutta interpreted as confirming its corollary right to issue passes and *dastaks*, transferring that right to others. Customs obligations were replaced in both Bengal and Surat for fixed annual payments, which bolstered the Company's claims of independence from the impositions of other Mughal officials.[128] Bombay's coins were finally permitted to circulate freely in Mughal territory, including a new rupee stamped in Persian in Farrukhsiyar's name—though the council remained anxious that the coin's inscription of "Emperor of the Sea and Land" might be taken erroneously to "[insinuate] the Jurisdiction not only of this Island but the whole world to belong to him."[129] Madras received back its five villages as well as a grant for Divi Island.[130] The Company also obtained thirty-eight additional villages in Calcutta's environs and immunity, in theory, from the demands of neighboring *zamindars* and other Mughal office and title holders. In short, the directors regarded that with the *farman*, "the Circumstances of Affairs are greatly altered," rendering the Company a greater power in Bengal than "a Duan or any inferiour Officer."[131] As Robert Orme, the mid-eighteenth century Company historian, put it, it was the "Magna Charta of the Company in India."[132]

However, the power of a *farman* was not the same in 1717 as in 1680, especially as the ouster and death of Farrukhsiyar in 1719 was followed by the quick succession of three emperors over the following year. In this context, Murshid Quli Khan, now *nawab* of Bengal, in particular managed to absorb a remarkable amount of power, consolidating the responsibilities of a number of previously separate roles, such as those of *subahdar* and *diwan*. By his death in 1727, the *nawabi*, with its seat in his eponymous Murshidabad, had evolved into the chief political and fiscal officer in the wealthiest Mughal province, and Bengal had become a sovereign state in its own right.[133]

Conflict between these two rising powers in Bengal—the Company and the Bengal *nawabi*—was perhaps inevitable. A series of *nawabs* would reject Calcutta's claim to a right to coin money and resist the Company's efforts to take control over the thirty-eight villages. Meanwhile, friction increased over the increasingly liberal use by private traders at Calcutta of *dastaks* for immunities from taxes on a range of commodities, such as salt, that the *nawab* and others considered inappropriate and a violation of their prerogative. The Court of Directors saw in the accession of Mohammad Shah as emperor in 1720 an opportunity to settle these affairs once and for all, and resolved to press for both a firm settlement of the mint and the towns. Although "not fond of much Territory," the directors gave the council leave to expand as opportunity presented itself, if they had "a moral assurance it will contribute directly or in consequence to our real benefit."[134] However, the invasion of Delhi by the Persian king Nadir Shah in 1739 and Maratha raids into Bengal in the next decade only further weakened the hold of the Mughal center, while consequently strengthening both the Company and the *nawabi*. Part of the conflict between the Company and the *nawab* rested in rival interpretations of the *farman*, which English officials clearly expected to function as a property right, which could be alienated and inherited.[135] Yet, the Company was not insensitive to the reality of power politics. As John Deane, a former governor of Calcutta, put it in 1732, without the "Nabobs Sunnud [*sanad*] all the Phirmaunds from Court signify little."[136] On at least seven occasions between 1727 and 1749, Calcutta was forced to add significantly to the annual 3,000 rupee payment required by the *farman*, simply to be sure the Bengal *nawabs* would honor it.[137]

Company officials also seemed willing to defend by force what they understood as a sovereign right. Emboldened by the grant, Joseph Collet led Madras in 1717 into armed conflict with Diaram, the chief revenue farmer at Trivitore, to ensure the promised return of its five villages; a settlement with the *nawab* of Arcot the following year confirmed the Company's rights to the villages, Divi, as well as other immunities from Mughal impositions in Madras's environs. In 1719 Calcutta seized hostages and engaged in open skirmishes with a neighboring *zamindar* in order to retrieve a Hindu merchant of Calcutta who owed the Company unpaid rent, which the council hoped would convince others "not only to refuse protection to any of our tenants, but also to deliver them up to us when demanded."[138] The Company's focus remained more on rights and privileges than land, but it was often hard to keep them separate. The directors, reminding their subordinates of their commercial responsibilities, remained reluctant to "be incumber'd" with the thirty-eight villages but ultimately left it to the Calcutta council to determine what would be best to safeguard its jurisdiction.[139] In 1749 Fort William "assured" London "that if the country Government endeavours to encroach on any of the privileges granted you by the royal phirmaund we shall support them with our utmost efforts," and a few years later, sent the 1717 *farman* and copies of "all grants to Your Honours from the Mogull."[140]

Tensions in Bengal had reached a fever pitch by 1756. The *nawab*, Siraj-ud-daula, was as eager as his predecessors to establish his own authority and resist the Company's growing demands; he had also, somewhat by default, grown into an alliance with the French. Siraj's aggression had deep roots in his resentment of a variety of Company practices, which he regarded as offenses to his sovereignty, including the Company's general growing impertinence, its continuing fortification at Calcutta, and the increasing entanglements of English private traders in Bengal's economy, particularly their liberal use of *dastaks*. In June, he invaded and occupied Calcutta and Fort William. The town and fort were famously recovered just a year later, when in July 1757 the same team that had defeated Tulaji the previous year, Admiral Watson and Robert Clive, now deputy governor of Fort St. David, arrived in Bengal and as much through intrigue as force definitively defeated the *nawab's* forces at Plassey (Palasi), a mango grove near Murshidabad.

The conflict in Bengal was shaped from start to finish directly by the expectations established in the *farman*. This was made abundantly clear in the peace treaty settled between Siraj, Watson, and Clive. Each clause of this agreement was related to some issue with which the Company had been concerned over the previous century: that the Company have its privileges by virtue of its *farmans*, including its villages and *zamindari* in Calcuta; that its *dastaks* be respected; that restitution be made for seizures; that the Company be allowed to fortify in Calcutta "without any Hindrance or Obstruction"; that Calcutta have more authority over the land within and without its bordering ditch; and that its coins pass current and without deduction.[141] Similarly, the subsequent treaty with Mir Jaffar, the puppet *nawab* Clive installed in Siraj's place, reconfirmed and enlarged the *zamindari* of Calcutta into the so-called twenty-four *parganas*, a much larger unit of towns grouped for revenue assessment; it also restricted the *nawab* from building any new fortifications below Hugli.[142] The demands and concessions that followed from this would also have hardly seemed shocking to earlier Company leadership: a *sanad* for the *zamindari* that included clauses requiring the Company to keep good order in its jurisdiction; a reconfirmation of Calcutta's exemption from the jurisdiction of the *faujdar*; and finally, a subsequent grant from the *diwan* forgiving Calcutta's revenue obligations, interpreted by the English as having granted a "free tenure" of the town, specifically on the grounds that the Company needed such revenues for the town's infrastructure and defense.[143] Notoriously, Clive also acquired a personal *jagir* in Bengal, and the Company itself received one not long after from the *nawab* of Arcot.[144]

As C. R. Wilson put it almost a century ago, with Clive's victory at Plassey, "the soldier completed and more than completed what the ambassador began."[145] Following a series of conflicts, culminating in a bloody victory over Mir Kasim, Mir Jafar's successor, at Buxar in 1764, Calcutta's growing power had left the Company the most formidable political actor in eastern India. This was recognized by Shah Alam II in 1765, when he made the Company *diwan* in Bengal, Bihar, and Orissa. Although the directors had resisted the post when it had been offered three times earlier, the idea itself was not unprecedented. The conceptual and legal possibility of the English East India Company becoming a corporate Mughal tributary could be found in proposals and ideas from George Oxinden and Gerald Aungier to Samuel Annesley and John Gayer. Its foundations lay, several steps removed, in the aggressive efforts of John Child and others to assert the Company's authority over its colonies and British subjects throughout Asia, in a series of grants for rights of government at Madras and elsewhere, and in the Company's more recent assumption of other Mughal offices, the *zamindari* at Calcutta and *qilidari* at Surat. The *diwani* represented something of a different order, as it was a grant not just of rights to revenue and urban jurisdiction but of sovereign administrative and juridical authority over the great expanse of eastern India and its great populations of peasants and landlords. Nonetheless, a century of Company efforts to render itself a sovereign state in India had in a sense come to fruition—in fits and starts, rearticulated, transformed, and in a form hardly imaginable by Oxinden, Aungier, Annesley, Gayer, or Child—when in 1772, London sent Calcutta's governor Warren Hastings his orders to "stand forth as duan."

Conclusion

"A Great and Famous Superstructure"

In early 1756, virtually on the eve of the *nawab* of Bengal's invasion, the Calcutta council discovered to their horror that parts of the diary of John Surman's embassy to Emperor Farrukhsiyar were missing. Losing the official diplomatic record of the acquisition of the Company's "Magna Charta" in India should have been awkward enough. It was not nearly as embarrassing, however, as where one of its leaves ultimately resurfaced: stuck away, evidently unnoticed, in the factory's "publick necessary house."[1] How Surman's diary ended up in the latrine used by the factory's bureaucrats was, and remains, a mystery. Still, there may have been no finer metaphor for the place Company politics of the previous century would soon come to occupy in the annals of the British Empire. The *nawab's* invasion was regarded by Edmund Burke as marking "a memorable era in the history of the world"; his defeat at the Battle of Plassey in 1757 came quickly to be considered a "revolution," and the *diwani* grant that followed from it in 1765 the moment when, as Thomas Pownall put it in 1773, "the merchant" had "become the sovereign."[2] The Company's acquisition of territorial sovereignty in Bengal thus marked for many, then and since, a firm break from the past and, consequently, the political institutions, behaviors, and ideologies of its previous century and a half figured as part of a commercial prehistory—mislaid in the dustbin, or perhaps the necessary house, of political, intellectual, and imperial history.

Despite this persistent perception, the so-called Company "Raj" that emerged in the wake of Plassey and *diwani* was constantly negotiating the legacies of its past politics. That a British corporation could become a Mughal *diwan*, what Burke decried as a "dual sovereignty," with responsibilities over vast territorial revenues, the administration of justice, and the maintenance of "a large army for the protection of the provinces" had clear antecedents in pre-Plassey Company governance, in fantasies of an Indian Ocean *faujdari* and the realities of the acquisition of a *qilidari*, in shipping passes and *dastaks*, in Josiah Child's battles for Company charters and John Child's wars for his *farman*, not to mention John Surman's successful acquisition of it through diplomacy decades later.[3] The

Company's subsequent successful military campaigns in southern and western India and its defeat of the Marathas on land by the 1810s relied on the Company's power at sea, which in turn grew out of a system of passes designed to combat interloping and compete with rivals and a seventeenth-century struggle against Anglo-American "pirates" that gave way to an eighteenth-century "war" against Indian ones. That same process made possible subsequent Company dominance in the Arabian peninsula and the Indian Ocean, and particularly the conversion in the early nineteenth century of the Arabian "Pirate Coast" into the "Trucial Coast." In 1765, Company India still had corporations and Mayor's Courts, Madras was still struggling with assessments for street sweeping more than a century after Streynsham Master first tried to impose them in the 1670s, and Bombay still continued to battle the Portuguese over their claims to "spiritual jurisdiction" on the island well into the late eighteenth century.[4] In the 1820s there were also still *bichara* at Sumatra, which clearly displeased its governor Stamford Raffles, who derisively dismissed them as "little better than a palaver of North American Indians."[5]

Well into its "colonial" period, the Company-State in India remained in any number of ways an early modern regime.[6] This regime had been built out of the ambitions of seventeenth-century Company leadership to erect what they understood as "foundations as must in time induce a great & famous superstructure."[7] They did not set out to create a vast territorial empire in India nor would they have been particularly comfortable with one. Their efforts were directed towards protecting a particular form of hybrid and composite sovereignty over a system that was at its core urban, coastal, and maritime in its orientation and rooted in the Company's constitution as a corporate body politic, a jurisdiction over trade and people, a colonial proprietor, and eventually a Mughal tributary officeholder. This typically early modern regime seemed exceedingly well-suited to navigating the decentralized politics of eighteenth-century India, but it sat increasingly uncomfortably next to the notion of a more centralized, national state and empire, which was emerging in eighteenth-century Britain. *Diwani* thus raised in stark terms a crucial "question of sovereignty," not only about Bengal but the Company as well.[8] Was it proper for a corporation to exercise the prerogatives of empire or was it a matter of degree, and the *diwani*, in Robert Clive's words, simply "so large a sovereignty" that it had been "too extensive for a mercantile Company"?[9] How could one, in the context of expanding British state claims to exclusive sovereignty, understand an East India Company that was both a chartered British corporation under Crown and Parliament and a titled officeholder under the Mughal emperor? What were the implications of a Company empire in Asia for a British empire that had just come to understand itself as "Protestant, commercial, maritime, and free" but which now had to confront the possibility of becoming a "free though conquering people"?[10]

While some vigorously defended the Company and its "antient system" in the wake of Plassey,[11] a great many more, for a variety of reasons, came to agree with Pownall that governing Bengal was a trust for which a corporate body was "not adequate" and with which its servants "should not be trusted."[12] Fairly quickly, the commercial and political autonomy the Company had so vigilantly defended for centuries would fall to Parliamentary intervention, understood as "reform."[13] The Company's negotiations with the ministry and the king's lawyers in the aftermath of 1757, which allowed it to retain sovereignty in Bengal in exchange for an annual tribute of £400,000, gave way a decade later to an ad hoc Parliamentary committee of inquiry investigating its administration both at home and abroad. Lord North's so-called "Regulating Act" of 1773 introduced a Supreme Court and the office of governor-general into Calcutta. Charles Fox's failed India Bill of 1783 was followed by William Pitt's India Act of 1784, which created a Parliamentary-appointed Board of Control to regulate the Company's directors at home and its government abroad. Burke and others indicted the Company's entire system in form of the impeachment of its first governor-general, Warren Hastings, beginning in 1786 and lasting into the 1790s. Charter renewals in 1794, 1813, and 1833 progressively dismembered the Company's independence, ultimately eliminating the Company itself in the wake of the Indian Rebellion of 1857–58.

Of course, this too was not unprecedented. The assault on the Company's constitution, in Parliament and the press alike, in the wake of *diwani* repeated all of the categories of critique of the "old" Company that had come into focus following the Glorious Revolution. The Company was accused of excess and corruption and of novelty and innovation in its political ambitions. It was investigated by ad hoc Parliamentary committees of inquiry, "regulated" by new legislation and charters, imposed upon by state agencies, all against the backdrop of ambitious rivals impatient to have access either to its commercial profits or political jurisdiction and an expanding Parliamentary imperial state, involved in a costly European war, eager to assert its authority over its competitors and capitalize on its revenue.[14] This process only continued and accelerated through the eighteenth century. The union of Great Britain, the expansion of the British military-fiscal state, the transformations of the British Empire in its mid-century wars, and the political and ideological expansion of a centralized, territorial state left increasingly little room for an East India Company political constitution, especially as that state came to make new and expansive claims over its empire. It was not an accident that the assault on the East India Company coincided with the establishment of a range of ideas and institutions designed to assert greater control and supervision over legal and political affairs of the British Atlantic, such as the Board of Trade, vice-Admiralty courts, the renewal of the Navigation Acts, a new piracy statute, and increasingly successful techniques of collecting, controlling, and disseminating information throughout the colonies. The process of absorbing a corporate and hybrid Atlantic colonial world into a more coherent British Empire was similarly neither linear nor always successful. Jersey lost its proprietorship (though not its property) in 1702 and Carolina in 1729, while the Penns, the Calverts, Rhode Island, and Connecticut managed to hold onto their government for longer. The charter for Georgia symbolized this transition, creating a proprietary corporation responsible for planting and governing the colony, but one which was determined from the start to dissolve into Crown rule after twenty-one years. The Seven Years' War catalyzed this process, compounding the political impulse for control with a fiscal need for revenue, while complicating the problem of legal uniformity in North America with the addition of French-speaking Quebec into the Crown's dominions. The "long eighteenth century," with its assault on Atlantic proprietary charters, clamping down on colonial autonomy, and imposition of a new regime of military expansion, political intervention, "intolerable" taxes and duties, and efforts to reform American colonial jurisprudence, all pointed toward the extension of metropolitan power and thus the expansion of both the British state over those corporate and chartered bodies that in fact had done the business of governing the early modern "empire."[15]

As P. J. Marshall has noted, in the mid-eighteenth century, "dealing with the Company was not unlike dealing with an American colony," with its chartered rights, representative governing body, and (much greater) political ties in London.[16] Efforts to rein it in similarly developed over time. The first blows to the Company's autonomy came amid the debates of the 1690s and their resolution in the creation of the United East India Company. This set the stage for a gradual assault on the Company's independence from the state across the eighteenth century. When Calcutta, Bombay, and Bengkulu were finally incorporated as municipalities (the former two in 1726, confirmed in 1727 and 1753, and the last in 1760), it was by royal, not Company, charter.[17] The new charter for the Madras corporation now included a number of alterations including for the first time a direct right of appeal from the Mayor's Court to the king and Privy Council; the Mayor's Court was officially, if not practically, stripped of its jurisdiction over non-Europeans in 1753.[18] Under these conditions, the Mayor's Court rapidly began to lose the hybrid character that had characterized it in the seventeenth century, giving way instead to forms of justice in all three presidency towns that increasingly separated European and Asian subjects.[19] A Supreme Court replaced the Mayor's Court and its municipal authority over Britons in Calcutta in 1773. A Recorder's Court in 1798 and then a Supreme Court in 1800–01 in Madras ultimately replaced its Mayor's Court, a process repeated for Bombay in 1823.[20] In the 1760s, Crown lawyers could still recognize the original Madras municipal charter as a legal precedent; just two decades later, even the

Company's own counsel could not definitively determine the grounds and authority on which the Company administered justice at St. Helena and recommended that the Company obtain a new royal charter of justice for that island as well.[21]

The legal and political assault on the Company in eighteenth-century Britain, particularly after Plassey, took aim at two of its most coveted rights and responsibilities: extraterritorial authority over British subjects in Asia and autonomous government of its possessions abroad. In 1757 Solicitor-General Charles Yorke, himself a former Company lawyer, was of the opinion that while the Company retained the right to send its own servants back to England at will, other Britons who had lived in Company settlements for "a considerable time," traded there, and participated in their government and its courts could be said to have "a license, though not in form" by prescription. In 1767 another official legal opinion held that the Company could not tax anyone other than its employees without their own consent or that of Parliament.[22] The 1773 Supreme Court interposed Crown-appointed judges in the administration of justice over Europeans. The so-called pious clause of the Company's 1813 charter permitted any British missionary to travel to and within Asia and established an archbishopric at Calcutta, formally incorporating the Company's ministry into the Anglican episcopacy.[23]

Though his opinion had been more ambiguous just years earlier, Yorke, as attorney general in 1761, insisted that any "Settlements, Fortresses or Territories" taken in the East Indies from a European power fell immediately under the king's prerogative.[24] The following year, he advised the Company that it should not pursue a potential treaty to purchase Salsette from the Marathas, who had seized it from the Portuguese in 1737, "without apprizing his Majesty's ministers of their inclinations."[25] In 1798 the Company's conquest of Ceylon from the Dutch was deemed to be a Crown, not a Company, possession, since it was from a European power.[26] In 1824 the British state ceded Bengkulu to the Dutch and in 1835 absorbed St. Helena as a Crown colony. By the nineteenth century, the Company flew only the Union Flag at its settlements as it was finally forbidden from flying anything but the red mercantile ensign on its ships, one hundred and fifty years after it had seemingly settled the issue with Samuel Pepys.[27] Persian gave way to English as British India's language of state, and William IV became the first British monarch to have his image on a Company coin.[28]

This was not accomplished without constant struggle; even the final, formal transition to Crown rule in India in 1858 was marked by conflicts between Company authorities and the British officers that replaced them, which were almost reminiscent of the days of Pigot and Watson, Waite and Harland, Child and St. John.[29] Yet, by the nineteenth century, such reforms, interventions, and incorporations began to seem natural. That the Company had changed fundamentally at

Plassey had become an historiographical truism, and the notion that the nation-state was the prime representative of the public and agent of empire largely indisputable. Although his views on the Company's history were in fact complex and at times contradictory, Thomas Babington Macaulay's extremely popular essay on Robert Clive embodied what had become the prevailing understanding of the Company's past.[30] When Clive first signed up for Company service, it was "purely a trading corporation. Its territory consisted of a few square miles, for which rent was paid to the native governments. Its troops were scarcely numerous enough to man the batteries of three or four ill-constructed forts, which had been erected for the protection of the warehouses." Madras—which "had arisen on a barren spot beaten by a raging surf"—governed itself with a wide latitude, but only by the permission of the local government, and indeed it was an authority no greater than "every great Indian landowner exercised within his own domain." Plassey, in his estimation, transformed the Company into "not merely an anomaly but a nuisance." It was only rendered a "beneficial anomaly" by Parliamentary regulation. For Macaulay, the British Empire in India had become a territorial power in India commanded by "mere traders, ignorant of general politics, ignorant of the peculiarities of the empire which had strangely become subject to them."[31]

This version of the early Company has had remarkable staying power. For all the work in recent decades incorporating empire into the fields of political, cultural, and intellectual history, our thinking about the nature of political communities outside the state continues to be deeply affected by the general assumptions at the core of that state's own expectations and ideologies. The Company's political institutions have tended to be approached *prima facie* as incomplete, instrumental, or simply curious, and the ideas behind them something akin to Macaulay's sarcastic disdain for the Company's "admirable code of political ethics": superficial, disingenuous, or simply self-interested. In the process, the wide scope of possibilities for the history of political thought in and, perhaps most directly, of the specific historical processes by which the British empire itself was made in India and around the globe, has been lost. The early modern East India Company was of course radically different from the modern British Empire in India. However, the process of making that empire—both in the sense of its foundations of the Company empire in the East Indies and its slow and painful transformation into a *British* empire in Asia—was deeply rooted in its early modern past. This is not to say that the earlier empire made the later one inevitable or was sufficient for its formation. It is to suggest, however, that the question as to whether the "revolution" at Plassey was a fundamental break or a moment of gradual transition ought at least to be open to the same sort of debate available across the Age of Revolutions, especially that famous "revolution" against the British empire in America.[32]

If such a political and intellectual approach to the early Company casts a different light on the nature of the evolution of British India, it also proposes a different reading to the discussion of the relationship between state and empire formation.[33] The East India Company was indeed important in shaping the ideas about modern, multinational commercial practice.[34] Yet, its fall was inseparable from the broader shifts in debates between corporate and individual foundations to society, understandings of property as economic rather than a political right, and, ironically, the alliance of capital and the state that came after, not before, the financial revolution.[35] It was a casualty of evolving definitions of public and private, and the growing consensus that the economy were "fields of intervention" for the polity rather than sites of government in their own right.[36] Companies became economic units and "corporation" came most readily to signify a commercial firm more readily than a body politic. The history of modern state formation was a history of one form of corporation, the nation-state, triumphing over its rivals, both within and without its borders, from the East India Company to pirates, mercenaries, composite monarchies, municipal corporations, monasteries, even the church.[37] In this sense, perhaps the "merchant-sovereign and the sovereign merchant" threatened so many in the late eighteenth century not because it was a novelty or an aberration but precisely because it was so very old, a vestige of the way politics and particularly empire used to be organized.[38] For there to have been a *British* Empire in India, not only did the East India Company have to conquer India but the British state also had to conquer the East India Company; the "conquests" in India became *British* only when Parliament asserted its rights to them, and the Company, after the fact.[39] Seen from this perspective, the rise of the modern British Empire in India becomes less an anomalous story of a commercial company that exceeded its mandate, and more an integral part of an even larger story about the historical processes by which modern states and empires themselves emerged.

A political and intellectual history of the East India Company on its own terms suggests even further the possibility of a history of political thought born out of the practices of governors, bureaucrats, and technicians who are responsible for implementing lofty ideals, negotiating between the wishes of the governors and the demands of the governed, and adapting and modifying sentiment to the distinct realities of governing over alien places and alien peoples. John Locke's proposition that there was a fundamental difference in form between "Church and State; A Commonwealth and an Army; or between a Family and the *East-India* Company" was as ideologically charged as Hobbes's belief that corporations were parasites within the body politic: neither were descriptions of the way things were but prescriptions for the way their authors believed things ought to be.[40] Early modern states and empires were not clearly defined structures but sets of de-centered processes, the product of the fuzzy tension among various legitimate rivals for power and sovereignty that defined early modern empire globally. Corporations, from towns to overseas colonial companies, can have political and intellectual histories because they were by nature public authorities and governments in their own right, which were not always quiescently subject to the nation-state. Correspondence, minutes, and administrative documents can be legitimate repositories of political thought because bureaucracies, networks, and institutions can be as legitimately political as those monarchies, republics, and others that came to speak on behalf of the "nation."

Realizing the political ambition and potential implicit in the attitudes and policies of late seventeenth-century Company officials in London and Asia also suggests a long narrative of the making of the British Empire that rests on historical continuities and historiographical comparisons. It defies the usual distinctions between a "colonial" Atlantic and a "trading world" of Asia, the "capitalist" northern Europeans and supposedly "medieval" Iberian models of empire in Asia, and, of course, between a "commercial" and "imperial" era in the Company's history and its analogue, the "first" and "second" British empires. Thus, when the Victorian imperial historian Sir John Seeley saw that the expansion of India "was not the act of a state and not accomplished by the army and the money of a state," and became the act of a state only with the intervention of the *British* state into Company affairs, he was partly right.[41] The "fit of absence of mind," to borrow Seeley's famous phrase, was neither that Britain accidentally backed into its Indian empire nor that eighteenth-century Britons did not notice it happening; it was that the foundations of that empire rested in the hard ideological work of the emerging modern state to forget that its roots lay in a very different form of body politic. Perhaps instead it takes a postmodern, postcolonial age to see the early modern age a bit more clearly, one in which empire, globalization, hybridity, and fragmentation are so very much on the mind and in which one finds a host of corporations and non-state actors resisting national sovereignty and doing the business of government. Whatever the reason, it just seems more plausible now than it did in the days of Burke, Macaulay, or Seeley to see the origins of the modern British Empire in India in the very distinctly *early* modern English East India Company-State.

ABBREVIATIONS

All manuscript and archival citations are from the India Office Records (IOR), Asia, Pacific and Africa Collections (formerly Oriental and India Office Collections), British Library, unless otherwise indicated.

Unpublished Sources

Add.MS	Additional Manuscripts, Manuscript Collections, British Library
Eg	Egerton Manuscripts, Manuscripts Collections, British Library
GL	Guildhall Library Manuscripts, London Metropolitan Archives
Harl.	Harleian Manuscripts, Manuscripts Collections, British Library
King's	King's Manuscripts, Manuscripts Collections, British Library
Lambeth	Lambeth Palace Library Archives
Lansdowne	Lansdowne Manuscripts, Manuscripts Department, British Library
NAS	National Archives of Scotland
NLS	National Library of Scotland
MS. Rawl.	Rawlinson Manuscripts, Bodleian Library, Oxford University
MSSEur	European Manuscripts, Asia, Pacific, and Africa Collections, British Library
PA	Parliamentary Archives of the United Kingdom
Sloane	Sloane Manuscripts, Manuscripts Collections, British Library
Stowe	Stowe Manuscripts, Manuscripts Collections, British Library
TNA	National Archives of the United Kingdom (formerly PRO)
Yale	Beinecke Rare Books and Manuscript Library, Yale University

Printed Records

BS	George Forrest, ed., *Selections from the Letters, Despatches, and Other State Papers Preserved in the Bombay Secretariat*, 2 vols. (Bombay: Government Central Press, 1887).

CCM   Ethel Bruce Sainsbury, ed., *A Calendar of the Court Minutes of the East India Company*, 11 vols. (Oxford: Clarendon Press, 1938).

EFI   Charles Fawcett, *The English Factories in India (New Series)*, 4 vols. (Oxford: Clarendon Press, 1936–55).

EFS   Anthony Farrington and Dhiravat na Pombejra, eds., *The English Factory in Siam*, 2 vols. (London: British Library, 2007).

LBJC   H.H. Dodwell, ed., *The Private Letter Books of Joseph Collet* (London: Longmans, Green and Co., 1933).

Boyle   Michael Hunter, Antonio Clericuzio, and Lawrence M. Principe, eds. *The Correspondence of Robert Boyle*. 6 vols. (London: Pickering and Chatto, 2001).

JHOC   *Journal of the House of Commons* (1802), *electronic edition*: http://www.british-history.ac.uk/catalogue.aspx?gid=43

RFSG: D&C   *Records of Fort St. George: Diary and Consultation Book*, 86 vols. (Madras: Superintendent, Government Press, 1910–1946).

RFSG: FSD   *Records of Fort St. George: Fort St. David Consultations* (Madras: Superintendent, Government Press, 1933–1937).

RFSG: LF   *Records of Fort St. George: Letters from Fort St. George*, 37 vols. (Madras: Superintendent, Government Press, 1915–1941).

Yule   Henry Yule, ed., *The Diary of William Hedges, Esq. (Afterwards Sir William Hedges), During His Agency in Bengal; As Well as On His Voyage Out and Return Overland (1681–1687)*, 3 vols. (London: The Hakluyt Society, 1888).

NOTES

Preface

1. I have explored some of these trends elsewhere; see Philip Stern, "History and Historiography of the English East India Company: Past, Present, and Future!" *History Compass* 7, no. 4 (2009): 1146–80.
2. Samuel Purchas, *Purchas His Pilgrimes, In Five Bookes* (London: William Stansby for Henrie Fetherstone, 1625), 1:630.
3. James Mill, *The History of British India*, 2nd ed. (London: Baldwin, Cradock, and Joy, 1820), 1:iii.

Introduction

1. Thomas Babington Macaulay, "Government of India (10 July 1833)," in *Speeches of Lord Macaulay, Corrected By Himself* (London: Longman, Green, and Company, 1877), 65–66.
2. Adam Smith, *An Inquiry into the Nature and Causes of the Wealth of Nations* (London, 1776), 2:4, 479.
3. Edmund Burke, *The Works of the Right Honourable Edmund Burke*, vol. 7: *Speeches on the Impeachment of Warren Hastings* (London: Bell and Daldy, 1870), 23.
4. An exception is Robert Travers, *Ideology and Empire in Eighteenth-Century India: The British In Bengal* (Cambridge: Cambridge University Press, 2007).
5. Such sentiments are omnipresent in the literature, even among the Company's most accomplished and prolific historians. For a sampling, see C. A. Bayly, "The British Military-Fiscal State and Indigenous Resistance: India 1750–1820," in Lawrence Stone, ed., *An Imperial State at War: Britain from 1689 to 1815* (London and New York: Routledge, 1994), 325–26; H. V. Bowen, "'No Longer Mere Traders': Continuities and Change in the Metropolitan Development of the East India Company, 1600–1834," in H. V. Bowen, Margarette Lincoln, and Nigel Rigby, eds., *The Worlds of the East India Company* (Woodbridge, Suffolk: Boydell Press, 2002), 19; K. N. Chaudhuri, *The Trading World of Asia and the English East India Company, 1660–1760* (Cambridge: Cambridge University Press, 1978), 20, 113; Bruce Lenman, *England's Colonial Wars: 1550–1688: Conflicts, Empire, and National Identity* (Harlow, Essex, 2001), 207; Sudipta Sen, *Empire of Free Trade: The East India Company and the Making of the Colonial Marketplace* (Philadelphia: University of Pennsylvania Press, 1998), 80; S. Sen, *Distant Sovereignty: National Imperialism and the Origins of British India* (New York: Routledge, 2002), 6; Niels Steensgaard, *The Asian Trade Revolution of the Seventeenth Century: The East India Companies and the Decline of the Caravan Trade* (Chicago: University of Chicago Press, 1973), 114.

6. Hints for such an approach can be found in gestures throughout the literature on the Company, but often such sentiments have tended to be articulated only suggestively, found only in short articles, in passing, or as exceptions within larger bodies of work or even the very same pieces. See Bayly, "British Military-Fiscal State," 324–25; Holden Furber, "The Growth of British Power in India 1708–1748," (1969) in Rosane Rocher, ed., *Private Fortunes and Company Profits in the India Trade in the 18th Century* (Aldershot, Hampshire: Variorum, 1997), 16; Furber, *Rival Empires of Trade in the Orient, 1600–1800* (Minneapolis: University of Minnesota Press, 1976), 198; R. Kemal, "The Evolution of British Sovereignty in India," *Indian Year Book of International Affairs* 6 (1957): 144. G. Z. Refai, "Sir George Oxinden and Bombay, 1662–1669," *English Historical Review* 92 (1977); Sanjay Subrahmanyam, "Frank Submissions: The Company and the Mughals Between Sir Thomas Roe and Sir William Norris," in Bowen, Lincoln, and Rigby, eds., *Worlds of the East India Company*, 70; Ian Bruce Watson, "Fortifications and the 'Idea' of Force in Early English East India Company Relations with India," *Past and Present* 88 (1980); Philip Woodruff [Mason], *The Men Who Ruled India: The Founders* (London: Jonathan Cape, 1953), 74.

7. See Alison Games, Philip Stern, Paul Mapp, and Peter Coclanis, "Forum: Beyond the Atlantic," *William and Mary Quarterly* (October 2006); Nicholas Canny, "Atlantic History and Global History" in Jack P. Greene and Philip D. Morgan, eds., *Atlantic History: A Critical Appraisal* (Oxford: Oxford University Press, 2009), 317–36. There is an ever-growing literature, particularly from the Atlantic perspective, on these intersections. For a summary, see Philip Stern, "History and Historiography of the English East India Company: Past, Present, and Future!" *History Compass* 7, no. 4 (2009): 1157–60.

8. Sanjay Subrahmanyam, *The Portuguese Empire in Asia, 1500–1700: A Political and Economic History* (London: Longman, 1993), 270–77; Kenneth McPherson, "Anglo-Portuguese Commercial Relations in the Eastern Indian Ocean from the Seventeenth to the Eighteenth Centuries," *South Asia* 19 (1996): 41–44; Glenn Ames, "The Carreira da India, 1668–1682: Maritime Enterprise and the Quest for Stability in Portugal's Asian Empire," *Journal of European Economic History* 20 (1991). See also the sort of comparative work, like that of Holden Furber, Sinnappah Arasaratnam, and Kenneth McPherson, collected in Sanjay Subrahmanyam, ed., *Maritime India* (Delhi: Oxford University Press, 2004); Om Prakash, ed., *European Commercial Expansion in Early Modern Asia* (Aldershot, Hampshire: Variorum, 1997); Leonard Blussé and Femme Gaastra, *Companies and Trade: Essays on Overseas Trading Companies During the Ancien Régime* (Leiden: Leiden University Press, 1981).

9. For one of many examples, compare the accounts of Philip Lawson, *The East India Company: A History* (London: Longman, 1993), 56; and Peter Borschberg, "Hugo Grotius, East India Trade and the King of Johor," *Journal of Southeast Asian Studies* 30 (1999): 226.

10. E.g., J. H. Elliott, *Empires of the Atlantic World: Britain and Spain in America 1492–1830* (New Haven, CT: Yale University Press, 2006); Richard Helgerson, *Forms of Nationhood: The Elizabethan Writing of England* (Chicago: University of Chicago, 1992), esp. 182; Kenneth McPherson, "Anglo-Portuguese Commercial Relations in the Eastern Indian Ocean from the Seventeenth to the Eighteenth Centuries," *South Asia* 19 (1996): 41–57. On "entangled empires," see along with the other essays in the "AHR Forum: Entangled Empires in the Atlantic World," Eliga H. Gould, "Entangled Histories, Entangled Worlds: The English-Speaking Atlantic as a Spanish Periphery," *American Historical Review* 112, no. 3 (June 2007): 764–86.

11. Charter, 43 Eliz I, 31 December [1600], in *Charters Granted to the East-India Company From 1601, Also The Treaties and Grants, Made with, or obtained from, the Princes and Powers in India, From the Year 1756 to 1772* (London, 1773), 5–6.

12. William Blackstone, *Commentaries on the Laws of England* (Oxford, 1765), vol. 1, chap. 18; Cecil T. Carr, ed., *Select Charters of Trading Companies* (New York: Burt Franklin, 1913), xii–xiv, xix; Harold Laski, "The Early History of the Corporation in England," *Harvard Law Review* 30, no. 6 (1917); William Robert Scott, *The Constitution and Finance of English,*

Scottish and Irish Joint-Stock Companies to 1720, 3 vols. (London: 1912; repr., Gloucester, MA: Peter Smith, 1968).

13. Ernst Kantorowicz, *The King's Two Bodies: A Study in Medieval Political Theology* (Princeton, NJ: Princeton University Press, 1957); F. W. Maitland, "The Crown as Corporation," *Law Quarterly Review* 17 (1901): 133; Maitland, "The Corporation Sole," *Law Quarterly Review* 16 (1900); Martin van Creveld, *The Rise and Decline of the State* (Cambridge: Cambridge University Press, 1999), 1.

14. Blackstone, *Commentaries*, 1:455–56

15. *The law of corporations: containing the laws and customs of all the corporations and inferior courts of record in England* (London, 1702), 2.

16. Catherine F. Patterson, "Corporations, Cathedrals and the Crown: Local Dispute and Royal Interest in Early Stuart England," *History* 85 (2000): 546–71; Phyllis Riddle, "Political Authority and University Formation in Europe, 1200–1800," *Sociological Perspectives* 36, no. 1 (1993): 45–62; Alexandra Shepard, "Contesting communities? 'Town' and 'gown' in Cambridge, c. 1560–1640," in Alexandra Shepard and Phil Withington, eds., *Communities in Early Modern England* (Manchester: Manchester University Press, 2000), 216–34.

17. Blackstone, *Commentaries*, 1:2, 6–7, 455–56; Paul D. Halliday, *Dismembering the Body Politic: Partisan Politics in England's Towns, 1650–1730* (Cambridge: Cambridge University Press, 1998), 32–33.

18. Blackstone, *Commentaries*, 1:460–61; Charles Molloy, *De jure maritime et navali, or, A treatise of affaires maritime and of commerce in three books* (London, 1677), 431.

19. Charter, 43 Eliz I, 31 December [1600], in *Charters*, 12; Otto von Gierke, *Community in Historical Perspective: A Translation of Selections from Das deutsche Genossenschaftsrecht (The German Law of Fellowship)*, (1868), trans. Mary Fischer, ed. Antony Black (Cambridge: Cambridge University Press, 1990). For a discussion of Gierke in this context, see Eric Wilson, "The VOC, Corporate Sovereignty and the Republican Sub-Text of *De iure praedae*," in Hans W. Blom, *Property, Piracy and Punishment: Hugo Grotius on War and Booty in De iure praedae—Concepts and Contexts* (Leiden: Brill, 2009), 337–38.

20. Phil Withington, "Company and Sociability in Early Modern England," *Social History* 32, no. 3 (August 2007): 291–307. See also Withington, *Society in Early Modern England: The Vernacular Origins of Some Powerful Ideas* (Cambridge: Polity Press, 2010).

21. Edward Coke, *The First Part of the Institutes of the Laws of England, Or, A Commentary Upon Littleton, Not the name of the Author Only, but of the Law Itself* (Philadelphia: Robert H. Small, 1853), 2:250a (1.3, c.6, sec. 413).

22. Timothy L. Alborn, *Conceiving Companies: Joint-Stock Politics in Victorian England* (London: Routledge, 1998), 3–4; Halliday, *Dismembering the Body Politic*, 29–55; Jacqueline Hill, "Corporatist ideology and practice in Ireland, 1660–1800," in S. J. Connolly, ed., *Political Ideas in Eighteenth-Century Ireland*, (Dublin: Four Courts Press, 2000), 65–82; Phil Withington, *The Politics of Commonwealth: Citizens and Freemen in Early Modern England* (Cambridge: Cambridge University Press, 2005); Withington, "Public Discourse, Corporate Citizenship, and State Formation in Early Modern England," *American Historical Review*, 112, no. 4 (October 2007): 1016–38.

23. Harold Laski, "The Personality of Associations," *Harvard Law Review* 29, no. 4 (1916): 407, 425.

24. Thomas Hobbes, *Leviathan, or The Matter, Forme, and Power of a Common Wealth, Ecclesiastical and Civil* (London, 1651), pt. 2, chap. 29, 174. For Hobbes's critique of mercantile corporations and bodies politic "subordinate," see chap. 22, esp. 119–21.

25. Stephen Krasner, "Compromising Westphalia," *International Security* 20, no. 3 (1995–96): 115–51; Andrias Osiander, "Sovereignty, International Relations, and the Westphalian Myth," *International Organization* 55, no. 2 (2001): 251–87; Robert Jackson, *Quasi-States: Sovereignty, International Relations and the Third World* (Cambridge: Cambridge University Press, 1990); Thomas J. Biersteker and Cynthia Weber, eds., *State Sovereignty as Social Construct* (Cambridge: Cambridge University Press, 1996).

26. Carl Schmitt, *The Concept of the Political*, trans. George Schwab (Chicago: University of Chicago, 1996), 26–28. On corporate sovereignty, see Alfred D. Chandler Jr. and Bruce

Mazlish, "Introduction," in *Leviathans: Multinational Corporations and the New Global History* (Cambridge: Cambridge University Press, 2005), 10–11; David Vogel, "The Corporation as Government: Challenges and Dilemmas," *Polity* 8, no. 1 (1975): 5–37; Joshua Evdasin Barkan, "A Genealogy of the Corporation: Articulating Sovereign Power and Capitalism" (PhD diss., University of Minnesota, 2006).

27. von Gierke, *Community in Historical Perspective*, 111, 198–204.

28. See Rodney Barker, *Political Ideas in Modern Britain: In and After the Twentieth Century* (London: Routledge, 1997), 100–104; F. W. Maitland, *State, Trust and Corporation*, ed. David Runciman and Magnus Ryan (Cambridge: Cambridge University Press, 2003); Jeanne Morefield, "States Are Not People: Harold Laski on Unsettling Sovereignty, Rediscovering Democracy," *Political Research Quarterly* 58, no. 4 (2005): 659–69; Morefield, "Harold Laski on the Habits of Imperialism," in Duncan Kelly, ed., *Lineages of Empire: The Historical Roots of British Imperial Thought* (Oxford: Oxford University Press, 2009), 215.

29. Laski, "Early History of the Corporation," 561.

30. Laski, "Personality of Associations," 425.

31. Sanjay Subrahmanyam, "Holding the World in Balance: The Connected Histories of the Iberian Overseas Empires, 1500–1640," *American Historical Review* 112, 5 (December 2007): 1359. See also, C. A. Bayly, *The Birth of the Modern World, 1780–1914: Global Connections and Comparisons* (Maiden, MA: Blackwell, 2004), esp. chaps. 1–2; Hendrik Spruyt, *The Sovereign State and its Competitors: An Analysis of Systems Change* (Princeton, NJ: Princeton University Press, 1994); Sanjay Subrahmanyam, *Explorations in Connected History: From the Tagus to the Ganges* (Delhi: Oxford University Press, 2005).

32. Lauren Benton, *A Search for Sovereignty: Law and Geography in European Empires, 1400–1900* (Cambridge: Cambridge University Press, 2009); Philip E. Steinberg, *The Social Construction of the Ocean* (Cambridge: Cambridge University Press, 2001); Richard Tuck, *The Rights of War and Peace: Political Thought and the International Order from Grotius to Kant* (Oxford: Oxford University Press, 1999), esp. 107; Wilson, "The VOC," 312, 322–27. See also Kathleen Wilson, "Re-thinking the British Colonial State: Gender and Governmentality in the Long Eighteenth Century," *American Historical Review* (forthcoming); Elizabeth Mancke, "Sites of Sovereignty: The Body of the Subject and the Making of the British Empire," in *Imperial Identities*, vol 1, *Global Rivals*, ed. Edward Farmer and Elizabeth Mancke (forthcoming). Many thanks to Professors Wilson and Mancke for allowing me to consult and cite their work-in-progress.

33. J. H. Elliott, "A Europe of Composite Monarchies," *Past and Present* 137 (1992): 48–71. See also Muzaffar Alam and Sanjay Subrahmanyam, eds., *The Mughal State* (Delhi: Oxford University Press, 1998); Karen Barkey, *Bandits and Bureaucrats: The Ottoman Route to State Centralization* (Ithaca, NY: Cornell, 1997) and *Empire of Difference: The Ottomans in Comparative Perspective* (Cambridge: Cambridge University Press, 2008); Sugata Bose, *A Hundred Horizons: The Indian Ocean in the Age of Global Empire* (Cambridge, MA: Harvard University Press, 2006), 55, 291n37; Harald Gustafsson, "The Conglomerate State: A Perspective on State Formation in Early Modern Europe," *Scandinavian Journal of History* 23 (1998): 189, 193–97, 211; Farhat Hasan, *State and Locality in Mughal India: Power Relations in Western India, c. 1572–1730* (Cambridge: Cambridge University Press, 2004); H. G. Koenigsberger, "*Dominium Regale* or *Dominium Politicum et Regale*: Monarchies and Parliaments in Early Modern Europe," in *Politicians and Virtuosi: Essays in Early Modern History* (London: Hambledon Press, 1986), 12; Conrad Russell, "Composite Monarchies in Early Modern Europe: The British and Irish Example," in Alexander Grant and Keith J. Stringer, eds., *Uniting the Kingdom? The Making of British History* (London: Routledge, 1995); Burton Stein, "State Formation and Economy Reconsidered: Part One," *Modern Asian Studies* 19 (1985): esp. 388.

34. Charles Ingrao, *The Hessian Mercenary State: Ides, Institutions, and Reform Under Frederick II, 1760–1785* (Cambridge: Cambridge University Press, 1987); Paul Christopher Manuel, Lawrence C. Reardon, and Clyde Wilcox, eds., *The Catholic Church and the*

Nation-State: Comparative Perspectives (Washington, DC: Georgetown University Press, 2006); Dauril Alden, *The Making of an Enterprise: The Society of Jesus in Portugal, Its Empire, and Beyond, 1540–1750* (Stanford, CA: Stanford University Press, 1996); John Jeffries Martin, "The Venetian Territorial State: Constructing Boundaries in the Shadow of Spain," in Thomas James Dandelet and John A. Marino, eds., *Spain in Italy: Politics, Society, and Religion 1500–1700* (Leiden: Brill, 2007); Janice Thomson, *Mercenaries, Pirates, and Sovereigns: State-Building and Extraterritorial Violence in Early Modern Europe* (Princeton, NJ: Princeton University Press, 1994).

35. Michael J. Braddick, *State Formation in Early Modern England, c. 1550–1700* (Cambridge: Cambridge University Press, 2000); Michael Braddick and John Walter, eds., *Negotiating Power in Early Modern Society: Order, Hierarchy and Subordination in Britain and Ireland* (Cambridge: Cambridge University Press, 2001); Mark Goldie, "The Unacknowledged Republic: Officeholding in Early Modern England," in Tim Harris, ed., *The Politics of the Excluded, c. 1500–1850* (Houndmills: Palgrave, 2001), 155, 156; Patrick Collinson, "De Republica Anglorum: Or, History with the Politics Put Back," (1989) in Collinson, ed., *Elizabethan Essays* (London: The Hambledon Press, 1994); Andrea Finkelstein, *Harmony and the Balance: An Intellectual History of Seventeenth-Century English Economic Thought* (Ann Arbor: University of Michigan, 2000), 34.

36. Edward Keene, *Beyond the Anarchical Society: Grotius, Colonialism, and Order in World Politics* (Cambridge: Cambridge University Press, 2002), 4, 69; Lauren Benton, *Law and Colonial Cultures: Legal Regimes in World History, 1400–1900* (Cambridge: Cambridge University Press, 2001); J. H. Elliott, *Empires of the Atlantic World*, 118; Alison Games, *Web of Empire: English Cosmopolitans in an Age of Expansion 1560–1660* (New York: Oxford University Press, 2008).

37. Mary Sarah Bilder, *The Transatlantic Constitution: Colonial Legal Culture and the Empire* (Cambridge, MA: Harvard University Press, 2004); Bilder, "English Settlement and Local Governance," in Michael Grossberg and Christopher Tomlins, eds., *Cambridge History of Law in America*, vol 1, *Early America, 1580–1815* (Cambridge: Cambridge University Press, 2008), 67–79; Christine Daniels and Michael V. Kennedy, eds., *Negotiated Empires: Centers and Peripheries in the Americas, 1500–1820* (New York: Routledge, 2002); Jack P. Greene, *Negotiated Authorities: Essays in Colonial Political and Constitutional History* (Charlottesville: University of Virginia Press, 1994); Vicki Hsueh, *Hybrid Constitutions: Challenging Legacies of Law, Privilege, and Culture in Colonial America* (Durham, NC: Duke University Press, 2010); Ian K. Steele, "The Anointed, the Appointed, and the Elected: Governance of the British Empire, 1689–1784," in P. J. Marshall, ed., *Oxford History of the British Empire: The Eighteenth Century* (Oxford: Oxford University Press, 1998), 105–27.

38. Andrew Fitzmaurice, *Humanism and America: An Intellectual History of English Colonisation, 1500–1625* (Cambridge: Cambridge University Press, 2003); Alexander B. Haskell, "'The Affections of the People': Ideology and the Politics of Colonial Virginia, 1607–1757," (PhD diss., The Johns Hopkins University, 2005); Karen Kupperman, *Providence Island, 1630–1641: The Other Puritan Colony* (Cambridge, 1993); Peter E. Pope, *Fish into Wine: The Newfoundland Plantation in the Seventeenth Century* (Chapel Hill: University of North Carolina, 2004).

39. Virginia DeJohn Anderson, "New England in the Seventeenth Century," in Nicholas Canny, ed., *Oxford History of the British Empire*, vol 1, *Origins of Empire* (Oxford: Oxford University Press, 1998), 196, 198; Bilder, "English Settlement," 70–71.

40. Maitland, "Crown as Corporation," 140.

41. Phil Withington, "Citizens, community and political culture in Restoration England," in Alexandra Shepard and Phil Withington, eds., *Communities in Early Modern England* (Manchester: Manchester University Press, 2000), 138.

42. K. G. Davies, "Joint-Stock Investment in the Later Seventeenth Century," *Economic History Review* 4 (1952): 294.

43. As in a commissioner, or one to whom a trust or responsibility is committed.

44. Huw V. Bowen, "The 'Little Parliament': The General Court of the East India Company, 1750–1784," *Historical Journal* 34, no. 4 (1991): esp. 861.

45. On the India House, see William Foster, *The East India House: Its History and Associations* (London: John Lane, 1924), esp. chap. 6.

46. John Guy, "The Rhetoric of Counsel in Early Modern England," in Dale Hoak, ed., *Tudor Political Culture* (Cambridge: Cambridge University Press, 1995), 310; Linda Levy Peck, "Kingship, counsel and law in early Stuart Britain," in J. G. A. Pocock, ed., *The Varieties of British Political Thought, 1500–1800* (Cambridge: Cambridge University Press, 1993), 98–102; Finkelstein, *The Harmony and the Balance,* 127–28.

47. London to Pariaman, 25 November 1685, E/3/91 f. 11; Miles Ogborn, *Indian Ink: Script and Print in the Making of the English East India Company* (Chicago: University of Chicago Press, 2007), 52–57, 76–83; Michael Clanchy, "Does Writing Construct the State?" *Journal of Historical Sociology* 15, 1 (2002): 68–70.

48. See, for example, Julia Adams, *The Familial State: Ruling Families and Merchant Capitalism in Early Modern Europe* (Ithaca, NY: Cornell University Press, 2005); William Barber, *British Economic Thought and India 1600–1858: A Study in the History of Development Economics* (Oxford: Clarendon Press, 1975); James Bohun, "Protecting Prerogative: William III and the East India Trade Debate, 1689–1698," *Past Imperfect* 2 (1993); Robert Brenner, *Merchants and Revolution: Commercial Change, Political Conflict, and London's Overseas Traders 1550–1653* (Princeton, NJ: Princeton University Press, 1993); Margaret Bauer Havlik, "Power and Politics in the East India Company 1681–1709" (PhD diss., University of Akron [Ohio], 1998); Henry Horwitz, "The East India Trade, the Politicians, and the Constitution: 1689–1702," *Journal of British Studies* 17 (1978); Steve Pincus, *1688: The First Modern Revolution* (New Haven, CT: Yale University Press, 2009), 372–81; Arnold A. Sherman, "Pressure from Leadenhall: The East India Company Lobby, 1660–1678," *Business History Review* 50 (1976); Robert Walcott, "The East India Interest in the General Election of 1700–01," *English Historical Review* 71 (1956); James Vaughn, "The Politics of Empire: Metropolitan Socio-Political Development and the Imperial Transformation of the British East India Company, 1675–1775," (PhD diss., University of Chicago, 2009).

49. Chaudhuri, *Trading World,* 22, 113–14; Shafaat Ahmad Khan, *The East India Trade in the XVIIth Century in its Political and Economic Aspects* (London: Oxford University Press, 1923). See also, K. N. Chaudhuri, "The English East India Company and Its Decision-Making," in Kenneth Ballhatchet and John Harrison, eds., *East India Company Studies: Papers Presented to Professor Cyril Philips* (Hong Kong: Asian Research Service, 1986); K. N. Chaudhuri, "The English East India Company in the 17th and 18th Centuries: A Pre-Modern Multinational Organization," in Leonard Blussé and Femme Gaastra, eds., *Companies and Trade* (The Hague: Leiden University Press, 1981), 32; Chaudhuri, *The English East India Company; The Study of an Early Joint-Stock Company 1600–1640* (London: Frank Cass and Co., 1965); Emily Erikson and Peter Bearman, "Malfeasance and the Foundations for Global Trade: The Structure of English Trade in the East Indies, 1601–1833," *American Journal of Sociology* 112, no. 1 (2006): 195–230; Santhi Hejeebu, "Contract Enforcement in the English East India Company," *Journal of Economic History* 65, no. 2 (2005); Nick Robins, *The Corporation that Changed the World: How the East India Company Shaped the Modern Multinational* (Ann Arbor, MI: Pluto Press, 2006). On the "agency" problem, see Julia Adams, "Principals and Agents, Colonialists and Company men: The Decay of Colonial Control in the Dutch East Indies," *American Sociological Review* 61, no. 1 (1996): 12–28; Ann Carlos and Stephen Nicholas, "Agency Problems in Early Chartered Companies: The Case of the Hudson's Bay Company," *Journal of Economic History* 50, no. 4 (1990): esp. 857, 863; Carlos and Nicholas, "Giants of an Earlier Capitalism: The Chartered Companies as Modern Multinationals," *Business History Review* 62 (1988). For a critique similar to the one offered here, see Ogborn, *Indian Ink,* 70.

50. Thomas Babington Macaulay, "Warren Hastings," (1841) in, *Critical and Historical Essays contributed to 'The Edinburgh Review'* (London, 1884), 606; Cf. Chaudhuri, *Trading World,* 113.

51. Søren Mentz, *The English Gentleman Merchant at Work: Madras and the City of London 1660–1740* (Copenhagen: Museum Tusculanum Press, 2005), 262. See also I. B. Watson, *Foundation for Empire: English Private Trade in India, 1659–1760* (New Delhi: Vikas, 1980); P. J. Marshall, *East Indian Fortunes: The British in Bengal in the Eighteenth Century* (Oxford: Clarendon Press, 1976); Holden Furber, *Private Fortunes and Company Profits in the India Trade in the 18th Century* (Brookfield, VT: Variorum, 1997).

52. See *Charters,* 1–139; Charles II, warrant to Attorney General, 24 March 1661/2, Sloane 856 f. 10.

53. Thomas Pownall, *The Right, Interest, and Duty, of Government, as Concerned in the affairs of the East Indies* (London, 1773), 7.

54. Steensgaard, *Asian Trade Revolution,* 115; Steensgaard, "The Companies as a Specific Institution in the History of European Expansion," in Leonard Blussé and Femme Gaastra eds. *Companies and Trade,* 237.

55. René Barendse, "To be a Servant of his Catholic Majesty: Indian Troops of the *Estado da India* in the Eighteenth Century," in Jos Gommans and Om Prakash, eds., *Circumambulations in South Asian History* (Leiden: Brill, 2003), 70; J. van Goor, "Seapower, Trade, and State Formation: Pontianak and the Dutch," in *Trading Companies in Asia 1600–1830,* ed., J. van Goor (Utrecht, 1986), 85; Wilson, "The VOC," 331–38.

56. C. H. Alexandrowicz, *An Introduction to the History of the Law of Nations in the East Indies (16th, 17th, and 18th Centuries)* (Oxford: Clarendon Press, 1967).

57. Chaudhuri, *Trading World,* 120–25; Sen, *Empire of Free Trade,* 77.

58. E.g., Paul D. Halliday, "'A Clashing of Jurisdictions': Commissions of Association in Restoration Corporations," *Historical Journal* 41 (1998): 427, 428, 448–55; Hasan, *State and Locality in Mughal India,* 115; Catherine Patterson, "Quo Warranto and Borough Corporations in Early Stuart England: Royal Prerogative and Local Privileges in the Central Courts," *English Historical Review* 120, no. 488 (2005): 879–906.

59. Compare, for example, Sudipta Sen's description of the process of obtaining a *farman* with G. R. Elton's account of a charter. Sen, *Empire of Free Trade,* 68, 77; G. R. Elton, *The Tudor Constitution: Documents and Commentary* (Cambridge: Cambridge University Press, 1960), 117–19.

60. For a similar point, though one emphasizing the importance of personal relationships in navigating among these varieties of governance, see Mattison Mines, "Courts of Law and Styles of Self in Eighteenth-Century Madras: From Hybrid to Colonial Self," *Modern Asian Studies* 35 (2001): 45.

61. The model here draws upon Georg Simmel's notion of a "tertius gaudens"—a third party that "rejoices," that is benefits, from its role as intermediary in an exchange between two other parties—as well as Ronald Burt's notion that the *tertius,* in filling in the "structural holes" in a network between those two parties can construct for itself a form of "structural autonomy," although it seems that such a usage is not what Burt, who focuses on economic transactions, exactly had in mind. Georg Simmel, *The Sociology of Georg Simmel,* ed. and trans. Kurt Wolff (Glencoe, IL: Free Press, 1950), 154–69; Ronald S. Burt, *Structural Holes: The Social Structure of Competition* (Cambridge, MA: Harvard University Press, 1992), 47–48. I owe a great debt to (now) Professor Emily Erikson for first setting me on the path to this work almost a decade ago.

62. David Armitage, *The Ideological Origins of the British Empire* (Cambridge: Cambridge University Press, 2000), 3–4; Andrew Fitzmaurice, "The Ideology of Early Modern Colonisation," *History Compass* 2 (2004): 9.

63. This book thus comprehends institutions as crucial in shaping attitudes, intentions, fantasies, languages, assumptions, expectations, and rules that shaped and guided, but perhaps did not always determine, behavior. In this sense, it is a study of an institution and its political

culture, defined as one less concerned with the "players of the game" than "what the players presume the nature and limits of their game to be." Dale Hoak, "Introduction," in Hoak, ed., *Tudor Political Culture*, 1–2. See also Clifford Geertz, "Ideology as a Cultural System," in David Apter, ed., *Ideology and Discontent* (London: The Free Press of Glencoe, 1964), 53; James G. March and Johan P. Olsen, *Rediscovering Institutions: The Organizational Basis of Politics* (New York: The Free Press, 1989), esp. 22; Stephen D. Krasner, "Sovereignty: An Institutional Perspective," in James A. Caporaso, ed., *The Elusive State: International and Comparative Perspectives* (Newbury Park, CA: Sage, 1989), 70, 74–93.

64. On approaching political thought "in the world" in late eighteenth-century British India, see Jon Wilson, *The Domination of Strangers: Modern Governance in Eastern India, 1780–1835* (Basingstoke: Palgrave Macmillan, 2008); see also Philip J. Stern, "Rethinking Institutional Transformations in the Making of Modern Empire: The East India Company in Madras," *Journal of Colonialism and Colonial History* 9, no. 2 (Fall 2008).

65. *Proposals for Setling the East-India Trade* (London, 1696), 9.

Chapter 1

1. "Commission for appointing President and Council of Fort St. George," 21 January 1708/9, E/3/96, 425.

2. Henry Davison Love, *Vestiges of Old Madras, 1640–1800* (London: John Murray, 1913, repr. New York: AMS, 1968), 1:1, 12–19, 23, 27, 28, 34–35; V. Mahalingam, "The Grant of Madraspatam to the English East India Company," *Indian Year Book of International Affairs* 2 (1953): 160–65. See also William Foster, *The Founding of Fort St. George* (London: Eyre & Spottiswoode, 1902).

3. London to Madras, 5 July 1682, E/3/90 f. 3.

4. Love, *Vestiges*, 1:68, 71, 89.

5. Madras Consultation, 11 April 1672, in *RFSG: D&C, 1672–1678*, 3; Madras Consultation, 3 June 1678, in *RFSG: D&C, 1678–79*, 76; Sinnappah Arasaratnam, *Merchants, Companies and Commerce on the Coromandel Coast, 1650–1740* (Delhi: Oxford University Press, 1986), 83–86; Love, *Vestiges*, 1:352.

6. Niels Steensgaard, *The Asian Trade Revolution of the Seventeenth Century: The East India Companies and the Decline of the Caravan Trade* (Chicago: University of Chicago, 1973), 117.

7. Alison Games, *The Web of Empire: English Cosmopolitans in an Age of Expansion, 1560–1660* (New York: Oxford University Press, 2008), 208–17.

8. Philip Lawson, *The East India Company: A History* (London: Longman, 1993), 39–40.

9. Court Minutes, 18 December 1657, in *CCM*, 5:199; Court Minutes, 25 July 1660, in *CCM*, 6:25; Margaret Makepeace, ed., *Trade on the Guinea Coast 1657–1666: The Correspondence of the English East India Company* (Madison: African Studies Program, University of Wisconsin, 1991); Shafaat Ahmad Khan, *The East India Trade in the XVIIth Century In its Political and Economic Aspects* (London: Oxford University Press, 1923, repr. New Delhi: S. Chand and Co., 1975), 90–91.

10. D. K. Bassett, "Early English Trade and Settlement in Asia," repr. in Patrick Tuck, ed., *The East India Company 1600–1858*, vol. 4: *Trade, Finance, and Power* (London: Routledge, 1998), 14.

11. Committees for Pulo Run to Thomas Gee, 5 January 1655 in *CCM*, 5:2.

12. John Dutton, "Briefe Relation of a Voyage from St. Helena on the Coast of Africa to Bantam in India, begun the 6th Day of May 1661 and from thence to England," Lansdowne MS 213 no. 39; William Foster, "The Acquisition of St. Helena," *English Historical Review* 34 (1919): 282–84; Philip Gosse, *St. Helena, 1502–1938* (London: Cassell, 1938, repr. Owestry: Anthony Nelson, 1990), 44–49; A. H. Schulenburg, "St Helena: British Local History in the Context of Empire," *Local Historian* 2 (1998): 108–9; Stephen Royle, *The Company's Island: St Helena, Company Colonies and the Colonial Endeavour* (London: IB Tauris, 2007),

17–19. See also P. J. Stern, "Politics and Ideology in the Early East India Company-State: The Case of St. Helena, 1673–1709," *Journal of Imperial and Commonwealth History* 35, 1 (March 2007): 1–23.

13. Royle, *Company's Island*, 21–23.

14. Richard Boothby, *A True Declaration of the Intollerable Wrongs done to Richard Boothby, Merchant of India, by Two Lewd Servants of the Honorable East India Company* (London, 1644), 24; Games, *Web of Empire*, 181, 190–208.

15. See, for example, Circular Letter to Dutch Factories, 2 October 1682, E/3/90 f. 34.

16. Court Minutes, 11 June 1680, B/36 f. 11; London to St. Helena, 6 May 1685, E/3/90 f. 272–74.

17. Samuel T. Sheppard, *Bombay* (Bombay: Times of India Press, 1932), 6; London to Lord Protector [1654], TNA CO/77, vii, no. 92 in *CCM*, 4:374; Bassett, "Early English trade and settlement," 13–14; G. Z. Refai, "Sir George Oxinden and Bombay, 1662–1669," *English Historical Review* 92 (1977): 574.

18. Court Minutes, 7 April 1658, in *CCM*, 5:250.

19. On the ongoing disputes over the treaty, see Shafaat Ahmad Khan, *Anglo-Portuguese Negotiations Relating to Bombay, 1660–1677* (Oxford: Humphrey Milford, 1922).

20. Clarendon quoted by J. P. De Souza, "The Population of Bombay at the Beginning of British Rule," *Journal of Indian History* 50 (1972): 90; Pepys cited by Linda Colley, *Captives* (New York: Pantheon Books, 2002), 25.

21. Sir Abraham Shipman's Commission, H/48, f. 4. For the most recent and innovative perspectives on the English colony at Tangier, see Games, *Web of Empire*, esp. 293–98; William Bulman, "Constantine's Enlightenment; Culture and Religious Politics in the Early British Empire, c. 1649–1710" (PhD diss., Princeton University, 2009), part 2, and Tristan Stein's forthcoming dissertation, "The Mediterranean in the English Empire of Trade, 1640–1740" (Harvard University).

22. Charles Fawcett, *The First Century of British Justice in India* (Oxford: Clarendon Press, 1934), 1–2n; M. D. David, *History of Bombay 1661–1708* (Bombay: University of Bombay, 1973), 24–38; Bombay to Surat, 28 September 1668, H/49 f. 38; Privy Council Minutes, 13 December 1667, TNA CO 77/10 [copy, OIOC EurMSS PhotoEur 149/10], f. 633

23. John Fryer, *A New Account of East-India and Persia in Eight Letters Being Nine Years Travels, Begun 1672 and Finished 1681* (London: R. R. for Rt. Chiswell, 1698), 64.

24. Court Minutes, 6 November 1674, in *CCM*, X:107–8; *EFI*, 44; London to Surat, 19 March 1668/9, H/49 f. 17.

25. London to Surat, 24 August 1668, H/49 f. 9.

26. Sir Courtenay Ilbert, *The Government of India Being a Digest of the Statute Law Relating Thereto, With Historical Introduction and Explanatory Matter* (Oxford: Clarendon Press, 1898), 18.

27. Letters Patents, 27 March 1669, in *Charters Granted to the East-India Company From 1601, Also The Treaties and Grants, Made with, or obtained from, the Princes and Powers in India, From the Year 1756 to 1772* (London, 1773), 83–85, 88–91.

28. St. George Tucker, *Blackstone's Commentaries: With Notes of Reference, to the Constitution and Laws, of the Federal Government of the United States; And of the Commonwealth of Virginia* (Philadelphia, 1803), 1:405. See Mary Sarah Bilder, *The Transatlantic Constitution: Colonial Legal Culture and the Empire* (Cambridge, MA: Harvard University Press, 2004); Lauren Benton, *Law and Colonial Cultures: Legal Regimes in World History, 1400–1900* (Cambridge: Cambridge University Press, 2001).

29. Letters Patents, 27 March 1669, in *Charters*, 83.

30. B. H. McPherson, "Revisiting the Manor of East Greenwich," *American Journal of Legal History* 42 (1998): 35–56; Michael Craton, "Property and propriety. Land tenure and slave property in the creation of a British West Indian plantocracy, 1612–1740," in Susan Staves and John Brewer, eds., *Early modern Conceptions of Property* (London: Routledge, 1996), 499; Edward Keene, *Beyond the Anarchical Society: Grotius, Colonialism and Order in World Politics* (Cambridge: Cambridge University Press, 2002), 62–68.

31. London to Bombay, 25 August 1686, E/3/91 f. 84.

32. Keene, *Beyond the Anarchical Society,* 67.

33. This issue arose perhaps most famously a century later in the context of the American Revolution. See Benjamin Franklin, "On the Tenure of the Manor of East Greenwich," *Gazetteer and New Daily Advertiser,* 11 January 1766; James Muldoon, "Discovery, Grant, Charter, Conquest, or Purchase: John Adams on the Legal Basis for English Possession of North America," in Bruce H. Mann and Christopher L. Tomlins, eds., *The Many Legalities of Early America* (Chapel Hill: University of North Carolina Press, 2001); Richard Tuck, *The Rights of War and Peace: Political Thought and the International Order from Grotius to Kant* (Oxford: Oxford University Press, 1999), 121–22.

34. London to Surat, 13 December 1672, H/50 f. 11; Madras Consultation, 19 December 1677, in *RFSG:D&C, 1672–1678,* 127.

35. London to St. Helena, 5 April 1689, E/3/92 f. 17; London to Bombay, 28 July 1686, IOR E/3/91 f. 83; Report of the Attorney General, 16 November 1681, TNA CO 77/49 f. 247.

36. London to Surat, 16 February 1669, H/49 f. 116.

37. London to St. Helena, 3 August 1687, E/3/91 ff. 180–81.

38. London to Lords Committees for Trade and Plantations, 4 September 1677, in *CCM,* 11:78–79; London to Surat, 19 March 1668/9, H/49 f. 21; Surat to London, 30 March 1670, H/49 f. 221.

39. London to Surat, 19 March 1668/9, H/49 ff. 11–12; Surat to London, 26 November 1669, H/49 f. 175.

40. Court Minutes, 11 June 1680, B/36 f. 11; London to St. Helena, 10 March 1681, G/32/1, 16–32.

41. London to Surat, 22 February 1670/71, H/49 f. 298; Bombay to Surat, 6 October 1668, H/49 f. 62.

42. Bombay to London, 12 July 1672, H/50 f. 34–35.

43. G. Wilcox, "On the Establishment of English Law on Bombay 30 December 1672," Add. MS 39,255 ff. 41–44, 46; Surat to London, 30 March 1670, H/49 f. 219; John Burnell, *Bombay in the Days of Queen Anne: Being an Account of the Settlement,* ed., Samuel Sheppard (London: Hakluyt Society, 1933), 6; *EFI,* I, 2–3, 45–47; Fawcett, *First Century,* 14, 49; Arnold Wright, *Annesley of Surat and His Times: The True Story of the Mythical Wesley Fortune* (London: Andrew Melrose, Ltd., 1918), 54; Surat to Bombay, 16 May 1672, in *BS,* 1:64.

44. Quoted in *EFI,* 1:12.

45. London to Surat, 19 March 1668/9, H/49 f. 14–15.

46. G. Wilcox, "On the Establishment of English Law in Bombay 30 December 1672," Add.MS 39,255 f. 45; Fawcett, *First Century,* 74.

47. "Proposals Touching Bombay Island Recommended to the Honourable Company by their President & Councell at Surratt," nd, *BS,* I, 51–53; Frank Conlon, "Functions of Ethnicity in a Colonial Port City: British Initiatives and Policies in Early Bombay," in Dilip K. Basu, ed., *The Rise and Growth of the Colonial Port Cities in Asia* (Berkeley: Center for South and Southeast Asia Studies, University of California, 1985), 50; *EFI,* 80.

48. Consultation, 18 and 27 March and 5 September 1678, in *RFSG: D&C, 1678–79,* 58–60.

49. St. Helena Consultations, 13 October 1684, IOR G/32/2, 3, n.p.

50. Surat Consultations, 27 March 1683 and 5 and 7 May 1683, IOR G/36/5 f. 21, 33.

51. Wilcox, "English Law in Bombay," ff. 45, 46.

52. Madras Consultation, 24 November 1687, *RFSG:D&C, 1687,* 182.

53. Madras to London, 6 September 1671, E/3/32 f. 40.

54. Madras Consultation, 25 November 1678, in *RFSG: D&C, 1678–79,* 140; Kanakalatha Mukund, *The View from Below: Indigenous Society, Temples and the Early Colonial State in Tamilnadu, 1700–1835* (New Delhi: Orient Longman, 2005), 53.

55. Surat to George Cooke and Barker Hibbins, 13 September 1690, G/36/92 f. 169; Fawcett, *First Century,* 35.

56. Court Minutes, 15 June 1677, in *CCM*, 11:51. On similar concerns over appeals in the Atlantic, see Bilder, *Transatlantic Constitution*, esp. 48–49.

57. For example, see, London to Bombay, 25 August 1686, E/3/91 f. 84; London to Madras, 9 June 1686, E/3/91 f. 71; Richard Grove, *Green Imperialism: Colonial Expansion, Tropical Island Edens, and the Origins of Environmentalism, 1660–1860* (Cambridge: Cambridge University Press, 1995), 96. For examples of the movements of slaves, see, e.g., London to Madras, 18 February 1690/1, E/3/92 f. 140–41; London to Madras, 13 June 1683, E/3/90 f. 83; Consultations, 4 October 1686, 15 February 1687/8, and 14 May 1688 in *RFSG: D&C, 1686*, 83; *RFSG: D&C, 1688*, 30, 78–79; Extract of London to FSG, 27 November 1668 and London to Fort St. David, 6 March 1694/5, reprinted in *Yule*, 2:cccliv, ccclvi.

58. Consultation, 24 September 1687, in *RFSG, 1687*, 149–50.

59. London to Madras, 7 January 1686/7, E/3/91 f. 121.

60. Surat to Bombay, 18 December 1675, in *BS*, 73; "A List of all the English both men and Women on the Island of Bombay together with a List of what men and Women are Deceased and the time when for the space of yeares past taken this 30th August 1675," E/3/36 ff. 45, 47.

61. Alan Harding, "The Origins of the Concept of the State," *History of Political Thought* 15 (1994): 57–58; Miles Ogborn, *Indian Ink: Script and Print in the Making of the English East India Company* (Chicago: University of Chicago Press, 2007), 58–59; Kevin Sharpe, *Selling the Tudor Monarchy: Authority and Image in Sixteenth-Century England* (New Haven, CT: Yale University Press, 2009); Quentin Skinner, "The state," in Terence Ball, James Farr, and Russell Hanson, eds., *Political Innovation and Conceptual Change* (Cambridge: Cambridge University Press, 1989), 91–95, 125–26; For a contemporary reflection, see *The Grounds of Sovereignty and Greatness* (London: Printed by T. R. & N. T., 1675), 12.

62. Surat to London, 10 January 1671/2, E/3/32 f. 141.

63. See, for example, London to St. Helena, 5 December 1698, G/32/1, 52; Madras Consultation, 24 November 1687, in *RFSG: D&C, 1687*, 183; Love, *Vestiges*, 1:445–46.

64. Wilcox, "English Law in Bombay," ff. 43–45.

65. Fryer, *New Account*, 68.

66. London to Madras, 21 December 1683, E/3/90 f. 140; "Embarkation Order to Captain John North," 23 December 1679, in Love, *Vestiges*, 1:448; *Yule*, 1:158; Fryer, *New Account*, 38; Thomas Salmon, *Modern History: Or the Present State of All Nations* (London, 1739), 1:277; Joseph Collett to Joseph Harding, 28 August 1718, in *LBJC*, 186.

67. Robert Travers, "Death and the Nabob: Imperialism and Commemoration in Eighteenth-Century India," *Past and Present* 196 (August 2007): 92, 94.

68. Peter Borsay, *The English Urban Renaissance: Culture and Society in the Provincial Town 1660–1770* (Oxford: Clarendon Press, 1989), 85–101; J. H. Elliott, *Empires of the Atlantic World: Britain and Spain in America, 1492–1830* (New Haven, CT: Yale University Press, 2006), 43; Diane Shafer Graham, "Planting, Planning and Design: A Comparative Study of English Colonial Cities Founded in India, North America, and the Caribbean 1660–1710" (PhD diss., Binghamton University, 2001). As Partha Mitter has observed, such patterns could be found in East and South Asian architectural writing and urban plans as well. Partha Mitter, "The Early British Port Cities of India: Their Planning and Architecture Circa 1640–1757," *Journal of the Society of Architectural Historians* 45 (1986): 99–101.

69. Susan J. Lewandowski, "Changing Form and Function in the Ceremonial and the Colonial Port City in India: An Historical Analysis of Madurai and Madras," *Modern Asian Studies* 11, no. 2 (1977): 202.

70. London to Surat, 24 August 1668, H/49 f. 13; Graham, "Planting, Planning and Design," 192–94; *EFI*, 26.

71. London to St. Helena, 1 August 1683, E/3/90 f. 90–91.

72. Partha Mitter, "Architectural Planning and Other Building Activities of the British in Madras, Bombay, and Calcutta," in Basu, ed., *Colonial Port Cities*, 194–95.

73. Claude Guillot, "Urban Patterns and Polities in Malay Trading Cities, Fifteenth through Seventeenth Centuries," *Indonesia* 80 (2005): 44; Lewandowski, "Madurai and Madras," 200; P. J. Marshall, "The White Town of Calcutta Under the Rule of the East India Company," *Modern Asian Studies* 34 (2000); Carl H. Nightingale, "Before Race Mattered: Geographies of the Color Line in Early Colonial Madras and New York," *American Historical Review* 113, no. 1 (February 2008): 52–56; George Winius, "A Tale of Two Coromandel Towns: Madraspatam (Fort St. George) and São Thomé de Meliapur," *Itinerario* 18 (1994): 61.

74. Partha Mitter, "Early British Port Cities of India," 102–7.

75. Madras Consultation, 10 June 1672, 1 October 1675, and 19 May 1677 in *RFSG, D&C, 1672–1678*, 5, 76, 115.

76. Madras Consultation, 27 February 1687/8, in *RFSG, D&C, 1688*, 35–36; Mukund, *View from Below*, 13.

77. Madras Consultation, 12 November 1683, in *RFSG: D&C, 1683*, 102; Patricia Seed, *Ceremonies of Possession in Europe's Conquest of the New World, 1492–1640* (Cambridge: Cambridge University Press, 1995), 25–40. See also, Richard Drayton, *Nature's Government: Science, Imperial Britain, and the "Improvement" of the World* (New Haven, CT: Yale University Press, 2000), 55–67.

78. Partha Mitter, "Architectural Planning," 194; Fryer, *New Account*, 40.

79. Bombay to London, 6 January 1672/3, H/50 ff. 67–68.

80. London to Madras, 29 February 1683/4 E/3/90 f. 154.

81. London to St. Helena, 5 April 1684, E/3/90 f. 175.

82. London to Surat, 7 April 1684 E/3/90 f. 165; London to Bengal, 5 March 1683/4, E/3/90 f. 159.

83. Extract of London to Madras, 27 November 1668, reprinted in *Yule*, 2:cccliv.

84. Court Minutes, 10 August 1688, B/39 f. 138; London to St. Helena, 11 January 1709, G/32/1, 156–57; London to St. Helena, 5 March 1713/14, E/3/98, 291; J. Ovington, *A Voyage to Suratt in the Year, 1689* (London, 1696), 89, 97. On the Company's Atlantic wine trade more broadly, see David Hancock, "'An Undiscovered Ocean of Commerce Laid Open': India, Wine and the Emerging Atlantic Economy, 1703–1813," in H. V. Bowen, Margarette Lincoln, and Nigel Rigby eds. *The Worlds of the East India Company* (Woodbridge, Suffolk: Boydell Press in association with the National Maritime Museum and University of Leicester, 2002), esp. 155–56.

85. London to Bengal, 20 June 1683, London to St. Helena, 1 August 1683, and 5 August 1684, E/3/90 f. 83, 95, 175–77.

86. Patrick Peebles, "Captain Robert Knox and The East India Company, 1681–1700" (unpublished paper, 2001). Many thanks to Professor Peebles for sharing this paper with me and allowing me to cite it.

87. I have discussed these issues in more detail in Philip J. Stern, "From the Fringes of History: The Early East India Company and the Birth of the British Empire in India," in Elizabeth Kolsky and Sameetah Agah, eds., *Fringes of Empire* (Delhi: Oxford University Press, 2009), 19–44.

88. Shubhra Chakrabarti, "Intransigents *Shroffs* and the English East India Company's Currency Reforms in Bengal, 1757–1800," *Indian Economic and Social History Review* 34 (1997): 71–72; K. N. Chaudhuri, *The Trading World of Asia and the English East India Company, 1660–1760* (Cambridge: Cambridge University Press, 1978), 175; Balkrishna Govind Gokhale, *Surat in the Seventeenth Century: A Study in Urban History of pre-modern India* (London: Curzon Press, 1979), 129–32.

89. London to Bombay, 14 July 1686, E/3/91, f. 79.

90. London to Bombay, 3 August 1687, IOR E/3/91, f. 161.

91. London to Surat, 22 February 1670/71, H/49 f. 290.

92. Letters Patents, 5 October [1676], in *Charters*, 111; London to Bombay, 18 February 1688/9, E/3/92 f. 11.

93. Surat to Bombay, 23 March 1675/6, in *BS*, 1:83–85; Pridmore, *Coins*, 148, 156–57, 166.

94. *CCM*, 11:xii n 2; Court Minutes, 9 February 1676/7, 21 February 1676/7, 23 January 1678, in *CCM*, 11:14, 18, 141.

95. F. Pridmore, *The Coins of the British Commonwealth of Nations to the End of the Reign of George VI 1952:pt. 4, India*, vol. 1, *East India Company Presidency Series c. 1642–1835* (London: Spink and Son, 1975), 105–7, 149–50; *EFI*, 182n.

96. Commission and Instruction from Bombay to Captain John Shaxton and Captain Richard Clifton, 30 November 1687, E/3/47 f. 155; Pridmore, *Coins*, 150.

97. John S. Deyell and R. E. Frykenberg, "Sovereignty and the 'SIKKA' under Company Raj: Minting Prerogative and Imperial Legitimacy in India," *Indian Economic and Social History Review* 19 (1982): 13; Pridmore, *Coins*, 4.

98. Alexander Hamilton, *A New Account of the East Indies, being the observations and remarks of Captain Alexander Hamilton, who spent his time there from the year 1688 to 1723*, 2 vols. (Edinburgh: Printed by John Mosman, 1727), 1:365; George Birdwood, *Report on the Old Records of the India Office, With Supplementary Note and Appendices*. (London: W. H. Allen, 1891), 223n; Deyell and Frykenberg, "Sovereignty and the "SIKKA,"" 13; Pridmore, *Coins*, 11, 57–59, 65.

99. London to Madras, 26 August 1685, E/3/90 f. 293

100. Deyell and Frykenberg, "Sovereignty and the "SIKKA," 13–15.

101. Gerald Aungier to London, 15 January 1673/4, H/50 f. 143.

102. E.g., Court Minutes, 21 February 1677, in *CCM*, 11:18.

103. London to Surat, 19 March 1668/9, H/49 ff. 12–13.

104. "Resolves of the Court Touching the Peopling of the Island Bombay," 1674, H/50 f. 270; London to St. Helena, 15 March 1677/8, in *CCM*, 11:162.

105. "Proposals Touching Bombay Island Recommended to the Honourable Company by their P & Councell at Surratt," nd. [3 February 1671/2], in *BS*, 1:53.

106. For example, Dutch Batavia and the English Atlantic. Joyce Chaplin, *Subject Matter: Technology, the Body, and Science on the Anglo-American Frontier, 1500–1676* (Cambridge, MA: Harvard University Press, 2001), 156; Ann Laura Stoler, *Carnal Knowledge and Imperial Power* (Berkeley: University of California Press, 2002), 47; Karen Kupperman, *The Jamestown Project* (Cambridge, MA: Harvard University Press, 2007), 287.

107. Court Minutes, 21 August 1674, 26 August 1674, 5 January 1677, in *CCM*, 10:74–77, 11:2; Bombay to London, 8 January 1675/6, H/51 f. 11; London to Surat, 7 March 1676/7, H/51 f. 18.

108. Love, *Vestiges*, 1:449–50; Richard Grassby, *Kinship and Capitalism: Marriage, Family, and Business in the English-Speaking World, 1580–1740* (Cambridge: Cambridge University Press, 1991), 76.

109. Surat to London, 7 November 1671, E/3/32 ff. 95–96; Surat to London, 3 February 1671, in *BS*, 56.

110. "A List of all the English both men and Women on the Island of Bombay together with a List of what men and Women are Deceased and the time when for the space of yeares past taken this 30th August 1675," E/3/36 ff. 45–48; Bombay to London, 23 January 1669/70, H/49 f. 263.

111. Ovington, *Voyage to Suratt*, 146.

112. Bombay to London, 26 November 1675, H/51 f. 6; London to Surat, 7 March 1676/7, H/51 f. 17.

113. Søren Mentz, *The English Gentleman Merchant at Work: Madras and the City of London 1660–1740* (Copenhagen: Museum Tusculanum Press, 2005), 244.

114. London to Surat, 19 March 1668/9, H/49 f. 21.

115. Ibid., f. 16.

116. Andrea Finkelstein, *Harmony and the Balance: An Intellectual History of Seventeenth-Century English Economic Thought* (Ann Arbor: University of Michigan, 2000), 143.

117. Conlon, "Early Bombay," 50; *EFI*, 15.

118. London (Secret) to Madras, 31 October 1683, E/3/90 f. 123; London to Madras, 8 April 1687, E/3/91, f. 144; Yogesh Sharma, "Changing Destinies, Evolving Identities: The

Indo-Portuguese Community at Madras in the Seventeenth Century," in Yogesh Sharma
and José Leal Ferreira, eds., *Portuguese Presence in India during the Sixteenth and Seventeenth
Centuries* (New Delhi: Viva Books, 2008), 114–15; Winius, "A Tale of Two Coromandel
Towns," 55, 61–62; Fryer, *New Account*, 69. On the Dutch and Portuguese, see Stoler, *Carnal Knowledge*, 46–51; L. A. Rodrigues, "The Portuguese Army of India," *Journal of Indian
History* 57, no. 1 (1979): 81. On Petty's intermarriage project, see Ted McCormick, *William Petty and the Ambitions of Political Arithmetic* (Oxford: Oxford University Press, 2009),
238–40, though on the general rejection of the notion in the English Atlantic until the
eighteenth century, see Chaplin, *Subject Matter*, 159, 189.

119. Douglas E. Haynes and Tirthankar Roy, "Conceiving Mobility: Weavers' Migrations in
Pre-colonial and Colonial India," *Indian Economic and Social History Review* 36 (1999):
38–49.

120. Surat to London, 1 June 1671, E/3/32 f. 14.

121. Love, *Vestiges* 1:1, 12–19, 23, 27, 28, 34–35, 68; See also William Foster, *The Founding of
Fort St. George* (London: Eyre and Spottiswoode, 1902).

122. Madras Consultations, 18 February 1675/6, in *RFSG, 1672–1678*, 87; Mukund, *View from
Below*, 11–12.

123. "Proposals Touching Bombay Island," nd., *BS*, 51–53; Conlon, " Early Bombay," 50.

124. London to Bombay, 12 December 1687, E/3/91 f. 234; London to Madras, 12 January
1687/8, E/3/91 f. 239–40; London to Bombay, 27 August 1688, E/3/91 f. 274; Bombay
to London, 7 June 1689, E/3/48 f. 19–20.

125. London to Surat, 7 March 1676/7, H/51 f. 21; Bombay to Surat, 16 August 1694, G/3/10
f. 67.

126. London to Chief and Council at Taiwan, 2 July 1684, E/3/90 f. 195; Madras Consultation,
14 August 1684, in *RFSG: D&C, 1684*, 89.

127. Surat to London, 1 June 1671, E/3/32, f. 14.

128. London to Madras, 3 January 1693/4, E/3/92 f. 306; London to Madras, 16 April 1697,
E/3/92 f. 541; Josiah Child to Robert Blackborne, 3 May 1693, H/40 f. 130.

129. London to Persia, 6 June 1694, E/3/92 f. 375; Court Minutes, 22 June 1688, B/39 ff.
134–35; Vahé Baladouni, "Armenian Trade with the English East India Company: An
Aperçu," *Journal of European Economic History* 15 (1986): 158–62; Ina Baghdiantz
McCabe, *The Shah's Silk for Europe's Silver: The Eurasian Trade of the Julfa Armenians in
Safavid Iran and India* (Atlanta, GA: Scholars Press, 1999), 342; R. W. Ferrier, "The Armenians and the East India Company in Persia in the Seventeenth and Early Eighteenth Centuries," *Economic History Review* 26 (1973): 49–51.

130. London to Madras, 29 February 1691/2, E/3/92 f. 193.

131. E.g., Walter Fischel, "The Jewish Merchant-Colony in Madras (Fort St. George) During the
17th and 18th Centuries: A Contribution to the Economic and Social History of the Jews
in India," *Journal of the Economic and Social History of the Orient* 3, no. 1 (1960): 78–107,
continued in *JESHO* 3, no. 2 (1960): 175–95; Mentz, *English Gentleman Merchant at Work*,
esp. 41–49; Gedalia Yogev, *Diamonds and Coral: Anglo-Dutch Jews and Eighteenth-Century
Trade* (Leicester: Leicester University Press, 1978); Sebouh Aslanian, "'The Salt in a Merchant's Letter': The Culture of Julfan Correspondence in the Indian Ocean and the Mediterranean," *Journal of World History* 19, no. 2 (2008): 127–88; Aslanian, "Social Capital,
'Trust' and the Role of Networks in Julfan Trade: Informal and Semi-formal Institutions at
Work," *Journal of Global History* 1 (2006): 387–88; Aslanian, "Trade Diaspora versus Colo-
nial State: Armenian Merchants, the English East India Company, and the High Court of
Admiralty in London, 1748–1752," *Diaspora* 13, no. 1 (2004): 37–100.

132. London to Surat, 5 March 1674/5, H/50 f. 256.

133. Swally Marine to London, 17 January 1675/6, E/3/36 f. 147. The same is quoted by
Arnold Wright in his biography of Samuel Annesley, although one might speculate with
relation to contemporary imperial politics why he chose to leave out the line "to be liberall."
See Wright, *Annesley of Surat and His Times: The True Story of the Mythical Wesley Fortune*

(London: Andrew Melrose, Ltd., 1918), 56–57. On both the letter from London and the reply from Aungier, see also *EFI*, 1:135–36.

134. Oxinden to William Rider, 30 December 1665, BL Add.MS 40,707 f. 8 quoted by Refai, "George Oxinden," 578.

Chapter 2

1. *Charters Granted to the East-India Company, from 1601; also the treaties and grants, made with, or obtained form, the princes and powers in India, from the year 1756 to 1772* ([London, 1773]), 82, 97.

2. Opinion of G. Petrords, CO 77/8, f. 143.

3. Court Minutes, 6 December 1676, in *CCM*, X, 385; Timothy Wilson, *Flags at Sea* (London: Her Majesty's Stationary Office, 1986), 36–37. On the flag, see Sir Charles Fawcett, "The Striped Flag of the East India Company and its Connexion with the American 'Stars and Stripes,'" *The Mariner's Mirror* 23 (1937), esp. 449–50n1, 473; Henry W. Moeller, *Shattering an American Myth: Unfurling the History of the Stars and Stripes* (Mattituck, NY: Amereon House, 1992), esp. 8–9, 22–23.

4. Court Minutes, 11 June 1680, B/36 f. 11; London to St. Helena, 10 March 1681, G/32/1, 16–32; London to St. Helena, 3 August 1687, E/3/91 ff. 180–81.

5. Harold Laski, "The Early History of the Corporation in England," *Harvard Law Review* 30, no. 6 (1917): 585.

6. Quoted by Andrea Finkelstein, *Harmony and the Balance: An Intellectual History of Seventeenth-Century English Economic Thought* (Ann Arbor: University of Michigan Press, 2000), 47.

7. Charter, 43 Eliz I, 31 December [1600], in *Charters*, 5, 12, 21.

8. Luís Filipe F. R. Thomaz, "Portuguese Control Over the Arabian Sea and the Bay of Bengal: A Comparative Study," in Om Prakash and Denys Lombard, eds., *Commerce and Culture in the Bay of Bengal, 1500–1800* (New Delhi: Manohar, 1999), 115–62, esp. 127; K. S. Mathew, "Trade in the Indian Ocean and the Portuguese System of Cartazes," *The First Portuguese Colonial Empire*, ed. Malyn Newitt (Exeter: University of Exeter Press, 1986), 75–77; Sugata Bose, *A Hundred Horizons: The Indian Ocean in the Age of Global Empire* (Cambridge, MA: Harvard University Press, 2006), 45; Sinnappah Arasaratnam, "Mare Clausum: The Dutch and Regional Trade in the Indian Ocean 1650–1740," *Journal of Indian History* 61 (1983): 73–91.

9. Lauren Benton, *A Search for Sovereignty: Law and Geography in European Empires, 1400–1900* (Cambridge: Cambridge University Press, 2009), 141; Philip Steinberg, *The Social Construction of the Ocean* (Cambridge: Cambridge University Press, 2001); Hendrik Spruyt, "Institutional Selection in International Relations: State Anarchy as Order," *International Organization* 48 (1994); C.H. Alexandrowicz, *An Introduction to the History of the Law of Nations in the East Indies (16th, 17th, and 18th Centuries)* (Oxford: Clarendon Press, 1967); Sanjay Subrahmanyam, "Holding the World in Balance: The Connected Histories of the Iberian Overseas Empires, 1500–1640," *American Historical Review* 112, no. 5 (2007): 1367. On protection rackets and state formation more generally, see Charles Tilly, "War Making and State Making as Organized Crime," in Peter Evans, Dietrich Rueschemeyer, and Theda Scocpol, eds., *Bringing the State Back In* (Cambridge: Cambridge University Press, 1985), 169–91.

10. See, e.g., Form of a Pass, February 1679/80, in *RFSG: D&C, 1679–80*, 75, 77; Madras Council, License to Thomas Bowrey et al., 7 February 1686/7, and Pass for Ship Adventure, 12 December 1682, Yale Gen MSS MISC Group 2317 Item F-4 and F-7 OS.

11. John Goldsborough to Christian Poke, 17 June 1693, E/3/50 f. 106.

12. Edward Misselden, *The Circle of Commerce, Or, The Ballance of Trade in Defence of Free Trade* (London, 1623), 37.

13. London to Madras, 15 January 1688/9, E/3/92 f. 6; Surat to Bombay, 28 April 1696, G/3/23 bk II, f. 42; Bombay to EIC, 15 December 1696, E/3/52 f. 287–88; Secret Committee to Charles II, 15 August 1684, E/3/90 f. 200.
14. London to Surat, 29 February 1691/2, E/3/92 f. 208; Surat to London, 29 April 1695, E/3/51 f. 40; Bombay to Madras, 5 December 1688, E/3/47 f. 202.
15. Deposition of Zephaniah Rathband, 27 October 1684, E/3/44 f. 227.
16. William Robert Scott, *The Constitution and Finance of English, Scottish and Irish Joint-Stock Companies to 1720*, 3 vols. (London: 1912; repr., Gloucester, MA: Peter Smith, 1968), 2:135.
17. Bombay to Captain Jonathan Andrews, 24 December 1687, E/3/47 f. 168.
18. Deposition of John Hakney, 15 October 1684, E/3/44 f. 202.
19. John Petit to Captain Hilder, 19 April 1683, E/3/43 f. 37.
20. Bengal to Captain Henry Udall, 24 July 1683, E/3/43 f. 91; Bengal to London, 22 April 1684, E/3/44 f. 40; Thomas Haggerston[e] to London, 31 April 1684, E/3/44 f. 53; William Hedges to London, 8 August 1684, E/3/44 f. 98.
21. *RFSG: D&C 1682*, vi; Scott, *Constitution and Finance*, 2:136, 146.
22. Court Minutes, 8 October 1680, B/36 f. 48.
23. Court Minutes, 28 September 1681, B/36 f. 162; General Court, 5 October 1681, B/36 f. 164; Court Minutes, 15 August 1683, B/37 f. 161.
24. Minutes, 30 April 1684, B/38, f. 2; Martin Moir, *A General Guide to the India Office Records* (London: British Library, 1988), 9.
25. "Sands contra Exton," Hillary Term, 34 Car II, GL MS 14187/2 f. 1; Lauren Benton, "Legal Spaces of Empire: Piracy and the Origins of Ocean Regionalism," *Comparative Study of Society and History* 47 (2005): 717.
26. *Cases Argued and Adjudged in the High Court of Chancery, Published from the Manuscripts of Thomas Vernon, Late of the* Middle Temple, *Esq., By Order of the High Court of Chancery* (Dublin, 1726), 1:128.
27. While *quo warranto* was mainly used against urban corporations, the Commissioners for Trade and Plantations did contemplate its use against the Bermuda Company in 1679. Paul D. Halliday, *Dismembering the Body Politic: Partisan Politics in England's Towns, 1650–1730* (Cambridge, Cambridge University Press, 1998), esp. 138–39, 200. On the prominence of these lawyers in the late seventeenth century more generally, see David Lemmings, *Gentlemen and Barristers: The Inns of Court and the English Bar 1680–1730* (Oxford: Oxford University Press, 1990), esp. 267–75. On the general context for the *quo warranto* cases and attempts on corporate liberties, see Tim Harris, *Restoration: Charles II and His Kingdoms, 1660–1685* (London: Allen Lane, 2005), esp. 293–300.
28. William Barber, *British Economic Thought and India 1600–1858: A Study in the History of Development Economics* (Oxford: Clarendon Press, 1975), 49; Robert B. Ekelund Jr. and Robert D. Tollison, *Politicized Economies: Monarchy, Monopoly, and Mercantilism* (College Station, TX: Texas A&M University Press, 1997), 184; Steve Pincus, *1688: The First Modern Revolution* (New Haven, CT: Yale University Press, 2009), 376–78.
29. *Cases Argued and Adjudged in the High Court of Chancery*, 1:128.
30. T. B. Howell, ed., *A Complete Collection of State Trials and Proceedings for High Treason and Other Crimes and Misdemeanors from the Earliest Period to the Year 1783, With Notes and Other Illustrations*, 21 vols. (London: T. C. Hansard, 1816), 10:380–81, 517. On monopoly and the late Elizabethan Parliament, see David Sacks, "The Countervailing of Benefits: Monopoly, Liberty and Benevolence in Elizabethan England," in Dale Hoak, ed., *Tudor Political Culture* (Cambridge: Cambridge University Press, 1995), 272–91.
31. See example, *An Answer to Two Letters Concerning the East-India Company* (London, 1676), 9–10.
32. Finkelstein, *Harmony and the Balance*, 67; Joyce Appleby, *Economic Thought and Ideology in Seventeenth-Century England* (Princeton, NJ: Princeton University Press, 1978), chap. 5.
33. Finkelstein, *Harmony and the Balance*, 66, 145.

34. Benton, *Search for Sovereignty*, 114; Eliga Gould, "Zones of Law, Zones of Violence: The Legal Geography of the British Atlantic, circa 1772," *William and Mary Quarterly* 60, 3 (July 2003): 471–510; Edward Keene, *Beyond the Anarchical Society; Grotius, Colonialism, and Order in World Politics* (Cambridge: Cambridge University Press, 2002), 2–3, 40–96, esp. 54; Richard Tuck, *The Rights of War and Peace: Political Thought and the International Order from Grotius to Kant* (Oxford: Oxford University Press, 1999), 8–9, 90–91, 137.

35. Samuel Fortrey, *Englands Interest and Improvement Consisting in the Increase of the Store, and Trade, of this Kingdom* (Cambridge, 1663), 4.

36. Philopatris, *A Treatise Wherein is Demonstrated That the East-India Trade is the Most National of Foreign Trades* (London, 1681), 1–2, 34. The pamphlet is often credited to Josiah Child, who repeated the same arguments in his work, though William Letwin, for one, argued emphatically that this is a misattribution. See Letwin, *Sir Josiah Child, Merchant Economist* (Boston, MA: Kress Library of Business and Economics, 1959), 33–35.

37. Josiah Child, *A New Discourse of Trade* (London, 1694), 106, 110.

38. [Robert Ferguson], *The East-India-Trade A Most Profitable Trade to the Kingdom And Best Secured and Improved in a Company and a Joint-Stock* (London, 1677), 15. Thomas Papillon, still then in Company leadership—and to whom the pamphlet is often misattributed, likely as a result of an attribution of his patronage in a 1696 reprinting—requested the pamphlet from Ferguson, who was also paid a gratuity from the court of committees. William Letwin, *The Origins of Scientific Economics: English Economic Thought 1660–1776* (London, 1963; repr., Abingdon: Routledge, 2003) 33, 234.

39. Philopatris, *Treatise*, 34.

40. *State Trials*, 373.

41. J[osiah] C[hild], *Brief Observations Concerning Trade, and interest of money* (London, 1668), 3; Child, *A Discourse Concerning Trade And in Particular of the East Indies* (London, 1689), 1.

42. [Ferguson], *East-India-Trade*, 25; [Nathaniel Tenche], *A Modest and Just Apology for; or, Defence of the Present East-India-Company Against the Accusations of their Adversaries* (London, 1690), 14.

43. Charles Molloy, *De Jure Maritimo et Navali: Or, A Treatise of Affaires Maritime and of Commerce* (London, 1677), 434; Child, *New Discourse of Trade*, 103.

44. London to Bengal, 30 May 1683, E/3/90 f. 80.

45. Bartholomew Harris to John Vauxe and Samuel Annesley, 28 June 1692, E/3/49 f. 92.

46. Philopatris, *Treatise*, 35.

47. London to Persia, 23 December 1685, E/3/91 f. 12.

48. Enoch Walsh to London, 11 May 1697, E/3/53 f. 45.

49. Attestation of Sir John Gayer, 12 June 1695, E/3/51 f. 87.

50. *Cases Argued and Adjudged in the High Court of Chancery*, 127.

51. "Sands contra Exton," Hillary Term, 34 Car II, GL MS 14187/2 f. 1.

52. Child, *New Discourse of Trade*, 103, 105.

53. Philopatris, *Treatise*, 36.

54. Surat Consultations, 19 July 1683, G/36/5 f. 55; Surat to London, 30 November 1683, E/3/43 f. 208; Surat to London, 29 November 1684, E/3/44 f. 319; Francis Day and Bartholomew Harris to John Child, 29 November 1684, E/3/44 f. 321.

55. George Bowcher [to Thomas Grantham], 16 January 1684/5, E/3/44 f. 378; T[homas] G[rantham] to George Bowcher, 18 January 1684/5, E/3/44 f. 380.

56. Alexandrowicz, *Law of Nations*, 55–57.

57. Report of the Attorney General Concerning Interlopers, 16 November 1681, TNA CO 77/49 f. 247.

58. "Sands contra Exton," Hillary Term, 34 Car II, GL MS 14187/2 f. 2.

59. *State Trials.*, 381, 484; Ludwell H. Johnson III, "The Business of War: Trading with the Enemy in English and Early American Law," *Proceedings of the American Philosophical Society*, 118, no. 5 (1974): 459–60; James Muldoon, "Papal Responsibility for the Infidel: Another Look at Alexander VI's *Inter Caetera.*" *Catholic Historical Review* 64, no. 2 (1978):

181; H. S. Q. Henriques, "The Jews and the English Law, VI," *Jewish Quarterly Review*, 16, no. 4 (1904): 625.

60. *State Trials*, 484.
61. "The Attorney General's Arguments in The Governour and Company of the Merchants of London Trading to the East Indies, Plaintiffs, vs. Thomas Saunds, Defendant," MS. Rawl.D.747 ff. 110–11; *State Trials*, 488–89.
62. *State Trials*, 477.
63. Ibid., 379–80.
64. *The Argument of the Lord Chief Justice of the Court of King's Bench concerning the Great Case of Monopolies between the East-India Company, Plaintiff, and Thomas Sandys, Defendant* (London, 1689), 4; Ken MacMillan "Common *and* Civil Law? Taking Possession of the English Empire in America, 1575–1630." *Canadian Journal of History* 38, no. 3 (2003): 415–22.
65. *State Trials*, 394; *The Argument of a Learned Counsel Upon an Action of the Case Brought by the East-India-Company, Against Mr. Thomas Sands, an Interloper* (London, 1696), 53–54.
66. *State Trials*, 386, 392.
67. "The Humble Reply of Several Merchants and Others," in *A Journal of Some Remarkable Passages Before the Honourable House of Commons and the Right Honourable the Lords of their Majesties Most Honourable Privy Council* (London, 1693), 26.
68. Halliday, *Dismembering the Body Politic*, 210.
69. Ken MacMillan, *Sovereignty and Possession in the English New World: The Legal Foundations of Empire, 1576–1640* (Cambridge: Cambridge University Press, 2006), esp. 106–19; James Muldoon, "Discovery, Grant, Charter, Conquest, or Purchase: John Adams on the Legal Basis for English Possession of North America," in Bruce H. Mann and Christopher L. Tomlins, eds., *The Many Legalities of Early America* (Chapel Hill: University of North Carolina Press, 2001), 31, 36; Muldoon, "The Contribution of the Medieval Canon Lawyers to the Formation of International Law," *Traditio* 28 (1972): 497. See also, Peter Borschberg, "Hugo Grotius, East India Trade and the King of Johor," *Journal of Southeast Asian Studies* 30, no. 2 (1999): 239n74; Anthony Pagden, *Lords of all the World: Ideologies of Empire in Spain, Britain and France c.1500–c.1800* (New Haven, CT: Yale University Press, 1995), 64; Steinberg, *Social Construction of the Ocean*, 79; Charles-Martial de Witte, "Les bulles pontificales et l'expansion portugaise au XVᵉ siècle," *Revue d'histoire ecclésiastique* 48 (1953).
70. Muldoon, "Papal Responsibility," 168n1, 169–70, 184.
71. *State Trials.*, 385, 392, 501–2, 504.
72. Ibid., 498.
73. Ibid., 441.
74. *Argument of a Learned Counsel*, 52–53.
75. Ibid., 32–34; Barber, *British Economic Thought and India*, 31n8; *State Trials*, 431.
76. *Two Letters Concerning the East India Company* (London, 1676), 3; Richard Grassby, "Pollexfen, John (1636–1715)," Oxford Dictionary of National Biography (Oxford University Press, 2004, online ed., January 2008), http://www.oxforddnb.com/view/article/22475.
77. Daniel Goffman, *Britons in the Ottoman Empire, 1642–1660* (Seattle: University of Washington, 1998), 14; Niels Steensgaard, "Consuls and Nations in the Levant from 1570 to 1650," *Scandinavian Economic History Review* 15 (1967) in Sanjay Subrahmanyam, ed., *Merchant Networks in the Early Modern World* (Aldershot, Hampshire: Variorum, 1996), 216–17, 220–21.
78. Scott, *Constitution and Finance*, 2:142, 166.
79. *The Allegations of the Turky Company and Others Against the East-India-Company, Relating to the Management of that Trade* (London, 1681), 2.
80. Quoted by Gary De Krey, *London and the Restoration 1659–1683* (Cambridge: Cambridge University Press, 2005), 370; Halliday, *Dismembering the Body Politic*, 206–8, 229–32.
81. *State Trials*, 498, 507; The fact that some Italian merchants ironically had, a few decades earlier, also indicted the Levant Company for acting like a "little Republique," particularly

for insisting on attempting to choose their own ambassadors, went unnoticed. "Narrative of some of the Levant Companies Proceedings with his Late Majestie & Your Crowne," SP 97/19 f. 266. Many thanks to Tristan Stein for making me aware of this reference.

82. *State Trials*, 452.

83. Barber, *British Economic Thought and India*, 39–40.

84. *Allegations of the Turky Company*, 5; *Britannia Languens: Or, A Discourse of Trade* (London, 1689), 137–38.

85. Roger Coke, *Reflections upon the East-Indy and Royal African Companies* (London, 1695), 6–7.

86. Keene, *Beyond the Anarchical Society*, 53; Pagden, *Lords of all the World*, 67–88; Richard Tuck, *Rights of War and Peace: Political Thought and the International Order from Grotius to Kant* (Oxford: Oxford University Press, 1999), 90, 104–8, 174–75.

87. [Richard Hakluyt], "Notes of information one the behaulfe of the Merchants entending trade to the Easte Indies," Huntington Library MSS El 2360; Heidi Brayman Hackel and Peter C. Mancall, "Richard Hakluyt the Younger's Notes for the East India Company in 1601: A Transcription of Huntington Library Manuscript EL 2360," *Huntington Library Quarterly* 67, no. 3 (2004). See also Alexandrowicz, *Law of Nations*, 58–59; David Armitage, "Introduction," in Hugo Grotius, *The Free Sea, or A Disputation Concerning the Right which the Hollanders Ought to Have to the Indian Merchandise for Trading*, trans. Richard Hakluyt, ed. David Armitage (Indianapolis, IN: Liberty Fund, 2004), xxii; Sinnappah Arasaratnam, *Pre-Modern Commerce and Society in Southern Asia: An Inaugural Lecture delivered at the University of Malaya on 21 December 1971* (Kuala Lumpur: University of Malaya Press, 1972), 9; Borschberg, "Hugo Grotius," 227–28, 241–48; G. Norman Clark, "Grotius's East India Mission to England," *Transactions of the Grotius Society* 20 (1934); Tuck, *Rights of War and Peace*, 93–94; George Winius, "A Tale of Two Coromandel Towns: Madraspatam (Fort St. George) and São Thomé de Meliapur," *Itinerario* 18 (1994): 58–59.

88. *Cases Argued and Adjudged in the High Court of Chancery*, 1:127.

89. *State Trials*, 411, 493–95.

90. Patricia Seed, *Ceremonies of Possession: Europe's Conquest of the New World, 1492–1640* (Cambridge: Cambridge University Press, 1995), 154–60; Steinberg, *Social Construction of the Ocean*, chs. 2–3, esp. 66.

91. Philopatris, *Treatise*, 15.

92. London to Madras, 13 February 1684/5, E/3/90 f. 257.

93. *State Trials*, 455, 517–18.

94. *Argument of the Lord Chief Justice*, 20, 29.

95. London to Madras, 13 February 1684/5, E/3/90 f. 257.

96. *Argument of the Lord Chief Justice*, 3–4.

97. *State Trials*, 526–33, 538; Tuck, *Rights of War and Peace*, 116–17.

98. This very same argument underscored the recent royal *quo warranto* assault on municipal corporations, which Jeffreys himself had spearheaded, only here he maintained the corporation did fulfill its obligation. See Halliday, *Dismembering the Body Politic*, 162, 205.

99. *Argument of the Lord Chief Justice.*, 8, 17–18, 24; *State Trials*, 520, 545, 553–54.

100. "Totum integrum et solum Commercium et Negotiationem habere, uti et gaudere." *State Trials*, 486.

101. *The Case of Charles Price, Merchant, and Others; Owners and Freighters of the Ship Andaluzia* (London, 1689?).

102. London to Surat, 26 July 1683, E/3/90 f. 86.

103. Court Minutes, 4 February 1684/5, B/38 f. 81.

104. Committees for Lawsuits, 7 May 1685, H/23 f. 1–2, 3–4.

105. London to Madras, 13 February 1684/5, E/3/90 f. 257; London to Bengal, 13 February 1684/5, E/3/90 f. 262.

106. Court Minutes, 30 November and 7 December 1687, B/39 f. 81–82; *JHOC*, vol. 10, 28 May 1689.

107. London to Bombay, 28 September 1687, E/3/91 f. 196.

108. Secret Committee to Madras, 19 October 1683, E/3/90 f. 120; London to Madras, 24 February 1685/6, E/3/91 f. 54; London to Surat, 26 March 1686, E/3/91 f. 57; Surat to London, 10 February 1686/7, E/3/46 f. 151; London to Bombay, 13 May 1687, E/3/91 f. 149; Bengal to Bombay, 10 September 1687, E/3/47 f. 94; Gombroone to Isfahan, 20 March 1694/5, E/3/50 f. 377 (postscript); Isfahan to London, 30 September 1695, E/3/51 f. 200.

109. *Charters*, 116–40.

110. London to Surat, 7 April 1684, E/3/90 f. 170.

111. Benton, *Search for Sovereignty*, 148. "His Majesties Commission to D[o]c[t]or St. John," (Latin and "Englished"), 6 February 1684, and "The Company's Commission to Doctor St. John," 7 April 1684, E/3/90 f. 185–86; Commission to John Gray, 14 January 1685/6, E/3/91 f. 20; London to Bombay, 22 October 1686, E/3/91 f. 101; "Commission to Sir John Biggs," 22 October 1686, E/3/91 f. 115; London to Madras, 7 January 1686/7, E/3/91 ff. 118–19; London to Madras, 28 September 1687, E/3/91 f. 213; Madras Consultations, 24 February 1686/7, 26 and 28 July, and 1 December 1687, in *RFSG: D&C 1687*, 35, 103–6, 188; Charles Lockyer, *An Account of the Trade in India* (London, 1711), 7.

112. London to Surat, 23 March 1686/87, E/3/91 f. 135.

Chapter 3

1. London to Madras, 28 September 1687, E/3/91 f. 214.

2. Bombay to London, 14 June 1672, H/50 f. 19–20; on claims over rivers, passages, and waterways more generally, see Lauren Benton, *A Search for Sovereignty: Law and Geography in European Empires, 1400–1900* (Cambridge: Cambridge University Press, 2009), chaps. 2–3.

3. Surat to London, 14 December 1683, E/3/43 f. 261; Surat to London, 23 April 1683, E/3/43 f. 40; John Richards, *The Mughal Empire* (Cambridge: Cambridge University Press, 1993), 218–20; I. B. Watson, "Fortifications and the 'Idea' of Force in Early English East India Company Relations with India," *Past and Present* 88 (1980).

4. Madhais Yasin, "Sivaji's Naval Experiment," in K. S. Mathew, ed., *Mariners, Merchants and Oceans: Studies in Maritime History* (New Delhi: Manohar, 1995), 253–56; R. R. S. Chauhan, *Africans in India: From Slavery to Royalty* (New Delhi: Asian Publication Services, 1995), chaps. 4–5.

5. Surat to London, 18 November 1679 H/51 ff. 184–86; London to Surat, 15 March 1680/81, H/51 f. 252.

6. Bombay to London, 6 January 1672/3, H/50 f. 67.

7. "Instructions to be observed by Mr. Stephen Ustick in his Treaty with Sevagee," 25 September 1671, E/3/32, f. 31; Instructions to Henry Oxinden and Journal, 11 May 1674, H/50 ff. 273–80; "Journal or Narrative of what occurred in Henry Oxinden's Journey to the Castle of Rairy," May–June 1674, H/50 ff. 281–93; John Fryer, *A New Account of East-India and Persia in Eight Letters Being Nine Years Travels, Begun 1672 and Finished 1681* (London: R. R. for Rt. Chiswell, 1698), 77–82.

8. *EFI*, I, 112.

9. It was inscribed on a gold medal given to Streynsham Master for his service at Surat during Sivaji's invasion, recommended to Madras as it redoubled its fortifications in 1684, and evidently quoted offhand by a Company factor to the circumnavigator William Dampier a decade later. *Yule*, 2:ccxxvi; London to Madras, 2 July 1684, E/3/90 f. 192; William Dampier, *Voyages and descriptions. in three parts: to which is added a general index to both volumes* (London: Printed for James Knapton, 1699), 102.

10. Court Minutes, 21 and 26 January 1680/1, B/36 f. 83–84; London to Surat, 15 March 1680/81, H/51 f. 261; London to Bombay, 31 January 1681/2 H/51 f. 290–91.

11. Surat to London, 8 April 1680 H/51 f. 220; Surat to London, 23 January 1681/2, H/51 f. 302.

12. Bombay to London, 8 January 1682/3, H/51 f. 316; Surat to London, 8 April 1680 H/51 f. 223–24.
13. Surat to London, 8 April 1680, H/51 f. 224.
14. Surat to London, 23 January 1681/2, H/51 f. 303–4.
15. Bombay to London, 22 September 1683, E/3/43 f. 140; Surat to London, 30 November 1683, E/3/43 f. 206.
16. Bombay to London, 22 September 1683, E/3/43 f. 140; "Henry Smith's Objections," 27 October 1683, E/3/43 f. 166; Surat to London, 30 November 1683, E/3/43 f. 205–6.
17. For the instructions, see London to Surat, 15 March 1680/81, H/51 f. 254–55.
18. Court Minutes, 2 February 1680/1, B/36 f. 85; London to Surat, 15 March 1680/81, H/51 f. 253, 256.
19. "Henry Smith's Objections," 27 October 1683, f. 168.
20. For in-depth detail of the rebellion, its prelude, and aftermath, see Oliver Strachey and Ray Strachey, *Keigwin's Rebellion (1683–4): An Episode in the History of Bombay* (Oxford: Clarendon Press, 1916).
21. Declaration of John Church [26 January 1683/4], E/3/43 f. 321.
22. Bombay (Keigwin) to Charles II [27 December 1683–8 February 1684], E/3/43 f. 369–75.
23. Benton, *Search for Sovereignty*, 99.
24. Commission and Instructions for Capt. Stephen Adderton, 6 March, 1683/4, E/3/43 f. 289–90.
25. Bombay (Keigwin) to Charles II, ff. 370–71; John Petit to Henry Smith, 15 March 1683/4, E/3/43 f. 489.
26. Bombay (Keigwin) to Charles II, f. 374.
27. Bombay (Keigwin) to Surat, 1 January 1683/4, E/3/43 f. 285.
28. Surat Consultations, 19 July 1683, G/36/5, I, f. 55.
29. Francis Day's report on his meeting with the rebels, 25 January 1683/4, E/3/43, f. 319; Deposition of Francis Day, 25 September 1684 E/3/44 f. 147; John St. John to Charles II, 20 October 1684, TNA CO 77/14 f. 141.
30. John Turner to Henry Smith, 30 December 1683, E/3/43 f. 282.
31. Declaration of John Church, E/3/43 f. 320.
32. "A Proclamation For the Liberty Felicity & Tranquility of the Inhabitants & Indwellers of Bombay," 29 December 1683, E/3/43 f. 277.
33. Keigwin to Charles II, 15 September 1684, E/3/44 f. 128.
34. "Articles of Agreement between the Governor and Inhabitants of Bombay," nd, E/3/43 f. 278; Declaration of John Church [26 January 1683/4], E/3/43 f. 320.
35. See, for example, "Pass to Monmock Parsee," 6 January 1683/4, E/3/43 f. 323; "Pass to Ship Ruparell," nd, E/3/43 f. 421.
36. London to Surat, 26 March 1686, E/3/91 f. 58.
37. Attestations of Henry Smith, Ralph Lambton, Roger Carr, and John Beere, 10 and 11 January 1683/4, E/3/43 f. 352–58.
38. "The Narrative of Thomas Spenser Chirurgion," 21 October 1684, E/3/44 f. 208–9; Extract of London Secret Committee to the King, 15 August 1684, in *Yule*, 2:ccclvii.
39. London Secret Committee to General, President and Council at Surat, 26 September 1684, E/3/90 f. 207–8; Surat to London, 31 January 1684/5, E/3/44 f. 400.
40. Letters patents, 9 August 1683, in *Charters granted to the East-India Company, from 1601; also the treaties and grants, made with, or obtained, from the Princes and Powers in India, from the year 1756 to 1772* (London, 1773), 121.
41. London to Bengal, 21 December 1683, E/3/90 f. 149; Bruce Lenman, "The East India Company and the Emperor Aurangzeb," 37 (1987), 27; *Yule*, clxi–clxii. See also Sir Thomas Grantham, *An Historical Account of Some Memorable Actions Performed for the Service of his Prince and Country* (London, 1714).
42. Surat to London, 26 April 1684, E/3/44 f. 164.
43. John St. John to Charles II, 20 October 1684, TNA CO 77/14 f. 141.

44. Order under the Privy Seal to John Petit, Geo Bowcher, Simon Cracroft and Edwd. Littleton, 12 November 1684, A/1/39.
45. "Copy of the Pardon Granted by Sr Thomas Grantham to Richard Keigwin, etc.," 18 December 1684 E/3/44 f. 290; Journal of Thomas Grantham's Voyage, Harl 4753, ff. 13–19.
46. Proceedings of the Admiralty Court at Swally Marine, September–October 1684, E/3/44 f. 132–40; Journal of Thomas Grantham's Voyage, Harl 4753, ff. 25, 32; Charles Fawcett, *The First Century of British Justice in India* (Oxford: Clarendon Press, 1934), 121.
47. J. K. Laughton, "Keigwin, Richard (d. 1690)," rev. Søren Mentz, *Oxford Dictionary of National Biography* (Oxford University Press, 2004), online ed., January 2008, www.oxforddnb.com/view/article/15254.
48. Sir Gervase Lucas's Reports, TNA CO/77 f. 90, quoted in Shafaat Ahmad Khan, *Sources for the History of British India in the Seventeenth Century* (London, 1926; repr., London: Curzon Press, 1975), 116.
49. London to Bombay, 14 July 1686, E/3/91, f. 79; London to Bombay, 6 January 1687/8, E/3/91 f. 249.
50. Surat to London, 21 April 1685, E/3/45 f. 34; Bombay to London, 9 May 1685, E/3/45 f. 60.
51. Commission to Commanders of Ships, 26 November 1684, E/3/90 f. 252; London Secret Committee to Charles II, 15 August 1684, E/3/90 f. 200–201.
52. London to Surat, 28 October 1685, E/3/91 f. 5.
53. London to St. Helena, 6 May 1685, E/3/90, f. 272–74; Journal of Thomas Grantham's Voyage, Harl 4753, f. 37; Shafaat Ahmad Khan, *The East India Trade in the XVIIth Century in its Political and Economic Aspects* (London: Oxford University Press, 1923), 200.
54. London to Madras, 6 June 1687, E/3/91 f. 154.
55. Abd-al Kahar to Charles II (trans. Thomas Hyde), nd, CO 77/14, ff. 58–50; London to Banten, 15 July 1692, E/3/90 f. 6; *London Gazette* (8–11 May 1682); *The Historian's Guide, or, Britain's Rememberancer* (London, 1690), 141, 143–46; Daniel Lysons, *The Environs of London: Being An Historical Account of the Towns, Villages, and Hamlets, within Twelve Miles of that Capital: Volume the Fourth: Counties of Herts, Essex & Kent* (London, 1795–96), 242.
56. Josiah Child to Laurence Hyde, 2 June 1682, TNA CO 77/14 f. 53.
57. See Claude Guillot, "Banten and the Bay of Bengal during the Sixteenth and Seventeenth Centuries," in Om Prakash and Denys Lombard, eds., *Commerce and Culture in the Bay of Bengal, 1500–1800* (Manohar: Indian Council of Historical Research, 1999), 163–82; London to Pangeran Deepa Penerat, 7 July 1682, E/3/90 f. 8.
58. London to Banten, 15 July 1692, E/3/90 f. 5; London to Abd-al Kahar, 7 July 1682, E/3/90 f. 7
59. Claude Guillot, *The Sultanate of Banten* (Jakarta: Gramedia Book Publishing Division, 1990), 52–53; "Relations of what passed at Bantam, March 1682," Lansdowne 1152, f. 84–85; Josiah Child and Benjamin Bathurst to James II, Court Minutes, 29 June 1687, B/39 f. 24: Femme Gaastra, "War, Competition and Collaboration: Relations Between the English and Dutch East India Companies in the Seventeenth and Eighteenth Centuries," in H. V. Bowen, Margarette Lincoln and Nigel Rigby, eds. *The Worlds of the East India Company* (Woodbridge, Suffolk: Boydell Press, 2002), 50–55. The flag in this case fared somewhat better than it did in a similar incident in 1617, when one seized by the Dutch from an English ship in Japan was said to have been used for toilet paper. Alison Games, *The Web of Empire: English Cosmopolitans in an Age of Expansion, 1560–1660* (New York: Oxford University Press, 2008), 111.
60. Pieter van Dam, *A Justification of the Directors of the Netherlands East-India Company as it was Delivered Over Unto the High and Mighty Lords of the States General of the United Provinces, the 22d of July, 1686* (London, 1688), 10–11.
61. See, e.g., *The Civil Wars of Bantam: Or, An Impartial Relation of all the Battels, Sieges, and the Remarkable Transctions, Revolutions, and Accidents that happened in the late Civil Wars between that King and his Eldest Son, commonly called by them The Young King* (London,

1683); *A Short Account of the Seige of Bantam: And its Surrender to the Rebels, who were Assisted by the DUTCH, and their Fleet, in the East-Indies, In a Letter from an English Factor to a Merchant of London* (London, 1683).

62. 6 September 1683, Add.MS 41,822 f. 28.

63. Commission to Capt. John Ely from Surat Council, 26 April 1684, E/3/44 f. 46.

64. London to Abu'l Fatah, 27 July 1683, E/3/90 f. 104; Petition to the king, nd. Add.MS 41,822 f. 5; Josia Child to [secretary of state], 1 September 1683 and 6 September 1683, Add.MS 41,822 ff. 25–26, 28–29; East India Company to Charles II, nd, Add.MS 41,822 f. 35; List of Company's complaints, 1685, BL Add.MS 41,822 f. 80; K. N. Chaudhuri and Jonathan Israel, "The English and Dutch East India Companies and the Glorious Revolution of 1688–9," in Jonathan Israel, ed. *The Anglo-Dutch Moment: Essays on the Glorious Revolution and its World Impact* (Cambridge: Cambridge University Press, 1991), 414–16.

65. *An Impartial Vindication of the English East-India-Company, From the Unjust and Slanderous Imputations Cast Upon them in a Treaties Intituled, A Justification of the Directors of the Netherlands East-India-Company; As it was delivered over unto the High and Mighty Lords the States General of the United Provinces* (London: Printed by J. Richardson, 1688).

66. Memorial of Marquess D'Albeville, 1 August 1687, Add.MS 41,822 f. 115.

67. London to Madras, 5 July 1682, E/3/90 f. 3; Letter of Introduction for Captain John Preston to VOC Factory Governors, 2 October 1682, E/3/90 f. 34; London to Bengal, 21 December 1683, E/3/90 f. 150.

68. London to Charles II, 9 July 1684, Add.MS 41,822 f. 47–48; Gaastra, "War, Competition and Collaboration," 53–54. See also Karen Chancey, "The Amboyna Massacre in English Politics, 1624–1632," *Albion* 30, no. 4 (1998): 583–98; Adam Clulow, "Unjust, Cruel and Barbarous Proceedings: Japanese Mercenaries and the Amboina Incident of 1623," *Itinerario* 31, no. 1 (2007): 15–34; Anthony Milton, "Marketing a Massacre: Amboyna, The East India Company and the Public Sphere in Early Modern England," in Peter Lake and Steve Pincus, eds., *Politics of the Public Sphere in Early Modern England* (Manchester: Manchester University Press, 2008); Benjamin Schmidt, *Innocence Abroad: The Dutch Imagination and the New World, 1570–1670* (Cambridge: Cambridge University Press, 2001), 296–300. For an example of the popularization of Amboina during the Anglo-Dutch wars, see John Dryden, *Amboyna: A Tragedy, As it is Acted at the Theatre-Royal* (London: Printed by T. N. for Henry Herringman, 1673).

69. "A Brief Memorial of the Late Transactions at Bantam," 2 April 1683, TNA CO 77/17 f. 122; Surat to Secret Committee, 26 September 1684, E/3/44, f. 151.

70. London to Bengal, 14 January 1685/6, E/3/91 f. 24; London to Pariaman, 20 January 1685/6, E/3/91 f. 13; London to Queen of Atcheen, 1 October 1684, E/3/90 f. 231; London to King of Mindanoa, 19 October 1684, E/3/90 f. 243; L. E. Pennington, "Samuel Purchas: His Reputation and the Uses of His Works," in L.E. Pennington, ed., *The Purchas Handbook: Studies of the life, times and writings of Samuel Purchas 1577–1626* (London: The Hakluyt Society, 1997), 10.

71. Court Minutes, 29 June 1687, B/39 f. 24.

72. Secret Committee to Madras, 5 September 1683 and 19 October 1683, E/3/90 ff. 111–12, 117–20; Secret Committee Transactions about Bombay, 15 August 1684, E/3/90 ff. 200ff; Court Minutes, 9 June and 22 October 1686, B/38 ff. 216–17, 256; C.H. Philips, "The Secret Committee of the East India Company," *Bulletin of the School of Oriental Studies* 10 (1940): 299–304.

73. Secret Committee's Transactions About Bombay, August–October 1684, E/3/90 f. 205; London to Surat, 6 May 1685, E/3/90 f. 278–79; "Commission to Sir John Child to be General and Admiral &c.," 3 February 1684/5, E/3/90 f. 280; John Bruce, *Annals of the Honorable East-India Company from their Establishment by the Charter of Queen Elizabeth, 1600, to the Union of the London and English East-India Companies, 1707–8*, 3 vols. (London: Black, Parry, and Kingsbury, 1810), 2:568.

74. K. N. Chaudhuri, *The Trading World of Asia and the English East India Company, 1660–1760* (Cambridge: Cambridge University Press, 1978), 116–17; London to Surat, 2 July 1684, E/3/90 f. 196.

75. Bombay to London, 23 January 1669/70, H/49 f. 258; Surat to London, 3 February 1671/2, E/3/32 f. 164; London to Surat, 28 October 1685, E/3/91 f. 5–6; London to Bombay, E/3/91 f. 250; Philip Lawson, *The East India Company: A History* (London: Longman 1993), 47; Ruby Maloni, "Surat to Bombay: Transfer of Commercial Power." *Itinerario* 26, no. 1 (2002): 61–73.

76. London to Bombay, 15 August 1683, E/3/90 f. 107; London to Surat, 7 April 1684 and 6 May 1685, E/3/90 f. 165, 278.

77. London to Bombay, 27 August 1688, E/3/91, f. 272. On the later usage of the phrase "brightest jewel in the Crown," see M. E. Yapp, "'The Brightest Jewel': The Origins of a Phrase," in Kenneth Ballhatchet and John Harrison, eds., *East India Company Studies: Papers Presented to Professor Sir Cyril Philips* (Hong Kong: Asian Research Service, 1986).

78. Surat to London, 26 September 1684, E/3/44 f. 159.

79. London to St. Helena, 3 August 1687, E/3/91 f. 183.

80. London to Madras, 6 March 1684/5 and 2 July 1684, E/3/90, ff. 266, 289.

81. London to Surat, 3 October 1684, E/3/90 f. 218.

82. London to Bombay, 3 August 1687, E/3/91 f. 160–61, 163.

83. London to Madras, 22 October 1686, E/3/91 f. 108.

84. Surat Council to London, 6 May 1684, E/3/44 f. 57; Arnold Wright, *Annesley of Surat and His Times: The True Story of the Mythical Wesley Fortune* (London: Andrew Melrose, Ltd., 1918), 87.

85. London to Madras, 2 July 1684, E/3/90 f. 192; London to Madras, 28 August 1682, 20 September 1682, 2 July 1684, 2 July 1683, 3 September 1684, E/3/90 f. 9, 26, 189, 192, 198, 224.

86. London to Captain John Gayer, 7 April 1684, E/3/90 f. 173.

87. London to Captain Robert Knox, 4 April 1684, E/3/90 f. 183; Anna Winterbottom, "Producing and Using the *Historical Relation of Ceylon*: Robert Knox, the East India Company, and the Royal Society," *British Journal for the History of Science* 42 (2009).

88. Secret Committee to Surat, 16 November 1683, E/3/90 f. 133.

89. Thomas Grantham to [London], 23 August 1684, E/3/44 f. 110; Journal of Thomas Grantham's Voyage, Harl 4753, ff. 2–3, 6–7.

90. London to "Queen of Atcheen," 1 October 1684, E/3/90 f. 231. For a narrative of the early events in founding the Sumatran settlement, see Alan Harfield, *Bencoolen: A History of the Honourable East India Company's Garrison on the West Coast of Sumatra (1685–1825)* (Barton-on-Sea: A and J Partnership, 1995).

91. London to Madras, 2 July 1684, E/3/90 f. 192.

92. Bengkulu to Madras, 3 October 1685, G/35/1 f. 12 [10].

93. Benjamin Bloome and Joshua Charlton to Ralph Ord, [October] 1685, repr. in John Bastin, ed., *The British in West Sumatra (1685–1825)* (Kuala Lampur: University of Malaya Press, 1965), 13–14.

94. William Dampier, *A New Voyage Round the World* (London, 1697), 183.

95. London to Bombay, 31 January 1689/90, E/3/92 f. 78.

96. London to Madras, 2 July 1684, E/3/90 f. 192.

97. Court Minutes, 27 July 1687 and 3 August 1687, B/39 f. 29–30; Bengkulu to Court of Committees, 6 February 1685/6, repr. in John Bastin, ed., *British in West Sumatra*, 32; Harfield, *Bencoolen*, 22.

98. London to Bengkulu, 31 August 1687, E/3/91, f. 192; Secret Committee to Madras, 19 October 1683, E/3/90 f. 117; Anthony Farrington, "Bengkulu: An Anglo-Chinese Partnership," in Bowen, Lincoln, and Rigby, eds., *Worlds of the East India Company*, 112–13.

99. London to Bengkulu, 1 March 1692/3, in *RFSG: LF 1693–94*, 14.

100. London to Pariaman, 21 October 1685, E/3/91 f. 1; John Bruce, *Annals*, 598.

101. London to Madras, 6 March 1694/5, E/3/92 f. 392, 394; Anthony Farrington, "Bengkulu," 114–15.

102. Anthony Reid, *Charting the Shape of Early Modern Southeast Asia* (Singapore: Institute of Southeast Asian Studies, 2000), 199; Bengkulu to Court of Committees, 6 February 1685/6, repr. in Bastin, ed., *British in West Sumatra*, 28.

103. London to Bengkulu, 22 January 1713/14, E/3/98, 257; Frenise A. Logan, "The East India Company and African Slavery in Benkulen, Sumatra, 1687–1792," *Journal of Negro History* 41, no. 4 (1956): 339–48; Harfield, *Bencoolen*, 7–15.

104. London to Fort St. David, 6 March 1694/5, E/3/92 ff. 400–401.

105. York Fort Consultations, 27 September 1709, G/35/56, n.p.

106. London to Bengal, 27 August 1688, E/3/91 f. 286; Madras to Surat, 28 June 1686, f. 34; London to Bengkulu, 29 February 1691/2, E/3/92 f. 203.

107. London to Pariaman, 21 October 1685, E/3/91 f. 1; London to Madras, 29 February 1683/4, E/3/90 f. 155; London to king of Mindinao, 19 October 1684, E/3/90 f. 243.

108. "Transactions of the Committees for Secrecy in Reference to the Affairs in the Bay of Bengalla," 14 January 1685/6, E/3/91 f. 33.

109. Surat to London, 30 November 1686, E/3/46 f. 99.

110. Surat to London, 26 April 1684, E/3/44 f. 43.

111. London to Surat, 7 April 1684, E/3/90 f. 167; I. Bruce Watson, "Fortifications and the 'Idea' of Force in Early English East India Company Relations with India," *Past and Present* 88 (1980).

112. London to Surat, 6 May 1685, E/3/90 f. 278.

113. Surat to London, 21 April 1685, E/3/45 f. 31; D.K. Bassett. "British 'Country' Trade and Local Trade networks in the Thai and Malay States, c. 1680–1770," *Modern Asian Studies*, 23, no. 4 (1989): 628–29; *EFS*, 1:12.

114. Madras to London, 5 February 1685, in *EFS*, 2:889.

115. Surat to London, 29 November 1684 in *EFS*, 2:888.

116. Surat to London, 23 April 1683, E/3/43 f. 41; Peter Crouch to Surat, 16 December 1683, E/3/43 f. 276; William Strangh to London, 11 May 1684, E/3/44 ff. 65–66; Madras to Surat, 8 March 1686/7, E/3/46 f. 168.

117. Madras Consultations, 14 and 15 April 1686 in *EFS*, 2:933–34.

118. Bombay's Instructions to Captain Joseph Eaton, 23 May 1687, E/3/47 ff. 56–58; Bombay to Madras, 30 November 1687, E/3/47 f. 143; *Yule*, 1:135; London to Madras, 9 June 1686 in *EFS*, 2:939.

119. *By the King. A Proclamation For the Recalling All His Majesties Subjects from the Service of Foreign Princes in East India, 2 James II; 17 July 1686* (London, 1686).

120. Madras Consultations, 27 and 28 July and 3 August 1687 in *RFSG: D&C 1687*, 103, 105–6.

121. Commission Forms, in ibid., 204–6.

122. Chaudhuri and Israel, "English and Dutch East India Companies," 438; Chaudhuri, *Trading World*, 109, 113–14; Steve Pincus, *1688: The First Modern Revolution* (New Haven, CT: Yale University Press, 2009), 378.

123. Instructions to Captain Joseph Eaton, 23 May 1687, f. 56.

124. Madras Consultations, 5 March 1687/8 in *RFSG: D&C 1688*, 42; "His Majesty the King of Syam his just declaration against the Honorable Governor & Company of Merchants of London trading to the East Indies & the Governor & Councill of Fort St. George," 11 August 1687, in *EFS*, 2:1068–77.

125. Phaulkon to Madras, 29 October 1686, in *EFS*, 2:976.

126. Maurice Collins, *Siamese White* (London: Faber and Faber, 1936).

127. London to Bombay, 11 April 1688, E/3/91 f. 263.

128. London to Madras, 22 October 1686, E/3/91 f. 109–110.

129. London to Bombay, 14 July 1686, E/3/91 f. 79–80.

130. Pincus, *1688*, 326, 380.

131. Madras Consultations, 11–12 June 1688, in *RFSG: D&C, 1688*, 93–94.

132. Proclamation of Joseph Eaton and Officers, 16 March 1685/6, E/3/45 f. 242.
133. Proceedings of the Court of Admiralty, 12 December 1687, E/3/47 f. 160; Sentence of Condemnation of Ship Streights Merchant, 9 November 1687, E/3/47 f. 176; John Wyborne to London, 6 January 1687/8, E/3/47 ff. 178–81.
134. London to Elihu Yale, 12 December 1687, E/3/91 f. 231.
135. London to Madras, 29 February 1683/4, E/3/90 f. 155.
136. London to Madras, 22 October 1686, E/3/90 f. 110.
137. London to Surat, 17 June 1685, E/3/90 f. 288; London to Madras, 14 January 1685/6 and 22 October 1686, E/3/91 ff. 18, 109–10; Commission and instructions to William Hodges, Anthony Weltden, John Hill, and James Perrimen, 22 August 1687, in *EFS*, 2:1081.
138. Madras to Richard Burnaby and Samuel White, 27 August 1687, in *RFSG, D&C, 1687*, 133; London to Madras, 22 October 1686, E/3/91 f. 110; Bombay to Madras, 30 November 1687, E/3/47 f. 142. White served as a local contact for King Narai's 1684 embassy to France, facilitating the gift offered to Charles II en route and coordinating the re-export of presents and other equipage for the envoys. See Henry Guy to Customs Commissioners, 26 and 27 August 1684 in *EFS*, 2:874–75.
139. London to Madras, 6 February 1687/8, E/3/91 f. 251.
140. Madras to London, [?] January 1688/9, E/3/47 f. 214.
141. Madras to Surat, 19 December 1687 in *EFS*, 2:1103.
142. Madras Consultation, 26 December 1687 in ibid., 2:1106.
143. Madras to London, 1 February 1689/90, E/3/48 f. 130.
144. Madras Consultations, 11 and 12 January 1687/8, in *RFSG: D&C, 1688*, 7–8; Samuel White, *A True Account of the Passages at MERGEN in the KINGDOM of Syam, After Captain Anthony Weltden arrived at that Port in the Curtana Frigat, for Account of the EAST-INDIA Company* ([London], [1688]), 5–7; Samuel White, *The Case of Samuel White, Humbly Presented, to the Honourable, the Knights, Citizens, and Burgesses in Parliament Assembled* ([London], [1688]), 2–3.
145. London to Madras, 27 August 1688, E/3/91 f. 282.
146. London to Bengal, 21 December 1683, E/3/90 f. 148; London to Bengal, 5 March 1683/4, E/3/90 f. 158.
147. London (secret) to Madras, 14 January 1685/6, E/3/91 f. 30–31.
148. London to Madras, 9 June 1686, E/3/91 f. 72; London to Bengal, 17 June 1685, E/3/90 f. 289.
149. *Yule*, 1:133–34, 161.
150. "The Governor and Company of Merchants of London Trading into the East Indies To the Most Noble & Illustrious Prince the Nabob of Decca," 20 January 1685/6, E/3/91 f. 42.
151. See "The Governor and Company of Merchants of London trading into the East Indies to the most famous, Glorious, and Renouned King of RACAN," 20 January 1685/6, E/3/91 f. 42; Commission and Instructions to Joan Perera Faria Junior, 23 February 1679/80 and "Articles of Commerce to be Proposed to the King of Barma and Pegu in behalfe of the English Nation for the settling a Trade in those Countrys," in Madras Consultations, 23 February 1679/80, in *RFSG: D&C, 1680–1681*, 9–10; Madras to London, 9 October 1684, E/3/44 f. 195; Madras Consultations, 8 March 1687/8, *RFSG: D&C, 1688*, 46.
152. Job Charnock and Francis Ellis to London, 22 November 1686, E/3/46 f. 93.
153. Proceedings of the Admiralty Court held aboard ship Beaufort, 18 April 1687, 24 May 1687, 1 November 1687, 17 November 1687, E/3/47 ff. 2–12.
154. Madras Consultations, 10 January, 28 February 1686/7, 16 June 1687, and 5 December 1687, in *RFSG: D&C, 1687*, 6, 38–39, 88, 190.
155. *The East Indian Chronologist* (Calcutta, 1801), 11. Job Charnock et al., to Surat, 24 November 1686, E/3/46 f. 95–97; "Translate of Nabob Shaesta Caun's Perwanna," 4 September 1687 (received), E/3/47 f. 95; Bruce, *Annals*, II:557–59; William Foster, "The East India Company, 1600–1740," in H. H. Dodwell, ed., *The Cambridge History of India*, vol 5: *British India, 1497–1858* (Cambridge, 1929; repr., Delhi: S. Chand and Co., 1963), 108.

156. "Transactions of the Committees for Secrecy in Reference to the Affairs in the Bay of Bengala in London to Madras," 14 January 1685/6, E/3/91 ff. 30–33.

Chapter 4

1. London to Madras, 28 September 1687, E/3/91 f. 209
2. Surat to London, 17 January 1675/6, E/3/36 f. 147.
3. London to Madras, 22 January 1691/2, E/3/92 f. 171.
4. London to Bombay, 3 February 1686/7, E/3/91, f. 131; Josiah Child, *A Discourse Concerning Trade And in Particular of the East Indies* (London, 1689), 2. On the English love-hate relationship with the Dutch in the seventeenth century, see, among others, Joyce Appleby, *Economic Thought and Ideology in Seventeenth-Century England* (Princeton, NJ: Princeton University Press, 1978), chap. 4; Lisa Jardine, *Going Dutch: How England Plundered Holland's Glory* (New York: Harper, 2008); Steven C. A. Pincus, "From Butterboxes to Wooden Shoes: The Shift in English Popular Sentiment from Anti-Dutch to Anti-French in the 1670s," *Historical Journal* 38, no. 2 (1995): 331–61.
5. London to Surat, 28 October 1685, E/3/91 f. 7; London to Bombay and Surat, July 1686, E/3/91, f. 80.
6. Daniel Statt, *Foreigners and Englishmen: The Controversy over Immigration and Population, 1660–1760* (Newark: University of Delaware, 1995), chaps. 2–3.
7. Josiah Child, "A Discourse concerning Plantations," (1692) in *Select Tracts Relating to Colonies* (London, 1732), 32; Statt, *Foreigners and Englishmen*, 76–77.
8. London to Surat, 28 October 1685, E/3/91 f. 7; London to Surat, 13 May 1691, E/3/92 f. 162; London to Madras, 26 January 1697/8, E/3/93 f. 16.
9. London to Abd-al Kahar, 7 July 1682, E/3/90 f. 7; London to Pangeran Deepa Penerat, 7 July 1682, E/3/90 f. 8.
10. London to Bombay, 29 February 1691/2, E/3/92 ff. 215–16; London to Bombay, 6 January 1687/8, E/3/91 f. 248; for one instance of the analogy to the Thames, see London to Bombay, 11 September 1689, E/3/92 f. 32.
11. Cf. H. V. Bowen, "Company, State, and Empire: Government and the East India Company during the Eighteenth Century," in Simonetta Cavaciocchi, ed., *Poteri Economici e Poteri Politici Secc. XIII–XVIII* (Prato: Instituto Internazionale di Storia Economica "F. Datini," 1999), 682.
12. E.g., Philopatris, *A Treatise Wherein is Demonstrated That the East-India Trade is the Most National of Foreign Trades* (London, 1681), 24–29; William Langhorne, *Considerations Humbly Tendred, Concerning the East-India Company* ([London], 1688).
13. Swally Marine to London, 17 January 1675/6, E/3/36 f. 149.
14. London to Surat, 22 February 1670/71, H/49 f. 291; Surat to London, 7 November 1671, H/49 f. 384.
15. Madras Consultations, 2 February 1687/8, in *RFSG: D&C, 1688*, 19.
16. London to St. Helena, 1 August 1683, E/3/90 f. 92.
17. London to Bombay, 6 January 1687/8, E/3/91 f. 250.
18. London to Bombay, 11 September 1689, E/3/92 f. 64.
19. Gerald Aungier to London, 15 January 1673/4, H/50 f. 141. In his mid-nineteenth-century history of the East India Company's administration, Sir John Kaye even suggested that the instructions in 1679–80 for Bombay to recover its civil and military expenses from local sources were the first "scheme of general administration, embracing the whole question of Inland Revenue" in British India. John William Kaye, *The Administration of the East India Company: A History of Indian Progress* (London: R. Bentley, 1853), 70.
20. London to Madras, 26 August 1685, E/3/90 f. 293.
21. René Barendse, "To be a Servant of his Catholic Majesty: Indian Troops of the *Estado da India* in the Eighteenth Century," in Jos Gommans and Om Prakash, eds., *Circumambulations in South Asian History* (Leiden: Brill, 2003), 72–74.

22. London to Madras, 20 July 1683, E/3/90 f. 87; London to Madras, 22 January 1691/2, E/3/92 f. 171; London to Fort St. David, 6 March 1694/5, E/3/92 f. 400.

23. London to Bombay, 11 September 1689, E/3/92 f. 64.

24. London to Madras, 9 June 1686, E/3/91, f. 72.

25. London to Bombay, 6 January 1687/8, E/3/91 f. 248.

26. Jacob Viner, "Power Versus Plenty as Objectives of Foreign Policy in the Seventeenth and Eighteenth Centuries," *World Politics* 1, no. 1 (1948): 1–29; Ronald Findlay and Kevin O'Rourke, *Power and Plenty: Trade, War, and the World Economy in the Second Millennium* (Princeton, NJ: Princeton University Press, 2007).

27. See Richard Tuck, *The Rights of War and Peace: Political Thought and the International Order from Grotius to Kant* (Oxford: Oxford University Press, 1999), 90, 104–8, 174–75; Anthony Pagden, *Lords of all the World: Ideologies of Empire in Spain, Britain and France c.1500–c.1800* (New Haven, CT: Yale University Press, 1995), 67–88.

28. London to Madras, 6 June 1687, E/3/91 f. 154.

29. London to Abd al-Kahar, 7 July 1682, E/3/90 f. 8.

30. London to Bombay, 29 February 1691/2, E/3/92 f. 216.

31. Madras Consultations, 3 January 1685/6, in *RFSG, D&C, 1686*, 3; Kanakalatha Mukund, *The View from Below: Indigenous Society, Temples and the Early Colonial State in Tamilnadu, 1700–1835* (New Delhi: Orient Longman, 2005), 14.

32. Though the rate cap of 8 or 9 percent was a fair bit higher than what Child and others wanted in England. London to Madras, 5 July 1682, E/3/90 f. 3; J[osiah] C[hild], *Brief Observations Concerning Trade, and interest of money* (London, 1668), 6–16.

33. Quoted by Mukund, *View from Below*, 16.

34. London to Madras, 31 May 1683, E/3/90 f. 81.

35. London to Thomas Pitt, 21 November 1699, E/3/93 f. 230.

36. London to Madras, 16 March 1684/5, E/3/90 f. 266.

37. London to St. Helena, 1 August 1683, E/3/90 f. 95.

38. London to Bombay, 29 February 1691/2, E/3/92 f. 215.

39. London to Bombay, 11 September 1688, E/3/91 f. 294.

40. London to Madras, 22 January 1691/2, E/3/92 f. 175.

41. See London to Surat, 3 October 1684, E/3/90 f. 220.

42. London to Surat, 26 March 1686, E/3/91 f. 58.

43. Secret Committee to Surat, 26 September 1684, E/3/90 f. 210.

44. Ibid., f. 208; London to Madras, 20 September 1682, E/3/90 f. 26.

45. Istvan Hont, "Free trade and the economic limits to national politics: neo-Machivaellian political economy reconsidered," in John Dunn, ed., *The Economic Limits to Modern Politics* (Cambridge: Cambridge University Press, 1990), 62–63.

46. J. G. A. Pocock, *The Machiavellian Moment: Florentine Political Thought and the Atlantic Republican Tradition* (Princeton, NJ: Princeton University Press, 1975), 414.

47. Philip J. Stern, "'Defending their Country on Horsback': Soldiers, Settlers, and Citizens in the Seventeenth-Century East India Company," *Journal of Early Modern History* 15 (2011), 1–22. See also, e.g., Ronald L. Boucher, "The Colonial Militia as a Social Institution: Salem, Massachusetts 1764–1775," *Military Affairs* 37, no. 4 (1973): 125–30; J. E. Cookson, "Service without Politics? Army, Militia and Volunteers in Britain during the American and French Revolutionary Wars," *War in History* 10, no. 4 (2003): 381–97; John Morgan Dederer, *War in America to 1775: Before Yankee Doodle* (New York: New York University Press, 1990), 182; Jack S. Radabaugh, "The Militia of Colonial Massachusetts," in A. J. R. Russell-Wood, ed., *Local Government in European Overseas Empires, 1450–1800* (Aldershot: Ashgate, 1999).

48. Copy of the First Commission, 19 December 1673, G/32/1, 5.

49. Michael J. Braddick, "Civility and Authority," in David Armitage and Michael J. Braddick, eds., *The British Atlantic World, 1500–1800* (Houndmills: Palgrave Macmillan, 2002); Michael Craton, "Property and Propriety. Land Tenure and Slave Property in the Creation

of a British West Indian Plantocracy, 1612–1740," in J. Brewer and S. Staves, eds., *Early Modern Conceptions of Property* (London: Routledge, 1996), 518; Craton, "Reluctant Creoles: The Planters' World in the British West Indies," in Bernard Bailyn and Philip Morgan, eds., *Strangers within the Realm: Cultural Margins of the First British Empire* (Chapel Hill: Institute of Early American History and Culture and University of North Carolina Press, 1991), 326–27.

50. London to St. Helena, 1 August 1683, E/3/90 f. 90–91, 93. On the failures of this project, particularly in the early days, see Royle, *Company's Island*, 37.

51. London to Madras, 14 January 1685/6, E/3/91, f. 17.

52. London to Bombay, 27 August 1688, E/3/91 f. 272.

53. Jean Gelman Taylor, *The Social World of Batavia: European and Eurasian in Dutch Asia* (Madison: University of Wisconsin Press, 1983; repr., 2009), 6, 10, 18; Barendse, "To be a Servant of his Catholic Majesty," 73–74.

54. London to Surat, 19 March 1668/9, H/49 f. 14–15; Surat to London, 22 January 1676/7, H/51 f. 34; Bombay to London, 24 January 1676/7 in *BS*, I, 119; S. M. Edwardes, *The Bombay City Police: A Historical Sketch, 1672–1916* (London: Oxford University Press, 1923), 1–19.

55. Surat to London, 26 September 1684, IOR E/3/44 f. 160.

56. Articles of Agreement, [December 1683], E/3/43 f. 278.

57. Madras Consultations, 18 February 1675/6, in *RFSG: D&C, 1672–1678*, 87.

58. London to Madras, 6 June 1687 and 3 August 1687, E/3/91 f. 153, 173.

59. *EFI*, I, 60; Bombay to London, 18 March 1672/3, H/50 f. 82–85.

60. *CCM*, XI, 9–11, 13, 49, 51–52, 71, 79, 97–99, 115, 125–26; Bombay to London, 18 March 1672/3, H/50 f. 86; "Copy of Order Concerning Petition of Alvaro Pirez," 17 October 1677, Yale OSB MSS 41 Box 2; Sir Charles Fawcett, *The First Century of British Justice in India* (Oxford, 1934; repr., Aalen: Scientia Verlag, 1979), 84–86.

61. *CCM*, XI, 244–46; Surat to London, 21 January 1678/9, H/51 f. 149–50.

62. London to Surat, 19 March 1679/80 H/51 f. 174.

63. Petition on Behalf of Manoell Brandao de Lima, 19/29 September 1678, in *RFSG: D&C 1678–79*, 165–66; Yogesh Sharma, "Changing Destinies, Evolving Identities: The Indo-Portuguese Community at Madras in the Seventeenth Century," in Yogesh Sharma and José Leal Ferreira, eds., *Portuguese Presence in India during the Sixteenth and Seventeenth Centuries* (New Delhi: Viva Books, 2008), 121–22, 125.

64. Philip J. Stern, "Politics and Ideology in the Early East India Company-State: The Case of St Helena, 1673–1709," *Journal of Imperial and Commonwealth History* 35, no. 1 (2007): 15.

65. Madras Consultation, 9 July 1688, in *RFSG: D&C, 1688*, 107.

66. London to Surat, 19 March 1668/9, H/49 f. 19–20.

67. Sanjay Subrahmanyam, *The Political Economy of Commerce: Southern India 1500–1650* (Cambridge: Cambridge University Press, 1990), 330–32; C. A. Bayly and Sanjay Subrahmanyam, "Portfolio Capitalists and the Political Economy of Early Modern India," *Indian Economic and Social History Review* 25 (1988): 401–24.

68. Bombay Consultations, 25 March 1685, G/3/3, I, f. 43.

69. Maurizio Viroli, "Machiavelli and the Republican Idea of Politics," in Gisela Bock, Quentin Skinner, and Maurizio Viroli, eds., *Machiavelli and Republicanism* (Cambridge: Cambridge University Press, 1990), 158; Mark Goldie, "The Unacknowledged Republic: Officeholding in Early Modern England," in Tim Harris, ed., *The Politics of the Excluded, c. 1500–1850* (Houndmills: Palgrave, 2001), esp. 175–80.

70. London to Elihu Yale, 12 December 1687, E/3/91 f. 231.

71. Copy, "Letters Patent of the Governor and Company of Merchants of London, trading into the East-Indies, to the Mayor, Aldermen, and Burgesses of Madras, granting the power to establish a municipality and Mayor's Court at Madras," 30 December 1687, A/1/41 (38). For a (somewhat unflattering) description of the court in action, see Alexander Hamilton, *A New Account of the East Indies, being the observations and remarks of Captain Alexander*

Hamilton, who spent his time there from the year 1688 to 1723, 2 vols. (Edinburgh: Printed by John Mosman, 1727), 1:361.

72. Madras to John Child, 29 September 1688, in *RFSG: LF, 1688*, 60; "Report for the first Duke of Leeds, Lord High Treasurer, on the State of Madras," 30 September 1688, Eg 3340 f. 181.

73. Love, *Vestiges*, 1:499.

74. London to Madras, 18 February 1690/1, E/3/92 f. 141.

75. See Phil Withington, *The Politics of Commonwealth: Citizens and Freemen in Early Modern England* (Cambridge: Cambridge University Press, 2005).

76. London to Madras, 22 January 1691/2, 3 January 1693/4, and 6 March 1694/5, E/3/92 f. 174, 301, 390; Love, *Vestiges*, 1:497–503; Child, *Brief Observations*, 4–5.

77. London to Bombay, 6 January 1687/8, E/3/91 f. 250.

78. "At a General Sessions Held at the Town Hall on Wednesday the 11th of December 1689," in *Records of Fort St. George: Minutes of Proceedings in the Mayor's Court of Madraspatam (June to December 1689 and July 1716 to March 1719* (Madras: Superintendent Government Press, 1915), 12. The dissertation work of Mitch Fraas has done much to explain the role of these courts in eighteenth-century British India. See A.M. Fraas, "'They Have Travailed Into a Wrong Latitude': The Laws of England, Indian Settlements, and the British Imperial constitution 1726–1773" (PhD dissertation, Duke University, forthcoming).

79. Fawcett, *First Century*, 57; London to Bombay, 6 January 1687/8, E/3/91 f. 249.

80. See Elizabeth Mancke, "Negotiating an Empire: Britain and its Overseas Peripheries, c. 1550–1780," in Christine Daniels and Michael Kennedy, eds., *Negotiated Empires: Centers and Peripheries in the Americas, 1500–1820* (London: Routledge, 2002); Michael Braddick and John Walter, eds., *Negotiating Power in Early Modern Society: Order, Heirarchy and Subordination in Britain and Ireland* (Cambridge: Cambridge University Press, 2001).

81. Mukund, *View from Below*, chap. 3; H. J. Leue, "Legal Expansion in the Age of the Companies: Aspects of the Administration of Justice in the English and Dutch Settlements of Maritime Asia, c.1600–1750," in W. J. Mommsen and J. A. de Moor, eds., *European Expansion and Law: The Encounter of European and Indigenous Law in Nineteenth and Twentieth-Century Africa and Asia* (Oxford: Berg, 1992), 134–35; Mattison Mines, "Courts of Law and Styles of Self in Eighteenth-Century Madras: From Hybrid to Colonial Self," *Modern Asian Studies* 35 (2001): 38; Patrick A. Roche, "Caste and the British Merchant Government in Madras, 1639–1749," *Indian Economic and Social History Review* 12 (1975).

82. On Viranna and his predecessors, see Joseph J. Brennig, "Chief Merchants and the European Enclaves of Seventeenth-Century Coromandel," *Modern Asian Studies* 11, no. 3 (1977): 321–40; Sinnappah Arasaratnam, *Merchants, Companies and Commerce on the Coromandel Coast, 1650–1740* (Delhi: Oxford University Press, 1986); Miles Ogborn, *Global Lives: Britain and the World, 1550–1800* (Cambridge: Cambridge University Press, 2008), 80–83, 90–93.

83. Madras Consultation, 27 November 1678, in *RFSG: D&C 1678–79*, 142–44.

84. MSS Eur E210/1 f. 38; Madras Consultation, 2 December 1678, in *RFSG; D&C, 1678–79*, 145.

85. Madras Consultations, 11 July and 1 August 1678 in *RFSG: D&C, 1678–79*, 86–87, 93.

86. Quoted by Ogborn, *Global Lives*, 90.

87. York Fort Consultations, 11 January 1699/1700, G/35/4 f. 15.

88. York Fort Consultations, 1 July 1695, G/35/3 f. 16; York Fort Consultations, 1 May 1705, G/35/5, Consultation Diary 1 February 1704/5 to 29 August 1706, f. 29; Joseph Collet to Samuel Collet, 23 August 1714, in *LBJC*, 98.

89. London to Bengkulu, 9 May 1690, E/3/92 f. 94.

90. London to Bengkulu, 29 February 1691/2, E/3/92 f. 202; London to Bengkulu, 21 November 1699, E/3/93 f. 235; Bengkulu to London, 5 July 1703, bk. 3, 88–89.

91. London to Surat, 19 March 1668/9, H/49 f. 19–20; London to Madras, 22 January 1691/2, E/3/92 f. 173; London to Thomas Pitt, 21 November 1699, E/3/93 f. 229.

92. Roche, "Caste and the British Merchant Government in Madras," 381–407.

93. London to Elihu Yale, 12 December 1687, E/3/91 f. 231.

94. Ted McCormick, *William Petty and the Ambitions of Political Arithmetic* (Oxford: Oxford University Press, 2009); Julian Hoppit, "Political Arithmetic in Eighteenth-Century England," *Economic History Review* 49, no. 3 (1996): 16–18.

95. See, among others, Bernard S. Cohn, "The Census, Social Structure and Objectification in South Asia," in *An Anthropologist Among the Historians and Other Essays* (Delhi and New York: Oxford University Press, 1987); Nicholas Dirks, *Castes of Mind: Colonialism and the Making of Modern India* (Princeton NJ: Princeton University Press, 2001), 198–227.

96. London to Yale, 12 December 1687, E/3/91 f. 231.

97. Andrea Finkelstein, *Harmony and the Balance: An Intellectual History of Seventeenth-Century English Economic Thought* (Ann Arbor: University of Michigan, 2000), 180–85.

98. Instructions for Sir John Gayer, 26 May 1693, E/3/92 f. 272; Arnold Wright, *Annesley of Surat and His Times: The True Story of the Mythical Wesley Fortune* (London: Andrew Melrose, Ltd., 1918), 152. See Patrick Collinson, "The Monarchical Republic of Queen Elizabeth I," (J. E. Neale Memorial Lecture, 8 May 1986), in Patrick Collinson, ed., *Elizabethan Essays* (London: The Hambledon Press, 1994), 38; Pocock, *Machiavellian Moment*, 408.

99. Madras Consultations, 18 February 1675/6, in *RFSG: D&C, 1672–1678*, 89; Sharma, "Changing Destinies, Evolving Identities," 119–21.

100. London to Surat, 28 October 1685, E/3/91 f. 7.

101. London to Bengkulu, 29 February 1691/2, E/3/92 f. 202; Alan Harfield, *Bencoolen: A History of the Honourable East India Company's Garrison on the West Coast of Sumatra (1685–1825)* (Barton-on-Sea: A and J Partnership, 1995), 36–37.

102. London to Madras, 1 July 1696, E/3/92 f. 487–88.

103. London to Surat, 19 March 1668/9, H/49 f. 19–20; London to Madras, 22 January 1691/2, E/3/92 f. 173; London to Thomas Pitt, 21 November 1699, E/3/93 f. 229.

104. Gerald Aungier to London, 15 January 1673/4, H/50 f. 138–39.

105. London to Bombay, 14 July 1686, E/3/91 f. 79.

106. Court of Directors to Bengkulu, 13 January 1713/14, E/3/98, 238.

107. Joseph Collet to Moses Lowman, 14 November 1712, in *LBJC*, 43.

Chapter 5

1. David Armitage, *The Ideological Origins of the British Empire* (Cambridge: Cambridge University Press, 2000), 36; Lesley Cormack, "The Fashioning of an Empire: Geography and the State in Elizabethan England," in Neil Smith and Anne Godlewska, eds., *Geography and Empire* (Cambridge, MA: Blackwell, 1994), 17; Sanjay Subrahmanyam, "Connected Histories: Notes Towards a Reconfiguration of Early Modern Eurasia," *Modern Asian Studies* 31 (1997): 736; Sanjay Subrahmanyam, "Turning the Stones Over: Sixteenth-century Millenarianism from the Tagus to the Ganges," *Indian Economic and Social History Review* 40 (2003). On the "confessional state" more broadly, see Michael J. Braddick, *State Formation in Early Modern England, c. 1550–1700* (Cambridge: Cambridge University Press, 2000), pt. 4; Gerhard Oestreich, *Neostoicism and the Early Modern State*, ed. Brigitta Oestreich and H. G. Koenigsberger, trans. David McLintock (Cambridge: Cambridge University Press, 1982), 135–272.

2. *A Complete Collection of State Trials and Proceedings for High Treason and Other Crimes and Misdemeanors from the Earliest Period to the Year 1783, With Notes and Other Illustrations*, ed. T. B. Howell, 21 vols., vol. 10 (London: Printed by T. C. Hansard, 1816), 375.

3. See Penelope Carson, "An Imperial Dilemma: The Propagation of Christianity in Early Colonial India," *Journal of Imperial and Commonwealth History* 18 (1990).

4. Blair Worden, "Providence and Politics in Cromwellian England," *Past and Present* 109 (1985): 55; Keith Thomas, *Religion and the Decline of Magic* (New York: Oxford University

Press, 1971), 109–10. On "biblical culture" in the Atlantic world, see J. H. Elliott, *Empires of the Atlantic World: Britain and Spain in America, 1492–1830* (New Haven, CT: Yale, 2006), chap. 7.

5. Geoffrey Clark, *Betting on Lives: The Culture of Life Insurance in England, 1695–1775* (Manchester: Manchester University Press, 1999).

6. Bombay to London, 26 September 1687, E/3/47 f. 99.

7. Alison Games, *The Web of Empire: English Cosmopolitans in an Age of Expansion, 1560–1660* (New York: Oxford University Press, 2008), 240; John W. McKenna, "How God became an Englishman," in Delloyd J. Guth and John W. McKenna, eds., *Tudor Rule and Revolution: Essays for G. R. Elton from his American Friends* (Cambridge: Cambridge University Press, 1982), 34; Paul Stevens, "'Leviticus Thinking' and the Rhetoric of Early Modern Colonialism," *Criticism* 35 (1993): 441, 448. On similar Dutch attitudes, see Simon Schama, *The Embarrassment of Riches: An Interpretation of Dutch Culture in the Golden Age* (Berkeley: University of California Press, 1988), 93–125.

8. London to Bengal, 30 May 1683, E/3/90 f. 80; London to Madras, 31 May 1683, E/3/90 f. 81; Bombay to London, 1 December 1702, E/3/70 no. 8636.

9. *An Answer to Two Letters, Concerning the East-India Company* (London, 1676), 4.

10. Bombay to London, 12 July 1672, H/50 f. 34–35; "G. Willcox on the Establishment of English Law on Bombay 30 December 1672," BL Add.MS 39,255 f. 41.

11. Ibid., f. 45.

12. Gerald Aungier to London, 15 January 1673/4, H/50 f. 138; Glenn Ames, "The Role of Religion in the Transfer and Rise of Bombay, c. 1661–1687," *Historical Journal* 46 (2003): 338.

13. London to Madras, 13 February 1684/5, E/3/90 f. 256.

14. Josiah Child, *A New Discourse of Trade* (London, 1694), 103, 201; Daniel Statt, *Foreigners and Englishmen: The Controversy over Immigration and Population, 1660–1760* (Newark: University of Delaware, 1995), 88–91.

15. Ames, "Role of Religion," 317–30.

16. Archbishop of Isfahan to Thomas Pitt, 17 May 1709, Add.MS 59,481 f. 133; Vahé Baladouni, "Armenian Trade with the English East India Company: An Aperçu," *Journal of European Economic History* 15 (1986): 160; P. J. Marshall, "The White Town of Calcutta Under the Rule of the East India Company," *Modern Asian Studies* 34 (2000): 315.

17. London to Madras, 14 January 1685/6, E/3/91 f. 17.

18. Kanakalatha Mukund, *The View from Below: Indigenous Society, Temples and the Early Colonial State in Tamilnadu, 1700–1835* (New Delhi: Orient Longman, 2005), 52.

19. Copy of the Laws for Bombay, repr. in Sir Charles Fawcett, *The First Century of British Justice in India* (Oxford, 1934; repr., Aalen: Scientia Verlag, 1979), 20–21.

20. "For what nation is there so great, who hath God so nigh unto them, as the Lord our God is in all things that we call upon him for?"

21. M. D. David, *History of Bombay 1661–1708* (Bombay: University of Bombay, 1973), 438–39; *EFI*, 1:35–36.

22. Instructions to Bengal, 14 January 1685/6, E/3/91 f. 36.

23. London to Bombay, 6 January 1687/8, E/3/91 f. 250.

24. London to Surat, 24 August 1668 and 19 March 1668/9, H/49 f. 7, 17; Glenn Ames, "Serving God, Mammon, Or Both? Religious vis-à-vis Economic Priorities in the Portuguese *Estado da India*, c. 1600–1700," *Catholic Historical Review* 86, 2 (2000): 216; Yogesh Sharma, "Changing Destinies, Evolving Identities: The Indo-Portuguese Community at Madras in the Seventeenth Century," in Yogesh Sharma and José Leal Ferreira, eds., *Portuguese Presence in India during the Sixteenth and Seventeenth Centuries* (New Delhi: Viva Books, 2008), 111; Stephen Neill, *A History of Christianity in India: The Beginnings to AD 1707*, 2 vols. (Cambridge: Cambridge University Press, 1984), 1:231.

25. Bombay (Keigwin) to Charles II, 27 December to 8 February 1683/4, E/3/43 f. 374; "Articles of Agreement between the Governor and Inhabitants of Bombay," [29 December 1683], E/3/43 f. 278.

26. [Streynsham Master], "A Letter from Suratt in India, giving an account of the Manners of the English Factors, their Way of Civill Converse and Pious Comportment and Behaviour in these Partes," MSS Eur E.210/2, f. 4, also repr. in *Yule*, 2:cccv; John Villiers, "Doing Business with the Infidel: Merchants, Missionaries and Monarchs in Sixteenth Century Southeast Asia," in Karl Anton Sprengard and Roderich Ptak, eds., *Maritime Asia: Profit Maximisation, Ethics and Trade Structure c. 1300–1800* (Wisbaden: Harrassowitz, 1994), 160–70.

27. For contemporary drawings and accounts of the pagoda and lodge at Salsette, see Add.MS 15,505 f. 1; King's 198, f. 1–4.

28. K. N. Chaudhuri, "From the Barbarian and the Civilised to the Dialectics of Colour: An Archaeology of Self-Identities," in Peter Robb, ed., *Society and Ideology: Essays in South Asian History Presented to Professor K. A. Ballhatchet* (Delhi: Oxford University Press, 1993), 31–32; Peter Kirsch, "VOC—Trade without Ethics?," in Karl Anton Sprengard and Roderich Ptak, eds., *Maritime Asia: Profit Maximisation, Ethics and Trade Structure c. 1300–1800* (Wisbaden: Harrassowitz, 1994), 194.

29. Ole Peter Grell, Jonathan Israel, and Nicholas Tyacke, eds., *From Persecution to Toleration: The Glorious Revolution and Religion in England* (Oxford: Clarendon Press, 1991); John Coffey, *Persecution and Toleration in Protestant England 1558–1689* (London: Longman, 2000); R. Po-Chia Hsia and Henk van Nierop, eds., *Calvinism and Religious Toleration in the Dutch Golden Age* (Cambridge: Cambridge University Press, 2002); Stuart Schwartz, *All Can Be Saved: Religious Tolerance and Salvation in the Iberian Atlantic World* (New Haven, CT: Yale University Press, 2008).

30. Mukund, *View from Below*, 54–55.

31. Orders to William Aislaby, Bombay Diary, 12 November 1694, G/3/10a; David, *History of Bombay*, 438–39; *EFI*, 1:35–36.

32. Charles Marsham to Thomas Tenison, 29 November 1705, Lambeth MS 929 no. 52.

33. Joseph Collet to Samuel Collet, 28 August 1718, and Joseph Collet to Daniel Dolins, 28 August 1718, in *LBJC*, 183, 196.

34. See extract from Conde de Villa Verde to Don Gaspar Alfonso, 28 June 1696, H/59, 19–20.

35. Markus Vink, "Church and State in Seventeenth-Century Colonial Asia: Dutch Parava Relations in Southeast India in a Comparative Perspective," *Journal of Early Modern History* 4 (2000): 43.

36. Madras to Fort St. David, 5 April 1694, and Madras to Bishop of St. Thomé, 7 April 1694, in *RFSG: LF, 1694*, 33–34.

37. Madras Consultations, 22 and 24 January 1704, in *RFSG: D&C, 1704*, 6–7.

38. G/1/21 f. 4.

39. London to Bombay, 21 February 1717/18, E/3/99 f. 213; London to Bombay, 4 November 1719, E/3/100 f. 14.

40. Don John Baptist Milton to the Court of Directors, 26 October 1712, H/59 ff. 1–6.

41. Kenneth Ballhatchet, "Roman Catholic Missionaries and Indian Society: The Carmelites in Bombay, 1786–1857," in Kenneth Ballhatchet and John Harrison, eds., *East India Company Studies: Papers Presented to Professor Sir Cyril Philips* (Hong Kong: Asian Research Service, 1986), 255; Neill, *History of Christianity in India*, 1:361.

42. London to Bombay, 24 March 1721/2, E/3/101 f. 120.

43. "Proposals Touching Bombay Island," in Surat to London, 3 February 1671, repr. in *BS*, 1:55.

44. Madras Consultations, 4 April 1678 in *RFSG: D&C, 1678–79*, 65–66.

45. Bombay to Surat in *BS*, I, 158; Fawcett, *First Century*, 137.

46. For comparisons of contemporary English attitudes about Catholics and Muslims, see Linda Colley, *Captives* (New York: Pantheon Books, 2002), 104–34.

47. *State Trials*, 375.

48. Surat to Captain Tyrell, 3 November 1685, E/3/45 f. 150; G. V. Scammell, "European Exiles, Renegades and Outlaws and the Maritime Economy of Asia c. 1500–1750," *Modern Asian Studies* 26 (1992).

49. Surat Consultation, 4 April 1683, G/36/5 f. 24–25. For another case in Persia, see Gombroone to London, 9 October 1688, E/3/47 f. 196; London to Bombay, 11 September 1689, E/3/92 f. 33.

50. Surat Consultations, 24 May 1696, G/36/5 f. 105.

51. Games, *Web of Empire*, chap. 7; Randy Richard Wood, "English Protestantism in Maritime Context: Merchants, Planters, and Preachers, c. 1560–1660" (PhD diss., Pennsylvania State University, 2003), 216–366.

52. "From the Court, a Circular," 13 February 1657/8, repr. in *Yule*, 2:cccli.

53. Henry Barry Hyde, *Parochial Annals of Bengal, Being a History of the Bengal Ecclesiastical Establishment of the Honourable East India Company* (Calcutta: Bengal Secretariat Book Depot, 1901), 1–2.

54. "A List of Persons in the Service of the Right Honourable English East India Company in Fort St. George Madraspatnam, According to their Degrees by the Rules," 1686, in *RFSG: D&C, 1686*, 116–17.

55. Court Minutes, 16 August 1682, B/37 f. 24; Games, *Web of Empire*, 224–25.

56. Add.MS 39,255 f. 42; St. Helena Consultations, 20 April 1696, G/32/2, 5:n.p.

57. St. Helena Consultation, 12 February 1682/3, G/32/2, 1:82.

58. Madras Consultations, 10 April 1686, in *RFSG: D&C, 1686*, 33.

59. London to St. Helena, 1 August 1683, E/3/90 f. 95; London to St. Helena, 3 August 1687, E/3/91 f. 179.

60. Surat to London, 18 March 1677/78, H/51 f. 82; *EFI*, 1:42–43.

61. Madras Consultation, 1 April 1678 in *RFSG: D&C, 1678–79*, 65; List of Subscriptions for the Erection of the Fort Church, 26 September 1677, MSS Eur E 210/1 f. 20; London to Madras, 22 January 1691/2, E/3/92 f. 177; Henry Davison Love, *Vestiges of Old Madras, 1640–1800* (London: John Murray, 1913; repr., New York: AMS, 1968), 1:423–27.

62. William Anderson and Benjamin Adams, "A Narrative of the Proceedings Relating to the Building a Church in the English Settlement at Fort William in the Kingdom of Bengall," Lambeth MS 935 no. 7.

63. London to Bombay, 11 September 1689, E/3/92 f. 33.

64. Surat to London, 17 January 1675/6, E/3/36 f. 148; London to Surat, 2 July 1684, E/3/90 f. 198; London to Surat, 26 March 1686, E/3/91 f. 57; David, *History of Bombay*, 135, 410–16; *EFI*, 1:81, 185.

65. Court Minutes, 15 August 1679, in *CCM*, 11:286.

66. London to Bengal, 7 April 1708, E/3/96, 267; Anderson and Adams, "Narrative," f. 2; Charles Robert Wilson, *The Early Annals of the English in Bengal* (London and Calcutta: W. Thacker & Co. 1900), 2:li.

67. London to Bengal, 14 January 1685/6, E/3/91 f. 24; London to Governor and Council of Pryaman, 20 January 1685/6, E/3/91 f. 13; London to Madras, extract in *Yule*, 2:cccliii; Wood, "English Protestantism," 332–33.

68. Court Minutes, 5 December 1677 and 2 January 1678, in *CCM*, 11:120, 132.

69. Thomas Salmon, *Modern History: Or the Present State of All Nations* (London, 1739), 1:277; Charles Lockyer, *An Account of the Trade in India* (London, 1711), 20; J. Talboys Wheeler, *Madras in the Olden Time: Being a History of the Presidency from the First Foundation of Fort St. George to the French Occupation of Madras* (Madras: Graves and Co., 1861), 2:223.

70. Bombay to London, 7 December 1679, H/51 f. 244; Court Minutes, 27 March 1679, in *CCM*, 11:259; "A List of the Honourable Companise bookes packt up in the Chest, wrote upon Library Bantam," n.d., E/3/43 f. 444.

71. London to Bengal, 20 December 1699, E/3/93 f. 252.

72. Salmon, *Modern History*, 1:275; Love, *Vestiges*, 1:425.

73. Joseph Collet to Mary Collet, 13 December 1716, in *LBJC*, 139.

74. London to Surat, 19 March 1668/9, H/49 f. 17.

75. Commission and Instructions to Sir George Oxinden, 19 March 1661[/2], H/48 f. 19.

76. [Streynsham Master], "A Letter from Bombay in the East Indies," 18 January 1671, MSS Eur E 210/2 f. 2.
77. Madras to London, 23 September 1648; repr. in Love, *Vestiges*, 1:74; London to St. Helena, 20 February 1677, G/32/1, 8, 10; London to Bombay, 15 March 1680/81, H/51 ff. 269–70.
78. S. D. Amussen, "Gender, Family and the Social Order," in A. J. Fletcher and J. Stevenson, eds., *Order and Disorder in Early Modern England* (Cambridge: Cambridge University Press, 1985), esp. 203–4; Philip S. Gorski, *The Disciplinary Revolution: Calvinism and the Rise of the State in Early Modern Europe* (Chicago: University of Chicago, 2003); R. Po-chia Hsia, *Social Discipline in the Reformation: Central Europe 1550–1750* (London: Routledge, 1989); Lamar M. Hill, "The Privy Council and Private Morality," in Charles Carlton, with Robert L. Woods, Mary L. Robertson, and Joseph S. Block, *States, Sovereigns and Society In Early Modern England: Essays in Honour of A. J. Slavin* (New York: St. Martin's Press, 1998), 216.
79. London to Bengkulu, 16 April 1697, E/3/92 f. 669.
80. [Streynsham Master], "A Letter from Suratt," MSS Eur E.210 f. 4; *Yule*, 2:cccvi.
81. Surat to London, 1 June 1671, E/3/32 f. 11; "Rules to be observed by all English men that Lie in the Factory of Suratt," 2 July 1696, G/36/95 f. 46–47.
82. Love, *Vestiges*, 1:402; J. Talboys Wheeler, *Annals of the Madras Presidency, Being a History of the Presidency from the First Foundation of Fort St. George to the French Occupation of Madras*, 3 vols. (London, 1861; repr., Delhi: B. R. Publishing Corporation, 1985), 3:336–53.
83. Madras Consultations, 15 April, in *RFSG, D&C 1678–79*, 68; York Fort Consultations, 18 July 1695, G/35/3 f. 41.
84. The act cited is 12 Car II c.25. Madras Consultations, [7] May 1675, in *RFSG: D&C, 1672–1678*, 42; Madras Consultations, 21 August and 2 and 11 September 1678, in *RFSG: D&C, 1678–79* (Madras: Superintendent, Government Press, 1911), 105, 108–10, 113; Love, *Vestiges*, 1:377.
85. London to St. Helena, 20 December 1699, E/3/93 f. 264.
86. "Copy of the First Commission of the Government after the Retaking the Island [St. Helena] from the Dutch, "19 December 1673, G/32/1, 5–7.
87. London to St. Helena, 10 March 1681, G/32/1, 18–19.
88. Recital of Laws and Ordinances, nd [1707?], G/32/1, 96.
89. Fawcett, *First Century*, 14, 19–25; David, *History of Bombay*, 119, 135.
90. "Laws and Ordinances of warr for the better governing the Militia now under the Government and in the service of the Honorable East India Company," H/49 f. 71, 75–78.
91. *EFI*, 1:80, 111.
92. Order to Ensign William Shaw, Bombay Diary, 8 April 1695, G/3/10a.
93. "G. Wilcox on the Establishment of English Law in Bombay 30 December 1672," Add.MS 39,255 f. 46.
94. *EFI*, 1:80, 111.
95. John Anderson, *English Intercourse with Siam* (London: Kegan Paul, Trench, Trübner and Co., 1890), 403–4; David, *History of Bombay*, 424; Fawcett, *First Century*, 74–75; *EFI*, 1:35.
96. Madras Consultation, 5 June 1682, in *RFSG: D&C, 1682*, 40.
97. D. E. Underdown, "The Taming of the Scold: The Enforcement of Patriarchal Authority in Early Modern England," in Fletcher and Stevenson, *Order and Disorder*, 116–36. On the role of gender, specifically at St. Helena and elsewhere, in helping to define colonial subjecthood, see Kathleen Wilson, "Re-thinking the British Colonial State: Gender and Governmentality in the Long Eighteenth Century," *American Historical Review* (forthcoming).
98. St. Helena Consultation, 1 April 1676, G/32/2, 1:5. On ducking for "gender-related offenses" in early modern England, see Underdown, "Taming of the Scold," 123.
99. St. Helena Consultation, 1 April 1676, G/32/2, 1:5.
100. Faramerz Dabhoiwala, "Sex, Social Relations and the Law in Seventeenth- and Eighteenth-century London," in Michael J. Braddick and John Walter, eds., *Negotiating Power in Early Modern Society: Order, Hierarchy, and Subordination in Britain and Ireland* (Cambridge: Cambridge University Press, 2001), 87–94.

101. St. Helena Consultation, 23 October 1682, G/32/2 1:42–43; St. Helena Consultation, 28 August, 23 October, 18 December 1682, and 19 March 1682/3, G/32/2 2:27, 42–43, 70, 89–90.
102. London to St. Helena, 10 March 1681, G/32/1, 18–19.
103. Charles Marsham to Thomas Tenison, 29 November 1705, Lambeth MS 929 no. 52.
104. Surat to London, 26 November 1669, H/49 ff. 177–79; Streynsham Masters [*sic*] to Samuel Masters [*sic*], 9 December 1678, in *Boyle*, 6:446; [Master], "A Letter from Suratt," MSS Eur E.210 ff. 4–5; *Yule*, 2:cccxvii–cccxviii.
105. *Yule*, 1:149–50; London to Madras, 21 December 1683, E/3/90 f. 140.
106. Joseph Collet to Moses Lowman, 3 January 1714/15, and Collet to John Bedwell, 14 December 1716 in *LBJC*, 115, 143.
107. Joseph Collet to Samuel Collet, 31 October 1713, in ibid., 67.
108. Joseph Collet to Samuel Collet, 22 September 1712, and Collet to Milton, 23 June 1713, in ibid., 22–23, 50.
109. Charles Marsham to Thomas Tenison, 29 November 1705, Lambeth MS 929 no. 52.
110. Surat to London, 26 November 1669, H/49 f. 177–78.
111. Bombay to London, 23 January 1669/70, H/49 f. 266–67.
112. London to St. Helena, 15 March 1678, in *CCM*, 11:163; London to Surat, 7 March 1676/7, H/51 f. 25.
113. London to Surat, 19 March 1668/9, H/49 f. 14, 19; London to Bombay, 10 March 1668/9, H/49 f. 26–27; Secret Committee to Madras, 31 October 1683, E/3/90 f. 123; London to Madras, 8 April 1687, E/3/91, f. 144. On similar Dutch practices, see Vink, "Church and State in Seventeenth-Century Colonial Asia," 33, 36–43.
114. Frank Penny, *The Church in Madras, Being the History of the Ecclesiastical and Missionary Action of the East India Company in the Presidency of Madras in the Seventeenth and Eighteenth Centuries* (London: John Murray, 1904), 73.
115. Ibid., viii; Maurice Thomson et al. to Connett, Owen, Goodwin, Wilkinson, Tuckney, and Arrowsmith, 13 February 1657, in *Yule*, 2:ccli–cclii; Hyde, *Parochial Annals*, 1.
116. *The Argument of the Lord Chief Justice of the Court of King's Bench concerning the Great Case of Monopolies between the East-India Company, Plaintiff, and Thomas Sandys, Defendant, Wherein their Patent for Trading to the East-Indies, Exclusive of all others, is adjudged good* (London, 1689), ii; See also Villiers, "Doing Business with the Infidel," 161n27; John Villiers, "De um caminho ganhar almas e fazenda: Motives of Portuguese Expansion in Eastern Indonesia in the Sixteenth Century," *Terrae Incognitae* 14 (1982); Patricia Seed, *Ceremonies of Possession in Europe's Conquest of the New World, 1492–1640* (Cambridge: Cambridge University Press, 1995), 33–34.
117. London to Bengal, 26 January 1697/8, E/3/93 f. 24.
118. Gerald Aungier, quoted in Fawcett, *First Century*, 78.
119. Joseph Collet to Daniel Dolins, 30 August 1713, in *LBJC*, 59.
120. Laws of Bombay, in Fawcett, *First Century*, 20.
121. Surat to London, 17 January 1675/6, E/3/36 f. 148–49.
122. Streynsham Masters [*sic*] to Samuel Masters [*sic*], 9 December 1678, in *Boyle*, 6:446.
123. Surat to Bombay, 2 August 1690, G/36/92 f. 166.
124. Wheeler, *Madras in the Olden Time*, 2:40–41.
125. Madras to London, 6 September 1671, E/3/32 f. 39; Penny, *Church in Madras*, 71–72.
126. Extract of Mr. Adams's Letter, Chaplain at Calcutta, printed in *Yule*, 2:cccxix.
127. Wood, "English Protestantism," 357.
128. "Report by Henry Prideaux on the state of factories and plantations in the East Indies with proposals for improving provision for the spread of religion," Lambeth MS 933 no. 2; Cotton Mather, *A Pillar of Gratitude, A Brief Recapitulation, of the Matchless favours with which the God of Heaven hath obliged the Hearty Praises of His New-English Israel* (Boston: B. Green and J. Allen, 1700), 45–48.
129. Fell to archbishop of Canterbury, 21 June 1681, in Neill, *History of Christianity in India*, 367.

130. General Court Minutes, 27 April 1677, in *CCM*, 11:40.
131. Court Minutes, 3 October 1677, in *CCM*, 11:89.
132. Thomas Hyde to Robert Boyle, 29 November 1677, in *Boyle*, 6:469.
133. Court Minutes, 25 April and 26 September 1679 in *CCM*, 11:268, 296.
134. Robert Boyle to Robert Thompson, 5 March 1677, in *Boyle*, 6:436–38.
135. Court Minutes, 6 July 1670, repr. in *Yule*, 2:cccliv.
136. Streynsham Masters [*sic*] to Samuel Masters [*sic*], 9 December 1678, printed in *Boyle*, 6:446.
137. The book was published, with a dedication to Boyle, in 1660. Hugo Grotius, *De Veritate Religionis Christianae Editio Nova cum Annotationibus, Cui accessit versio Arabica*, trans. Edward Pococke (Oxford: Gulielm. Hall, 1660); the Court reported it was "very ready to promote so pious a Worke, soe they may be first satisfied that these Bookes have the Allowance of Authoritie." Application of Richard Baxter to the Court of Committees, repr. in *Yule*, 2:cccliii. See also Baxter to Boyle, 14 June 1665, in *Boyle*, 2:473.
138. Boyle to Robert Thompson, 5 March 1677, in *Boyle*, 6:436–38.
139. Court Minutes, 17 June 1681, B/36 f. 126; Josiah Woodward to Thomas Woolley, 21 November 1710, H/59 f. 191–93. Some years later, the patronage of this work also led Robert Huntington, chaplain to the Levant Company in Aleppo, to recommend Boyle support Pococke in a translation of the Book of Common Prayer into Arabic as well. See Huntington to Boyle, 8 September 1673, in *Boyle*, 4:359–60.
140. Court Minutes, 6 July 1681, B/36 f. 130.
141. Court Minutes, 8 February 1681/2, B/36, f. 192; Court Minutes, 3 May 1682, B/37 f. 4.
142. London to Bengkulu, 19 December 1690, E/3/92 f. 121; Thomas Hyde, *Jang Ampat Evangelia Derri Tyan Kita Jesu Christi daan Berboatan Derri Japostoli Ber Sacti, Beisalin dallam Baffa Malayo, That is, the Four Gospels of Our Lord Jesus Christ and the Acts of the Holy Apostles, Translated into the Malayan tongue* (Oxford: Printed by H. Hall, 1677). The book was dedicated to Boyle.
143. London to Madras, 18 February 1690/1, E/3/92 f. 141.
144. London to Madras, 22 January 1691/2, E/3/92 f. 176.
145. For greater complexity on this, see Gauri Viswanathan, "Yale College and the Culture of British Imperialism," *Yale Journal of Criticism* 7 (1994): esp. 24.
146. Thomas Hyde to Robert Boyle, 5 March 1691 and 11 June 1691, in *Boyle*, 6:331, 334.
147. Josiah Child to Robert Blackborne, 22 December 1693, MS Rawl A.303 f. 259.
148. Penny, *Church in Madras*, 109.
149. London to Madras, 22 January 1691/2, E/3/92 f. 176; London to Madras, 29 February 1691/2, E/3/92 f. 195; Robert Blackborne to Captain John Dorrill, 13 May 1696, H/36 f. 170; London to Bengal, 18 January 1716/17, E/3/99, f. 45.
150. Benjamin Woodroffe to Josiah Child, 17 October 1693, H/59 f. 187.
151. London to Surat, 13 September 1695, E/3/92 f. 446; London to Madras, 16 April 1697, E/3/92 f. 552; Robert Blackborne to Benjamin Woodroffe, 25 February 1694/5, H/36 f. 65; Sir John Fleet to Dr. Woodroffe, 7 March 1694/5, H/36 f. 66; Robert Blackborne to Benjamin Woodroffe, 14 November 1695, H/36 f. 123; Court Minutes, 29 December 1693, B/40 f. 223; Court Minutes, 30 December 1695, B/41 f. 46; Bombay Consultations, 17 September 1700, G/3/5, 3, f. 27; Fort St. David Consultations, 29 November 1697, in *RFSG: FSD, 1697*, 43.
152. Sir John Fleet to Benjamin Woodroff, 3 July 1695, H/36 f. 87
153. Henry Prideaux to Thomas Tenison, 27 March 1695, Lambeth MS 933 no. 1.
154. Report by Henry Prideaux on the state of factories and plantations in the East Indies with proposals for improving provision for the spread of religion, [March 1695], Lambeth MS 933 no. 2.
155. Josiah Woodward to Thomas Woolley, 21 November 1710, H/59 f. 193.
156. London to Bombay, 21 February 1717/18, E/3/99 f. 212.
157. George Lewis to Henry Newman, 1 February 1712/3, Lambeth MS 933 no. 115.

158. Court of Managers to Madras, 7 April 1708, E/3/96, 240.
159. London to Madras, 25 January 1716/17, E/3/99 f. 58; Joseph Collet to Daniel Dolins, 13 July 1717, in *LBJC,* 155–56; Penny, *Church in Madras,* chap. 9.
160. Richard Cobbe, *Bombay Church: Or, A True Account of the Building an Finishing the English Church at Bombay in the East Indies* (London, 1766), 26–27, 115–19.
161. Henry Newman to Thomas Woolley, 15 January 1710/11, E/1/3 f. 30; Newman to Court of Directors, 28 November 1711, E/1/3 f. 411; Newman to Court of Directors, 3 December 1712, E/1/4 f. 286; London to Madras, 25 January 1716/17, E/3/99 f. 62.
162. Edward Harrison to Johann Ernest Gründler, 25 October 1715, and William Stevenson to Henry Newman, 3 February 1715/16 in Bartholomaeus Ziegenbalg, *Propagation of the Gospel in the East: Being a Collection of Letters from the Protestant Missionaries and other Worthy Persons in the East-Indies, &c.* (London, 1718), 180–81, 200.
163. Joseph Collet to Newman, 19 September 1717, in *LBJC,* 165–66; Newman to Woolley, 16 December 1726, 13 January 1730/31, H/59 f. 203, 207, 211; Newman to Mole, 2 December 1736 and 8 January 1740/1, H/59 f. 213, 229; Newman to John Lewis, 9 September 1741, Lambeth MS 3017, f. 217; James Thomas, *The East India Company and the Provinces in the Eighteenth Century,* vol. 1, *Portsmouth and the East India Company 1700–1815* (Lewiston, NY: Edwin Mellon Press, 1999), 83–85.
164. Carson, "Imperial Dilemma," 171–73.

Chapter 6

1. "Demands made on behalfe of the Right Honorable Company by their Generall Sir. John Child Barontt. sent to the Governr. of Suratt by Cozee Ebram and Dungi Vorah, two Persons sent hither to treat," 7 October 1687, E/3/47 ff. 115–18.
2. London to Bombay, 27 August 1688, E/3/91 f. 272.
3. Secret Committee to Bombay, 31 March 1686, E/3/91 f. 49.
4. John Child to Mahmut Khan, 27 February 1686/7, E/3/46, f. 166.
5. London to Aurangzeb, 7 September 1688, E/3/91 f. 291.
6. Cf. Steve Pincus, *1688: The First Modern Revolution* (New Haven, CT: Yale University Press, 2009), 378.
7. London to Surat, 26 March 1686, E/3/91 f. 56; Surat to London, 10 February 1686/7, E/3/46, f. 149.
8. London to Madras, 9 June 1686, E/3/91 f. 70.
9. Surat to Secret Committee, 10 February 1686/7, E/3/46 f. 157.
10. Bombay to Bartholomew Harris, 24 December 1687, E/3/48 f. 164.
11. Secret Committee to Bombay, 31 March 1686, E/3/91 f. 49; London to Bombay, 5 December 1688, E/3/91 f. 297; John Bruce, *Annals of the Honorable East-India Company from their Establishment by the Charter of Queen Elizabeth, 1600, to the Union of the London and English East-India Companies, 1707–8,* 3 vols. (London: Black, Parry, and Kingsbury, 1810), 2:612.
12. London to Madras, 25 January 1687/8, E/3/91 f. 246; London to Bombay, 13 May 1687, E/3/91 f. 149.
13. Bombay to London, 5 December 1688, E/3/47 f. 200.
14. Bombay to London, 26 September 1687, E/3/47 f. 100.
15. Bombay Consultations, 15 February 1688/9, G/3/3 f. 1. One estimate from a visitor to Bombay just after the invasion reported the Sidi's force to have been as large as 25,000 men, but this seems a gross exaggeration. See J. Ovington, *A Voyage to Suratt in the Year, 1689* (London, 1696), 152.
16. Edward Barlow, *Barlow's Journal of His Life at Sea in King's Ships, East & West Indiamen & Other Merchantmen from 1659 to 1703,* ed. Basil Lubbock, 2 vols. (London: Hurst and Blackett, [1934]), 2:434.

17. On the day-to-day course of the war on Bombay itself, see [Captain James Hilton], "Diary Booke 1690," 15 February 1688/9 to 22 June 1690, Bombay Consultations, G/3/3 (3), ff. 1–45; Bombay to London, 26 December 1689, E/3/48 f. 99; Bombay to London, 7 June 1689, E/3/48 f. 18.

18. "Proposalls made by the Nabob Mucteer Caune and sent to the Generall by ye Reverend Padree Superiore of Bandara and Seignr. Ant De Vuardo Conto," 27 April 1689, E/3/48 f. 7.

19. Instructions to Expedition to Daman, 29 May 1689, E/3/48 f. 13–15; "H[e]ads of a Phirmand to be procured from the Great Mogull Orung Zeeb, drawn out by the Gennerall & Councell of Bombay," 4 December 1689, E/3/48 f. 77–84; Diary of George Weldon and Abraham Navarro's embassy to the Mughal Court, Sloane MSS 1910 ff. 47–53.

20. Diary of George Weldon and Abraham Navarro's embassy to the Mughal Court, Sloane MSS 1910 ff. 45–47.

21. As described by John Burnell, *Bombay in the Days of Queen Anne: Being an Account of the Settlement*, ed. Samuel Sheppard (London: Hakluyt Society, 1933), 30.

22. Bombay Consultations, [?] February 1689/90, E/3/48 ff. 157–58; 28 February 1689/90, G/3/3 (3), f. 33; London to Surat, 18 February 1690/1, E/3/92 f. 128.

23. Surat to Bombay, 30 June 1690, E/3/48 f. 186.

24. Surat to London, 28 April 1690, E/3/48 f. 168–70; Bombay Consultations, 10–12 April 1690, G/3/3 (3) ff. 38–39.

25. "A coppy of a Phirmaund the 23th day of the month Jummaudull Auvul in the 33 year of a most glorious Reign, [February 1689/90]," E/3/48 f. 156.

26. Bombay Consultations, G/3/3 (3) ff. 43–45.

27. Bombay to London, 15 January 1690/1, E/3/48 f. 232.

28. Bombay to London, 1 April 1696, E/3/52 f. 22.

29. Bombay Consultations, 23 July 1694, G/3/4 (1), ff. 7–8. However, by 1697, there were multiple bidders for the tobacco, oil, and arrack farms, all selling higher than the opening price and even higher rates the following year. Bombay Consultations, 1 March 1696/7, G/3/5 f. 15; Bombay Consultations, 1 March 1697/8, G/3/5 f. 48.

30. Bombay to London, 25 January 1697/8, E/3/53 f. 225–26.

31. Harris to Christovara de Sousa, 26 February 1690/1, G/36/93 f. 21.

32. London to Surat, 13 May 1691, E/3/92 f. 161.

33. Richard Tuck, *The Rights of War and Peace: Political Thought and the International Order from Grotius to Kant* (Oxford: Oxford University Press, 1999), esp. 18–31; John Robertson, "Empire and Union: Two Concepts of the Early Modern European Political Order," in *A Union for Empire: Political Thought and the British Union of 1707* (Cambridge: Cambridge University Press, 1995), 19. For a contemporary defense, see Nathanial Tench, *A Modest and Just Apology for, or, Defence of the Present East-India-Company Against the Accusations of their Adversaries* (London, 1690), 9, 15–16.

34. Bombay to London, 10 February 1688/9, E/3/47 f. 220–23.

35. London to Madras, 15 February 1688/9, E/3/92 f. 4.

36. Surat to London, 30 June 1690, E/3/48 f. 180.

37. Bombay to London, 15 January 1690/1, E/3/48 f. 233; Bombay to Surat, 22 June 1690, E/3/48 f. 179; Surat to London, 30 June 1690, E/3/48 f. 180–83.

38. Bombay to London, 15 January 1690/1, E/3/48 f. 232.

39. Ibid., f. 233.

40. Surat to London, 30 June 1690, E/3/48 f. 180–83.

41. Bombay to London, 9 February 1690/1, E/3/48 f. 261.

42. London to Bombay, 3 October 1690, E/3/92 f. 57.

43. Child to Blackborne, 9 January 1691/2, H/40 f. 121.

44. "Commission to Sr. Jn Goldsborough Knt.," 10 February 1691/2, IOR E/3/92 f. 185–86; "Instructions to Sr. Jn Goldsborough Knt.," 29 February 1691/2, E/3/92 f. 186–90.

45. London to Bombay, 29 February 1691/2, E/3/92 f. 215.

46. London to Madras, 10 April 1693, E/3/92 f. 247, 251.

47. His first attempt at resigning came in early 1697. Gayer to London, 18 February 1696/7, E/3/52 f. 334; Gayer to London, 10 March 1697/8, E/3/53 f. 381.
48. Bombay to London, 15 January 1690/1, E/3/48 f. 232.
49. Sir Charles Fawcett, *The First Century of British Justice in India* (Oxford, 1934; repr., Aalen: Scientia Verlag, 1979), 157–60; See Surat to London, 11 February 1692/3, E/3/49 f. 193.
50. John Gayer and George Weldon to London, 3 October 1694, E/3/50 f. 244.
51. Bombay Consultation, 16 and 21 August 1694, G/3/4 f. 16, 25.
52. See Bombay Diary, 14 February 1690, G/3/3, no. 3, f. 31.
53. Bombay Consultation, 23 June 1694 and 25 July 1694, G/3/4 ff. 6–7, 9; 23 June and 21 December 1694, G/3/10a.
54. London to Surat, 13 May 1691, E/3/92 f. 162; Bombay to London, 5 June 1695, E/3/51 f. 78.
55. Bombay Consultations, 28 August 1694, G/3/4 f. 25.
56. Bombay Consultations, 21 August 1694, G/3/4 f. 23.
57. Petition, 24 August 1694, E/3/50 f. 251.
58. Jesuit priests to Sir John Gayer [August 1694], E/3/50 f. 232–36; Court Minutes, 18 March 1691/2 and 27 August 1695, B/40 ff. 19, 103–4; Memorial of Vicomte de Fonte Arcada, 15 May 1695, H/36 f. 99; Duke of Shrewsbury to John Fleet, 27 August 1695, H/36 f. 99; John Fleet to Duke of Shrewsbury, 10 September 1695, H/36 f. 97; Earl of Dartmouth to London, 1 November 1711, E/1/3 f. 388; Portuguese Envoy Memorial, 23 September/4 October 1711, E/1/3 f. 390–91; Ovington, *Voyage to Suratt*, 156.
59. John Gayer to Samuel Annesley, 1 March 1694/5, E/3/50 f. 355.
60. Surat to John Gayer, 7 January 1690/1, G/36/93 f. 9.
61. Bombay to London, 5 May 1692, E/3/49 f. 79.
62. Madras to Bombay, 29 September and 13 October 1687, E/3/47 ff. 109, 128.
63. London to Madras, 22 January 1691/2, E/3/92 f. 172.
64. Alexander Hamilton, *A New Account of the East Indies, being the observations and remarks of Captain Alexander Hamilton, who spent his time there from the year 1688 to 1723*, 2 vols. (Edinburgh: Printed by John Mosman, 1727), 1:360.
65. Abstract of Madras to London, 10 January 1709/10, E/4/1, 228; William Foster, "The East India Company, 1600–1740," in H. H. Dodwell, ed., *The Cambridge History of India*, vol 5, *British India, 1497–1858* (Cambridge, 1929; repr., Delhi: S. Chand and Co., 1963), 104; J. Talboys Wheeler, *Madras in the Olden Time: Being a History of the Presidency from the First Foundation of Fort St. George to the French Occupation of Madras* (Madras: Graves and Co., 1862), 1:246–47.
66. Bengal Consultations, 7 March 1696/7, extracted in H/68, 3.
67. Bengal to London, 14 December 1694, E/3/50 f. 283; Commission to Francis Ellis et al., 10 April 1693, E/3/92 ff. 259–60; Fawcett, *First Century*, 208–9.
68. London to Bengal, 26 January 1697/8, E/3/93 f. 27.
69. Bengal Consultations, 31 October 1698, extracted in H/68, 10–11; Farhat Hasan, "Indigenous Cooperation and the Birth of a Colonial City: Calcutta, c. 1698–1750," *Modern Asian Studies* 26, no. 1 (1992): 68–69, 75.
70. Instructions to Charles Eyre &ca. Council, 20 December 1699, E/3/93 f. 259.
71. Minutes of the Court of Committees, 26 February 1696/7, B/41 f. 152; London to Bengal, 20 December 1699, E/3/93 f. 249.
72. London to Madras, 11 September 1689, E/3/92 f. 74.
73. Madras to London, 25 May 1691, E/3/49 f. 22.
74. Diary of Sir John Goldsborough, 13 June to 29 August 1693, E/3/50 f. 90–97; Goldsborough to London, 26 June 1693, E/3/50 f. 109–11.
75. Fort St. David Consultations, 5 March 1695/6, in *RFSG: FSD, 1696*, 27; F. Pridmore, *The Coins of the British Commonwealth of Nations to the end of the reign of George VI 1952: Part 4, India*, vol. 1, *East India Company Presidency Series c. 1642–1835* (London: Spink and Son, 1975), 85.
76. Fort St. David Consultations, 18 October 1687, in *RFSG: FSD, 1697*, 21.

77. Madras Consultations, 23 April to 1 May 1696, in *RFSG: FSD, 1696*, 52–56.
78. Fort St. David Consultations, 20 July 1696, in *RFSG: FSD, 1696*, 88; Madras to Laurens Pit and Council (VOC, Negapatam), 17 June 1696, in *RFSG: LF, 1696*, 57–59.
79. Sinnappah Arasaratnam, "Mare Clausum: The Dutch and Regional Trade in the Indian Ocean 1650–1740," *Journal of Indian History* 61 (1983): 85.
80. Surat to Bombay, 28 June 1675, E/3/36 f. 23; Court Minutes, 15 February 1677, in *CCM*, 11:16.
81. Surat to London, 5 April 1679 H/51 f. 160–61.
82. Surat to Karwar, 6 November 1685, G/3/92 f. 95.
83. Commission and Instruction from Bombay to Captain John Shaxton and Captain Richard Clifton, 30 November 1687, E/3/47 f. 152.
84. London to Bombay, 11 January 1688/9, E/3/92 f. 1.
85. Surat to Madras, 19 May 1691, G/36/93 f. 42.
86. Goldsborough to London, 26 June 1693, E/3/50 f. 111; Goldsborough to Rani of Attingal, 25 July 1693, E/3/50 f. 114; Goldsborough to Daniel Acworth, 26 July 1693, E/3/50 f. 114–14; Goldsborough to Rani of Attingal, 26 July 1693, E/3/50 f. 117; Commission to Brabourn and Acworth, 29 July 1693, E/3/50 f. 118–21.
87. "Translate of an Ola given by her Highness ye Queen of Attinga to ye Rt. Hon. English East India Company," 29 July 1694, E/3/50 f. 223.
88. John Gayer to Rani of Attingal, 22 April 1695, E/3/51 f. 32.
89. Ceylon (VOC) to John Brabourn, 12 February 1696/7, E/3/52 f. 306.
90. Anjengo to Bombay, 11 March 1695/6, G/3/23 bk. 2, f. 86; Bombay to London, 3 October 1694, E/3/50 f. 242–43; "An Insinuation made by John Brabourn Comodore &ca. Council," 30 January 1694/5, E/3/50 f. 318–19; "A Description of the Southern part of the Peninsula of India intra Ganges Containing an Acct. of the present State Governmt. & Traffique of the Coast de Pescaria & ye Mallabarr Coast of the affairs of the English & Dutch East India Compas. there And more particularly of the Queen of Attingas Country, And the English Fort at Anjengo," June 1704, G/1/21 f. 7.
91. General Court Minutes, 6 December 1689, B/39 f. 234; Declaration and Protest made by John Brabourn, Commodore, 22 August 1695, E/3/51 ff. 166–67.
92. Anjengo to Bombay, 21 March 1691/2, G/3/22 ff. 27–28.
93. Anjengo to Bombay, 29 December 1694, G/3/21 f. 65.
94. Anjengo to Bombay, 6 March 1694/5, G/3/22 ff. 19–21.
95. "A Description of the Southern part of the Peninsula of India," f. 7.
96. Surat to Calicut, 28 March 1691/2, G/36/93 f. 131.
97. London to Bombay, 1 September 1697, E/3/92 f. 606; John Gladman, Edward Owen, and Thomas Harbin to Captain Benjamin Brangwin et al., 20 March 1694/5, E/3/50 f. 374–77; Vahé Baladouni, "Armenian Trade with the English East India Company: An Aperçu," *Journal of European Economic History* 15 (1986): 156.
98. Surat to Bombay, 4 October 1698, G/36/96 f. 193–94.
99. London to Bombay, 28 July 1699, E/3/93 f. 187–88; London to Persia, 2 August 1699, E/3/93 f. 200.
100. Robert Blackborne to Captain William Erle, 11 May 1696, H/36 f. 165.
101. Secret Committee to Nathaniel Higginson, 1 May 1696, E/3/93 ff. 23–27
102. London to Bombay, 28 July 1699, E/3/93 f. 187.
103. To corrupt Robinson and Gallagher's famous formula, that is. John Gallagher and Ronald Robinson, "The Imperialism of Free Trade," *Economic History Review*, 2nd series, 6, no. 1 (1953): 3.
104. Farhat Hasan, "Conflict and Cooperation in Anglo-Mughal Trade Relations during the Reign of Aurangzeb," *Journal of the Economic and Social History of the Orient* 34, no. 4 (1991): 360.
105. Surat to London, 5 December 1696, E/3/52 f. 228; Bombay to London, 15 December 1696, E/3/52 f. 289; John Richards, *The Mughal Empire* (Cambridge: Cambridge University Press,

1993), 240–48; Richards, "European City-States on the Coromandel Coast," in P. M. Joshi, ed., *Studies in the Foreign Relations of India* (Hyderabad: Andhra Pradesh State Archives, 1975), 515.

106. Nathanial Higginson to "Assid Caun the Grand Vissere," 23 January 1693/4, in *RFSG: LF, 1693–94* (Madras: Superintendent, Government Press, 1921), 90.

107. Surat to John Gayer, 12 October 1695, E/3/51 f. 182–83. On al-Ghafur see Ashin Das Gupta, "A Note on the Shipowning Merchants of Surat, c. 1700," (1987) repr. in Ashin Das Gupta, *Merchants of Maritime India* (Aldershot: Variorum, 1994).

108. Bombay to Surat, 30 September 1695, E/3/51 f. 202; Ashin Das Gupta, "Some Problems of the Reconstructing the History of India's West Coast from European Sources," in Uma Das Gupta, ed., *The World of the Indian Ocean Merchant 1500–1800: Collected Essays of Ashin Das Gupta* (New Delhi: Oxford University Press, 2001), 257.

109. Surat to Adam Gronen, 4 September 1695, G/36/94 f. 162; Surat to John Gayer, 12 October 1695, E/3/51 f. 181.

110. "Translation of the Kings Husbul Hookum to Ettimut Caune under Asset Caunes Seal concerning the Gunswejs being taken," [February 1696], E/3/51 f. 331; Surat to Bombay, 18 December 1695, G/3/23 f. 23; Surat to Bombay 23 December 1695, G/3/23 f. 28.

111. Surat to Bengal, 31 August 1698, G/36/96 f. 48.

112. London to Lord Arlington, 6 April 1669, H/36, 24–25.

113. Bombay to London, 3 December 1695, E/3/51 f. 270; Surat to Bombay, 15 June 1698, G/36/96 f. 160; Bombay Consultations, 29 June 1698, G/3/5 f. 62; Bonbay to London, 15 January 1697/8, E/3/53 f. 221–22; Pridmore, *Coins*, 108; Khafi Khan, *Khafi Khan's History of 'Alamgir, Being an English translation of the relevant portions of Muntakhab al-Lubab with notes and an introduction*, ed. S. Moinul Haq (Karachi: Pakistan Historical Society, 1975), 420–21.

114. John Wheeler and John Cockroft to John Gayer, 13 July 1701, E/3/70 no. 8585; Surat to Dianat Khan, 13 January 1701/2, Surat Factory Diary (3), copy, G/36/5a, n.p.; John Gayer to John Wheeler and John Cockroft, 28 March 1702, G/36/100, 41.

115. Annseley to Louis de Keiser, 21 February 1695/6, G/36/95 f. 21; Surat to Captain South, 12 October 1698, G/36/96 f. 55.

116. Bombay to London, 15 October 1696, E/3/52 f. 190; Surat to Gayer, 12 October 1695, E/3/51 f. 182; Surat to London, 2 November 1696, E/3/52 f. 224; Ashin Das Gupta, "Gujarati Merchants and the Red Sea Trade, 1700–1725," in Das Gupta, ed., *World of the Indian Ocean Merchant*, 370.

117. Annesley to Peter Ketting, 18/28 August 1698, G/36/95 f. 54, and 2/12 September 1698, G/36/95 f. 57; Surat to Bombay, 29 July 1696, G/3/23 f. 146.

118. Court Minutes, 3 February 1696/7, IOR B/41 f. 146; D. Luis da Cunza to William III, 22 June 1699, H/60 f. 18; Robert Blackborne to D. Luis da Cunza, 23 June 1699, H/36 f. 448–49.

119. Samuel Annesley to Aurangzeb, 9 August 1698, G/36/96 f. 51–52. On Kidd, see Robert C. Ritchie, *Captain Kidd and the War against the Pirates* (Cambridge, MA: 1986).

120. John Gayer to Surat, 29 October 1695, E/3/51 f. 232.

121. Michael Kempe, "Beyond the Law. The Image of Piracy in the Legal Writings of Hugo Grotius," in Hans W. Blom, ed., *Property, Piracy and Punishment: Hugo Grotius on War and Booty in De iure praedae—Concepts and Contexts* (Leiden: Brill, 2009), 383.

122. Lauren Benton, *A Search for Sovereignty: Law and Geography in European Empires, 1400–1900* (Cambridge: Cambridge University Press, 2009), 125.

123. Samuel Annesley to Peter Ketting, 22 April 1696, G/36/95 f. 38; John Gayer to Samuel Annesley, 1 March 1694/5, E/3/50 f. 355.

124. John Goldsborough to Ibrahim Khan and Khafi Khan, 6 September 1693, E/3/50 f. 125.

125. Bombay to Surat, 8 November 1695, E/3/51 f. 245; Gayer to Aurangzeb, 16 September 1695, E/3/51 f. 252

126. Surat to Bombay, 8 July 1698, E/3/54 f. 166.

127. Papers relating to convoy obligations, 12 October 1696, G/36/95 f. 64.

128. Bombay to London, 18 March 1695/6, E/3/51 f. 382.

129. Surat to Bombay, 30 October 1695, E/3/51 f. 242–43; Surat to Bombay, 8 August 1694, G/36/94 f. 59. On the office of the *faujdar*, see Nouman Ahmad Siddiqi, "The Faujdar and Faujdari under the Mughals," in Muzaffar Alam and Sanjay Subrahmanyam, eds., *The Mughal State (1526–1750)* (Delhi: Oxford University Press, 1998).

130. Bombay to Surat, 8 November 1695, E/3/51 f. 245; Surat to Bombay, 6 January 1696/7, E/3/52 f. 256.

131. Samuel Annesley to Louis de Keiser, 21 February 1695/6, IOR G/36/95 f. 21.

132. Georg Cavallar, *The Rights of Strangers: Theories of International Hospitality, the Global Community, and Political Justice since Vitoria* (Aldershot: Ashgate, 2002), 150. Winston Churchill famously used a similar metaphor centuries later to describe the English battleship fleet. See Robert Massie, *Castles of Steel: Britain, Germany, and the Winning of the Great War at Sea* (New York: Random House, 2003).

133. C. H. Alexandrowicz, "Freitas Versus Grotius," (1960) in David Armitage, ed., *Theories of Empire, 1450–1800* (Aldershot: Ashgate, 1998), 251–52.

134. They ultimately agreed on an obvious compromise: English out, Dutch return. Surat Consultation, 6 and 20 March 1696/7, G/36/5 f. 133, 137.

135. Bombay to London, 18 February 1696/7, E/3/52 f. 328; Bombay to London, 25 January 1697/8, E/3/53 f. 221.

136. London to Bombay, 3 October 1690, E/3/92 f. 55, 58.

137. It appears his early success can be credited more to the tenacity of his mother's advocacy on his behalf than the Company's inherent magnanimity. Court Minutes, 21 October 1696 and 19 January 1696/7, B/41 f. 105, 143; Blackborne to [Popple], 18 December 1696, TNA CO 323/2, f. 109.

138. Court Minutes, 19 June 1696, B/41 f. 75; Company's Petition, (delivered) 16 July 1696, H/36 f. 191.

139. Privy Council Register, 16 and 17 July 1696 TNA PC 2/76 ff. 474–75; Proclamation for apprehending pirates, 17 July 1696, H/36 ff. 201–3.

140. Court Minutes, 17 July 1696, B/41 f. 78–79; Company's Declaration, 22 July 1696, H/36 f. 203–4.

141. Lords Justices Proclamation, 10 August 1696, H/36 f. 205–7.

142. Blackbourne to Chester, 4 August 1696, H/36 f. 195–96.

143. Court Minutes, 19 August and 23 September 1696, 18 February 1696/7, B/41 ff. 86, 97, 252.

144. Court Minutes, B/41 ff. 107, 110, 125, 149, 153.

145. Arnold A. Sherman, "Pressure from Leadenhall: The East India Company Lobby, 1660–1678," *Business History Review* 50, no. 3 (1976): 329–55.

146. "Advices received . . . 28 September 1697," TNA CO 323/2 ff. 215–18 (and H/36, f. 291–95); "Extract of Surat Generall . . . received the 28th January 1697," TNA CO 323/2, ff. 232 (and H/36, f. 325). "Narrative of the Pyracyes committed in India," [5 October 1697], H/36, f. 291–95.

147. Court Minutes, 26 August 1696, B/41 f. 88.

148. Privy Council Register, 28 May 1687, TNA PC 2/72 ff. 461–62; Privy Council Register, 27 February 1689/90, TNA PC 2/73 ff. 393.

149. Court Minutes, 19 August 1696, B/41 f. 86; "Representation to the King," 18 March 1697/8, TNA CO 324/6, ff. 129–30; Privy Council Register, 6 March 1700/01, TNA PC 2/78 ff. 162–63; Board of Trade to William III, 4 March 1700/01, TNA CO 324/7 ff. 376–77.

150. Privy Council Register, 27 August 1696, TNA PC 2/76 f. 506–7.

151. Blackborne to Popple, 4 August 1698, H/36 f. 360.

152. Blackborne to Warren, 23 November 1697, H/36 f. 303; Vernon to Board of Trade, 21 December 1697, TNA CO 323/2, f214; "Extract of a letter to the East India Company from Capt. Thomas Warren Commander of His Maj. Ship Windsor, Dated at Blackstakes

the 28 November 1697," TNA CO 323/2, f. 218; Vernon to Privy Council, 21 December 1697, TNA CO 324/6 f. 114; "Representation to the King," 13 January 1697/8, TNA CO 324/6 f. 112–13; "Representation to the King," 26 February 1697/8, TNA CO 324/6, f123–25; Journal of the Board of Trade, 1 February 1697/8, TNA CO 391/10 f. 207; Journal of the Board of Trade, 17 February 1697/8, TNA CO 391/10 f. 217.

153. On the negotiations for payment, see Popple to Blackborne, 2 August 1698, TNA CO 324/6 f157; Blackborne to Popple, 4 August 1698, TNA CO 324/6, f. 158; Privy Council Register, 8 December 1698, TNA PC 2/77 f. 276–77; Vernon to Blackborne, 21 November 1697, H/36 f. 392.

154. Ritchie, *Captain Kidd*, chap. 6; Janice Thomson, *Mercenaries, Pirates, and Sovereigns: State-Building and Extraterritorial Violence in Early Modern Europe* (Princeton: Princeton University Press, 1994), 109; Petition to Lords Justices of England, 21 September 1699, H/36 f. 461–62; London (NC) to Surat, 30 December 1699, E/3/94, 130.

155. Court of Committees, 1 October 1697, B/41 f. 201; Petition to the Lords Justices of England, 5 October 1696, H/36 f. 291; "Narrative of ye Pyracyes committed in India," [5 October 1697], H/36 f. 291–95.

156. Ian K. Steele, "The Anointed, the Appointed, and the Elected: Governance of the British Empire, 1689–1784," in *Oxford History of the British Empire: The Eighteenth Century*, ed. P. J. Marshall, Oxford History of the British Empire series (Oxford: Oxford University Press, 1998), 107.

157. Randolph to Board of Trade, "Names of Pyrates which came into Pensilvania," n.d., TNA CO 323/2, A.14. f. 43; Steele, "Anointed," 107.

158. "Extracts of Letters Concerning Pirates," 12 February 1697/8, H/36 f. 325.

159. Ian K. Steele, *Politics of Colonial Policy: The Board of Trade in Colonial Administration, 1696–1720* (Oxford: Oxford University Press), chap. 3; Douglas Burgess, "Piracy in the Public Sphere: The Henry Every Trials and the Battle for Meaning in Seventeenth-Century Print Culture," *Journal of British Studies* 48 (2009): 887–913; Philip J. Stern, "British Asia and British Atlantic: Comparisons and Connections," *William and Mary Quarterly*, 3rd series, 63, no. 4 (2006): 708–12.

160. Report of the Commissioners of the Customs, 17 January 1695/6, TNA CO 324/5 f. 368–69; Randolph to Board of Trade, 26 April, 30 May, and 6 June 1698, TNA CO 324/6, ff. 151, 181–83; Randolph to Popple, 25 April 1698, TNA CO 324/6, f. 152–53; Privy Council Register, 31 December 1696, f 562; Journal of the Board of Trade, 15 April, 1 October, and 8 October 1697, TNA CO 391/10 f. 38, 148, 151.

161. P. Bradley Nutting, "The Madagascar Connection: Parliament and Piracy, 1690–1701." *American Journal of Legal History* 22, no. 3 (1978): 214.

162. Report of the Commissioners of the Customs, 17 January 1695/6, TNA CO 324/5 f. 367.

163. Privy Council Register, 28 April 1699, TNA PC 2/77 f. 330; Court Minutes, 28 September and 8 October 1697, B/41 f. 200, 202.

164. Journal of the Board of Trade, 10 March 1697/8, TNA CO 391/10 f. 229.

165. The commissions were granted to William Attwood Esqʳ and Sampson Shelton Broughton, 6 March 1700/01, TNA PC 2/78 f. 166–67.

166. Board of Trade to George Larkin, 19 April 1701, TNA CO 324/7 f. 417–18; General Heads of Enquiry, 19 April 1701, TNA CO 324/7 f. 418–24.

167. See, for example, Blackborne to Board of Trade, H/36, f. 347–48; Board of Trade to Attorney and Solicitor General, 21 April 1698, TNA CO 324/6, f. 139; Charles Hedges to Board of Trade, 22 April 1698, TNA CO 324/6, f. 139–40; Thomas Trevor and John Hawles to Board of Trade, 3 May 1698, TNA CO 324/6, f. 142; Popple to John Fleet, 5 May 1698, H/36 f. 142; Blackborne to Board of Trade, 17 March 1697/8, TNA CO 323/2, f. 282.

168. Court Minutes, 5 February 1696/7 and 14 May 1697, B/41, f. 148, 178; Petition to the Admiralty, 26 February 1696/7, H/36 f. 228–29; Blackborne to Admiralty, 15 May 1697, H/36 f. 251.

169. "Representation to the King," 13 January 1697/8, TNA CO 324/6, f. 112–13; Vernon to Board of Trade, 28 February 1697/8, TNA CO 324/6, f125; "East India Company's

Memorial relating to Instructions for the Men of War," 7 March 1697/8, TNA CO 324/6, Bundle B no. 28; "Representation to the King," 18 March 1697/8, TNA CO 324/6, f. 127–31; Warren to Board of Trade, 22 July 1698, CO 324/6 f. 156; Board of Trade to Lords Justices, 28 July 1698, TNA CO 324/6 f. 156–57; Robert Blackborne to William Couper, 17 February 1695/6, H/36 f. 135.

170. R. Yard to Popple, 7 September 1698, TNA CO 323/2 f. 395–96
171. Surat to London, 2 November 1696 and 6 February 1696/7, E/3/52 f. 225, 315.

Chapter 7

1. Bombay Consultations, 28 May 1690, G/3/3 f. 40; Surat to Madras, 10 June 1690, G/36/92 ff. 141–42.
2. London to Madras, 5 July 1682, E/3/90 f. 3; Letter of Introduction for Captain John Preston to VOC Factory Governors, 2 October 1682, E/3/90 f. 34; on the proposals for union, see TNA CO 77/15 f. 2ff; Peter Borschberg, "Hugo Grotius, East India Trade, and the King of Johor," *Journal of Southeast Asian Studies* 30 (1999): 245.
3. Jonathan Israel, "England, the Dutch, and the Struggle for Mastery of World Trade in the Age of the Glorious Revolution (1682–1702)," in Dale Hoak and Mordechai Feingold, eds., *The World of William and Mary: Anglo-Dutch Perspectives on the Revolution of 1688–89* (Stanford, CA: Stanford University Press, 1996); K. N. Chaudhuri and Jonathan Israel, "The English and Dutch East India Companies and the Glorious Revolution of 1688–9," in Jonathan Israel, ed., *The Anglo-Dutch Moment: Essays on the Glorious Revolution and its World Impact* (Cambridge: Cambridge University Press, 1991), 421–29.
4. E.g., Robert Wilkinson, *The Stripping of Joseph, or The crueltie of Brethren to a Brother. In a Sermon before his Majestie at White-hall, by Robert Wilkinson . . . With a Consolatorie Espistle, to the English-East-India-Companie, for their unsufferable wrongs sustayned in Amboyna by the Dutch there* (London, 1625).
5. John Gayer to Surat, 29 October 1695, E/3/51, f. 231.
6. John Vauxe to Josiah Child, 20 March 1691/2, E/3/49 f. 73–74; Gombroone to London, 10 March 1690/1, E/3/48 f. 272, 275–77.
7. London to Bombay, 11 September 1689, E/3/92 f. 63–64.
8. Charles Davenant, "Reflections on the East India Trade," [1697], TNA PRO 30/24/50 f. 26.
9. John Bruce, *Annals of the Honorable East-India Company from their Establishment by the Charter of Queen Elizabeth, 1600, to the Union of the London and English East-India Companies, 1707-8*, 3 vols. (London: Black, Parry, and Kingsbury, 1810), 3:686. I have discussed some of these ideas elsewhere, in Philip J. Stern, "*Auspicio Regis et Senatus Angliae*: The Political Foundations of the East India Company's Incorporation into the British Military-Fiscal State," in Rafael Torres Sánchez, ed., *War, State, and Development: Fiscal-Military States in the Eighteenth Century* (Pamplona: Eunsa, 2007), 385–408.
10. James Vaughn, "The Politics of Empire: Metropolitan Socio-Political Development and the Imperial Transformation of the British East India Company, 1675–1775," (PhD diss., University of Chicago, 2009), chap. 3.
11. Thomas Babington Macaulay, *The History of England from the Accession of James II*, 5 vols. (London, 1848; repr., New York, 1871), 4:233.
12. Steve Pincus, *1688: The First Modern Revolution* (New Haven: Yale University Press, 2009), 373.
13. Court Minutes, 2 October 1691, B/40 f. 74.
14. James Bohun, "Protecting Prerogative: William III and the East India Trade Debate, 1689–1698," *Past Imperfect* 2 (1993): 64.
15. "A Reply on Behalf of the Present *East-India Company* to a Paper of Complaints, commonly called, *The Thirteen Articles*, delivered by their Adversaries, to the Members of the House of COMMONS," [1691] TNA CO 77/16 f. 11–12.

16. William Robert Scott, *The Constitution and Finance of English, Scottish and Irish Joint-Stock Companies to 1720* (London, 1912; repr., Gloucester, MA: Peter Smith, 1968), 2:150–51; Shafaat Ahmad Khan, *The East India Trade in the XVIIth Century in its Political and Economic Aspects* (London: Oxford University Press, 1923), 220–21n3. For the mariners' and widows' petitions, see *JHOC*, vol. 10, 13 November, 1691, 26 January 1692, 18 January 1693. The Company hired solicitors to respond; see Court Minutes, 11 August to 14 September 1693, B/40 ff. 193–96.

17. See *JHOC*, vol. 10, 23 April and 3 May 1689; Petition and Appeal of Thomas Skinner to the House of Lords, [1693], PA HL/PO/JO/10/3/186/21.

18. Court Minutes, 10 July 1689, B/39 f. 207; Court Minutes, 16 October 1691, B/40 f. 76; Court Minutes, 19 September 1696, 14 October 1696, B/41 ff. 99, 103.

19. E.g., the case of the ship "Redbridge," *JHOC*, vol. 11, 8 January 1694.

20. Andrea Finkelstein, *Harmony and the Balance: An Intellectual History of Seventeenth-Century English Economic Thought* (Ann Arbor: University of Michigan, 2000), 65.

21. E.g., John Pollexfen, *England and East-India Inconsistent in their Manufactures, being an answer to a treatise intituled, An essay on the East-India Trade by the Author of the Essay of Wayes and Means* (London, 1697); Richard Grassby, "Pollexfen, John (1636–1715)," *Oxford Dictionary of National Biography* (Oxford University Pres, 2004, online edn., January 2008), url: http://www.oxforddnb.com/view/article/22475.

22. London to Madras, 22 January 1691/2, E/3/92 f. 175.

23. London to General of India, and Council at Madras, 15 February 1688/9, E/3/91 f. 6.

24. London to Madras, 20 September 1682, E/3/90 f. 26; Arnold Sherman, "Pressure from Leadenhall: The East India Company Lobby, 1660–1678," *Business History Review* 50, no. 3 (1976): 352.

25. Miles Ogborn, *Indian Ink: Script and Print in the Making of the English East India Company* (Chicago: University of Chicago Press, 2007), 139–40.

26. London to Bombay, 31 January 1689/90, E/3/92 f. 78.

27. Proceedings of the Admiralty Court held aboard ship Beaufort (Bengal), 1 November 1687, E/3/47 ff. 5–7; Proceedings of the Court of Admiralty (Bombay), 12 December 1687, E/3/47 f. 160.

28. Secret Committee to Madras, 22 October 1686, E/3/90 f. 110; Samuel White, *A True Account of the Passages at MERGEN in the KINGDOM of Syam, After Captain Anthony Weltden arrived at that Port in the Curtana Frigat, for Account of the EAST-INDIA Company* ([London], [1688]), 7.

29. Samuel White, *The Case of Samuel White, Humbly Presented, to the Honourable, the Knights, Citizens, and Burgesses in Parliament Assembled* ([London], [1688]), 3–4; see also Samuel White, *An Account of the Articles Drawn up here in ENGLAND by the East-India-Company against the King of Siam* (London, 1689?).

30. Robert Travers, "Contested Despotism: Problems of Liberty in British India," in Jack P. Greene, ed., *Exclusionary Empire: English Liberty Overseas 1600–1900* (Cambridge: Cambridge University Press, 2010), 199–200.

31. Francis Davenport, *An historical abstract of Mr. Samuel White, his management of affairs, in his shahbandarship of Tenassery and Mergen, during Francis Davnports stay with him in quality of secretary* (London, 1688); [Nathanial Tenche,] *A Modest and Just Apology for, or, Defence of the Present East-India-Company Against the Accusations of their Adversaries* (London, 1690), 15–22.

32. George White, *Reflections on a Scandalous Paper, Entituled the Answer of the East-India-Company to Two Printed Papers of Mr. Samuel White: Together with the True Character of Francis Davenport, the Said Company's Historiographer* (London, 1689), 7.

33. Ibid., 4–5.

34. Ibid., 4.

35. George White, *There was a Paper publish'd on Friday last, Entituled Considerations humbly tender'd concerning the East-India-Company: And the Design of it is to offer some Arguments for continuing the said Company under the present Charter and Management* (London, 1689).

36. Court Minutes, 16 May 1690, B/40 f. 4.
37. *JHOC*, vol. 10, 16 May and 13 July 1689; *The deplorable case of the poor distressed planters in the island of St. Hellena, under the cruel oppressions of the East-India Company. Humbly presented to the charitable consideration of the honourable, the knights, citizens, and burgesses in Parliament assembled. By Dorothy Bowyer, and Martha Bolton widows, in behalf of themselves and their fellow-sufferers* (London, 1689); *The most deplorable case of the poor distressed planters in the island of St. Hellena, under the cruel oppressions of the East-India Company: humbly presented to the charitable consideration of the honourable, the knights, citizens, and burgesses in Parliament assembled. By Elizabeth, Martha, Grace, and Sarah, the mournful daughters of John Colson, who was one of those that were murthered by a pretended court-marshal at that place* (London, 1690).
38. London to St. Helena, 15 June 1689, E/3/92 f. 30.
39. White, *Reflections on a Scandalous Paper*, 5.
40. *JHOC*, vol. 10, 7–8 June 1689.
41. The committee, consisting of fifty members of Parliament, and endowed with subpoena power, was authorized on 6 November 1689 and convened the next day. See BL Add.MS 22,185 f. 15.
42. Court Minutes, 10 May 1689, 28 May 1689, 15 November 1689, B/39 f. 205–6, 231; *JHOC*, vol. 10, 25 May 1689.
43. General Court Minutes, 19 November 1689, B/39 f. 232.
44. W[illiam] A[twood], *An Apology for the East India Company: With an Account of Some Large Prerogatives of the Crown of England, Anciently Exercised and Allowed of in our Law, in Relaiton to Foreign Trade and Foreign Parts* (London, 1690), 33–34.
45. London to Bombay, 3 October 1690, E/3/92 f. 57.
46. London to Madras, 9 May 1690, E/3/92 f. 101.
47. New East India Company Minute Book, 6 October 1692, Bodl. MS Rawl. C. 449, f. 1; *A Journal of Some Remarkable Passages Before the Honourable House of Commons and the Right Honourable the Lords of their Majesties Most Honourable Privy Council* (London, 1693), 2; *JHOC*, vol. 10, 28 October 1691.
48. *JHOC*, vol. 10, 29 October 1691.
49. London to Surat, 29 February 1691/2, E/3/92 f. 210; Instructions for Sir John Gayer, 26 May 1693, E/3/92 f. 271; For the letter see, Copy of a Clause of John Vaux[e] to Thomas Vaux[e], 22 January 1690/1; Copy of a Clause of John Vaux[e] to Josiah Vaux[e], 22 January 1690/1, BL Add.MS 22,185 f. 25–26; Vauxe to London, 28 January 1692/3 E/3/49 f. 180–81; Journal of John Vaux[e], 15 October 1693, Add.MS 14,253 f. 14.
50. See Add.MS 22,185 f. 23–35; Surat to London, 28 April 1693, E/3/50 f. 21.
51. *An Account of Some Transactions in the Honourable* House of Commons *And Before the Right Honourable Lords of the King's Most Honourable Privy Council; Relating to The Late East-India Company* (London, 1693), 1.
52. *An Answer to a Late Tract Entituled An Essay on the East-India Trade* (London, 1697), 29–30; Roger Coke, *Reflections upon the East-Indy and Royal African Companies* (London, 1695), 1; Scott, *Joint-Stock Companies*, 152.
53. George White, *An Account of the Trade to the East-Indies* (London, 1691), 8; *Proposals for Setling the East-India Trade* (London, 1696), 17; *Some Remarks Upon the Present State of the East-India Company's Affairs* (London, 1691); *News from the East-Indies* (London, 1691). See also Ogborn, *Indian Ink*, 148–49.
54. Court Minutes, 25 November 1698, B/41 f. 350.
55. *Britannia Languens: Or, A Discourse of Trade* (London, 1689), 97–98; *Reasons Humbly Offered Against Establishing, by Act of Parliament, the East-India-Trade, in a Company, with a Joint-Stock, Exclusive of Others, the Subjects of England* (London, 1693), 1; *An ESSAY Towards a Scheme or Model for Erecting a National East-India Joynt-Stock or COMPANY More Generally Diffused and Enlarged for the Restoring, Establishing, and Better Carrying on that Most Important TRADE* (London, 1691); *Reasons Humbly Proposed for Asserting and Securing the Right of the Subjects to the Freedom of Trade, until they are Excluded from it by Act*

of Parliament (London, 1695); *An Account of the East India Companies War with the Great Mogul* ([London, 1690]); 3; *A Brief Abstract of the Great* Oppressions *and Injuries which the late MANAGERS of the East-India-Company Have Acted on the LIVES, LIBERTIES, and ESTATES of their Fellow-Subjects* ([London, 1698]).

56. ~~*Reasons Proposed for the Encouragement of all People to under-write to the New Subscriptions*~~, *appointed to be made to the late East-India Companyes Stock* (London, 1693?), 8. On eighteenth-century nabobs, see Tillman Nechtman, *Nabobs: Empire and Identity in Eighteenth-Century Britain* (Cambridge: Cambridge University Press, 2010).

57. Court Minutes, 18 March 1691/2, B/40 f. 104; *Some Equitable Considerations, Respecting the Present Controversie between the Present EAST INDIA COMPANY and the New Subscribers or PETITIONERS against them* (London, 1698); For an example of the Company's responses, see *The True Copy of a Letter from Two of the East-India-Companies Council Left at Surrat by their General Sir John Child Barronet, when he and the rest of the English Nation Departed the Indian Shoar, and Retired to Bombay to begin the late War against the Great Mogul and his Subjects* (London, 1688). Jeffreys' arguments in *Sandys* were printed as *The Argument of the Lord Chief Justice of the Court of King's Bench concerning the Great Case of Monopolies between the East-India Company, Plaintiff, and Thomas Sandys, Defendant* (London, 1689).

58. *Ten Considerations in Favour of the East-India Company* (London, 1698).

59. Court Minutes, 22 August and 19 September 1694, B/40 f. 254, 256; Tenche, *Modest and Just Apology*, 1.

60. London to Madras, 29 February 1691/2, E/3/92 f. 193; London to Bengal, 29 February 1691/2, E/3/92 f. 197.

61. Josiah Child to Robert Blackborne, 22 July 1692, Bold. MS Rawl A.303 f. 301.

62. Josiah Child to Robert Blackborne, 22 December 1692, MS Rawl A.303 f. 224.

63. "The Humble Answer of the Governour Deputy Governour and Court of Committees of the East India Company," 20 May 1692, H/40 ff. 175–79; Court Minutes, 29 February 1691/2, B/40 f. 102; *A Third Collection of Scarce and Valuable Tracts on the Most Interesting and Entertaining Subjects* (London, 1751), 178–99.

64. "The Judges Opinion," 17 November 1692, TNA CO 77/16 f. 17; *Account of Some Transactions*, 15–17; *JHOC*, vol. 10, 14 November 1692.

65. *JHOC*, vol. 10, 25 February and 3 March 1693.

66. Responses to the Company's petition, nd, Bodl. MS Rawl A.303 f. 159 (#3).

67. Margaret Bauer Havlik, "Power and Politics in the East India Company 1681–1709," (PhD diss., University of Akron, 1998), 84n50; Scott, *Constitution and Finance*, 2:157.

68. Privy Council Register, 13 April 1693, 3 August 1693, 17 August 1693, 31 August 1693, 7 September 1693, 21 September 1693, TNA PC 2/75 f. 132, 192, 197, 205, 228.

69. *Transactions in the Honourable* House *of* Commons, 17–25.

70. Ibid., 23.

71. *A Charter of Regulations Granted to the East-India Company by Their Sacred Majesties King William and Queen Mary, under the Great Seal of England, Dated the 11th of November, 1693, in the 5th Year of their Majesties Reign* (London, 1693); "The Matter of the Five Petitions against passing the Company's Restoring Charter and for a free Trade by Order of Council dated 7th September instant comes to be heard at Council Board on Thursday 14th Instant," [7 September 1693], n.p., A/2/8; D. W. Jones, "Defending the Revolution: The Economics, Logistics, and Finance of England's War Effort, 1688–1712," in Hoak and Feingold, eds. *World of William and Mary*, 66;

72. *By-Laws proposed by the Governour, Deputy Governour, and Committee of Nine, Pursuant to an Order of the General Court for the better Managing and Regulating the Companies Affairs* (London, 1695); Scott, *Joint-Stock Companies*, 153–54.

73. Court Minutes, 12 January 1693/4 and 26 March 1694, B/40 ff. 227, 242.

74. Court Minutes, 2 January 1693/4 and 22 August 1694, B/40 ff. 223, 255; Petition to Lords Justices, 8 August 1695, H/36 f. 91; "Reasons offered for not sending out one Moyety of the Manufacture of this Kingdome," n.d., H/36 f. 217.

75. Court Minutes, 22 January 1696/7 B/41 f. 144. On the weaver's riots of 1696 and 1697, see William Foster, *The East India House: Its History and Associations* (London: John Lane, 1924), 68–79.
76. Bombay to London, 15 December 1696, E/3/52 ff. 287–88.
77. Court Minutes, 9 November 1693, B/40 f. 213; Bombay to London, 15 December 1696, E/3/52 f. 289.
78. K. N. Chaudhuri, "The English East India Company's Shipping (c. 1660–1760)" in Jaap R. Bruijn and Femme Gaastra, eds., *Ships, Sailors, and Spices: East India Companies and their Shipping in the 16th, 17th and 18th Centuries* (Amsterdam: Neha, 1993), 58.
79. Petition to the House of Commons, 23 May 1698, B/41 f. 285.
80. General Court Minutes, 30 October 1695, B/41 f. 35–36.
81. Court Minutes, 28 June 1695, B/41 f. 13.
82. London to Surat, 18 February 1690/1, E/3/92 f. 128.
83. Committee for Buying Goods to Josiah Child, 14 May 1695, H/36 f. 76–77.
84. *JHOC*, vol. 11, 19 January 1694; Bodl. MS Rawl. D. 747, f145–52; MS Rawl. A. 303, f. 109–11; Philip Lawson, *The East India Company: A History* (London and New York: Longman, 1993), 53–54; Sir Courtenay Ilbert, *The Government of India Being a Digest of the Statute Law Relating Thereto, With Historical Introduction and Explanatory Matter*, 3rd ed. (Oxford: Clarendon Press, 1915), 26.
85. *A Collection of the Parliamentary Debates in England, from the year M,DC,LXVIII to the Present Time* (London and Dublin, 1739–42), 3:13.
86. "Report of the Committee appointed Jovis 7 Marty 1694 to inspect the Books of the East India Company immediately," Bodl. MS Rawl.D.747 ff145–52; *Parliamentary Debates*, 3:9, 13; William Barber, *British Economic Thought and India 1600–1858: A Study in the History of Development Economics* (Oxford: Clarendon Press, 1975), 45. News of all this reached India in late 1695. Bombay to Surat, 15 January 1695/6, G/3/11 f. 24.
87. Chaudhuri and Israel, "English and Dutch East India Companies," 437.
88. *An Answer to the Case of the Old East-India Company; As Represented by Themselves to the LORDS Spiritual and Temporal in Parliament Assembled* (London, 1700), 5.
89. *A Collection of the Debates and Proceedings in Parliament in 1694 and 1695 Upon the Inquiry into the Late Briberies and Corrupt Practices* (London, 1695), iii.
90. Lawson, *East India Company*, 52.
91. Petition of Thomas Cooke, 9, 11, and 17 April 1695, PA HL/PO/JO/10/1/475/930 f. 22, 23, 28.
92. PA HL/PO/JO/10/2/23A, NS I, no. 929, 8 April 1695; *An Act to Indemnifie Sir Thomas Cooke from Actions which he might be Liable to, by Reason of his Discovering to whom he Paid and Distributed several sums of Money therein mentioned, to be Received out of the Treasure of the East India Company, or for any Prosecution for such Distribution* (London: Printed by Charles Bill, 1695).
93. *Inquiry into the Late Briberies*, 61; "A True and Full Discovery Upon Oath Made by Sir Thomas Cooke," 23 April 1695, PA HL/PO/JO/10/1/475/930 f. 35–36; Deposition of Sir Bazil Firebrace, 25 April 1695, PA HL/PO/JO/10/1/475/930 f. 39–42.
94. Harold Laski, "The Early History of the Corporation in England," *Harvard Law Review* 30, no. 6 (1917): 561; Brian Weiser, *Charles II and the Politics of Access* (Woodbridge, Suffolk: Boydell Press, 2003); Scott, *Constitution and Finance*, 2:143.
95. Barber, *British Economic Thought and India*, 43; Weiser, *Charles II*, 125; Shafaat Ahmad Khan, *The East India Trade in the XVIIth Century In its Political and Economic Aspects* (London: Oxford University Press, 1923; repr., New Delhi: S. Chand and Co., 1975), 150.
96. London to Madras, 13 February 1684/5, E/3/90 f. 256. See also Philip Lawson, "Tea, Vice and the English State, 1660–1784," in *A Taste for Empire and Glory* (Aldershot, Hampshire: Variorum, 1997).
97. Court Minutes, 13 April 1693, B/40 f. 183.

98. Minutes of the Committee of Parliament to Hear and Examine Sir Thomas Cooke, PA HL/ PO/JO/10/1/475/930, f. 29–30; Chaudhuri and Israel, "English and Dutch East India Companies," 433.
99. "A True and Full Discovery Upon Oath Made by Sir Thomas Cooke," 23 April 1695, PA HL/PO/JO/10/1/475/930 f. 35.
100. *Parliamentary Debates*, 3:17–31.
101. Court Minutes, 16 March 1693/4, B/40 f240; 24 November 1697, B/41 f. 213.
102. Tench, *Modest and Just Apology*, 9.
103. Court Minutes, 23 March 1696/7 B/41 f. 156.
104. Court Minutes, 13 and 23 May 1698, B/41 f. 283–85.
105. Court Minutes, 25 May 1698, B/41 f. 285; *JHOC*, vol. 12, 26 May 1698.
106. Court Minutes, 27 May and 1 June 1698, B/41 f. 286.
107. General Court Minutes, 10 June, 20, and 22 June, B/41 ff. 286–87.
108. *Parliamentary Debates*, 3:109.
109. General Court, 27 June 1698, B/41 f. 287–88.
110. Proceedings of Commissioners Appointed for Raising Two Millions upon a Fund for Payment of Annuities, 14 July 1698, H/27, 1; General Court, 19 July 1698, B/41 f. 291.
111. *Parliamentary Debates*, 3:105–16.
112. Proceedings of Commissioners Appointed for Raising Two Millions upon a Fund for Payment of Annuities, 14 and 30 July and 3 August 1698, H/27, 6–7, 21, 23; Court Minutes (New Company), 24 September 1698, B/42 f. 20.
113. London to Bengal, 26 August 1698, E/3/93 f. 102.
114. "Company's Petition to the House of Commons," MS Rawl. A. 303, f. 147; Bill to continue the old Company, 1700, MS Rawl. A. 303 f. 113–14; General Court, 13 July 1698 B/41 f. 290.
115. Petition of the *New London*, 23 February 1699/1700, PA HL/PO/JO/10/6/4/1512 f. 3.
116. Lawson, *East India Company*, 55.
117. "The Dead Stock of the East India Company in India & Elsewhere Beyond the Seas," TNA CO 77/16 f. 73–74; Petition to the House of Commons, 23 May 1698, B/41 f. 285.
118. "East India Company's Response to Mr. Pollexfen's Paper," 1 April 1696, PA HL/PO/ JO/10/1/476/955 f. 122–23.
119. Minutes of the General Court, 12 March 1699/1700, B/43 f. 115; Robert Blackbourne to King William III, 13 March 1699/1700, TNA CO 77/16 f. 81.
120. Petition to the House of Commons and "Responses to the Company's Petition," Bodl. MS Rawl. A.303 f. 147–48, 159–60.
121. English East India Company petition, read in Privy Council 25 April 1700, TNA PC 1/1/54; Privy Council Register, 25 April 1700, TNA PC 2/78 f. 13.
122. Debate on the matter opened on September 7, and Norris was chosen on October 11. Court Minutes (New), B/42 ff. 9, 38. For an insightful comparison of the two embassies, see Sanjay Subrahmanyam, "Frank Submissions: The Company and the Mughals Between Sir Thomas Roe and Sir William Norris," in *The Worlds of the East India Company*, ed. H. V. Bowen, Margarette Lincoln, and Nigel Rigby (Woodbridge, Suffolk: Boydell Press, 2002).
123. Petition to William III, 11 January 1698/9, H/36 f. 409; "Draught of some Phirmaunds, &c.," n.d. [11 January 1698/9], H/36 ff. 410–11; Blackborne to Vernon, 11 January 1698/9, H/36 f. 409.
124. The Crown, avoiding conflict, issued such commissions to both Companies for southern and western India and for neither in Bengal. Privy Council Register, 2 and 16 May 1700, TNA PC 2/78 f. 19, 28–29.
125. Court Minutes, 18 June 1697, B/41 f. 183; London to Madras, 20 December 1698, E/3/93 f. 154; Court Minutes, 25 November 1698, B/41 f350; 28 November 1698, B/41 f350; Court Minutes, 19 April 1700, B/43 f. 128; 22 April 1700, B/43 f. 129; D. Waddell, "Charles Davenant (1656–1714), A Biographical Sketch," *Economic History Review* 11 (1958): 282.

126. London to John Gayer, 5 May 1699, E/3/93 f. 178; Court Minutes, 1 May 1700, B/43 f. 134; Court Minutes 10 July 1702, B/44 f. 17; Thomas Pitt to Simon Holcombe, 15 April 1701, Add.MS 22,843 f. 21–22.

127. Charles Davenant, "Reflections on the East India Trade," n.d. [1697?], TNA PRO 30/24/50 f. 31.

128. The literature on Darien is voluminous, though far more focuses on its role in the Atlantic and British politics than in the broader East India debate. Among others, see G. P. Insh, *The Company of Scotland Trading to Africa and the Indies* (London: Charles Scribner, 1932); John Prebble, *The Darien Disaster* (Martin Secker and Warburg, Ltd., 1968) repr. as *Darien: The Scottish Dream of Empire* (Edinburgh: Birlinn, 2000); David Armitage, "The Scottish Vision of Empire: Intellectual Origins of the Darien Venture," in John Robertson, ed., *A Union for Empire: Political Thought and the British Union of 1707* (Cambridge: Cambridge University Press, 1995); Andrew Mackillop, "Accessing Empire: Scotland, Europe, Britain, and the Asia Trade, 1695–c.1750," *Itinerario* 29, no. 3 (2005); Douglas Watt, *The Price of Scotland: Darien, Union and the Wealth of Nations* (Edinburgh: Luath, 2007). For a broad historiographical review, dating back to the eighteenth century itself, see Allan Macinnes, *Union and Empire: The Making of the United Kingdom in 1707* (Cambridge: Cambridge University Press, 2007), 12–52.

129. Lord Basil Hamilton to the Earl of Arran, 31 March 1696, NAS GD 406/1/7496; G. P. Insh, "The Founding of the Company of Scotland Trading to Africa and the Indies." *Scottish Historical Review* 21 (1924): 292; G. P. Insh, "The Founders of the Company of Scotland," *Scottish Historical Review* 25 (1928): 241–42; Philip J. Stern, "British Atlantic and British Asia: Comparisons and Connections," *William and Mary Quarterly* 63, no. 4 (October 2006): 705–7. The Scots had tried this once before, in 1618, but the project was arrested fairly quickly by James I. M. D. D. Newitt, "The East India Company in the Western Indian Ocean in the Early Seventeenth Century," *Journal of Imperial and Commonwealth History* 14 (1986): 22–23.

130. Unsigned proposal, nd, NLS ADV 83.7.4 f. 44–46; Martin Gregory to Captain James Gibson, 13 February 1699, NLS ADV 83.7.4 f. 138–39; Martin Gregory to the Court of Directors, 9 July 1699, NLS ADV 83.7.4 f. 190; Robert West to the Earl of Arran, 30 April 1700, NAS GD 406/1/4743.

131. Court Minutes (Scottish), 4 December 1695, H/30 f. 67.

132. *A Poem upon the Undertakeing of Company of Scotland Trading to Africa and the Indias*, n.d., Add.MS 35,068 f. 122.

133. William Paterson to Scottish Court of Directors, 17 January 1699/1700, NLS ADV 83.7.5 f. 56.

134. See the various petitions to the House of Lords, PA HL/PO/JO/10/1476/955.

135. General Court (old) Minutes, 11 November and 6 December 1695, B/41 f. 38, 41–42.

136. East India Company to William III, 3 January 1695/6, H/36 f. 124; Court Minutes, 3 and 8 January 1695/6, B/41 f. 45–46.

137. London to Bombay, 4 May 1696, E/3/92 f. 476; Court Minutes, 4 December 1695, and General Court Minutes, 9 December 1695, B/41 f. 41–42.

138. Orders of conference committee and Copy of address from Lords to William III, H/30 f. 41–44; "Notes on East India Trade from the Commons Journals," Stowe 246 f. 1.

139. H/30 ff. 46–50, 76; C.K., *Some Seasonable and Modest Thoughts, Partly Occasioned By, and Partly Concerning the Scots East-India Company* (Edinburgh, 1696), 32; Privy Council Register, 13 February 1695/6, PC 2/76 f. 285; "Notes on East India Trade from the Commons Journals," Stowe 246 ff. 1–2.

140. Walter Stewart to Sir John Maxwell, 4 February 1696, Glasgow City Archives, SMC T-PM/113/652.

141. *The Representation and Petition of the Council-General of the Indian and African Company to the Parliament* (Edinburgh, 1700), 7; "A Leurs Magnificences les Bourgomaîtres & à Messieurs les Conseillers de la Ville d'Hambourg," 7 April 1697, NLS ADV 83.7.4 f41; *The*

Original Papers and Letters Relating to the Scots Company, Trading to Africa and the Indies, From the Memorial given in against their taking Subscriptions at Hamburgh, *by* Sir Paul Ricaut, *His Majesty's Resident there, to their last Address sent up to His Majesty in December, 1699, Faithfully extracted from the Companies Books* (1700); Robert Blackbourne to Sir Paul Ricaut, 30 June 1697, H/36 f. 261; John Erskine and William Paterson to the Committee of Foreign Trade, 18/8 December 1696, NLS MS1914 f21.

142. *Original Papers and Letters*, 17

143. East India Company to House of Lords, 15 January 1695/6, PA HL/PO/JO/10/1/476/955 f. 88.

144. "Remedies humbly offered to the Lords Spirituall and Temporall in Parliament Assembled . . ." 13 December 1695, PA HL/PO/JO/10/1/476/955 f. 18.

145. *The Case of the Ship Annandale Belonging to the Company of Scotland, Trading to Africa and the Indies,* n.d., NLS ADV 83.7.6 f19.

146. Order of Francis Scott on behalf of the Company, 12 August 1704, NLS ADV 83.7.6 f. 53; Petition to the Judge of the HCA, nd, NLS ADV 83.7.6 f. 30; *The Tryal of Captain Thomas Green and his Crew* (Edinburgh, 1705), NAS GD 18/6072; Petition of Captain Thomas Green and his Crew, 1705, NAS GD 248/594/6/1.

147. Petition of Thomas Green to the Admiralty, 13 October 1704, NLS ADV 83.7.6 ff. 36–37.

148. *Act for a Company Tradeing to Affrica and the Indies* (26 June 1695).

149. Representation of the Scottish Company against Captain Green, [1704], NLS ADV 83.7.6 f. 38.

150. "Answers for Mr. Roderick Mackenzie and the African Company to this second Petition presented by Captain Green," 9 September 1704, NLS ADV 83.7.6 f. 50.

151. General Court Minutes, 6 July 1699, B/43 f. 16–18.

152. London to Madras, 29 October 1698, E/3/93 f. 115–16.

153. Minutes of the General Court, 12 March 1699/00, B/43 f. 115.

154. "Indenture Tripartite Between Her Majesty Queen Anne, and the Two East-India Companies, For Uniting the Said Companies," 22 July 1702, and "The Earl of Godolphin's Award, between the Old and New East-India Companies," 29 September 1708 in *Charters granted to the East-India Company, from 1601; also the treaties and grants, made with, or obtained from, the princes and powers in India, from the year 1756 to 1772* ([London], [1773]), 243–314, 343–57. For the financial intricacies of effecting union, see Scott, *Constitution and Finance*, 2:169–92.

155. Draft of letter to the Earl of Leven, 16 May 1706, NLS ADV 83.7.6 f. 58.

156. Macaulay, *History of England*, 4:238.

157. Michael J. Braddick, *State Formation in Early Modern England, c. 1550–1700* (Cambridge: Cambridge University Press, 2000); Paul D. Halliday, *Dismembering the Body Politic: Partisan Politics in England's Towns, 1650–1730* (Cambridge: Cambridge University Press, 1998), 212, 276–303.

158. Court Minutes, 25 February 1697/8, B/41 f. 253; "Proceedings of Commissioners Appointed for Raising Two Millions upon a Fund for Payment of Annuities," 9 August 1698, H/27, 65.

159. Ogborn, *Indian Ink*, esp. 150–51.

160. The Humble Petition of the Lord Mayor and Aldermen and Commonality of the City of London in Common Council Assembled, TNA PC 1/1/143/1; Opinion of Edward Northy TNA PC 1/1/143/5.

161. Both concerns were addressed publicly in *A Dialogue Between a Director Of the New-East India Company, and one of the Committee for preparing By-Laws for the said Company, in which Those for a Rotation of Directors, and the preventing of BRIBES are particularly debated* (London: Printed for Andrew Bell, 1699).

162. See Bruce G. Carruthers, *City of Capital: Politics and Markets in the English Financial Revolution* (Princeton: Princeton University Press, 1996).

163. Lawson, *East India Company*, 77.

Chapter 8

1. Surat (old) to London, 10 October 1702, E/3/70 no. 8630.
2. Surat (new) to William Norris, 20 January 1700/1, E/3/60 no. 7380; Surat (new) to new Company Court of Directors, 16 August 1700, E/3/58 no. 7144; Edward Norris to Court of Directors, 20 January 1700/1, E/3/60 no. 7377. William Norris accused Stephen Colt, the president of the old Company's Surat factory, of being a Jacobite and demanded he be turned over and be executed. See various letters and attestations on the matter, 15 January 1700/1 to 8 February 1700/1, E/3/60 nos. 7362–63.
3. Surat (old) to London (old), 18 October 1701, 1 and 20 April 1702, E/3/70 nos. 8591, 8618, 8615.
4. London (new) to William Norris, 12 April and 3 September 1700, Add.MS 31,302 f. 18, 21.
5. F. Pridmore, *The Coins of the British Commonwealth of Nations to the end of the reign of George VI 1952: Pt. 4, India*, vol. 1, *East India Company Presidency Series c 1642–1835* (London: Spink and Son, 1975), 84.
6. Bengal (new) to Nicholas Waite, 18 January 1700/1, E/3/60 no. 7374; See, e.g., "The forme of passes given by Sir Edward Littleton transmitted by him to this Presidency," nd, E/3/70 no. 8599; A. Karim, "Murshid Quli Khan's Relations with the East India Company from 1700–1707," *Journal of the Economic and Social History of the Orient* 4, no. 3 (December 1961): 267.
7. Waite to Mews and Brooke, 29 January 1699/00, E/3/56 no. 6863.
8. N[icholas] W[aite] to Bombay, 11 January 1699/00, E/3/56 no. 6823.
9. Nicholas Waite to Dianat Khan, 7 October 1700, E/3/58 no. 7170; Account of the Consul's envoy to the Nawab, nd [January 1699/1700], E/3/56 no. 6816; Declaration of Thomas Burges, 4 March 1699/00, E/3/56 no. 6935; Attestation of Benjamin Wyche, Samuel Richardson, and Philip Blower, 15 January 1700/01, E/3/60, no. 7361, f. 1.
10. Bombay to Waite, 15 January 1699/00, E/3/56 no. 6828.
11. Thomas Pitt to John Pitt, 12 November 1699, Add. MS 22,842 f. 3–4; Roger L'Estrange, *Fables of Æsop and other eminent mythologists with morals and reflexions*, 2 vols., (London, 1692), 1:19–20; Annabel Patterson, *Fables of Power: Aesopian Writing and Political Theory* (Durham, NC: Duke University Press, 1991), 91–94, 142; Mark Kishlansky, "Turning Frogs into Princes: Aesop's *Fables* and the Political Culture of Early Modern England," in Mark Kishlansky and Susan Amussen, eds., *Political Culture and Cultural Politics in Early Modern Europe: Essays Presented to David Underdown* (Manchester: Manchester University Press, 1995), 340, 354–55; Line Cottegnies, "'The Art of Schooling Mankind': The Uses of the Fable in Roger L'Estrange's *Aesop Fables* (1692)" in Anne Duncan-Page and Beth Lynch, *Roger L'Estrange and the Making of Restoration Culture* (Aldershot, Hampshire: Ashgate, 2008), 137–38, 140.
12. Waite to Stephen Colt and Council, 23 January 1699/00, E/3/56 no. 6844; Surat (old) to Waite, 25 January 1699/00, E/3/56 no. 6848; Attestation of Thomas Somaster and Francis Terne, 28 January 1699/00, E/3/56 no. 6858.
13. Harland to "Narabut Caune" 6 June 1704, E/3/70 no. 8665; London (Managers) to Bombay and Surat, 24 September 1702, E/3/95, 2.
14. London (new) to Surat (new), 11 June 1703, E/3/94, 459.
15. Edward Harrison to Thomas Pitt, 14 February 1702/3, Add.MS 22852 f. 73.
16. Surat to London, 18 October 1701, E/3/70 no. 8591.
17. John Burniston to "Abdell Gophore," [May? 1704], Bodl. MS Rawl A.303 f. 125; John Burniston to "Nezabut Cawne," [May? 1704], Bodl. MS Rawl A.303 f. 127.
18. Surat Consultations, 25 May 1704, Surat Factory Diary, copy, G/36/5a (3), n.p.
19. Surat Consultations, 26 May and 12 June 1704, and "Deposition of John Brangwin," Surat Factory Diary, G/36/5a, (3) n.p.
20. Bombay Consultations, 8 November 1704, P/341/2, 1:1; Surat Consultations, 21–24 May 1704, 30–31 May, 7 June, G/36/5a (3) n.p.

21. Surat Consultations, 7 August 1704, G/36/5a (3), n.p.
22. Bombay Consultations, 8 November 1704, P/341/2, 1:1; Bombay to Captain James Hanmer, 18 November 1704, P/341/2, 1:4.
23. Bombay Consultations, 26 December 1704, P/341/2, 1:60; Bombay Consultations, 17 November 1705, P/341/2, 2:84.
24. Thomas Pitt to London (old), 19 September 1706, repr. in *Yule*, 2:cxlvii.
25. Nicholas Waite to London (Managers), 28 November 1704, G/36/99a, n.p.
26. Bombay Consultations, 18 November 1704, P/341/2, 1:2–3; Bombay to London (Managers), 30 November 1704, P/341/2, 1:26.
27. Ephraim Bendall to Nicholas Waite, 5 December 1704, Ephriam Bendall to Jeremy Bonnell, 14 December 1704, and Nicholas Waite to Ephraim Bendall, 26 December 1704, P/341/2, 1:54–57; Bombay Consultations, 14 August 1705, 27 December 1705, P/341/2, 2:11, 126; Bombay to London (Managers), draft, 15 March 1704/5, P/341/2, 1:152.
28. Bombay Consultations, 22 May 1705, P/341/2, 1:204.
29. Robert Harland to Bombay, 22 November 1704, P/341/2, 1:32.
30. Bombay Consultations, 4 December 1704, P/341/2, 1:33.
31. Deposition of John Harrison, Copy, 12 December 1704, P/341/2, 1:44–45; Bombay Consultations, 29 January 1704/5, P/341/2, 1:117–18.
32. Abstract of Surat (new) to London, 28 July 1704, E/4/449, 30; Bombay Consultations, 4, 6, and 12 December 1704, P/341/2, 1:34–35, 42, 44. Emphasis added.
33. Bombay Consultations, 15 December 1704, P/341/2, 1:49–50.
34. Bombay to London (Managers), 30 December 1704, P/341/2, 1:67.
35. Bombay Consultations, 24 November 1704, P/341/2, 1:16–17.
36. Bombay Consultations, 13, 15, and 16 December 1707, P/321/3, n.p.; Bombay Consultations, 24 April, 14 June, 10 July 1705, P/341/2, 1:175, 215, 234–35; Waite to Jaunde Ali Khan, 14 June 1705, P/341/2, 1:217–18; Bombay Consultations, 4 September and 19 November 1705, P/341/2, 2:20, 88.
37. Surat (old) Consultations, 12 June 1702, G/36/5a, 3:n.p.
38. Bombay Consultations, 23 November 1704, 3 January 1704/5, 29 March 1705, P/341/2, 1:12–13, 87–93, 163; Bombay Consultations, 30 October 1705, P/341/2, 2:71–72.
39. Bombay Consultations, 11 December 1705, P/341/2, 2:110.
40. London (Managers) to Bombay, 4 June 1703 and 12 January 1704/5, E/3/95, 135, 408.
41. London (Managers) to Bombay, 12 January 1704/5, E/3/95, 408.
42. [S. M. Edwardes], *The Gazetteer of Bombay City and Island* (Bombay: Times Press, 1909), 1:152–53.
43. Bombay Consultations, 26 December 1704, P/341/2, 1:57–59.
44. Bombay Consultations, 20 November 1704, 5 April 1705, 10 May 1705, P/341/2, 1:6, 8, 167, 191; Surat (old) to London (old), 18 February 1703/4, G/36/100, 3:13.
45. Bombay Consultations, 23 August 1705, P/341/2, 2:14–15.
46. Bombay Consultations, 27 December 1705, P/341/2, 2:124.
47. Bombay Consultations, 1 November 1705, P/341/2, 2:75.
48. Bombay Consultations, 1 May 1705, P/341/2, 1:185–86; London to Bombay, 24 March 1709/10, E/3/96, 733–34; Committee of Correspondence, 8 October 1719, D/18 f. 30.
49. Bombay Consultations, 15 May 1705, P/341/2, 1:192–93.
50. Bombay Consultations, 4 December 1705, P/341/2, 2:103.
51. Proclamation of Bombay Council, 2 December 1704, P/341/2, 1:32; Bombay Consultations, 30 October 1705, P/341/2, 2:72–73; Surat to London, 30 March 1670, H/49 f. 220; Swally Marine to London, 7 November 1671, E/3/32 f. 95; Court Minutes, 19 April 1699, B/41 f. 393; London (Managers) to Bombay, 20 April 1708, E/3/96, 361.
52. Bombay Consultations, 23 August and 1 November 1705, P/341/2, 2:16, 75.
53. Bombay Consultations, 19 July 1705, P/341/2, 1:238.
54. See, for example, Committee of Correspondence, 15 May 1730, D/19 ff. 32–33; Samuel Sheppard, "Introduction," in John Burnell, *Bombay in the Days of Queen Anne, Being an*

Account of the Settlement, ed. Samuel Sheppard (London: Hakluyt Society, 1933; repr., New Delhi, Munshiram Manoharlal, 1997), xviii; London (Managers) to Bombay, 4 June 1703, E/3/95. 136; London (Managers) to Bombay, 20 April 1708, E/3/96, 361. The sentiment was repeated again in 1717; London to Bombay, 28 June 1717, E/3/99 f. 125.

55. London (Managers) to Bombay, 20 April 1708, E/3/96, 361.

56. Robert Markley, "Monsoon Cultures: Climate and Acculturation in Alexander Hamilton's *A New Account of the East Indies*," *New Literary History* 38 (2007): 543–44.

57. Court of Managers to Captain Charles Richards, 11 June 1703, E/3/95, 145–46; London to Bombay, 24 March 1709/10, E/3/96, 733–34.

58. Abstract of Bombay to London, 19 January 1710/11, E/4/449, 155; Representation to the Court of Managers, 1 March 1705/6, E/1/196, 335–40.

59. Aislabie to old Company committees, 5 January 1708/9, repr. in *Yule*, 2:cxlix.

60. London (old) to John Gayer, 20 April 1708, and London (old) to William Aislabie, 20 April 1708, repr. in *Yule*, 2:cxlvii–cxlviii.

61. On the church, and to a lesser extent the fish, see Richard Cobbe, *Bombay Church: Or, A True Account of the Building an Finishing the English Church at Bombay in the East Indies* (London, 1766).

62. Extract from letter, 5 May 1708, BL Add.MS 20,240 f. 3; London (Managers) to St. Helena, 5 May 1708, E/3/96, 386.

63. London to St. Helena, 21 March 1717/18, E/3/99 f. 250; Minutes of the Committee of Correspondence, 14 December 1719, D/18 f. 21; London to St. Helena, 24 February 1722/3, E/3/101 f. 249.

64. Edward Harrison to Thomas Pitt, 20 March 1702/3, Add.MS 22,852 f. 78.

65. Court of Directors (N.C.) to John Pitt, 9 March 1702, E/3/94, 450; Abstract of Madras to Bengal, 25 May 1703, postscript, E/4/1, 1.

66. London to Madras, 25 January 1716/17, E/3/99 f. 60.

67. "Commission and Instructions given by the Court of Managers for the United Trade to the East Indies to Mr. Nathaniel Halsey, Mr. Robert Hedges....," 26 February 1702/3, E/3/95, 47; London to Bengal, 9 January 1709/10, E/3/96 657; Commission to Anthony Weltden et al., 30 December 1709/10, E/3/96, 647–50; Court of Directors to Anthony Weltden, 9 January 1709/10, E/3/96, 675–81.

68. London to Bombay, 21 February 1717/18, E/3/99 f. 206; Court of Managers to Madras, 7 April 1708, E/3/96, 226; Court of Managers to Madras, 12 January 1704/5, E/3/95, 373.

69. Abstract of Madras to London, 17 and 30 January and 7 February 1708/9, and 10 January 1709/10, E/4/1, 179, 230; Kanakalatha Mukund, *The View from Below: Indigenous Society, Temples and the Early Colonial State in Tamilnadu, 1700–1835* (New Delhi: Orient Longman, 2005), 32.

70. A botching of the fortieth chapter of the Magna Carta: "*nulli vendemus, nulli negabimus, aut differemus, rectum vel justitiam*," or "to no one will we sell, refuse or delay, right or justice." It is tempting to believe the omission of the concept of "right" was intentional. London to Bombay, 27 February 1718/19, E/3/99 f. 342–43.

71. London (Managers) to Madras, 7 April 1708 and 4 February 1708/9, E/3/96, 277–28, 435; For similar sentiments, see Committee of Correspondence, 11 April 1721, D/18 f. 44.

72. London (Managers) to St. Helena, 5 May 1708, E/3/96, 436; Cornelius Neale Dalton, *The Life of Thomas Pitt* (Cambridge: Cambridge University Press, 1915), 276; compare with London to St. Helena, 6 May 1685, E/3/90 f. 272.

73. London to St. Helena, 13 March 1718/19, E/3/100 f. 362; London (Managers) to St. Helena, 30 November 1704, E/3/95, 303.

74. London to Bombay, 27 March 1714, E/3/98, 341.

75. The reference was to chap. 20 of the Magna Carta. London to Bombay, 4 November 1719, E/3/100 f. 15; Madras Consultations, 26 December 1707, in *RFSG: D&C, 1707*, 92; London to Bombay, 21 February 1717/18, E/3/99 f. 208; London to Bombay, 4 November 1719, E/3/100 f. 12.

76. London (Managers) to Madras, 18 January 1705/6, E/3/95, 489; London to Thomas Pitt, 21 November 1699, E/3/93 f. 230.

77. London to Bombay, 24 March 1721/2, E/3/101 ff. 123–24.

78. London to Bombay, 21 February 1717/18, E/3/99 f. 206; London (Managers) to Madras, 18 January 1705/6, E/3/95, 489; Abstract of Madras to London, 28 January 1703/4, E/4/1, 14 and 15 January 1704/5, E/4/1, 41; London to Madras, 14 February 1722/3, E/3/101 f. 221; J. Talboys Wheeler, *Madras in the Olden Time: Being a History of the Presidency from the First Foundation of Fort St. George to the French Occupation of Madras,* (Madras: Graves and Co., 1861), 2:17–21.

79. Court of Managers to Madras, 18 January 1705/6, E/3/95, 489–90.

80. London to Madras, 16 February 1721/2, E/3/101 f. 62.

81. See Niels Brimnes, *Constructing the Colonial Encounter: Right and Left Hand Castes in Early Colonial South India* (Richmond, Surrey: Curzon Press, 1999); Arjun Appadurai, "Right and Left Hand Castes in South India," *Indian Economic and Social History Review* 11, nos. 2–3 (1974): 216–59.

82. Brimnes, *Constructing,* 69–70, 72–73; Nicholas Dirks, "From Little King to Landlord: Colonial Discourse and Colonial Rule," in Dirks, ed., *Colonialism and Culture* (Ann Arbor, MI: University of Michigan, 1992), 175–208.

83. Abstract of Madras to London, 10 October 1707, E/4/1, 116–17; Madras Consultations, 26 June, 17 July, 14, 19, 22, 25, 29 August, 10 September, 28 November 1707 in *RFSG: D&C, 1707,* 36, 40–41, 50–51, 52–56, 58, 60, 84–86; Brimnes, *Constructing,* 59.

84. Madras Consultations, 14–16, 24 September and 1–2 October 1707 in *RFSG: D&C, 1707,* 62–63, 66, 68–69.

85. Abstract of Madras to London, 6 January 1709/10, E/4/1, 232; Madras Consultation, 15 January and 21 June 1708 in *RFSG: D&C, 1708,* 4–6, 34–35.

86. London to Madras, 9 January 1709/10, E/3/96, 624.

87. Abstract of Madras to London, 22 December 1707, E/4/1, 122–23; e.g., Madras Consultations, 30 October and 6 November, 1707 in *RFSG: D&C, 1707,* 75–80; Abstract of Thomas Frederick to London, 22 January 1707/8, E/4/1, 134.

88. See Brimnes, *Constructing,* 62–63, 72.

89. Joseph Collet to Samuel Baylie, 8 August 1717, Samuel Collet, 28 August 1718, and Daniel Dolins, 28 August 1718, in *LBJC,* 162, 183, 196.

90. John Richards, "European City-States on the Coromandel Coast," in P. M. Joshi, ed., *Studies in the Foreign Relations of India* (Hyderabad: Andhra Pradesh State Archives, 1975), 516; Richards, "The Hyderabad Karnatic, 1687–1707," *Modern Asian Studies* 9, no. 2 (1975): 251.

91. London (Managers) to Madras, 6 January 1703/4, E/3/95, 220; Abstract of Madras to London, 5 January 1710/11, E/4/1, 271; Abstract of E. Harrison to London, 3 September 1711, E/4/1, 304.

92. Abstract of Fort St. David to London, 8 February 1703/4, E/4/1, 22; Abstract of Madras to London, 6 January 1709/10, E/4/1, 230.

93. Madras to London, 5 January 1710/11, in *RFSG: DTE, 1701–02 to 1710–11,* 140–41; Gabriel Roberts to Arthur Moore, October 1708, Yale OSB MSS File Folder 16956, f. 2; Richard Farmer to Court of Directors, 12 January 1710/11, E/1/3 f. 25.

94. Abstract of Madras to London, 4 September 1711, E/4/1, 293; Abstract of Madras to London, 14 October 1712, E/4/1, 355.; Abstract of Fort St. David to London, 13 February 1712/13.

95. Abstract of E. Harrison to London, 13 October 1711, E/4/1, 305; Abstract of Madras to London, 22 December 1711 and 4 and 7 January 1711/12, E/4/1, 319.

96. Abstract of Madras to London, 4 September 1711, E/4/1, 293.

97. Abstract of Madras to London, 11 January 1712/13, E/4/1, 375; Abstract of Fort St. David to London, 13 February 1712/13, E/4/1, 405.

98. Court of Directors to Madras, 13 January 1713/14, E/3/98, 156, 160–61.

99. Anjengo to Court of Managers, 9 September 1704, G/1/21 f. 1; "A Description of the Southern part of the Peninsula of India intra Ganges Containing an Account of the present State Government & Traffique of the Coast de Pescaria & the Mallabarr Coast of the affairs of the English & Dutch East India Companies there And more particularly of the Queen of Attingas Country, And the English Fort at Anjengo," June 1704, G/1/21 ff. 3–8; Surat (old) to London (old), 18 February 1703/4, G/36/100, 3:13.

100. Clement Downing, *A Compendious History of the Indian Wars; With An Account of the Rise, Progress, Strength, and Forces of Angria the Pyrate* (London: T. Cooper, 1738), 42.

101. *Imperial Gazetteer of India, Provincial Series: Madras*, vol. 2, *The Southern and West Coast Districts, Native States, and French Possessions* (Madras: Superintendent of Government Printing, 1908), 354.

102. "By the Committee appointed to consider the State of Bencoolen and the West Coast of Sumatra," 6 November 1710, D/91 f. 486; York Fort to London, 14 April 1701, G/35/5 n.p; Bengkulu to London, 4 July 1710, G/35/6 no. 122.

103. Abstract of Madras to London, 14 February 1704/5, E/4/1, 46; Court of Managers to Madras, 12 January 1704/5, E/3/95, 378; Court of Managers to Bengal, 7 February 1706/7, E/3/96, 99.

104. Bengkulu to London, 5 July 1703, G/25/5 (3), 92; London (Managers) to Bengkulu, 2 February 1703/4, E/3/95, 266.

105. St. Helena Consultations, May 1716 to June 1717, G/32/5, 41; London (Managers) to St. Helena, 30 November 1704, E/3/95, 308; London (Managers) to St. Helena, 14 December 1705, E/3/96, 32; St. Helena Consultations, 20 December 1711, G/32/5 (1), 2; Fort William Consultations, 3 February 1706/7, P/1/1, pt. 3, f. 364; Madras Consultations, 19 August 1708 in *RFSG: D&C, 1708*, 46; London to St. Helena, 16 October 1713, E/3/98, 113; "A List of the Right Honourable United Companies Slaves, and how Employ'd," October 1710, G/36/5 no. 131; Bengkulu to London, 14 November 1710, G/35/6 no. 132.

106. List of the Militia Belonging to the Right Honourable United Company At York Fort, 31 December 1708, G/35/6 no. 62; List of the Right Honourable United Companies Covenantd Servants Here," 31 December 1708, G/35/6 no. 63.

107. Bengkulu to London, [January 1702/3], G/35/5 (3), 31.

108. London to Bengkulu, 21 April 1709, E/3/96, 535.

109. Bengkulu to Madras, 28 June 1701, G/35/5 n.p. (para. 6); 8 November 1701, n.p. (para 7); Bengkulu to London (Managers), 1 February 1704/5, G/35/6, no. 1, para 10; Court of Managers to Bengkulu, 11 March 1703/4, E/3/95, 279.

110. London to Bengkulu, 20 March 1712/13, E/3/98, 25–26.

111. John Bastin, ed., *The British in West Sumatra (1685–1825)* (Kuala Lumpur: University of Malaya Press, 1965), xxiii, 39n221.

112. Court of Directors to Bengkulu, 13 January 1713/14, E/3/98, 239.

113. Joseph Collet to Sultan Guillamott, 1 September 1712, in *LBJC*, 400.

114. Collet to Joseph Harding, 18 September 1712, and to Mary Quincy, 19 September 1712, in *LBJC*, 17, 19.

115. Joseph Collet to Samuel Collet, 1 March 1713/14, in *LBJC*, 78–79.

116. Joseph Collet to Daniel Dolins, 30 August 1713, and Joseph Collet to John Bedwell, 20 April 1714 in *LBJC*, 56, 85. Collet's "reformation of manners" is analyzed in more detail by Kathleen Wilson, "Re-thinking the British Colonial State: Gender and Governmentality in the Long Eighteenth Century," *American Historical Review* (forthcoming).

117. Alan Harfield, *Bencoolen: A History of the Honourable East India Company's Garrison on the West Coast of Sumatra (1685–1825)* (Barton-on-Sea: A and J Partnership, 1995), 77–79.

118. Joseph Collet to White, 23 September, 20 and 23 October 1713, and Joseph Collet to Gregory Page, 26 February 1713/14, in *LBJC*, 61, 65–66, 71–72; Harfield, *Bencoolen*, 79–80. See London to Surat, 7 April 1684, E/3/90 f. 167.

119. Bengkulu to London, [January 1702/3], G/35/5, 3:24–25, 28; Bengkulu to London, 4 July 1710, G/35/6 no. 122; James Clarke to London, 4 January 1708/9, G/35/6 no. 84; Bastin, ed., *British in West Sumatra*, 41

120. A. G. Harfield, "Fort Marlborough: The Honourable East India Company's Fort at Benkulen, Sumatra," *Society for Army Historical Research* 58, no. 236 (1980): 236; Joseph Collet to Samuel Collet, 23 August 1714, in *LBJC*, 97.

121. Joseph Collet to James Harding, 10 October 1715, in *LBJC*, 120.

122. Joseph Collet to Moses Lowman, 3 January 1714/15, in *LBJC*, 115.

123. Harfield, "Fort Marlborough," 241–42; Harfield, *Bencoolen*, 81–85.

124. Committee of Correspondence, 3 May 1720, D/18 f. 29.

125. Committee of Correspondence, 15 September 1730, D/19 f. 37.

126. Harfield, *Bencoolen*, 93; Committee of Correspondence, 21 September 1732, D/19 f. 81.

127. Anthony Farrington, "Bengkulu: An Anglo-Chinese Partnership," in H. V. Bowen, Margarette Lincoln, and Nigel Rigby, eds., *The Worlds of the East India Company* (Woodbridge, Suffolk: Boydell Press, 2002), 115; London to Bengkulu, 13 January 1713/14, E/3/98, 241.

128. Bengkulu to Madras, 28 June 1701, G/35/5 n.p.; Abstract of Madras to London, 15 January 1704/5 and 20 February 1705/6, E/4/1, 40, 78.

129. Thomas Bowrey to London, February 1698/9, Guildhall MS 03041/2.

130. Rodgett and Griffiths to London, 24 February 1703/4, G/35/7, 5.

131. Court Minutes (Managers), 16 December 1702, B/47 f. 64; London to St. Helena, 30 November 1704, E/3/95, 308; London to Borneo, 16 December 1704, E/3/95, 348–56; R. Suntharalingam, "The British in Banjarmasin: An Abortive Attempt at Settlement 1700–1707," *Journal of Southeast Asian History* 4, no. 2 (1963): 33–50; Marc Jason Gilbert, "The Collapse of the English Trade Nexus at Pulo Condore and Banjarmasin and the Legacy of the Early British East India Company Urban Network-Building in Southeast Asia," in Kennth R. Hall, *The Growth of Non-Western Cities: Primary and Secondary Urban Networking, c. 900–1900* (Lanham, MD: Rowman and Littlefield, 2010). Many thanks to Professor Gilbert for sharing an early draft of his essay.

132. John Bruce, *Annals of the Honorable East-India Company from their Establishment by the Charter of Queen Elizabeth, 1600, to the Union of the London and English East-India Companies, 1707–8*, 3 vols. (London: Black, Parry, and Kingsbury, 1810), 3:606–7; Ambrose Baldwin to London, 14 February 1705/6, G/35/7, 27–28.

133. Henry Barre to London, 23 March 1705/6, G/35/7, 29.

134. Banjar to London, 31 January and 3 February 1705/6, Henry Barre to London, and Banjar to London, 24 July 1707, G/35/7, 24–27, 32.

135. London to Madras, 13 January 1713/14, E/3/98, 154–56.

136. Banjar to London, 5 March 1707/8, G/35/7, 53.

137. Committee of Correspondence, 24 January 1720/1, D/18 f. 39.

138. Abstract of Bengal to London (Managers), 20 January 1703/4, E/4/1, 4; London (Managers) to Bengal, 18 January 1705/6, E/3/95, 521.

139. London to Bengal, 8 January 1717/18, E/3/99 f. 189.

140. London (Managers) to Bengal, 18 January 1705/6, E/3/95, 522.

141. London (Managers) to Bengal, 12 January 1714/15, E/3/98, 474.

142. London (Managers) to Bengal, 7 April 1708, E/3/96, 267; Abstract of Bengal to London (Managers), 31 December 1706, E/4/1, 96.

143. Abstract of Bengal to London, 18 February 1708/9, E/4/1, 199.

144. London (Managers) to Bengal, 2 March 1702/3 and to Madras, 9 March 1702/3, E/3/95, 61–63, 77.

145. London (Managers) to Bengal, 18 January 1705/6, E/3/95, 522; Abstract of Bengal to London (Managers), 31 December 1706, E/4/1, 96.

146. London (Managers) to Calcutta, 4 February 1708/9, E/3/96, 474–75; London (Managers) to Bengal, 18 January 1705/6, E/3/95, 522; Abstract of Bengal to London (Managers), 24

December 1707, E/4/1, 144; London (Managers) to Bengal, 7 April 1708, E/3/96, 268; London to Anthony Weltden, 9 January 1709/10, E/3/96, 680–81.

147. London (Managers) to Bengal, 7 April 1708, E/3/96, 264–66.

148. London to Anthony Weltden, 9 January 1709/10, E/3/96, 680.

149. P. J. Marshall, "The White Town of Calcutta Under the Rule of the East India Company." *Modern Asian Studies* 34, no. 2 (2000): 307–31; Swati Chattopadhyay, "Blurring Boundaries: The Limits of 'White Town' in Colonial Calcutta," *Journal of the Society of Architectural Historians* 59, no. 2 (2000): 154–79; Farhat Hasan, "Indigenous Cooperation and the Birth of a Colonial City: Calcutta, c. 1698–1750," *Modern Asian Studies* 26, no. 1 (1992): 77–78.

150. London (Managers) to Bengal, 18 January 1705/6, E/3/95, 522;

151. Abstract of Bengal to London, 7 January 1711/12, E/4/1, 338; London to Bengal, 16 February 1721/2, E/3/101 f. 86.

152. London (Managers) to Calcutta, 4 February 1708/9, E/3/96, 474.

153. London (Managers) to Bengal, 7 April 1708, E/3/96, 264–66.

154. Abstract of Bengal to London, 7 January 1711/12, E/4/1, 338; London to Bengal, 16 February 1721/2, E/3/101 f. 86.

155. Abstract of Bengal to London, 17 December 1709, E/4/1, 218; Rhoads Murphey, "The City in the Swamp: Aspects of the Site and Early Growth of Calcutta," *Geographical Journal* 130, no. 2 (1964): 253–55.

156. Abstract of Anthony Weltden to London, 13 February 1710/11, E/4/1, 264.

157. C. A. Bayly, *Indian Society and the Making of the British Empire* (Cambridge: Cambridge University Press, 1988), 68; William Foster, "The East India Company, 1600–1740," in H.H. Dodwell, ed., *The Cambridge History of India*, vol 5: *British India, 1497–1858* (Cambridge: Cambridge University Press, 1929; repr., Delhi: S. Chand and Co., 1963), 112; P. J. Marshall, *East Indian Fortunes: The British in Bengal in the Eighteenth Centry* (Oxford: Clarendon Press, 1976), 24.

158. P. J. Marshall, "British Expansion in India in the Eighteenth Century: A Historical Revision," (1975) in *Trade and Conquest: Studies on the Rise of British Dominance in India* (Aldershot, Hampshire: Variorum, 1993).

159. Fort William Consultations, 19 July 1708, P/1/1, pt. 3, f. 444; Abstract of Bengal to London, 6 November 1708, E/4/1, 154.

160. Hasan, "Indigenous Cooperation," 71–72, 79–81 (app. A).

161. Committee of Correspondence, 15 January 1723/4, D/18 f. 96–98; Committee of Correspondence, 11 March 1723/4, D/18 f. 100; Bengal Journals, 1709, P/174, no. 83, 58.

162. London to Bengal, 9 January 1709/10, E/3/96, 665.

163. London to Anthony Weltden, 9 January 1709/10, E/3/96, 680.

Chapter 9

1. London to Nathaniel Higginson, 28 January 1697/8, E/3/93 ff. 19–20; Thomas Harkwyck to London (new), 18 January 1700/01, E/3/60 no. 7372; Bengal to London, 13 October 1707, E/4/1, 139; Holden Furber, *Rival Empires of Trade in the Orient, 1600–1800* (Minneapolis: University of Minnesota Press, 1976), 199.

2. London (Managers) to Madras, 12 January 1704/5, E/3/95, 378; Daniel Heller-Roazen, *The Enemy of All: Piracy and the Law of Nations* (Brooklyn, NY: Zone Books, 2009); Anne Pérotin-Dumon, "The Pirate and the Emperor: Power and the Law on the Seas, 1450–1850," in James D. Tracy, ed., *The Political Economy of Merchant Empires: State Power and World Trade 1350–1750* (Cambridge: Cambridge University Press, 1991); Janice Thomson, *Mercenaries, Pirates, & Sovereigns: State-Building and Extraterritorial Violence in Early Modern Europe* (Princeton: Princeton University Press, 1994).

3. Arne Bialuschewski, "Thomas Bowrey's Madagascar Manuscript of 1708," *History in Africa* (2007): 42; Robert C. Ritchie, *Pirates: Myths and Realities* (Minneapolis: James Ford Bell

Library, 1986), 18–19; Bialuschewski, "The Golden Age of Piracy, 1695–1725: A Reassessment," in Luc François and Ann Katherine Isaacs, eds., *The Sea in European History* (Pisa: Edizioni Plus, Università di Pisa, 2001), 234; Marina Carter, "Pirates and Settlers: Economic Interactions on the Margins of Empire," in Sameetah Agha and Elizabeth Kolsky, eds., *Fringes of Empire* (Oxford: Oxford University Press, 2009), 55, 62–65.

4. Bombay Consultations, 18 September 1703, G/3/5 (5), f. 10.

5. "Proposals Touching Bombay Island Recommended to the Honourable Company by their President & Councell at Surratt," [3 February 1671/2], in *BS*, 1:53

6. Patricia Risso, "Cross-Cultural Perceptions of Piracy: Maritime Violence in the Western Indian Ocean and Persian Gulf Region during a Long Eighteenth Century," *Journal of World History* 12 (2001): 303.

7. See Bombay to London, 6 January 1699/1700, G/3/17 f. 2.

8. Risso, "Cross-Cultural Perceptions," 307; Stewart Gordon, *The Marathas, 1600–1818* (Cambridge: Cambridge University Press, 1993), 105, 109.

9. Bombay Consultations, 24 November 1704, P/341/2, 1:15, 17; Bombay to William Reynolds, 24 November 1704, P/341/2, 1:21.

10. Bombay Consultations, 2 December 1704, P/341/2, 1:30.

11. Bombay Consultations, 24 November and 2 December 1704, P/341/2, 1:15, 17, 30; Bombay to William Reynolds, 24 November 1704, P/341/2, 1:21.

12. William Reynolds, Randall Pye, John Van Duuren, Euclid Baker, Henry Cliffe, and John Collet to Nicholas Waite, 28 November 1704, P/341/2, 1:22–23; Bombay Consultation, 28 November 1704, P/341/2, 1:24.

13. Bombay to Robert Adams and Calicut Council, 30 December 1704, P/341/2, 1:68.

14. Bombay Consultations, 5 April 1705, P/341/2, 1:167.

15. Bombay Consultations, 30 October 1705, P/341/2, 2:69, 74.

16. London to Bombay, 24 March 1709/10, E/3/96, 733–34; London to Bombay, 27 March 1714, E/3/98, 339; London to Bombay, 21 February 1717/18, E/3/99 f. 204.

17. Clement Downing, *A Compendious History of the Indian Wars; With An Account of the Rise, Progress, Strength, and Forces of* Angria *the Pyrate* (London: T. Cooper, 1738), 10–11.

18. London to Bombay, 24 March 1721/2, E/3/101 f. 123.

19. Committee of Correspondence, 26 June 1719, D/18 f. 6.

20. See for example, London to Captain Daniel Small, 30 November 1722, E/3/101 f. 181–82; London to Captain Richard Holden, 11 January 1722/3, E/3/101 f. 211.

21. London to Bengal, 16 February 1721/2, E/3/101 f. 87; John Keay, *The Honourable Company: A History of the English East India Company* (London: Harper Collins, 1991), 259–62.

22. Expenses of Bombay, 1 August 1697–22 July 1702, MS Rawl.D.747 f. 210; Ruby Maloni, "Surat to Bombay: Transfer of Commercial Power," *Itinerario* 26, no. 1 (2002): 67; I. Bruce Watson, "Fortifications and the 'Idea' of Force in Early English East India Company Relations with India," *Past and Present* 88 (1980).

23. Committee of Correspondence, 11 March 1723/4, D/18 f. 101.

24. Bombay to London, 16 March 1724/5, E/4/459, 411.

25. Kanhoji Angre to William Phipps and Phipps to Angre, nd [June? 1724], in *BS*, 2:37–38.

26. Kanhoji Angre to William Phipps, 23 July 1724, in *BS*, 2:41.

27. Bombay to London, 9 April and 7 September 1725, E/4/459, 422–23, 440–41.

28. London to Bombay, 21 February 1717/18 and 27 February 1718/19, E/3/99 f. 205, 340.

29. Gayer to Annesley, 1 March 1694/5, E/3/50 f. 355; Risso, "Cross-Cultural Perceptions," 308–16; Muhammad Al-Qasimi, *The Myth of Arab Piracy in the Gulf* (London: Croom Helm, 1986); Charles E. Davies, *The Blood-Red Arab Flag: An Investigation into Qasimi Piracy 1797–1820* (Exeter: University of Exeter Press, 1997); L. E. Sweet, "Pirates or Polities? Arab Societies of the Persian or Arabian Gulf, 18th Century," *Ethnohistory* 11, no. 3 (1964): 262–80.

30. "Abstract of the Advices Received from Persia by the East India Company touching the Arabs of Muscatt," n.d., TNA CO 323/2, f. 305.

31. Isfahan to London, 19 July 1697, E/3/53 f. 90–93.

32. John Gayer to the Imam of Muscat, 15 January 1701/2, G/36/100, 6–7.
33. Surat (old) to Captain Charles Hill, Captain Robert Hudson and Mr. Samuel Goodman, 26 January 1701/2, G/36/100, 8.
34. J. Talboys Wheeler, *Madras in the Olden Time: Being a History of the Presidency from the First Foundation of Fort St. George to the French Occupation of Madras*, 2 vols. (Madras: Graves and Co., 1861), 2:5–8.
35. London to Madras, 9 January 1709/10, E/3/96, 624.
36. London to Bombay, 27 February 1718/19, E/3/99 f. 340.
37. Bombay to London, 7 September 1725, E/4/459, 442–43.
38. Bombay to Nazabutt Caun, 5 December 1704, P/341/2, 1:41.
39. London to Bombay, 24 March 1721/2, E/3/101 f. 119.
40. London to Bombay, 27 March 1714, E/3/98, 335.
41. London to Gombroone, 9 January 1709/10, E/3/96, 703; Committee of Correspondence, 20 February 1718/19, D/18 f. 4; London to Bombay, 4 November 1719, E/3/100 f. 10.
42. Abstract of Bengal to London, 11 December 1714, E/4/1, 538.
43. "Articles by which the English Nation and the Sceddees of Jingeera have adjusted an alliance, defensive and offensive, on the coast of India," 6 December 1733, in *BS*, 2:61–62.
44. Richard Bourchier to Robert Orme, "Account of the Morratoes," 11 July 1763, MSSEur Orme/India 3, f. 774; *The Arabian Pirate, or Authentic History and Fighting Adventures of Tulagee Angria* (Newcastle, [1795]); Keay, *Honourable Company*, 265–69.
45. Anne Bulley, *The Bombay Country Ships, 1790–1833* (Richmond, Surrey: Curzon Press, 2000), 12.
46. Risso, "Cross-Cultural Perceptions of Piracy," 309; Ashin Das Gupta, "India and the Indian Ocean in the Eighteenth Century," (1987) in Uma Das Gupta, ed., *The World of the Indian Ocean Merchant 1500–1800: The Collected Essays of Ashin Das Gupta* (Oxford: Oxford University Press, 2001), 200.
47. Bombay Consultations, 20 January 1741/42, in *BS*, 2:76.
48. The Company estimated the Sidi received 43,964 rupees per year from control of the castle, and 12,0141 from the *tanka*. See "A Representation made to the Mogul by John Spencer, in behalf of the Honourable East India Company," [4 March 1759], Add.MS 18,464 f. 98; "Firmaun under the Great Mogul's Seal, and undersealed by the Vizier, for the Honourable Company's holding the Government of the Castle of Surat," 4 September 1759, Add.MS 18,464 ff. 100–101; Dustuck (or Order) under the Khan Sumauor Steward's Seal for the Honourable Company's holding the King's Fleet, 26 August 1759, Add.MS 18,464 ff. 101–2; Extract of London to Bombay, 6 May 1761, Add.MS 18,464 f. 126.
49. Lakshmi Subramanian, "Power and the Weave: Weavers, Merchants and Rulers in Eighteenth-Century Surat," in Rudrangshu Mukherjee and Lakshmi Subramanian, eds., *Politics and Trade in the Indian Ocean World: Essays in Honour of Ashin Das Gupta* (New Delhi: Oxford University Press, 1998), 54–55; G. Z. Refai, "Sir George Oxinden and Bombay, 1662–1669," *English Historical Review* 92 (1977): 575.
50. Extract of Bombay to London, 27 March 1759, Add.MS 18,464 f. 123.
51. Extract of London to Bombay, 25 April 1760, Add.MS 18,464 f. 125.
52. State of the Case Presented to the Admiralty, 21 December 1710, D/91 f. 527.
53. Privy Council Register, 8 January 1701/02, TNA PC 2/78 f. 295; TNA CO/77/16 f. 158–62; H/93, f. 1, 2, 4, 5, 9, 81, 141, 199, 219, 288, 289; Court Minutes, 28 October 1715, B/53 f. 471; Court Minutes, 18 December 1717, 8 and 15 January 1717/8, B/54 f. 528, 548, 554; Warrant for a Bill to try Pirates in Madras, 8 March 1731/2, Add.MS 36,130 ff. 37–41 (Similar warrants for Bengal on ff. 43–48 and for Bombay on ff. 49–53); 11/12 William III c.7 (1698–99); 4 Geo I c.2/c.11 s.7 (1717–18); 8 Geo I c. 24 (1721–22); 18 Geo II c. 30 (1744–45). On the accessories omission, see Privy Council Register, 16 May 1700, TNA PC 2/78 f. 28–29.
54. Opinion of J. Paul, D. Ryder, and J. Strange, 10 August 1739, L/L/6/1 f. 10 (also TNA PC 1/5/52/1); Petition of the East India Company, PC 1/5/52/3; Lauren Benton, "Legal

Spaces of Empire: Piracy and the Origins of Ocean Regionalism," *Comparative Study of Society and History* 47 (2005): 719.

55. "An Act for the Encouragement of the Trade to America," in *Anno Regni Annae Reginae* (London, 1708), 464; Thomas Woolley to House of Lords, 20 March 1707/8, PA HL/PO/JO/10/6/149/2482 f. 1; HL/PO/JO/10/6/149/2482 f. 8.

56. Opinion of Edw. Northey and Jo. Hungerford, 3 December 1715, H/23 f. 127–28; Virginia Bever Platt, "The East India Company and the Madagascar Slave Trade," *William and Mary Quarterly* 26, no. 4 (1969): 555–56.

57. Committee of Correspondence, 21 September 1721, D/18 f. 57.

58. Philip Lawson, *The East India Company: A History* (London and New York: Longman, 1993), 71.

59. Court Minutes (Managers), 25 May, 6 June 15 August, 12 & 19 September 1705, B/48, 5, 7, 22, 30, 32–33.

60. Printed Broadside, London, 4 November 1709, in D/91 f. 145.

61. Blank charterparty form, D/1 f. 148.

62. London to Bengal, 16 February 1721/2, E/3/101 f. 87.

63. Bombay Consultations, 1 May 1705, P/341/2, 1:184–85.

64. London to Madras, 14 February 1722/3, E/3/101 f. 219.

65. Joseph Collet to Secret Committee, 3 August 1717, E/4/299 no. 735.

66. Andrew Mackillop, "Accessing Empire: Scotland, Europe, Britain, and the Asia Trade, 1695–c.1750," *Itinerario* 29, no. 3 (2005): 15–19.

67. London to Madras, 25 January 1716/17, E/3/99 f. 51.

68. Bombay to London, 2 November 1715, E/4/459, 33; Gerald B. Hertz, "England and the Ostend Company," *English Historical Review* 22, no. 86 (1907): 257; Marquis of Ruvigny and Raineval, *The Jacobite Peerage, Baronetage, Knightage, and Grants of Honour* (Edinburgh: T. C. & E. C. Jack, 1904), 206. See, for example, *The Importance of the Ostend-Company Consider'd* (London, 1726); Paul Monod, "Dangerous Merchandise: Smuggling, Jacobitism, and Commercial Culture in Southeast England, 1690–1760," *Journal of British Studies* 30, no. 2 (1991): 150–82, esp. 174; C. Koninckx, "La Compagnie Suédoise des Indes Orientales et les Pays-Bas Autrichiens," *Bulletin des Seances de l'Academie Royale des Sciences d'Outre-Mer* 3 (1978): 295–329.

69. London to Bengal, 21 December 1722, E/3/101 f. 185–86; Committee of Correspondence, 10 October 1721, D/18 f. 58.

70. London to Bengal, 18 January 1716/17, E/3/99 f. 36.

71. London to Madras, 25 January 1716/17, E/3/99 f. 51; See also miscellaneous drafts on the subject, H/74, 7–76.

72. Ellen T. Harris, "With Eyes on the East and Ears in the West: Handel's Orientalist Operas," *Journal of Interdisciplinary History* 36, no. 3 (Winter 2006): 423.

73. Proclamation, 18 October 1716, H/74, 5.

74. London to Bombay, 9 March 1719/20, E/3/100 f. 130.

75. Opinion of Philip Yorke, 3 November 1725, TNA CO 77/16 f. 195.

76. William Foster, "The East India Company, 1600–1740," in H. H. Dodwell, ed., *The Cambridge History of India*, vol. 5: *British India, 1497–1858* (Cambridge: Cambridge University Press, 1929; repr., Delhi: S. Chand and Co., 1963), 109.

77. Committee of Correspondence, 20 March 1727/8, D/19 f. 16.

78. H. Walpole to [Delafaye], 18 November 1728, TNA SP 78/188 f. 358.

79. See Brimley Skinner to Duke of Newcastle, 24 March 1731, H/74, 81–83.

80. Frederick I, Patents to Henry Konig and Company, 14 June 1731, H/74, 83–92; Monod, "Dangerous Merchandise," 174.

81. A. Westerrun to the States General, 9 May 1732, H/74, 163–67. See also Newcastle to East India Company, 24 April 1732, TNA SP 36/26 f. 84; Waldegrave to Newcastle, 9 August 1732, TNA SP 78/200 f. 299–303.

82. See, among other documents in the series, East India Company petition to Lords Justices (draft), 16 August 1723, H/60, 121–33; Jorge Manuel Flores, "Relic or Springboard?

A Note on the 'rebirth' of Portuguese Hughli, ca. 1632–1820," *Indian Economic and Social History Review* 39 (2002): 389.

83. P. J. Marshall, "British Assessments of the Dutch in Asia in the Age of Raffles," in Marshall et al., *India and Indonesia During the Ancien Regime: Essays* (Leiden: Brill, 1989), 12.

84. Wheeler, *Madras in the Olden Time*, 2:31.

85. Abstract of Madras to London, 19 December 1709, E/4/1, 228.

86. Madras Consultations, 31 January 1709/10, extracted in Wheeler, *Madras in the Olden Time*, 2:123–24.

87. P. J. Marshall, "British Expansion in India in the Eighteenth Century: A Historical Revision," (1975) in Marshall, *Trade and Conquest: Studies on the Rise of British Dominance in India* (Aldershot, Hampshire: Variorum, 1993).

88. Jim Phillips, "A Successor to the Moguls: The Nawab of the Carnatic and the East India Company, 1763–1785," *International History Review* 7 (1985): 364–89.

89. See Etrait des Articles du Projet de Neutralité, n.d. (May 1753), H/93 f. 110–11; EIC Secret Committee to the Earl of Holdernesse, 18 July 1754, H/93 f. 113–16; "The Copy referred to in the before going letter," n.d., H/93 f. 116–20; Earl of Albemarle to Holdernesse (marked seceret), 23 January 1754, Add.MS 32,848 ff. 101–3; Holdernesse to Albemarle, 24 January 1754, Add.MS 32,848 f. 114–20; Holdernesse to Albemarle, 14 February 1754, TNA SP 78/249 f. 110.

90. Fort William to Charles Watson, 14 January 1757, H/94 f. 364.

91. Add.MS 18,464 ff. 1–7.

92. Downing, *Compendious History*, 54; K. N. Chaudhuri, *Trading World of Asia and The East India Company, 1660–1760* (Cambridge: Cambridge University Press, 1978), 109.

93. Extract of a letter from George Pigot, 2 March 1756, H/94 f. 77–80; Keay, *Honourable Company*, 340.

94. Abstract of Bengal to London, 15 December 1703, E/4/1, 2; Abstract of Madras to London, 5 November 1704, E/4/1, 7.

95. London to Madras, 16 February 1721/2, E/3/101 f. 60; London to Bengal, 16 February 1721/2, E/3/101 ff. 81–82; Fort William Consultations, 28 April 1707, P/1/1, 3, f. 373; London (Managers) to Calcutta, 4 February 1708/9, E/3/96, 473–74; Abstract of Bengal to London, 24 December 1707, E/4/1, 145.

96. A. Karim, "Murshid Quli Khan's Relations with the East India Company from 1700–1707," *Journal of the Economic and Social History of the Orient*, 4, no. 3 (December 1961): 274–75, 283.

97. London (Managers) to Bombay, 9 March 1708/9, E/3/96, 491.

98. Abstract of Bengal to London, 28 August 1711, E/4/1, 283.

99. London to Bengal, 14 February 1722/3, E/3/101 f. 234.

100. London to Bengal, 12 January 1714/15, E/3/98, 470.

101. Abstract of Madras to London, 11 and 23 October 1709, E/4/1, 210. For the context of the wider politics of southern India in this period, see Sanjay Subrahmanyam, *Penumbral Visions: Making Polities in Early Modern South India* (Ann Arbor: University of Michigan Press, 2001).

102. Abstract of Madras to London, 20 August 1711, E/4/1, 292.

103. Madras Consultations, 31 July, 7 and 12 August, 1708 in *RFSG: D&C, 1708* 41–45; Abstract of Bengal to London, 6 November 1708, E/4/1, 156; Abstract of Madras to London, 1 October and 28 December 1708, E/4/1, 159, 162.

104. Abstract of Madras to London, 6 January 1709/10, E/4/1, 232. On Dau'ud Khan and his relationship with Europeans, see Subrahmanyam, *Penumbral Visions*, esp. 103–14.

105. Abstract of Madras to London, 22 January 1707/8, 1 October 1708, 11 & 23 October and 19 December 1709, and 6 January 1709/10, 14 October 1712, E/4/1, 129, 159, 213, 227, 232, 353; London to Madras, 9 January 1709/10, E/3/96, 624; Wheeler, *Madras in the Olden Time*: 2:94–104; P.J. Marshall, "British Expansion in India," 5; E/4/1, 129.

106. Abstract of Bengal to London, 16 October 1710, E/4/1, 257.

107. Abstract of Madras to London, 25 January 1709/10, E/4/1, 240; Abstract of Bengal to London, 28 August 1711, E/4/1, ,284.

108. Abstract of Madras to London, 14 October 1712, E/4/1, 354.

109. Abstract of Madras to London, 16 September 1713, E/4/1, 418.
110. Abstract of Bengal to London, 11 December 1714, E/4/1, 533–37.
111. Foster, "The East India Company," 111; Wheeler, *Madras in the Olden Time*, 2:95–107.
112. Abstract of Bengal to London, 11 December 1714, E/4/1. 533–37. Surman's diary of the embassy and other related correspondence and accounts can be found in H/69–71 and C. R. Wilson, *The Early Annals of the the English in Bengal*, vol. 2, pt. 2, *The Surman Embassy* (Calcutta: The Asiatic Society, 1911; repr. 1963).
113. Wilson, *Surman Embassy*, xxi.
114. Surman Diary and Consultations, 1 September 1714, H/69 f. 2.
115. Wilson, *Surman Embassy*, xxvii–xviii.
116. Ibid., xxi and appendix 1.
117. Surman Diary and Consultations, 5–8 July 1714, H/69, 54.
118. Wilson, *Surman Embassy*, xlvii, 71, 89.
119. Sudipta Sen, *Empire of Free Trade: The East India Company and the Making of the Colonial Marketplace* (Philadelphia: University of Pennsylvania Press, 1998), 75–76.
120. "A Translate of a General Petition to the King in order to our obtaining A Phirmaund," Surman Embassy Diary and Consultations, 28 August 1715, H/69, 66–69; London to Madras, 12 January 1714/15, E/3/98, 499; Wheeler, *Madras in the Olden Time*, 2:119, 128–31; Sen, *Empire of Free Trade*, 76.
121. "The Second Petition to His Imperiall Majesty," Surman Diary and Consultations, 29 January 1715/16, H/69, 89–90.
122. London to Madras, 25 January 1716/17, E/3/99 f. 57; Surman Diary and Consultations, 13–16 April 1716, H/69, 96.
123. Madras to London, H/68, 27–28.
124. Robert Orme, *A History of the Military Transactions of the British Nation in Indostan from the Year MDCCXLV. To which is prefixed A dissertation on the establishments made by Mahomedan conquerors in Indostan.* (London, 1763), 2:23.
125. Committee of Correspondence, 9 July 1719, D/18 f. 7; London to Bengal, 8 January 1717/8, E/3/99 f. 189; for the monthly accounts of the embassy, see H/71.
126. Keay, *Honourable Company*, 226–30.
127. Bombay Consultations, 24 and 29 January 1717/8, excerpted in *Yule*, 2:ccclix–ccclx.
128. Ramkrishna Mukherjee, *The Rise and Fall of the East India Company: A Sociological Appraisal* (New York and London: Monthly Review Press, 1974), 254.
129. F. Pridmore, *The Coins of the British Commonwealth of Nations to the end of the reign of George VI 1952: Pt. 4 India*, vol. 1, *East India Company Presidency Series c1642–1835* (London: Spink and Son, 1975), 112, 151.
130. Foster, "East India Company," 104.
131. London to Bengal, 8 January 1717/8, E/3/99 f. 189.
132. Orme quoted both in John Keay, *India: A History* (London: HarperCollins, 2000), 375 and in K. Datta, R. C. Majumdar, and H. C. Raychaudhuri, *An Advanced History of India* (London: Macmillan, 1967), 634.
133. P. J. Marshall, *East Indian Fortunes: The British in Bengal in the Eighteenth Century* (Oxford: Clarendon Press, 1976), 6; Kumkum Chatterjee, "Trade and Darbar Politics in the Bengal Subah, 1733–1757," *Modern Asian Studies* 26, no. 2 (1992): 237; John Richards, *The Mughal Empire* (Cambridge: Cambridge University Press, 1993), 277.
134. London to Bengal, 21 February 1721/2, E/3/101 f. 81.
135. Sen, *Empire of Free Trade*, 77.
136. Committee of Correspondence, 23 November 1732, D/19 f. 89.
137. Marshall, *East Indian Fortunes*, 7.
138. Keay, *Honourable Company*, 232–33, 242; Wheeler, *Madras in the Olden Time*, 283–90, 293–96.
139. London to Bengal, 3 February 1719/20, E/3/100 f. 118.
140. Calcutta to London, 24 February 1749/49 and 23 February 1751/52, in K. K. Datta, *Fort William-India House Correspondence*, vol. 1 (Delhi: National Archives of India, 1958), 332, 585.

141. "Treaty executed by the Nabob Serajah Dowla and of the Agreements of the President and Select Committee, and Colonel Clive, on the part of the Company," in February 1757, Add.MS 18,464 ff. 9–10; "Perwannahs from Nabob Serajah Dowla for erecting a Mint, and for the Currency of Business, and Copy of his Dustuck," dated in March 1757, Add.MS 18,464, ff. 11–12.

142. "Treaty between Nabob Meer Jaffier Ally Khan and the Company," June 1757, Add.MS 18,464 ff. 12–13; "Perwannah from Jaffier Ally Khan relating to the Zemindarry of the Lands South of Calcutta, granted to the Company by the Treaty with the Said Nabob," [20?] December 1757, Add.MS 18,464, ff. 14–15.

143. See copies of various grants and agreements, Add.MS 18,464 ff. 17–25.

144. "Sunnud from the Nabob of Arcot," 16 October 1763, Add.MS 18,464 f. 73; Bruce Lenman and Philip Lawson, "Robert Clive, the 'Black Jagir,' and British Politics," *Historical Journal* 26, no. 4 (1983): 801–29.

145. Wilson, *Surman Embassy*, lxix.

Conclusion

1. Bengal to London, 11 February 1756, in K. K. Datta, *Fort William-India House Correspondence*, vol. 1 (Delhi: National Archives of India, 1958), 156–57.

2. Edmund Burke, *The Works of the Right Honourable Edmund Burke, Vol. VII: Speeches on the Impeachment of Warren Hastings* (London: Bell & Daldy, 1870), 58; [William Watts], *Memoirs of the Revolution in Bengal Anno. Dom.* (London, 1760); Thomas Pownall, *The Right, Interest, and Duty, of Government, as Concerned in the affairs of the East Indies* (London: Printed for J. Almon, 1773), 3.

3. "Firmaun from the King Shah Aalum granting the Dewannee of Bengal, Bahar and Orissa, to the Company," H/68 f. 90.

4. Kanakalatha Mukund, *The View from Below: Indigenous Society, Temples and the Early Colonial State in Tamilnadu, 1700–1835* (New Delhi: Orient Longman, 2005), 18–25; Aparna Balachandran, "Christ and the Pariah: Colonialism, Religion and Outcaste Labor in Company Madras, 1780–1830" (PhD diss., Columbia University, 2008); "General View of a Memorial from the Portuguese Embassador," 20 December 1793, H/59, 89–91.

5. John Bastin, ed., *The British in West Sumatra (1685–1825)* (Kuala Lampur: University of Malaya Press, 1965), 34–35 n206.

6. Douglas M. Peers, "Gunpowder Empires and the Garrison State: Modernity, Hybridity, and the Political Economy of Colonial India, circa 1750–1860," *Comparative Studies of South Asia, Africa, and the Middle East* 27, no. 2 (2007): 248.

7. London to Madras, 14 January 1685/6, E/3/91 f. 17.

8. H. V. Bowen, "A Question of Sovereignty? The Bengal Land Revenue Issue, 1765–67," *Journal of Imperial and Commonwealth History* 16 (January 1988): 155–76.

9. Clive to William Pitt, 7 January 1759, in William Stanhope Taylor and John Henry Pringle, eds., *The Correspondence of William Pitt* (London: John Murray, 1840), 1:389–90.

10. David Armitage, *The Ideological Origins of the British Empire* (Cambridge: Cambridge University Press, 2000), 8; P. J. Marshall, "A Free Though Conquering People: Britain and Asia in the Eighteenth Century" (Inaugural Lecture, Rhodes Chair of Imperial History, King's College, 1981), reprinted in Marshall, *A Free Though Conquering People: Eighteenth-Century Britain and Its Empire* (Aldershot, Hampshire: Ashgate, 2003).

11. Alexander Dalrymple, *A Retrospective View of the Antient System of the East-India-Company: with a plan of regulation* (London, 1784). I explore the arguments of the Company's late eighteenth-century advocates more extensively in Philip J. Stern, "'This Dark Period of the Company's Affairs': History Writing, the English East India Company, and the Politics of Empire, 1757–1857," *Modern Intellectual History* (forthcoming).

12. Pownall, *Right, Interest, and Duty, of Government*, 3.

13. See H. V. Bowen, *Revenue and Reform: The Indian Problem in British Politics 1757–1773* (Cambridge: Cambridge University Press, 1991); Bowen, *The Business of Empire: The East*

India Company and Imperial Britain, 1756–1833 (Cambridge: Cambridge University Press, 2006); Philip Lawson, "Parliament and the First East India Inquiry, 1767," *Parliamentary History* 1 (1982); C. H. Philips, *The East India Company 1784–1834* (Manchester, 1961); Lucy Sutherland, *The East India Company in Eighteenth-Century Politics* (Oxford: Clarendon Press, 1952); Susan Staves, "The Construction of the Public Interest in the Debates over Fox's India Bill," *Prose Studies* 18 (1995).

14. Thomas Babington Macaulay, *The History of England from the Accession of James II*, 5 vols. (London, 1848; repr., New York, 1871), 4:228.

15. Mary Sarah Bilder, *The Transatlantic Constitution: Colonial Legal Culture and the Empire* (Cambridge, MA: Harvard University Press, 2004), 74; Bilder, "English Settlement and Local Governance," in Michael Grossberg and Christopher Tomlins, eds., *Cambridge History of Law in America*, vol 1, *Early America, 1580–1815* (Cambridge: Cambridge University Press, 2008), 81–82, 88–90; Richard Ross, "Legal Communications and Imperial Governance: British North America and Spanish America Considered," in Grossberg and Tomlins, eds., *Cambridge History of Law in America*, 105–9.

16. P. J. Marshall, *The Making and Unmaking of Empires: Britain, India, and America c.1750–1783* (Oxford: Oxford University Press, 2005), 208–9.

17. Sir Elijah Impey collected a good deal about the Bengkulu court in his tenure on the Calcutta Supreme Court; see the materials collected in Add.MS 16,268.

18. Minutes of the Committee of Correspondence, 1 November 1726, D/18 f. 126; William Foster, "The East India Company, 1600–1740," in H. H. Dodwell, ed., *The Cambridge History of India*, vol 5: *British India, 1497–1858* (Cambridge: Cambridge University Press, 1929; repr., Delhi: S. Chand and Co., 1963), 113; Mukund, *View from Below*, 28, 37–42.

19. Lauren Benton, *Law and Colonial Cultures: Legal Regimes in World History 1400–1900* (Cambridge: Cambridge University Press, 2001), 132–33.

20. Peter Auber, *An Analysis of the Constitution of the East-India Company and of the Laws Passed by Parliament for the Government of their Affairs, at Home and Abroad* (London: Kingsbury, Parbury, and Allen, 1826), 252; "Warrant for a Bill for Establishing a Court of Judicature at Madras," 19 January 1800, A/2/13; Robert Travers, *Ideology and Empire in Eighteenth-Century India: The British In Bengal* (Cambridge: Cambridge University Press, 2007), 144, 182ff.

21. See F. Norton on the Trial of Pirates at Fort St. George, 5 March 1761 and 21 April 1761, L/L/6/1 ff. 69–70; Yorke and Pratt on the Trial of Capital Offences at St. Helena and Appointing a Sheriff, 28 March 1761, 16 July 1761, 8 December 1761, and 8 December 1761, L/L/6/1 ff. 73–75; Company's Standing Council on Law Matters, 5 January 1781, Add.MS 20,240 ff. 9–10.

22. Opinion of Sayer on Recall of Military Officers and Residents in India also assessing Inhabitants of Calcutta, 12 October 1767, L/L/6/1 ff. 145–47.

23. See Penelope Carson, "An Imperial Dilemma: The Propagation of Christianity in Early Colonial India," *Journal of Imperial and Commonwealth History* 18 (1990): 171–73; John Burnell, *Bombay in the Days of Queen Anne: Being an Account of the Settlement*, ed. Samuel Sheppard (London: Hakluyt Society, 1933), 8n1.

24. C. Yorke, "Right of the King to Settlements Plunder & taken in the East Indies," 18 June 1761, L/L/6/1 ff. 76–77

25. C. Yorke on "Purchase or Cession of Salsette from the Mahratts," 7 August 1762, L/L/6/1 f. 82.

26. G. Rous on Government at Ceylon, 25 January 1798, IOR L/L/6/1 f. 611–12.

27. Sir Charles Fawcett, "The Striped Flag of the East India Company and its Connexion with the American 'Stars and Stripes,'" *Mariner's Mirror* 23 (1937). The issue of the flags in the settlements was raised as an issue as the Union flag underwent revision in anticipation of the Union with Ireland in 1801. See John Meheux to William Ramsay, 12 and 13 November 1800, H/67 f. 140, 153; Ramsay to Meheux, 12 November 1800, H/67 f. 141.

28. The Company's coinage with Mughal iconography in fact ceased much later than in other Mughal successor states. Jonathan Williams, Joe Cribb, and Elizabeth Errington, *Money:*

A History (New York: St. Martin's Press, 1997), 108–10; John S. Deyell and R. E. Fryken-berg, "Sovereignty and the 'SIKKA' under Company Raj: Minting Prerogative and Imperial Legitimacy in India," *Indian Economic and Social History Review* 19 (1982): 15–17; Kate Brittlebank, *Tipu Sultan's Search for Legitimacy: Islam and Kingship in a Hindu Domain* (Delhi: Oxford University Press, 1997), 65ff.

29. Peter Stanley, *White Mutiny: British Military Culture in India* (New York: New York University Press, 1998).

30. See, for example, Macaulay's historical account of the Company in his "Speech on the Government of India (July 10, 1833)," in *Speeches of Lord Macaulay, Corrected By Himself* (London: Longman, Green, and Company, 1877), 61.

31. Thomas Babington Macaulay, "Lord Clive," (1840) in *Critical and Historical Essays contributed to 'The Edinburgh Review'* (London, 1884), 498–99, 526.

32. See, e.g., Jack Greene, "The American Revolution," *American Historical Review* 105, no. 1 (2000): 93–102; "Colonial History and National History: Reflections on a Continuing Problem," *William and Mary Quarterly* 64, no. 2 (April 2007): 235–50.

33. See, among others John Brewer, *Sinews of Power: War, Money, and the English State* (New York: Alfred A. Knopf, 1989); Linda Colley, *Britons: Forging the Nation, 1707–1837* (New Haven: Yale University Press, 1992); Kathleen Wilson, *The Sense of the People: Politics, Culture, and Imperialism in England, 1715–1785* (Cambridge: Cambridge University Press, 1995); David Armitage, *The Ideological Origins of the British Empire* (Cambridge: Cambridge University Press, 2000); Michael J. Braddick, *State Formation in Early Modern England, c.1550–1700* (Cambridge: Cambridge University Press, 2000); Elizabeth Mancke, "Empire and State," in David Armitage and Michael Braddick, eds., *The British Atlantic World, 1500–1800* (Basingstoke: Palgrave Macmillan, 2002); Sudipta Sen, *Distant Sovereignty: National Imperialism and the Origins of British India* (New York: Routledge, 2002).

34. E.g., Robert Brenner, *Merchants and Revolution: Commercial Change, Political Conflict, and London's Overseas Traders, 1550–1653* (Princeton: Princeton University Press, 1993); K. N. Chaudhuri, "The English East India Company in the 17th and 18th Centuries: A Pre-Modern Multinational Organization," in Leonard Blussé and Femme Gaastra, eds. *Companies and Trade* (The Hague: Leiden University Press, 1981), 29–46; Nick Robins, *The Corporation that Changed the World: How the East India Company Shaped the Modern Multinational* (Ann Arbor: Pluto Press, 2006); Valerie Forman, "Transformations of Value and the Production of 'Investment' in the Early History of the English East India Company," *Journal of Medieval and Early Modern Studies* 34, no. 3 (Fall 2004): 611–41.

35. J. G. A. Pocock, *Virtue, Commerce, and History: Essays on Political Thought and History, Chiefly in the Eighteenth Century* (Cambridge: Cambridge University Press, 1985), 56–57, 66–69, 111–12.

36. Michel Foucault, *Security, Territory, Population: Lectures at the Collège fe France, 1977–1978* (New York: Picador Press, 2004), 95.

37. Harold Laski, "The Early History of the Corporation in England," *Harvard Law Review* 30, no. 6 (1917); Hendrik Spruyt, *The Sovereign State and its Competitors: An Analysis of Systems Change* (Princeton: Princeton University Press, 1994); Janice Thomson, *Mercenaries, Pirates, and Sovereigns: State-Building and Extraterritorial Violence in Early Modern Europe* (Princeton: Princeton University Press, 1994).

38. William Bolts, *Considerations on India Affairs; Particularly respecting the present state of Bengal and its dependencies* (London, 1772), vii.

39. J. R. Seeley, *The Expansion of England: Two Courses of Lecture* (London: Macmillan and Co., 1883), 170–71.

40. John Locke, *A Second Letter Concerning Toleration* (London, 1690), 51.

41. Seeley, *Expansion of England*, 170.

GLOSSARY

The following are some terms commonly used throughout the book and are intended only as a rough reference guide.

arrack   liquor or spirit, commonly distilled from coconut palm sap, rice, or sugarcane

bandar   port

banian   western Indian Hindu merchant

bhandari   western Indian Hindu maritime martial caste

bichara   local deliberative assemblies and law courts, usually Malay

buckshaw   dried bummalo fish; as a verb, the practice of fertilizing crops, particularly coconut trees, with fermented or rotten buckshaw

cartazes   Portuguese shipping passes

chop   seal or stamp, often used to mark official documents or passes

dastak   permit or pass, usually Mughal

diwan	provincial revenue farmer and administrator, usually Mughal
fanam	Southern Indian currency, gold or silver coin equivalent to about 3 d.
farman	lit., "command"; imperial grant, patent, charter
faujdar	lit., "army-holder"; head of tributary military or police force, usually Mughal
groab	small ship or galley
havaldar	lit., "office/charge-holder"; head of military or fort jurisdiction, usually Maratha
husb-ul-hukm	imperial order or instruction
jagir	assignment of revenue
kaul	grant or order, usually southern India
koli	laborer
mutasaddi	a Mughal port head or governor of a port town
muckadam	among other usages, a ship's pilot
nayak	Southern Indian ruler, often of a tributary state under Vijayanagara empire
nawab	a Mughal provincial governor or viceroy
ola	lit., "palm leaf"; Tamil grant or order
orang-kaya	Malay noble or merchant oligarchy
pagoda	Southern Indian currency, gold or silver coin equivalent to about 9 shillings; also, a Hindu temple

palanquin   a litter or sedan chair, often consisting of a covered box carried on poles

panchayat   local caste or village council

parwana   order, grant, or pass

peskash   offering, tribute, or gift, most often to a government official

phrakalang   in Burma and Siam, chief minister or foreign minister

qilidar   lit., "fort-holder"; commander of a fort or castle

rupee   Mughal currency, silver coin; exchange varied between 2s 3d and 2s 6d

sanad   grant or deed

saraf   money-changer

shahbandar   lit., "ruler of the port"; chief port and customs official

tanka   assignment of revenue

topass   slang for a *mestizo* Indo-Portuguese soldier

vakil   agent or representative (now, lit., "lawyer")

VOC   Vereenigde Oost-Indische Compagnie, or United (Dutch) East India Company

wazir   minister, often chief minister, to a Muslim king or emperor

xeraphin   western Indian currency; equivalent to between 1s 6d and 1s 8d

zamindar   lit., "land-holder"; regional Mughal revenue farmer with administrative, juridical, and police responsibilities

INDEX

CPSIA information can be obtained
at www.ICGtesting.com
Printed in the USA
BVOW08s0046101217
502178BV00003B/9/P